How to Use This Book

The Business Writer's Companion offers a concise yet thorough guide to business writing and communication in an easy-to-use format.

- **Twelve tabbed sections** organize the book's entries in thematic groups.
- A **brief table of contents** on the inside front cover provides a convenient listing of all twelve tabs.
- **Alphabetically arranged entries** within each tabbed section make it easy to find specific topics.
- At the beginning of each tab, a brief **Preview** discusses the entries in that section and lists them with page numbers.
- **Underlined cross-references** in each entry link to related entries both within and outside that tab. When a cross-reference directs to an entry outside its tab, the **tab number** appears in parentheses.
- A **complete table of contents** at the front of the book lists all entries, figures, Writer's Checklists, Digital Tips, and more.
- A **user-friendly index** provides a comprehensive list of terms and topics covered in the book, including topics that are not featured as main entries.
- A **complete list of model documents** in the book's final pages makes it easy to navigate examples and visuals.
- The inside back cover provides **instructions for accessing** *LaunchPad Solo for Professional Writing*, which gives you access to online video, audio, and practice activities.

About the Authors

Gerald J. Alred is Professor Emeritus of English at the University of Wisconsin–Milwaukee, where he is a teaching award recipient and an adviser to the Professional Writing Program. He is the author of numerous scholarly articles and several standard bibliographies on business and technical communication, and he is a founding member of the editorial board of the *Journal of Business Communication*. He is a recipient of the prestigious Jay R. Gould Award for "profound scholarly and textbook contributions to the teaching of business and technical writing."

Charles T. Brusaw served as a faculty member at NCR Corporation's Management College, where he developed and taught courses in professional writing, editing, and presentation skills for the corporation worldwide. He worked in advertising, technical writing, public relations, and curriculum development and was a communications consultant, an invited speaker at academic conferences, and a teacher of business writing at Sinclair Community College. He passed away in 2015.

Walter E. Oliu served as Chief of the Publishing Services Branch at the U.S. Nuclear Regulatory Commission, where he managed the agency's printing, graphics, editing, and publishing programs as well as daily operations of the agency's public website. He has taught at Miami University of Ohio, Slippery Rock State University, Montgomery College, and George Mason University.

Workplace Technology Adviser

Richard C. Hay is owner and manager of Twenty Six Design, LLC, a company that provides computer hosting, programming, and design solutions for organizations, including thousands of college writing, advising, and academic support centers across the United States. He is publisher of the peer-reviewed *Writing Lab Newsletter*, has taught business and technical writing at the University of Wisconsin–Milwaukee, sits on the boards of two nonprofits, and is president of Quest Theater Ensemble in Chicago.

EIGHTH EDITION

THE
BUSINESS WRITER'S
COMPANION

Gerald J. Alred

Charles T. Brusaw

Walter E. Oliu

bedford/st.martin's
Macmillan Learning

Boston | New York

For Bedford/St. Martin's
Vice President, Editorial, Macmillan Learning Humanities: Edwin Hill
Editorial Director, English: Karen S. Henry
Senior Publisher for Composition and Business and Technical Writing: Leasa
   Burton
Executive Editor: Molly Parke
Developmental Editor: Alicia Young
Media Producer: Melissa Skepko-Masi
Publishing Services Manager: Andrea Cava
Senior Production Supervisor: Lisa McDowell
Marketing Manager: Sophia Latorre-Zengierski
Project Management: Jouve
Senior Photo Editor: Martha Friedman
Permissions Manager: Kalina Ingham
Permissions Editor: Kerri Wilson
Senior Art Director: Anna Palchik
Text Design: Claire Seng-Niemoeller; Books By Design, Inc.
Cover Design: John Callahan
Cover Photo: Hero Images/Getty Images
Composition: Jouve
Printing and Binding: RR Donnelley and Sons — Shenzhen, PRC

Printed in China.

2   1   0   9   8   7

f   e   d   c   b   a

For information, write: Bedford/St. Martin's, 75 Arlington Street,
Boston, MA 02116   (617-399-4000)

ISBN 978-1-319-04476-3

Acknowledgments
Text acknowledgments and copyrights appear at the back of the book on page 441, which constitutes an extension of the copyright page. Art acknowledgments and copyrights appear on the same page as the art selections they cover.

At the time of publication all Internet URLs published in this text were found to accurately link to their intended Web site. If you do find a broken link, please forward the information to alicia.young@macmillan.com so that it can be corrected for the next printing.

Preface

The Business Writer's Companion is the best guide to the business writing essentials that help students land, navigate, and stand out on the job. A concise, topically arranged version of our popular *Business Writer's Handbook*, this easy-to-use guide addresses the most common types of business writing and communication. More than just a guide, however, the *Companion* places writing in a real-world context with quick access to more than 60 sample documents illustrating the most common types of business writing. With decades of combined academic and professional experience, we have developed the *Companion* as a reliable reference for both the classroom and the workplace.

Anticipating the needs of today's business writers, we have expanded our coverage of social media as a professional tool, including updated material throughout Tab 9, "Job Search and Application." Further, *LaunchPad Solo for Professional Writing* offers online tutorials on today's most relevant digital writing topics, from content management to personal branding. We also have been guided by the smart and generous reviews of colleagues and users across the country. In response to their suggestions, we've revised and updated entries throughout the book on topics such as layout and design, job search, résumés, and more.

The *Companion*'s Organization and Cross-Referencing System

The *Companion*'s entries are thematically organized into twelve tabbed sections. At the beginning of each tabbed section, a brief preview lists and introduces the entries, which are alphabetically arranged within that section. Within each entry, underlined cross-references link readers to related entries both within that section and in other tabbed sections. When referencing an entry in a different tabbed section, the cross-reference includes a tab number in parentheses.

Features

Concise, comprehensive coverage of the writing process along with in-depth treatment of grammar and usage provides detailed help for every stage of writing—from preparation, audience analysis, and research, to drafting, revising, and proofreading.

Real-world sample documents offer students authentic and effective models of business correspondence for a variety of workplace situations.

v

A popular quick-reference design makes information easy to find. In addition to the cross-references throughout the book that help students find related entries, the Complete List of Model Documents provides easy access to sample documents. Tips and checklists help students tackle complex tasks such as proofreading and revising, communicating with international audiences, and evaluating sources.

Emphasis on the latest workplace technologies stresses the importance of tailoring every document, post, and message to its purpose and medium. Up-to-date instruction gives students the latest advice on writing and designing for the Web, conducting Internet research, and approaching new software.

New to This Edition

Expanded coverage of "social media" discusses the growing importance of composing, collaborating, and constructing a professional identity in digital environments. Updates include discussion of how a strong social media presence on sites such as Twitter, Facebook, and LinkedIn can be seen as a boon to employers; a new sample résumé emphasizing social media fluency; and an updated Writer's Checklist for "Judicious Use of Social Media." In particular, Tab 9, "Job Search and Application," has been heavily revised to account for the role social media plays in the job search. Updated entries for "interviewing for a job" and "job search" take into account how businesses use social media in the interviewing and screening process and offer new strategies for finding jobs, including using social media channels to yield more fruitful results.

Revised entries for "global communication" and "international correspondence" include two new letters per entry modeling effective and ineffective techniques and emphasize the importance of recognizing, respecting, and adapting to the expectations of global audiences in the workplace.

New entries for "instant messaging" and "infographics" give guidance on communicating effectively via messaging programs and how text and visuals can be combined to clarify information.

Updated Professionalism and Ethics Notes throughout the book highlight tips that advise students on how to act courteously and conscientiously in the workplace.

Revised coverage of research and documentation reflects the most up-to-date changes in both MLA and APA styles.

Acknowledgments

We are deeply grateful to the many instructors, students, professional writers, and others who have helped shape *The Business Writer's Companion*, Eighth Edition. For their sound advice on this revision, we wish to express our thanks to the following reviewers who completed questionnaires: Judith Ann Ainsworth, University of Florida; Mildred Antenor, Seton Hall University; Candace Boeck, San Diego State University; George Fleet, Penn State University; Anne Harrington, Boston College; Dale Jacobson, University of North Dakota; Carolyn Leeb, DePaul University; Erica Lux, Chattanooga State Community College; Amanda McKendree, University of Notre Dame; Renee Rallo, Florida Gulf Coast University; Ashley Supinski, Penn State Lehigh Valley; Virginia Tucker, Old Dominion University; and Eric Albert Zimmer, University of Notre Dame.

We are also indebted to Richard C. Hay, owner and manager of Twenty Six LLC, who assessed the coverage and models throughout and provided specific advice to ensure that the book reflects the current use of workplace technology and business practice, including his review of the entry on adapting to new technologies and his insightful advice about the entry on blogs and forums. We thank Rachel Spilka, Renee Tegge, and Ulrike Mueller for advice about workplace writing, grammar and usage, global communication, and social media. We also thank Cynthia Ryan and Ashley Patriarca for their many contributions to this revision. Rachel and Ulrike have been consultants on previous editions, and we are grateful for their ongoing support. We are indebted to Eva Brumberger for her work on design principles and how it has enriched our instruction in the text.

For contributions to previous editions, we especially thank Quinn Warnick, Virginia Polytechnic Institute and State University, for developing the entry "adapting to new technologies." We also thank Erik Thelen for providing insights on workplace technology. For other special reviews and advice on the use and adaptation of workplace technology for business writing, we thank Michelle M. Schoenecker, Nick Carbone, and Paul Thomas. Finally, we thank Sally Stanton for expertly reviewing the "proposals" entry and developing the section on grant proposals.

We thank Rebekka Andersen for providing invaluable and fresh insights on many subjects, especially in the "proposals" entry. We thank Eileen Puechner, Senior Technical Editor at Johnson Controls, Inc., for her advice on workplace communication. We are also grateful to Kim Isaacs, Advanced Career Systems, Inc.; Matthias Jonas, Niceware International, LLC; Lisa Rivero, Milwaukee School of Engineering; and Peter Sands, University of Wisconsin–Milwaukee.

We most gratefully acknowledge the leadership of Bedford/St. Martin's and Macmillan Learning, beginning with Edwin Hill, Vice President of Editorial for the Humanities; Leasa Burton, Senior Publisher for Composition and Business and Technical Writing; Molly Parke, Executive Editor for Rhetorics and Business and Technical Writing; Karen Henry, Editorial Director for English; and Charles Christensen, retired president; for their support of this book. We would also like to acknowledge the contributions of others at Bedford/St. Martin's over the years—Nancy Lyman, who conceived the first edition of this book; Carla Samodulski, for her expert editorial guidance; Mimi Melek, for her editorial development of the second edition; Ellen Thibault, for editing the third edition; Caroline Thompson, for editing the fourth edition; Amy Gershman, for editing the fifth and sixth editions; and Alyssa Demirjian and Kate Mayhew, who edited the seventh edition.

For this edition, we thank Andrea Cava of Bedford/St. Martin's for ensuring the high-quality production of the book and Andrea Stefanowicz for her energy, care, and professionalism in turning manuscript into bound book. We are also pleased to acknowledge the guidance of Rachel Childs on related Bedford/St. Martin's titles, as well as the support of Alicia Young, development editor at Bedford/St. Martin's.

We gratefully acknowledge the ongoing contributions of many students and instructors at the University of Wisconsin–Milwaukee. Special thanks also go to Janice Alred for her many hours of substantive assistance and for continuing to hold everything together.

With sorrow, we mark the 2015 passing of our esteemed coauthor, Charles "Ted" Brusaw, and dedicate this edition of *The Business Writer's Companion* to honor his memory. Ted began his professional career as a freelance writer and moved on to a variety of positions in business and industry as a technical writer and corporate trainer, and for many years, he was manager of technical publications at the NCR Corporation. Ted coauthored *Practical Writing, The Business Writer's Handbook, Handbook of Technical Writing, The Professional Writer, The Business Writer's Companion*, and *Writing That Works*. He also independently authored a well-reviewed book of World War II military history (a Book of the Month Club selection), a Civil War novel, and a biography on Benedict Arnold. Ted was the consummate professional writer, teacher, and mentor (most especially to both of us) with whom we had the good fortune to work. He was also our friend. His standards were simply the highest.

Gerald J. Alred and Walter E. Oliu

With Bedford/St. Martin's, You Get More

At Bedford/St. Martin's, providing support to teachers and their students who use our books and digital tools is our top priority. The Bedford/St. Martin's English Community is now our home for professional resources, including Bedford *Bits*, our popular blog with new ideas for the composition classroom. Join us to connect with our authors and your colleagues at **community.macmillan.com** where you can download titles from our professional resource series, review projects in the pipeline, sign up for webinars, or start a discussion. In addition to this dynamic online community and book-specific instructor resources, we offer digital tools, custom solutions, and value packages to support both you and your students. We are committed to delivering the quality and value that you've come to expect from Bedford/St. Martin's, supported as always by the power of Macmillan Learning. To learn more about or to order any of the following products, contact your Bedford/St. Martin's sales representative or visit the Web site at **macmillanlearning.com**.

LaunchPad Solo for Professional Writing

launchpadworks.com

LaunchPad Solo for Professional Writing offers online tutorials on today's most relevant digital writing topics, from content management to personal branding, and allows students to work on whatever they need help with the most. Students develop the professional writing and communication skills they need to succeed both in the classroom and in the workplace and can explore today's technologies in clickable, assignable learning sequences organized by popular professional writing topics. *LaunchPad Solo for Professional Writing* features:

- **Digital Tips.** Step-by-step instruction for using technology to support workplace writing includes guidance for synchronizing data, assessing software and hardware, creating templates, and organizing productive online meetings.
- **Sample documents.** A wide range of effective professional writing models provides students with e-mail, résumés, cover letters, reports, proposals, brochures, and questionnaires (and more) to emulate.
- **Tutorials.** Screen captures walk students through maximizing free online tools to access projects across platforms, design dynamic presentations, develop podcasts, manage their personal brand, and build common citations in APA and MLA styles.
- **Adaptive quizzing for targeted learning, skills practice, and grammar help.** LearningCurve, a game-like adaptive quizzing

program, helps students focus on the writing and grammar skills for which they need the most help.

- **The ability to monitor student progress.** Use our gradebook to see which students are on track and which need additional help with specific topics.

LaunchPad Solo for Professional Writing can be packaged with *The Business Writer's Companion* at **a significant discount**. Order ISBN 978-1-319-12263-8 to ensure your students can take full advantage. Visit **launchpadworks.com** for more information. For technical support, visit **macmillanlearning.com/getsupport**.

Choose from Alternative Formats of *The Business Writer's Companion*

Bedford/St. Martin's offers a range of affordable formats, allowing students to choose the one that works best for them. For details about our e-book partners, visit **macmillanlearning.com/ebooks**.

Brief Contents

Complete Contents

Five Steps to Successful Writing

Successful writing on the job is not the product of inspiration, nor is it merely the spoken word converted to print. It is the result of knowing how to structure information using both text and design to achieve an intended purpose for a clearly defined audience. The best way to ensure that your writing will succeed—whether it is a proposal, a résumé, a Web page, or any other document—is to approach writing using the following steps:

1. Preparation
2. Research
3. Organization
4. Writing
5. Revision

You will very likely need to follow those steps consciously at first. The same is true the first time you use new software, interview a job candidate, or chair a committee meeting. With practice, the steps become nearly automatic. That is not to suggest that writing becomes easy. It does not. However, the easiest and most efficient way to write effectively is to do it systematically.

As you master the five steps, keep in mind that they are interrelated and often overlap. For example, your readers' needs and your purpose, which you determine in step 1, will affect decisions you make in subsequent steps. You may also need to retrace steps. When you conduct research, for example, you may realize that you need to revise your initial impression of a document's purpose and audience. Similarly, when you begin to organize your information, you may discover the need to return to the research step.

The time required for each step varies with different writing tasks. When writing an informal memo, for example, you might follow the first three steps (preparation, research, and organization) by simply listing the points in the order you want to cover them. In such situations, you gather and organize information mentally as you consider your purpose and audience. For a formal report, the first three steps require well-organized research, careful note-taking, and detailed outlining. For a routine e-mail message to a coworker, the first four steps might merge as you type the information on the screen. In short, the five steps expand, contract, and at times must be repeated to fit the complexity or context of the writing task.

Dividing the writing process into steps is especially useful for collaborative writing, in which you typically divide the work among team members, keep track of a project, and save time by not duplicating effort. When you collaborate, you can use e-mail to share text and other files, suggest improvements to each other's work, and generally keep everyone informed of your progress as you follow the steps in the writing process. See also collaborative writing (Tab 1).*

Preparation

Writing, like most professional tasks, requires solid preparation (Tab 1). In fact, adequate preparation is as important as writing a draft. In preparation for writing, your goal is to accomplish the following four major tasks:

- Establish your primary purpose.
- Assess your audience (or readers) and the context.
- Determine the scope of your coverage.
- Select the appropriate medium.

Establishing Your Purpose.   To establish your primary purpose (Tab 1), simply ask yourself what you want your readers to know, to believe, or to be able to do after they have finished reading what you have written. Be precise. Often a writer states a purpose so broadly that it is almost useless. A purpose such as "to report on possible locations for a new research facility" is too general. However, "to compare the relative advantages of Paris, Singapore, and San Francisco as possible locations for a new research facility so that top management can choose the best location" is a purpose statement that can guide you throughout the writing process. In addition to your primary purpose, consider possible secondary purposes for your document. For example, a secondary purpose of the research-facilities report might be to make corporate executive readers aware of the staffing needs of the new facility so that they can ensure its smooth operation in whichever location is selected.

Assessing Your Audience and Context.   The next task is to assess your audience (Tab 1). Again, be precise and ask key questions. Who exactly is your reader? Do you have multiple readers? Who needs to see or use the document? What are your readers' needs in relation to your subject? What are your readers' attitudes about the subject? (Are they skeptical? supportive? anxious? bored?) What do your readers already

---

*Throughout this book, words and phrases shown as links—underlined and set in an alternate typeface—refer to specific entries. The tab number in parentheses indicates the entry's location. If no tab number appears, the entry is in the same tabbed section as the entry you are reading.

know about the subject? Should you define basic terminology, or will such definitions merely bore, or even impede, your readers? Are you communicating with international readers and therefore dealing with issues inherent in global communication (Tab 1)?

For the research-facilities report, the readers are described as "top management." Who is included in that category? Will one of the people evaluating the report be the human resources manager? That person likely would be interested in the availability of qualified professionals as well as the presence of training, housing, and even recreational facilities available to employees in each city. The purchasing manager would be concerned about available sources for needed materials. The marketing manager would give priority to a facility's proximity to the primary markets and transportation to important clients. The chief financial officer would want to know about land and building costs and about each country's tax structure. The chief executive officer would be interested in all this information and perhaps more. As in this example, many workplace documents have audiences composed of multiple readers. You can accommodate their needs through one of a number of approaches described in the entry audience (Tab 1).

In addition to knowing the needs and interests of your readers, learn as much as you can about the context (Tab 1). Simply put, context is the environment or circumstances in which writers produce documents and within which readers interpret their meanings. Everything is written in a context, as illustrated in many entries and examples throughout this book. To determine the effect of context on the research-facilities report, you might ask both specific and general questions about the situation and about your readers' backgrounds: Is this the company's first new facility, or has the company chosen locations for new facilities before? Have the readers visited all three cities? Have they already seen

---

ESL TIP for Considering Audiences

In the United States, conciseness (Tab 10), coherence (Tab 10), and clarity characterize good writing. Make sure readers can follow your writing, and say only what is necessary to communicate your message. Of course, no writing style is inherently better than another, but, to be a successful writer in any language, you must understand the cultural values that underlie the language in which you are writing. See also global communication (Tab 1), copyright (Tab 5), plagiarism (Tab 5), and awkwardness (Tab 10).

Throughout this book, we have included ESL Tip boxes like this one with information that may be particularly helpful to nonnative speakers of English. The entry English as a second language (ESL) (Tab 11) includes a list of entries that may be of particular help to ESL writers.

other reports on the three cities? What is the corporate culture in which your readers work, and what are its key values? What specific factors, such as competition, finance, and regulation, are recognized as important within the organization?

Determining the Scope.   Determining your purpose and assessing your readers and context will help you decide what to include and what not to include in your writing. Those decisions establish the scope (Tab 1) of your writing project. If you do not clearly define the scope, you will spend needless hours on research because you will not be sure what kind of information you need or even how much. Given the purpose and audience established for the report on facility locations, the scope would include such information as land and building costs, available labor force, cultural issues, transportation options, and proximity to suppliers. However, it probably would not include the early history of the cities being considered or their climate and geological features, unless those aspects were directly related to your particular business.

Selecting the Medium.   Finally, you need to determine the most appropriate medium for communicating your message. Professionals on the job face a wide array of options—from e-mail, voice mail, videoconferencing, and blogs to more traditional means, such as letters, memos, reports, and face-to-face meetings.

The most important considerations in selecting the appropriate medium are the audience and the purpose of the communication. For example, if you need to collaborate with someone to solve a problem or if you need to establish rapport with someone, written exchanges could be far less efficient than a phone call or a face-to-face meeting. However, if you need precise wording or you need to provide a record of a complex message, communicate in writing. If you need to make frequently updated information accessible to employees at a large company, the best choice might be to place the information on the company's intranet site. If reviewers need to make handwritten comments on a proposal, you may need to provide paper copies that can be scanned or faxed, or you may use collaborative software to insert and route comments electronically. The comparative advantages and primary characteristics of the most typical means of communication are discussed in selecting the medium (Tab 2). See also writing for the Web (Tab 2) and the entries in Tab 4, "Business Writing Documents and Elements."

Research

The only way to be sure that you can write about a complex subject is to thoroughly understand it. To do that, you must conduct adequate research, whether that means conducting an extensive investigation for a major proposal—through interviewing, library and Internet research, careful note-taking, and documenting sources—or simply checking a company Web site and jotting down points before you send an e-mail message to a colleague. The entries in Tab 5, "Research and Documentation," will help you with the research process.

Methods of Research. Researchers frequently distinguish between primary and secondary <u>research</u> (Tab 5), depending on the types of sources consulted and the method of gathering information. *Primary research* refers to the gathering of raw data compiled from interviews, direct observation, surveys, experiments, questionnaires, and audio and video recordings, for example. In fact, direct observation and hands-on experience are the only ways to obtain certain kinds of information, such as the behavior of people and animals, certain natural phenomena, mechanical processes, and the operation of systems and equipment. *Secondary research* refers to gathering information that has been analyzed, assessed, evaluated, compiled, or otherwise organized into accessible form. Such sources include books, articles, reports, Web documents, e-mail discussions, business letters, minutes of meetings, and brochures. Use the methods most appropriate to your needs, recognizing that some projects will require several types of research and that collaborative projects may require those research tasks to be distributed among team members.

Sources of Information. As you conduct research, keep in mind all available information sources:

- Your own knowledge and that of your colleagues
- The knowledge of people outside your workplace, gathered through <u>interviewing for information</u> (Tab 5)
- Internet sources, including Web sites, directories, archives, and discussion groups
- Library resources, including databases and indexes of articles as well as books and reference works
- Printed and electronic sources in the workplace, such as brochures, memos, e-mail, and Web documents

The amount of research you will need to do depends on the scope of your project. Start by considering all of your potential sources, and then focus on those that are most useful.

Organization

Without organization, the material gathered during your research will be incoherent to your readers. To organize information effectively, you need to determine the best way to structure your ideas; that is, you must choose a primary method of development. The entry <u>organization </u>(Tab 1) describes typical methods of development used in on-the-job writing.

Methods of Development. To choose the development method best suited to your document, consider your subject, your readers' needs, and your purpose. An appropriate method will help focus your information and make it easy for readers to follow your presentation.

For example, if you are writing instructions for assembling office equipment, you might naturally present the steps of the process in the order readers should perform them: the sequential method of development. If you are writing about the history of an organization, your account might naturally go from the beginning to the present: the chronological method of development. If your subject naturally lends itself to a certain method of development, use it—do not attempt to impose another method on it.

Often you will need to combine methods of development. For example, a persuasive brochure for a charitable organization might combine a specific-to-general method of development with a cause-and-effect method of development. That is, you could begin with persuasive case histories of individual people in need and then move to general information about the positive effects of donations on recipients.

Outlining.   Once you have chosen a method of development, you are ready to prepare an outline. Outlining (Tab 1) breaks large or complex subjects into manageable parts. It also enables you to emphasize key points by placing them in the positions of greatest importance. By structuring your thinking at an early stage, a well-developed outline ensures that your document will be complete and logically organized, allowing you to focus exclusively on writing when you begin the rough draft. An outline can be especially helpful for maintaining a collaborative writing team's focus throughout a large project. However, even a short letter or memo needs the logic and structure that an outline provides, whether the outline exists in your mind, on a screen, or on paper.

At this point, consider layout-and-design elements that will be helpful to your readers and appropriate to your subject and purpose. For example, if visuals such as photographs or tables will be useful, think about where they may be deployed and what kinds of visual elements will be effective, especially if they need to be prepared by someone else while you write and revise the draft. The outline can also suggest where headings, lists, and other special design features may be useful. See Tab 7, "Design and Visuals."

Writing

When you have established your purpose, your readers' needs, and your scope, and you have completed your research and your outline, you will be well prepared to write a first draft. Expand your outline into paragraphs (Tab 1), without worrying about grammar, language refinements, or punctuation. Writing and revising are different activities; refinements come with revision.

Write the rough draft, concentrating entirely on converting your outline into sentences and paragraphs. You might try writing as though you were explaining your subject to a reader sitting across from you. Do not worry about a good opening. Just start. Do not be concerned in the rough draft about exact word choice unless it comes quickly and easily—concentrate instead on ideas.

Even with good preparation, writing the draft remains a chore for many writers. The most effective way to get started and keep going is to use your outline as a map for your first draft. Do not wait for inspiration—you need to treat writing a draft as you would any on-the-job task. The entry <u>writing a draft</u> (Tab 1) describes tactics used by experienced writers—discover which ones are best suited to you and your task.

Consider writing the introduction last because then you will know more precisely what is in the body of the draft. Your opening should announce the subject and give readers essential background information, such as the document's primary purpose. For longer documents, an introduction should serve as a frame into which readers can fit the detailed information that follows. See <u>introductions</u> (Tab 1).

Finally, write a conclusion that ties the main ideas together and emphatically makes a final, significant point. The final point may be to recommend a course of action, make a prediction or judgment, or merely summarize your main points—the way you conclude depends on the purpose of your writing and your readers' needs. See <u>conclusions</u> (Tab 1).

Revision

The clearer a finished piece of writing seems to the reader, the more effort the writer has likely put into its <u>revision</u> (Tab 1). If you have followed the steps of the writing process to this point, you will have a rough draft that needs to be revised. Revising, however, requires a different frame of mind than does writing the draft. During revision, be eager to find and correct faults and be honest. Be hard on yourself for the benefit of your readers. Read and evaluate the draft as if you were a reader seeing it for the first time.

Check your draft for accuracy, completeness, and effectiveness in achieving your purpose and meeting your readers' needs and expectations. Trim extraneous information: Your writing should give readers exactly what they need, but it should not burden them with unnecessary information or sidetrack them into loosely related subjects.

Do not try to revise for everything at once. Read your rough draft several times, each time looking for and correcting a different set of problems or errors. Concentrate first on larger issues, such as <u>unity</u> (Tab 10) and <u>coherence</u> (Tab 10); save mechanical corrections, like spelling and punctuation, for later proofreading. See also <u>ethics in writing</u> (Tab 1).

Finally, for important documents, consider having others review your writing and make suggestions for improvement. For collaborative writing, of course, team members must review each other's work on segments of the document as well as the final master draft. For further advice and useful checklists, see <u>revision</u> (Tab 1) and <u>proofreading</u> (Tab 1).

Style Guides and Standards

Organizations and professional associations often follow such guides as *The Chicago Manual of Style*, the *MLA Handbook*, *The Publication Manual of the American Psychological Association*, and *United States Government Printing Office Style Manual* to ensure consistency in their publications on issues of usage, format, and documentation. Because advice in such guides often varies, some organizations set their own standards for documents. Where such standards or specific style guides are recommended or required, you should follow those style guidelines.

The Writing Process

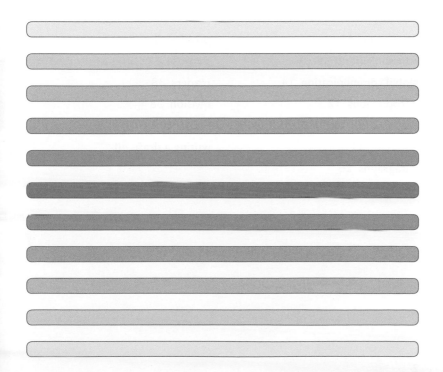

Preview

The "Five Steps to Successful Writing" essay (page xxvii) describes a systematic approach to writing and functions as a diagnostic tool for assessing problems. That is, when you find that a document is not achieving its primary purpose, the five steps can help you pinpoint where a problem occurred. Was the audience not fully assessed? Is additional research needed? Does the document need further revision? Many entries in this section expand on the topics introduced in the "Five Steps," such as **audience**, **collaborative writing**, **selecting the medium** (Tab 2), **writing a draft**, and others. Entries related to the research process, including such topics as finding, evaluating, and using sources, appear in Tab 5, "Research and Documentation."

audience

Considering the needs of your audience is crucial to achieving your purpose. When you are writing to a specific reader, for example, you may find it useful to visualize a reader sitting across from you as you write. (See correspondence, Tab 3.) Likewise, when writing to an audience composed of relatively homogeneous readers, you might create an image of a composite reader and write for *that* reader. In such cases, using the "you" viewpoint (Tab 10) and an appropriate tone (Tab 10) will help you meet the needs of your readers as well as achieve an effective business writing style (Tab 10). For meeting the needs of an audience composed of listeners, see presentations (Tab 8).

Analyzing Your Audience's Needs

Determine the readers' needs relative to your purpose and goals by asking key questions during preparation.

- Who specifically is your reader? Do you have multiple readers? Who needs to see or use the document?
- What do your readers already know about your subject? What are your readers' attitudes about the subject? (Are they skeptical? Supportive? Anxious? Bored?)
- What particular information about your readers (experience, training, and work habits, for example) might help you write at the appropriate level of detail? (See scope.)
- What does the context or medium suggest about meeting the readers' expectations for content? See layout and design (Tab 7) and selecting the medium (Tab 2).
- Do you need to adapt your message for international readers? If so, see global communication, global graphics (Tab 7), and international correspondence (Tab 3).

In the workplace, your readers are often less familiar with the subject than you are. Be careful, therefore, when writing on a topic that is unique to your area of specialization. Be sensitive to the needs of those whose training or experience lies in other areas; provide definitions of nonstandard terms and explanations of principles that you, as a specialist, take for granted. See also defining terms.

Writing for Varied and Multiple Audiences

In writing to a broad or varied audience, as in writing for the Web (Tab 2), visualize a few readers with different backgrounds but who share a purpose or need in reading your text. For documents aimed at multiple audiences with different needs, consider segmenting the document for different groups of readers: an <u>executive summary</u> (Tab 6) for top managers, an appendix with detailed data for technical specialists, and the body for those readers who need to make decisions based on a detailed discussion. See also <u>formal reports</u> (Tab 6) and <u>proposals</u> (Tab 4).

When you have multiple audiences with various needs but cannot segment your document, first determine your primary or most important readers—such as those who will make decisions based on your content—and be sure to meet their needs. Then meet the needs of secondary readers, such as those who need only some of the document's contents, as long as you do not sacrifice the needs of your primary readers. See also <u>persuasion</u> and "Five Steps to Successful Writing" (page xxvii).

collaborative writing

Collaborative writing occurs when two or more writers work together to produce a single document for which they share responsibility and decision-making authority. Collaborative writing teams are formed when (1) the size of a project or the time constraints imposed on it require collaboration, (2) the project involves multiple areas of expertise, or (3) the project requires the melding of divergent views into a single perspective that is acceptable to the whole team or to another group. Many types of collaborations are possible, from the collaboration of a primary writer with a variety of contributors and reviewers to a highly interactive collaboration in which everyone on a team plays a relatively equal role in shaping the document.

Tasks of the Collaborative Writing Team

The collaborating team strives to achieve a compatible working relationship by dividing the work in a way that uses each writer's expertise and experience to its advantage. The team should also designate a coordinator who will guide the team members' activities, organize the project, and ensure coherence and consistency within the document. The coordinator's duties can be determined by mutual agreement, assigned by management, or assigned on a rotating basis if the team often works together.

Planning.   The team members collectively identify the <u>audience</u>, <u>purpose</u>, <u>context</u>, and <u>scope</u> of the project. See also <u>meetings</u> (Tab 8).

At this stage, the team establishes a project plan that may include guidelines for communication among team members, version control (naming, dating, and managing document drafts), review procedures, and writing style standards that team members are expected to follow. The plan includes a schedule with due dates for completing initial research tasks, outlines, drafts, reviews, revisions, and the final document. Figure 7-11 (Tab 7) shows how project-schedule charts are typically organized.

▶ PROFESSIONALISM NOTE Deadlines must be met because team members rely on each other and one missed deadline can delay the entire project. A missed project deadline can result in a lost opportunity or, in the case of <u>proposals</u> (Tab 4), disqualify an application. Individual writers must adjust their schedules and focus on their own writing process to finish drafts and meet the deadline. See "Five Steps to Successful Writing" (page xxvii). ▶

Research and Writing. The team next completes initial research tasks, elicits comments from team members, creates a broad outline of the document (see <u>outlining</u>), and assigns writing tasks to individual team members, based on their expertise. Depending on the project, each team member further researches an assigned segment of the document, expands and develops the broad outline, and produces a draft from a detailed outline. See also <u>writing a draft</u> and <u>research</u> (Tab 5).

Reviewing. Keeping the audience's needs and the document's purpose in mind, each team member critically yet diplomatically reviews the other team members' drafts, from the overall organization to the clarity of each paragraph, and offers advice to help improve the writer's work. Team members can easily solicit feedback by sharing files and then working with track and comment features that allow reviewers to suggest changes without deleting the original text.

Revising. In this final stage, individual writers evaluate their colleagues' reviews and accept, reject, or build on their suggestions. Then, the team coordinator can consolidate all drafts into a final master copy and maintain and evaluate it for consistency and coherence. See also <u>revision</u>.

▶ PROFESSIONALISM NOTE As you collaborate, be ready to tolerate some disharmony, but temper it with mutual respect. Team members may not agree on every subject, and differing perspectives can easily lead to conflict, ranging from mild differences over minor points to major showdowns. However, creative differences resolved respectfully can energize the team and, in fact, strengthen a finished document by compelling writers to reexamine assumptions and issues in unanticipated ways. See also <u>listening</u> (Tab 8). ▶

Writer's Checklist: Writing Collaboratively

- ☑ Designate one person as the team coordinator.
- ☑ Identify the audience, purpose, context, and scope of the project.
- ☑ Create a project plan, including a schedule and style or format standards.
- ☑ Create a working outline of the document.
- ☑ Assign sections or tasks to each team member.
- ☑ Research and write drafts of each document section.
- ☑ Use the agreed-upon standards for style and format.
- ☑ Exchange sections for team member reviews.
- ☑ Revise sections as needed.
- ☑ Meet the established deadlines for drafts, revisions, and final versions.
- ☑ Consider online tools to facilitate the work of collaborating with team members.

conclusions

The conclusion of a document ties the main ideas together and can clinch a final significant point. This final point may, for example, make a prediction or offer a judgment, summarize key findings, or recommend a course of action. Figure 1–1 is a conclusion from a proposal to reduce health-care costs by increasing employee fitness through sponsoring health-club memberships. Notice that it summarizes key points, points to the benefits, and makes the recommendation.

The way you conclude depends on your <u>purpose</u>, the needs of your <u>audience</u>, and the <u>context</u>. For example, a lengthy sales proposal might conclude persuasively with a summary of the proposal's salient points and the company's relevant strengths. The following examples are typical concluding strategies.

RECOMMENDATION

Our findings suggest that you need to alter your marketing to adjust to the changing demographics for your products.

We recommend your placement of ads include . . . .

SUMMARY

As this report describes, we would attract more recent graduates with the following strategies:

1. Establish our presence on social media to reach more college students before they graduate.

Conclusion and Recommendation

Enrolling employees in the deluxe program at AeroFitness would allow them to receive a one-month free trial membership. Those interested in continuing could then join the club and receive a 30 percent discount on the $1,200 annual fee and pay only half of the one-time membership fee of $500. The other half of the membership fee ($250) would be paid for by ABO. If employees leave the company, they would have the option of purchasing ABO's share of the membership to continue at AeroFitness or selling their half of the membership to another ABO employee wishing to join AeroFitness.

Summarizes key points

Club membership allows employees at all five ABO warehouses to participate in the program. The more employees who participate, the greater the long-term savings in ABO's health-care costs. Overall, implementing this program will help ABO, Inc., reduce its health-care costs while building stronger employee relations by offering employees a desirable benefit. If this proposal is adopted, I have some additional thoughts about publicizing the program to encourage employee participation that I would be pleased to share.

Points to benefits

I recommend, therefore, that ABO, Inc., participate in the corporate membership program at AeroFitness Clubs, Inc., by subsidizing employee memberships. Offering this benefit to employees will demonstrate ABO's commitment to the importance of a healthy workforce.

Makes a recommendation

FIGURE 1–1. Conclusion

2. Increase our attendance at college career fairs.
3. Establish more internships and work-study programs.

JUDGMENT

Based on the scope and degree of the storm's damage, the current construction code for roofing on light industrial facilities is inadequate.

IMPLICATION

Although our estimate calls for a substantially higher budget than in the three previous years, we believe that it is reasonable given our planned expansion.

PREDICTION

Although I have exceeded my original estimate for equipment, I have reduced my labor costs; therefore, I will easily stay within the original bid.

The concluding statement may merely present ideas for consideration, may call for action, or may deliberately provoke thought.

IDEAS FOR CONSIDERATION

The new prices become effective at the first of the year. Price adjustments are routine for the company, but some of your customers will not consider them acceptable. Please bear in mind the needs of both your customers and the company as you implement these price adjustments.

CALL FOR ACTION

Please make a payment of $250 now if you wish to keep your account active. If you have not responded to our previous letters because of some special hardship, I will be glad to work out a solution with you.

THOUGHT-PROVOKING STATEMENT

Can we continue to accept the losses incurred by inefficiency? Or should we take the necessary steps to control it now?

Be especially careful not to introduce a new topic when you conclude. A conclusion should always relate to and reinforce the ideas presented earlier in your writing. Moreover, the conclusion must be consistent with what the introduction promised the report would examine (its purpose) and how it would do so (its method).

For guidance about the location of the conclusion section in a report, see formal reports (Tab 6). For letter and other short closings, see correspondence (Tab 3) and entries on specific types of documents throughout this book.

context

Context is the environment or circumstances in which writers produce documents and within which readers interpret the meanings of those documents, whether they are reports or correspondence. This entry considers the significance of context for workplace writing and suggests how you can be aware of it as you write. See also audience.

The context for any document is determined by interrelated events or circumstances both inside and outside an organization. For example, when you write a proposal to fund a project within your company, the economic condition of that company is part of the context that will determine how your proposal is received. If the company has recently laid off a dozen employees, its management may not be inclined to approve a proposal to expand its operations—regardless of how well the proposal is written.

When you correspond with someone, the events that prompted you to write shape the context of the message and affect what you say and how you say it. If you write to a customer in response to a complaint, for example, the tone and approach of your message will be determined by the context—what you find when you investigate the issue. Is your company fully or partly at fault? Has the customer incorrectly used a product? Contributed to a problem? (See also <u>adjustments</u>, Tab 3.) If you write instructions for office staff who must use high-volume document-processing equipment, other questions will reveal the context. What are the lighting and other physical conditions near the equipment? Will these physical conditions affect the layout and design of the instructions? What potential safety issues might the users encounter? See also <u>layout and design</u> (Tab 7).

Assessing Context

Each time you write, the context needs to be clearly in your mind so that your document will achieve its <u>purpose</u>. The following questions are starting points to help you become aware of the context, how it will influence your approach and your readers' interpretation of what you have written, and how it will affect the decisions you need to make during the writing process. See also "Five Steps to Successful Writing" (page xxvii).

- What is your professional relationship with your readers, and how might that affect the tone, style, and <u>scope</u> of your writing?
- What is "the story" behind the immediate reason you are writing; that is, what series of events or perhaps previous documents led to your need to write?
- What is the preferred medium of your readers, and which medium is best suited to your purpose? See also <u>selecting the medium</u> (Tab 2).
- What specific factors (such as competition, finance, and regulation) are important to your organization or department?
- What is the corporate culture in which your readers work, and what key values might you find in its mission statement?
- What current events within or outside an organization or a department may influence how readers interpret your writing?
- What national cultural differences might affect your readers' expectations or interpretations of the document? See also <u>global communication</u>.

As these questions suggest, context is specific each time you write and often involves, for example, the history of a specific organization or your past dealings with individual readers.

Signaling Context

Because context is so important, remind your reader in some way of the context for your writing, as in the following opening for a cover message to a proposal.

> ▶ During our meeting last week on improving quality, you mentioned that we have previously required usability testing only for documents going to high-profile clients because of the costs involved. The idea occurred to me that we might try less-extensive usability testing for many of our other clients. Because you asked for suggestions, I have proposed in the attached document a method of limited usability testing for a broad range of clients in order to improve overall quality while keeping costs at a minimum.

Of course, as described in <u>introductions</u>, providing context for a reader may require only a brief background statement or short reminders.

> ▶ Several weeks ago, a financial adviser noticed a recurring problem in the software developed by CGF Systems. Specifically, error messages repeatedly appeared when, in fact, no specific trouble . . .

> ▶ Jane, as I promised in my e-mail yesterday, I've attached the personnel budget estimates for the next fiscal year.

As the last example suggests, always provide context for attachments to <u>e-mail</u> (Tab 2).

defining terms

Defining key terms and concepts is often essential for clarity. Terms can be defined either formally or informally, depending on your <u>purpose</u>, <u>audience</u>, and <u>context</u>.

A *formal definition* is a form of classification. You define a term by placing it in a category and then identifying the features that distinguish it from other members of the same category.

TERM	CATEGORY	DISTINGUISHING FEATURES
An *auction* is	a public sale	in which property passes to the highest bidder through successively increased offers.

An *informal definition* explains a term by giving a more familiar word or phrase as a synonym.

- Plants have a *symbiotic*, or *mutually beneficial*, relationship with certain kinds of bacteria.

State definitions in a positive way; focus on what the term *is* rather than on what it is not.

NEGATIVE	In a legal transaction, *real property* is not personal property.
POSITIVE	*Real property* is legal terminology for the right or interest a person has in land and the permanent structures on that land.

Avoid circular definitions, which merely restate the term to be defined.

CIRCULAR	*Spontaneous combustion* is fire that begins spontaneously.
CLEAR	*Spontaneous combustion* is the self-ignition of a flammable material through a chemical reaction.

In addition, avoid "is when" and "is where" definitions. Such definitions fail to include the category and are too indirect.

- A *contract* is ~~when two or more parties agree to something.~~ *a binding agreement between two or more parties.*
                ^

description

The key to effective description is the accurate presentation of details, whether for simple or complex descriptions. In Figure 1–2, notice that the simple description contained in the purchase order includes five specific details (in addition to the part number) structured logically.

Shopping Cart		<u>Continue shopping</u>	<u>Print shopping cart</u>	
Part No.	**Description**	**Quantity**	**Item Price**	**Total**
IW 8421	Infectious-waste bags, 12″ × 14″, heavy-gauge polyethylene, red double closures with self-sealing adhesive strips	5 boxes containing 200 bags per box	$32.98	$164.90
			Subtotal	$164.90
			Shipping charges	$7.99
			Total	$172.89
				Submit order

FIGURE 1–2. Simple Description

Complex descriptions, of course, involve more details. In describing a mechanical device, for example, describe the whole device and its function before giving a detailed description of how each part works. The description should conclude with an explanation of how each part contributes to the functioning of the whole.

In descriptions intended for an <u>audience</u> unfamiliar with the topic, details are crucial. Details will help readers visualize specifics of the new image, object, or idea that the writer wants to convey. In the following description of a company's headquarters, notice the detailed discussion of colors, shapes, and features. The writer assumes that the reader knows such terms as *colonial design* and *haiku fountain*.

▶ Their company's headquarters, which reminded me of a rural college campus, are located north of the city in a 90-acre lush green wooded area. The complex consists of five three-story buildings of red-brick colonial design. The buildings are spaced about 50 feet apart and are built in a U-shape surrounding a reflection pool that frames a striking haiku fountain.

You can also use analogy to explain unfamiliar concepts in terms of familiar ones, such as "U-shape" in the previous example. See <u>figures of speech</u> (Tab 10).

Visuals can be powerful aids in descriptive writing. For a discussion of how to incorporate visual material into text, see Tab 7, "Design and Visuals."

ethics in writing

Ethics refers to the choices we make that affect others for good or ill. Ethical issues are inherent in writing and speaking because what we write and say can influence others. Further, how we express ideas affects our audience's perceptions of us and our organization's ethical stance. See also <u>audience</u>.

❖ ETHICS NOTE No book can describe how to act ethically in every situation, but this entry describes some typical ethical lapses to watch for during <u>revision</u>.* In other entries throughout this book, ethical issues are highlighted using the symbols surrounding this paragraph. ❖

Avoid language that attempts to evade responsibility. Some writers use the passive <u>voice</u> (Tab 11) because they hope to avoid responsibility

---

*Adapted from Brenda R. Sims, "Linking Ethics and Language in the Technical Communication Classroom," *Technical Communication Quarterly* 2, no. 3 (Summer 1993): 285–99.

or to obscure an issue: "It has been decided" (*Who* has decided?) or "Several mistakes were made" (*Who* made them?).

Avoid deceptive language. Do not use words with more than one meaning to circumvent the truth. Consider the company document that stated, "A nominal charge will be assessed for using our facilities." When clients objected that the charge was actually very high, the writer pointed out that the word *nominal* means "the named amount" as well as "very small." In that situation, clients had a strong case in accusing the company of attempting to be deceptive. Various <u>abstract words</u> (Tab 10), technical and legal <u>jargon</u> (Tab 10), and <u>euphemisms</u> (Tab 10) are unethical when they are used to mislead readers or to hide a serious or dangerous situation, even though technical or legal experts could interpret those words or terms as accurate. See also <u>word choice</u> (Tab 10).

Do not deemphasize or suppress important information. Not including information that a reader would want to have, such as potential safety hazards or hidden costs for which a customer might be responsible, is unethical and possibly illegal. Likewise, do not hide information in dense paragraphs with small type and little white space, as is common in credit-card contracts. Use <u>layout and design</u> (Tab 7) features such as legible type sizes, bulleted or numbered <u>lists</u> (Tab 7), and footnotes to highlight information that is important to readers.

Do not mislead with partial or self-serving information. For example, avoid the temptation to highlight a feature or service that readers would find attractive but that is available only with some product models or at extra cost. See also <u>logic errors</u> (Tab 10) and <u>positive writing</u> (Tab 10). Readers could justifiably object that you have given them a false impression to sell them a product or service, especially if you also deemphasize the extra cost or other special conditions.

In general, treat others—individuals, companies, groups—with fairness and with respect. Avoid language that is biased, racist, or sexist or that perpetuates stereotypes. See also <u>biased language</u> (Tab 10).

Finally, be aware that both <u>plagiarism</u> (Tab 5) and violations of <u>copyright</u> (Tab 5) not only are unethical but also can have serious professional and legal consequences for you in the classroom and on the job.

Writer's Checklist: Writing Ethically

Ask yourself the following questions:

- ☑ *Am I willing to take responsibility, publicly and privately, for what I have written?* Make sure you can stand behind what you have written.

- ☑ *Is the document or message honest and truthful?* Scrutinize findings and conclusions carefully. Make sure that the data support them.

(*continued*)

1

Writer's Checklist: Writing Ethically (continued)

☑ *Am I acting in my employer's, my client's, the public's, or my own best long-term interest?* Have an impartial and appropriate outsider review and comment on what you have written.

☑ *Does the document or message violate anyone's rights?* If information is confidential and you have serious concerns, consider a review by the company's legal staff or an attorney.

☑ *Am I ethically consistent in my writing?* Consistently apply the principles outlined here and those you have assimilated throughout your life.

☑ *What if everybody acted or communicated in this way?* If you were the intended reader, consider whether the message would be acceptable and respectful.

global communication

The continual expansion of the global marketplace and the growing need for many businesses to participate globally means that the ability to communicate with international audiences from varied backgrounds is essential. See <u>audience</u>.

Many entries in this book, such as <u>meetings</u> (Tab 8) and <u>résumés</u> (Tab 9), are based on dominant cultural patterns in the United States. The treatment of such topics might be very different in other cultures where leadership styles, persuasive strategies, and even legal constraints differ.

As illustrated in <u>international correspondence</u> (Tab 4), organizational patterns, forms of courtesy, and ideas about efficiency can vary significantly from culture to culture. What might be seen as direct and efficient in the United States could be considered blunt and even impolite in other cultures. The explanations for these differing ways of viewing communication are complex. Researchers often measure cultural differences through such concepts as the importance of honor or "face saving," perceptions of time, and preferences for avoiding uncertainty. Because cultures evolve and global communication affects cultural patterns, you must also be able to adapt to cultural variations. Figure 1–3 shows an ineffective global business communication, whereas Figure 1–4 demonstrates an effective global business communication. The checklist that follows offers useful approaches that can help you adapt. See also <u>global graphics</u> (Tab 7).

Use of first names varies among cultures and is not appropriate for initial contacts.

The writer does not provide context for the reader to judge this company's fit for Makos.

LoveModernInc.com
6828 W Grand Ave
Chicago, IL 60707

April 15, 2017

Rena Makos
Makos Contemporary Furniture
Xenokratous 7
Athina 106 75, Greece

Dear Rena,

Contractions ("I'm") are informal and might not appear in an English dictionary.

My name is Jesse Hernandez, and I'm an assistant director of sales at Love Modern, Inc., an interior design company in Chicago, Illinois. I'll be visiting Greece with some colleagues in two months and would like to touch base with you about the possibility of establishing a partnership with your company that would begin in Spring 2018.

The writer needs to introduce colleagues to be polite.

This is abrupt for many cultures.

The idiom "touch base" could be confusing.

We will be in Athens from 6/2/17 until 6/5/17 and from 6/8/17 until 6/11/17, and our schedule is very flexible. We'd like to meet with you if you have the time. If you believe that another company is better suited for this partnership, we'd greatly appreciate it if you forwarded this letter to them.

We look forward to your reply.

All the very best,

This sentence suggests the writer has not researched whether Makos is the best fit for a partnership.

Jesse Hernandez

The numerical month/day/year order is not universal outside of the United States.

FIGURE 1–3. Ineffective Global Business Communication

LoveModernInc.com
6828 W Grand Ave
Chicago, IL 60707

April 15, 2017

Rena Makos
Makos Contemporary Furniture
Xenokratous 7
Athina 106 75, Greece

Dear Ms. Makos:

I am writing to inquire about the possibility of a partnership between your company and Love Modern, Inc., an interior design company in Chicago, Illinois. Our director of sales, Kristina Roberts, saw your Modern Club chair at last year's Atlanta International Gifts & Home Furnishings Market and was impressed by its design and quality. We are interested in carrying products from your furniture line in our stores for the Spring 2018 season with the option of continuing that line in future seasons.

Our company offers an established customer base and a record of previous successes in partnerships such as the one we propose. Love Modern annually ranks in the top ten for furniture sales in the state, and we are known for providing excellent customer service and high-quality modern furniture. We are known for introducing new furniture designers, including rising international designers, to the Chicago metropolitan area. Your company has become highly regarded across Athens for innovative updates to classic designs, a quality that our customers appreciate. We believe that a partnership between our companies could benefit both equally.

Ms. Roberts and I will be in Athens June 2–5, 2017, and again June 8–11, 2017. If you are available to meet during our visits, please let me know, and I will arrange details for our meeting. During this meeting, we would begin negotiations for the details of this partnership. I expect that it will take no more than two hours. If you are not available to meet in person on the dates listed above, I would be pleased to set up alternate meeting times using Skype. If you would like to see a list of successful partnerships and industry rankings, go to LoveModernInc.com/mediafacts.php.

We at Love Modern are excited by the possibilities of working with Makos Contemporary Furniture. We look forward to your reply.

Sincerely,

Jesse Hernandez

Assistant Director of Sales
1 (555) 555-5555
jhernandez@LoveModernInc.com

FIGURE 1–4. Effective Global Business Communication

Writer's Checklist: Communicating Globally

☑ Discuss the differing cultures within your company or region to reinforce the idea that people can interpret verbal and nonverbal communications differently.

☑ Invite global and intercultural communication experts to speak at your workplace. Companies in your area may have employees who could be resources for cultural discussions.

☑ Understand that the key to effective communication with global audiences is recognizing that cultural differences, despite the challenges they may present, offer opportunities for growth for both you and your organization.

☑ Consult with someone from your intended audience's culture. Many phrases, gestures, and visual elements are so subtle that only someone who is very familiar with the culture can explain the effect they may have on others from that culture. See also <u>global graphics</u> (Tab 7).

☑ Intercultural Press publishes books on "intercultural, multicultural and cross-cultural studies and informative country guides to help you do business and form strong relationships in foreign countries." See *http://nicholasbrealey.com/boston/subjects/interculturalpress.html.* Geert Hofstede, a leading researcher in national and organizational culture, also offers cultural comparison tools and other resources on his Web site. See *https://geert-hofstede.com/.*

introductions

Every document must have either an opening or an introduction. An opening usually simply focuses the reader's attention on your topic and then proceeds to the body of your document. A full-scale introduction, discussed later in this entry, sets the stage by providing necessary information to understand the discussion that follows in the body. In general, <u>correspondence</u> (Tab 3) and routine <u>reports</u> (Tab 4) need only an opening; <u>formal reports</u> (Tab 6), major <u>proposals</u> (Tab 4), and other complex documents need a full-scale introduction. For a discussion of comparable sections for Web sites, see <u>writing for the Web</u> (Tab 2). See also <u>conclusions</u>.

Routine Openings

When your <u>audience</u> is familiar with your topic or if what you are writing is brief or routine, then a simple opening will provide adequate <u>context</u>, as shown in the following examples.

LETTER

Dear Mr. Ignatowski:
You will be happy to know that we have corrected the error in your bank balance. The new balance shows . . .

E-MAIL

Jane, as I promised in my e-mail yesterday, I've attached the human resources budget estimates for fiscal year 2018.

MEMO

To date, 18 of the 20 specimens your department submitted for analysis have been examined. Our preliminary analysis indicates . . .

Opening Strategies

Opening strategies are aimed at focusing the readers' attention and motivating them to read the entire document.

Objective.   In reporting on a project, you might open with a statement of the project's objective so that the readers have a basis for judging the results.

▶ The primary goal of this project was to develop new techniques to solve the problem of waste disposal. Our first step was to investigate . . .

Problem Statement.   One way to give readers the perspective of your report is to present a brief account of the problem that led to the study or project being reported.

▶ Several weeks ago a manager noticed a recurring problem in the software developed by Datacom Systems. Specifically, error messages repeatedly appeared when, in fact, no specific trouble. . . . After an extensive investigation, we found that Datacom Systems . . .

For proposals or formal reports, of course, problem statements may be more elaborate and a part of the full-scale introduction, which is discussed later in this entry.

Scope. You may want to present the <u>scope</u> of your document in your opening. By providing the parameters of your material, the limitations of the subject, or the amount of detail to be presented, you enable your readers to determine whether they want or need to read your document.

▶ This pamphlet provides a review of the requirements for obtaining a private pilot's license. It is not intended as a textbook to prepare you for the examination itself; rather, it outlines the steps you need to take and the costs involved.

Background. The background or history of a subject may be interesting and lend perspective and insight to a subject. Consider the following example from a newsletter describing the process of oil drilling:

▶ From the bamboo poles the Chinese used when the pyramids were young to today's giant rigs drilling in deep water, there has been considerable progress in the search for oil. But whether in ancient China or a modern city, underwater or on a mountaintop, the objective of drilling has always been the same — to manufacture a hole in the ground, inch by inch.

Summary. You can provide a summary opening by describing in abbreviated form the results, conclusions, or recommendations of your article or report. Be concise: Do not begin a summary by writing "This report summarizes. . . ."

CHANGE	This report summarizes the advantages offered by the photon as a means of examining the structural features of the atom.
TO	As a means of examining the structure of the atom, the photon offers several advantages.

Interesting Detail. Often an interesting detail will attract the readers' attention and pique their curiosity. Readers of an annual report for a manufacturer of telescopes and scientific instruments, for example, may be persuaded to invest if they believe that the company is developing innovative, cutting-edge products.

▶ The rings of Saturn have puzzled astronomers ever since they were discovered by Galileo in 1610 using the first telescope. Recently, even more rings have been discovered. . . .
    Our company's Scientific Instrument Division designs and manufactures research-quality, digitally controlled telescopes that

promise to solve the puzzles of Saturn's rings by enabling scientists to use multicolor differential photometry to determine the rings' origins and compositions.

Definition.   Although a definition can be useful as an opening, do not define something with which your audience is familiar or provide a definition that is obviously a contrived opening (such as "Webster defines *technology* as . . ."). A definition should be used as an opening only if it offers insight into what follows.

▶ *Risk* is often a loosely defined term. In this report, risk refers to a qualitative combination of the probability of an event and the severity of the consequences of that event. In fact, . . .

Anecdote.   An anecdote can be used to attract and build interest in a subject that may otherwise be mundane; however, this strategy is best suited to longer documents and <u>presentations</u> (Tab 8).

▶ In his poem "The Calf Path" (1895), Sam Walter Foss tells of a wandering, wobbly calf trying to find its way home at night through the lonesome woods. It made a crooked path, which was taken up the next day by a lone dog. Then "a bellwether sheep pursued the trail over vale and steep, drawing behind him the flock, too, as all good bellwethers do." This forest path became a country lane that bent and turned and turned again. The lane became a village street, and at last the main street of a flourishing city. The poet ends by saying, "A hundred thousand men were led by a calf near three centuries dead."

Many companies today follow a "calf path" because they react to events rather than planning. . . .

Quotation.   Occasionally, you can use a quotation to stimulate interest in your subject. To be effective, however, the quotation must be pertinent—not some loosely related remark selected from a book of quotations.

▶ Richard Smith, founder of PCS Corporation, recently said, "I believe that managers need to be more 'people smart' than ever before. The management style of today involves much more than just managing the operations of a department—it requires understanding the personalities that comprise a corporation." His statement represents a growing feeling among corporate leaders that . . .

Forecast.   Sometimes you can use a forecast of a new development or trend to gain the audience's attention and interest.

▶ In the not-too-distant future, we may be able to use a handheld medical diagnostic device similar to those in science fiction to assess the physical condition of accident victims. This project and others are now being developed at The Seldi Group, Inc.

Persuasive Hook.   Although all opening strategies contain persuasive elements, the hook uses <u>persuasion</u> most overtly. A Web site touting the newest innovation in tax-preparation software might address readers as follows:

▶ Welcome to the newest way to do your taxes! TaxPro EZ ends the headache of last-minute tax preparation with its unique TaxPro app.

Full-Scale Introductions

The purpose of a full-scale introduction is to give readers enough general information about the subject to enable them to understand the details in the body of the document. (See Figure 6–2, page 185.) An introduction should accomplish any or all of the following:

- *State the subject.* Provide background information, such as definition, history, or theory, to provide context for your readers.
- *State the purpose.* Make your readers aware of why the document exists and whether the material provides a new perspective or clarifies an existing perspective.
- *State the scope.* Tell readers the amount of detail you plan to cover.
- *Preview the development of the subject.* Especially in a longer document, outline how you plan to develop the subject. Providing such information allows readers to anticipate how the subject will be presented and helps them evaluate your conclusions or recommendations.

Consider writing an opening or introduction last. Many writers find that only after they have drafted the body of the document do they have a full enough perspective on the subject to introduce it adequately.

organization

A well-organized document enables your readers to grasp how the pieces of your subject fit together as a coherent whole. An organized document or presentation is based on an effective outline produced from a method of development that suits your subject, your <u>audience</u>, and your <u>purpose</u>. Following are the most common methods of developing any

document—from an e-mail to a formal report to a Web page. See also
<u>outlining</u>.

- *Cause-and-effect development* begins with either the cause or
  the effect of an event. For example, if you were reporting on
  the cause of the financial crisis in a company, you might start
  your report with the causes (perhaps investment decisions) and
  lead into the current financial circumstances. Conversely, you
  might start with a description of the financial crisis and trace
  the events back to the causes. This approach can also be used to
  develop a report that offers a solution to a problem, beginning
  with the problem and moving on to the solution, or vice versa.
- *Chronological development* emphasizes the time element of a
  sequence. For example, a Federal Aviation Administration (FAA)
  report on an airplane crash might begin with takeoff and proceed
  in segments of time to the eventual crash.
- *Comparison* is useful when writing about a new topic that is in
  many ways similar to another, more familiar topic. For example,
  an online tutorial for a new operating system might compare that
  system to one that is familiar to the users.
- *Division* separates a whole into component parts and discusses
  each part separately. Division could be used, for example, to
  report on a multinational organization by describing its operations
  in various countries.
- *Classification* groups parts into categories that clarify the relationship of the parts. For example, you might discuss local retail
  businesses by grouping them according to common demographic
  features of their target customers (such as age, household income,
  occupation).
- *General and specific development* proceeds either from general
  information to specific details or from specific information to a
  general conclusion. If you are writing about a new software product, for example, you might begin with a general statement of the
  function of the total software package, then explain the functions of the major routines in the package, and finally describe
  the functions of the various subroutines. Conversely, you might
  describe a software problem in a minor application and then
  trace it to a larger, more global problem with the software.
- *Order-of-importance development* presents information in either
  decreasing order of importance, as in a proposal that begins
  with the most important point, or increasing order of importance,
  as in a presentation that ends with your most important point.
- *Sequential development* emphasizes the order of elements in a
  process and is particularly useful when writing step-by-step
  instructions.

- *Spatial development* describes the physical appearance of an object or area (such as a room) from top to bottom, inside to outside, front to back, and so on. A crime-scene report might start at the site of the crime and proceed in concentric areas from that point.

Documents often blend methods of development. For example, in a report that describes the organization of a company, you might use elements from three methods of development. You could divide the larger topic (the company) into operations (division and classification), arrange the operations according to what you see as their impact within the company (order of importance), and present their manufacturing operations in the order they occur (sequential). As this example illustrates, when outlining a document, you may base your major division on one primary method of development appropriate to your purpose and then subordinate other methods to it.

During the organization stage of the writing process, consider a design and layout that will be helpful to your reader and a format appropriate to your subject and purpose. If you intend to include visuals with your writing, plan them as you create your outline, especially if they need to be prepared by someone else while you are writing and revising the draft. See also Tab 4, "Business Writing Documents and Elements," and Tab 7, "Design and Visuals."

outlining

An outline is the skeleton of the document you are going to write; at the least, it should list the main topics and subtopics of your subject in a logical organization.

Advantages of Outlining

An outline provides structure to your writing by ensuring that it has a beginning (introduction), a middle (main body), and an end (conclusion). Using an outline offers many other benefits.

- Larger and more complex subjects are easier to handle because an outline breaks them into manageable parts.
- Like a road map, an outline indicates a starting point and keeps you moving logically so that you do not lose your way before you arrive at your conclusion.
- Parts of an outline are easily moved around so that you can select the most effective arrangement of your ideas.
- Creating a good outline frees you from concerns of organization while you are writing a draft.

- An outline enables you to provide <u>coherence</u> (Tab 10) and <u>transition</u> (Tab 10) so that one part flows smoothly into the next without omitting important details.
- <u>Logic errors</u> (Tab 10) are much easier to detect and correct in an outline than in a draft.
- An outline helps with <u>collaborative writing</u> because it enables a team to refine a project's <u>scope</u>, divide responsibilities, and maintain focus.

Types of Outlines

Two types of outlines are most common: short topic outlines and lengthy sentence outlines. A *topic outline* consists of short phrases arranged to reflect your primary method of development. A topic outline is especially useful for short documents such as e-mails, letters, or memos. See Tab 3, "Correspondence."

For a large writing project, create a topic outline first, and then use it as a basis for creating a sentence outline. A *sentence outline* uses a complete sentence for each idea that may become the topic sentence for a paragraph in the rough draft. If most of your notes can be shaped into topic sentences for paragraphs, you can be relatively sure that your document will be well organized. See also <u>note-taking</u> (Tab 5) and <u>research</u> (Tab 5).

Creating an Outline

When you are outlining large and complex subjects with many pieces of information, the first step is to group related notes from your research into categories. Sort the notes by major and minor division headings. For example, the major divisions for this discussion of outlining could be as follows:

   I. Advantages of outlining
  II. Types of outlines
 III. Creating an outline

The second step is to establish your minor divisions within each major division. Arrange your minor points using a method of development under their major division and label them.

  II. Types of outlines
     A. Topic outlines   ] **Division and Classification**
     B. Sentence outlines

 III. Creating an outline
     A. Establish major and minor divisions.
     B. Sort notes by major and minor divisions.   ] **Sequential**
     C. Complete the sentence outline.

You will sometimes need more than two levels of headings. If your subject is complicated, you may need three or four levels of headings to better organize all your ideas in proper relationship to one another. In that event, use the following numbering scheme:

I. First-level heading
    A. Second-level heading
        1. Third-level heading
            a. Fourth-level heading

The third step is to mark each of your notes with the appropriate Roman numeral and capital letter. Arrange the notes logically within each minor heading, and mark each with the appropriate, sequential Arabic number. As you do, make sure your organization is logical and your headings have <u>parallel structure</u> (Tab 10). For example, all the second-level headings under "III. Creating an outline" are complete sentences in the active <u>voice</u> (Tab 11).

Treat <u>visuals</u> (Tab 7) as an integral part of your outline, and plan approximately where each should appear. Either include a rough sketch of the visual or write "illustration of . . ." at each place. As with other information in an outline, freely move, delete, or add visuals as needed.

The outline samples shown earlier use a combination of numbers and letters to differentiate the various levels of information. You could also use a decimal numbering system, such as the following, for your outline.

1. FIRST-LEVEL HEADING
    1.1 Second-level heading
    1.2 Second-level heading
        1.2.1 Third-level heading
        1.2.2 Third-level heading
            1.2.2.1 Fourth-level heading
            1.2.2.2 Fourth-level heading
    1.3 Second-level heading

2. FIRST-LEVEL HEADING

This system should not go beyond the fourth level because the numbers get too cumbersome beyond that point. In many documents, such as policies and procedures, the decimal numbering system is carried over from the outline to the final version of the document for ease of cross-referencing sections.

Create your draft by converting your notes into complete sentences and <u>paragraphs</u>. If you have a sentence outline, the most difficult part of the writing job is over. However, whether you have a topic or a sentence outline, remember that an outline is flexible; it may need to change as you write the draft, but it should always be your point of departure and return.

DIGITAL TIP

Formatting Your Outline

Using the outline feature of your word-processing software enables you to do the following:

- Format your outline automatically.
- Fill in, rearrange, and update your outline.
- Experiment with the organization and scope of information while retaining the outline format.
- Rearrange sections and subsections easily.
- Create Roman numeral or decimal numbering outline styles.

Experiment with the default settings of the outline feature to make the best use of this software.

paragraphs

A paragraph performs three functions: (1) It develops the unit of thought stated in the topic sentence; (2) it provides a logical break in the material; and (3) it creates a visual break on the page, which signals a new topic.

Topic Sentence

A topic sentence states the paragraph's main idea; the rest of the paragraph supports and develops that statement with related details. The topic sentence, which is often the first sentence, tells the reader what the paragraph is about.

▶ *The cost of training new employees is high.* In addition to the cost of classroom facilities and instructors, an organization must pay employees their regular salary while they sit in the classroom. For the companies to break even on this investment in their professional employees, those employees must stay in the job for which they have been trained for at least one year.

The topic sentence is usually most effective early in the paragraph, but a paragraph can lead to the topic sentence, which is sometimes done to achieve emphasis (Tab 10).

▶ Energy does far more than simply make our daily lives more comfortable and convenient. Suppose someone wanted to stop—and reverse—the economic progress of this nation. What would be the surest and quickest way to do it? Simply block the nation's ability to produce energy! The nation would face a devastating economic crisis. *Our economy, in short, is energy-based.*

On rare occasions, the topic sentence may logically fall in the middle of a paragraph.

▶ ... [It] is time to insist that science does not progress by carefully designed steps called "experiments," each of which has a well-defined beginning and end. *Science is a continuous and often a disorderly and accidental process.* We shall not do the young psychologist any favor if we agree to reconstruct our practices to fit the pattern demanded by current scientific methodology.

—B. F. Skinner, "A Case History in Scientific Method"

Paragraph Length

A paragraph should be just long enough to deal adequately with the subject of its topic sentence. A new paragraph should begin whenever the subject changes significantly. A series of short, undeveloped paragraphs can indicate poor <u>organization</u> by breaking a single idea into several pieces. A series of long paragraphs, however, can fail to provide the reader with manageable subdivisions of thought. Paragraph length should aid the reader's understanding of ideas.

Occasionally, a one-sentence paragraph is acceptable if it is used as a <u>transition</u> (Tab 10) between longer paragraphs or as a one-sentence <u>introduction</u> or <u>conclusion</u> in <u>correspondence</u> (Tab 3).

Writing Paragraphs

Careful paragraphing reflects the writer's logical organization and helps the reader follow the writer's thoughts. A good working outline makes it easy to group ideas into appropriate paragraphs. (See also <u>outlining</u>.) The following partial topic outline plots the course of the subsequent paragraphs:

TOPIC OUTLINE (PARTIAL)
1. Advantages of Chicago as location for new facility
   A. Transport infrastructure
      1. Rail
      2. Air
      3. Truck
      4. Sea (except in winter)
   B. Labor supply
      1. Engineering and scientific personnel
         a. Similar companies in area
         b. Major universities
      2. Technical and manufacturing personnel
         a. Community college programs
         b. Custom programs

RESULTING PARAGRAPHS

Probably the greatest advantage of Chicago as a location for our new facility is its excellent transport facilities. The city is served by three major railroads. Both domestic and international air-cargo service are available at O'Hare International Airport; Midway Airport's convenient location adds flexibility for domestic air-cargo service. Chicago is a major hub of the trucking industry, and most of the nation's large freight carriers have terminals there. Finally, except in the winter months when the Great Lakes are frozen, Chicago is a seaport, accessible through the St. Lawrence Seaway.

Chicago's second advantage is its abundant labor force. An ample supply of engineering and scientific staff is assured not only by the presence of many companies engaged in activities similar to ours but also by the presence of several major universities in the metropolitan area. Similarly, technicians and manufacturing personnel are in abundant supply. The colleges in the City Colleges of Chicago system, as well as half a dozen other two-year colleges in the outlying areas, produce graduates with associate's degrees in a wide variety of technical specialties appropriate to our needs. Moreover, three of the outlying colleges have expressed an interest in developing off-campus courses attuned specifically to our requirements.

Paragraph Unity and Coherence

A good paragraph has <u>unity</u> (Tab 10) and <u>coherence</u> (Tab 10) as well as adequate development. *Unity* is singleness of purpose, based on a topic sentence that states the core idea of the paragraph. When every sentence in the paragraph develops the core idea, the paragraph has unity. *Coherence* is holding to one point of view, one attitude, one tense; it is the joining of sentences into a logical pattern. Transitional words tie ideas together and lead to coherence, as shown by the boldfaced italicized words in the following paragraph.

TOPIC
SENTENCE

Over the past several months, I have heard complaints about the Merit Award Program. ***Specifically***, many employees feel that this program should be linked to annual ***salary increases***. They believe that ***salary increases*** would provide a much better incentive than the current $500 to $700 cash awards for exceptional service. ***In addition***, these ***employees believe*** that their supervisors consider the cash awards a satisfactory alternative to salary increases. Although I don't think this practice is widespread, the fact that the ***employees believe*** that it is justifies a reevaluation of the Merit Award Program.

Simple enumeration (*first, second, then, next,* and so on) also provides effective transition within paragraphs. Notice how the boldfaced italicized words and phrases give coherence to the following paragraph.

▶ Most adjustable office chairs have nylon tubes that hold metal spindle rods. To keep the chair operational, lubricate the spindle rods occasionally. ***First,*** loosen the set screw in the adjustable bell. ***Then*** lift the chair from the base. ***Next,*** apply the lubricant to the spindle rod and the nylon washer. ***When you have finished,*** replace the chair and tighten the set screw.

persuasion

Persuasive writing attempts to convince an <u>audience</u> to adopt the writer's point of view or take a particular action. Workplace writing often uses persuasion to reinforce ideas that readers already have, to convince readers to change their current ideas, or to lobby for a particular suggestion or policy (as in Figure 1–5). You may find yourself advocating for safer working conditions, justifying the expense of a new program, or writing a <u>proposal</u> (Tab 4) for a large purchase. See also <u>context</u> and <u>purpose</u>.

In persuasive writing, the way you present your ideas is as important as the ideas themselves. You must support your appeal with logic and a sound presentation of facts, statistics, and examples. See also <u>logic errors</u> (Tab 10).

A writer also gains credibility, and thus persuasiveness, through the readers' impressions of the document's appearance. For this reason, consider carefully a document's <u>layout and design</u> (Tab 7). See also <u>résumés</u> (Tab 9).

❖ ETHICS NOTE Avoid ambiguity. Do not wander from your main point and, above all, never make false claims. You should also acknowledge any real or potentially conflicting opinions, doing so allows you to anticipate and overcome objections and builds your credibility. See also <u>ethics in writing</u> and <u>promotional writing</u>. ❖

The <u>memo</u> (Tab 3) shown in Figure 1–5 was written to persuade the marketing staff to participate actively in a change to a new system (NRT/R4). Notice that not everything in this memo is presented in a positive light. Change brings disruption and challenges, and the writer acknowledges that fact.

A persuasive technique that places the focus on your reader's interest and perspective is discussed in the entry <u>"you" viewpoint</u> (Tab 10).

Interoffice Memo

TO: Marketing Staff
FROM: Harold Kawenski, MIS Administrator
DATE: April 21, 2017
SUBJECT: Changeover to the NRT/R4 System

As you all know, the merger with Datacom has resulted in dramatic growth in our workload—a 30 percent increase in our customer support services. To manage this expansion, we will soon install the NRT/R4 server and QCS Enterprise software with Web-based applications. You can contribute to making a smooth transition to the QCS system.

QCS Challenges
The changeover to the QCS system, understandably, will cause some disruption at first. We will need to (1) transfer many of our legacy programs and software applications to the new system and (2) learn to navigate in the R4 and QCS environments. Once we have made these adjustments, however, I am convinced we will welcome the changes.

QCS Benefits
The QCS system will provide smooth access to up-to-date marketing and product information when we need it. This system will speed processing dramatically and give us access to all relevant companywide databases. Because we anticipate that our workload will increase another 20 percent in the next several months, a timely conversion to the QCS system will be invaluable.

Training and Support
To cope with the changes, we will offer training sessions next week on our intranet. I have attached a schedule and sign-up form with specific class times. We will also provide a technical-support hotline at extension 4040, which will be available during business hours; e-mail support at qcs-support@conco.com; and online help documentation.

Response Date
Please return your form and e-mail me by Thursday, April 30, with suggestions or questions about the impact of the changeover on your department. I look forward to working with you to make this system a success.

Attachments: Training Schedule and Sign-Up Form

FIGURE 1–5. Persuasive Memo

point of view

Point of view is the writer's relation to the information presented, as reflected in the use of grammatical <u>person</u> (Tab 11). The writer usually expresses point of view in first-, second-, or third-person personal <u>pronouns</u> (Tab 11). Use of first person indicates that the writer is a participant or an observer. Use of second or third person indicates that the writer is giving directions, instructions, or advice, or is writing about other people or something impersonal.

FIRST PERSON	*I* scrolled down to find the settings option.
SECOND PERSON	*You* need to scroll down to find the settings option.
	[*You* is explicitly stated.]
	Scroll down to find the settings option.
	[*You* is understood in such an instruction.]
THIRD PERSON	*He* scrolled down to find the settings option.

Consider the following sentence, revised from an impersonal to a more personal point of view. Although the essential meaning of the sentence does not change, the revision indicates that people are involved in the communication. See also <u>voice</u> (Tab 11).

▶ ~~It is regrettable~~ that the equipment shipped on Friday ~~is unacceptable.~~
   I regret ... *we cannot accept*

Some people think they should avoid the pronoun *I* in business writing. However, doing so often leads to awkward sentences, with people referring to themselves in the third person as *one* or as *the writer* instead of as *I*.

▶ ~~The writer expects~~ that this project will be completed by July.
   I expect

However, do not use the personal point of view when an impersonal point of view would be more appropriate or more effective because you need to emphasize the subject matter over the writer or the reader. In the following example, it does not help to personalize the situation; in fact, the impersonal version may be more tactful.

PERSONAL	I received objections to my proposal from several of your managers.
IMPERSONAL	Several managers have raised objections to the proposal.

Whether you adopt a personal or an impersonal point of view depends on the **purpose** and the **audience** of the document. For example, in an informal e-mail to an associate, you would most likely adopt a personal point of view. However, in a report to a large group, you would probably emphasize the subject by using an impersonal point of view.

❖ **ETHICS NOTE** In company **correspondence** (Tab 3), use of the pronoun *we* may be interpreted as reflecting company policy, whereas *I* clearly reflects personal opinion. Which pronoun to use should be decided according to whether you are speaking for yourself (*I*) or for the company (*we*).

▶ *I* understand your frustration with the price increase, but *we* must now add the import tax to the sales price. ❖

ESL **TIP for Stating an Opinion**

In some cultures, stating an opinion in writing is considered impolite or unnecessary, but in the United States, readers expect to see a writer's opinion stated clearly and supported with logical reasoning. The opinion should be followed by specific examples to help the reader understand the writer's point of view. See also **logic errors** (Tab 10) and **"you" viewpoint** (Tab 10).

---

preparation

The preparation stage of the writing process is essential. By determining the needs of your **audience**, your **purpose**, the **context**, and the **scope** of coverage, you understand the information you will need to gather during **research** (Tab 5). See also **collaborative writing** and "Five Steps to Successful Writing" (page xxvii).

Writer's Checklist: Preparing to Write

☑ Determine who your readers are and learn certain key facts about them — their knowledge, attitudes, and needs relative to your subject.

☑ Determine the document's primary expectation: What exactly do you want your readers to know, to believe, or to do when they have finished reading your document?

☑ Consider the context of your message and how it should affect your writing.

Writer's Checklist: Preparing to Write (continued)

☑ Establish the scope of your document, not only by understanding your readers' needs and purpose but also by considering any external constraints, such as word limits for trade journal articles or how you might need to compress text, as in <u>writing for the Web</u> (Tab 2).

☑ Select the medium appropriate to your readers and purpose. See also <u>selecting the medium</u> (Tab 2).

process explanation

A process explanation may describe the steps in a process, an operation, or a procedure, such as the steps necessary in starting a small business. The <u>introduction</u> often presents a brief overview of the process or lets readers know why it is important for them to become familiar with the process you are explaining. Be sure to define terms that readers might not understand and provide appropriate <u>visuals</u> (Tab 7) to clarify the process. See also <u>defining terms</u>.

In describing a process, use transitional words and phrases to create unity within paragraphs, and select headings to provide <u>transition</u> (Tab 10) from one step to the next. Notice in the following example how a company tuition refund policy is described as a step-by-step process.

Tuition Refund Policy

1. PROCEDURES
   1.1 Tuition Reimbursement Approval
      1.1.1 An employee who meets school requirements and is interested in receiving tuition reimbursement should gain the approval of his or her manager and submit the request to the Human Resources Department (HR). HR may ask the manager to justify, in writing, the benefits of the academic work, if the reason is not obvious.
      1.1.2 After reaching an agreement, the employee should complete Sections I and II of Form F-6970.
      After HR has obtained two levels of management approval—from the employee's supervisor and the head of the department—it approves the employee's enrollment in the course or degree program.
      1.1.3 The employee who has been granted approval must submit to HR proof of enrollment and payment of appropriate fees to receive tuition reimbursement.

promotional writing

Promotional writing is vital to the success of any company or organization; high-quality, state-of-the-art products or services are of little value if customers and clients do not know they exist. Although you may not be a marketing or public relations specialist, you may be asked to prepare promotional (or marketing) materials, especially if you work for a small organization or are self-employed. Even at a large company, you may contribute to Web sites, <u>sales letters</u> (Tab 3), <u>blogs and forums</u> (Tab 2), or <u>social media</u> (Tab 2) feeds. See also <u>collaborative writing</u> (Tab 3) and <u>writing for the Web</u> (Tab 2.)

Many other documents described in this book often include the additional or secondary purpose of promoting an organization. For example, <u>adjustments</u> (Tab 3), which are usually concerned with resolving a specific problem, offer opportunities to promote your organization.

Writer's Checklist: Promotional Writing

- ☑ Analyze the needs, interests, concerns, makeup, and activities of your <u>audience</u>.

- ☑ Conduct adequate <u>research</u> (Tab 5) to understand your audience, especially by talking to those with firsthand knowledge of the product or service. (See <u>interviewing for information</u>, Tab 5.)

- ☑ Use the principles of <u>persuasion</u> to gain attention, build interest, reduce resistance, and motivate readers to act.

- ☑ Optimize your keywords, phrases, and search tags to reach the greatest number of interested readers.

- ☑ Make information visually appealing through strong <u>organization</u>, <u>layout and design</u>, and <u>visuals</u> that are well integrated with the text.

- ☑ Write with <u>clarity</u>, <u>coherence</u>, and <u>conciseness</u> to help your readers understand the message and to achieve your <u>purpose</u> (Tab 10).

❖ ETHICS NOTE Because readers are persuaded only if they believe the source is credible, be careful not to overstate claims and to avoid possible <u>logic errors</u> (Tab 10). See also <u>ethics in writing</u>. ❖

proofreading

Proofreading is essential whether you are writing a brief e-mail or a high-stakes résumé. Grammar and spell checkers are important aids to proofreading, but they can make writers overconfident. If a typographical error results in a legitimate English word (for example, *coarse* instead of *course*), the spell checker will not flag the misspelling. You may find some of the tactics discussed in revision useful when proofreading; in fact, you may find passages during proofreading that will require further revision.

▶ PROFESSIONALISM NOTE   Proofreading not only demonstrates that you respect readers (who can be distracted, irritated, or misled by errors in writing) but also reflects that you are professional in the way you approach all your work. ▶

Whether the material you proofread is your own writing or that of someone else, proofread in several stages. Although you need to tailor the stages to the specific document and to your own problem areas, the following *Writer's Checklist* should provide a useful starting point. For using Comment and Track Changes in word-processing programs, see *Digital Tip: Incorporating Tracked Changes* on page 40.

Traditional handwritten proofreaders' marks, shown in Figure 1–6, enable writers and editors to easily communicate in the production of publications.

Writer's Checklist: Proofreading in Stages

FIRST-STAGE REVIEW
- ☑ Appropriate format, as for reports or correspondence
- ☑ Consistent style, including headings, terminology, spacing, and fonts
- ☑ Correct numbering of figures and tables

SECOND-STAGE REVIEW
- ☑ Specific grammar and usage problems
- ☑ Appropriate punctuation
- ☑ Correct and consistent abbreviations and capitalization
- ☑ Correct spelling (including names and places)
- ☑ Accurate Web, e-mail, or other addresses
- ☑ Accurate data in tables, figures, and lists
- ☑ Cut-and-paste errors; for example, a result of moved or deleted text and numbers

(*continued*)

1

Writer's Checklist: Proofreading in Stages (continued)

FINAL-STAGE REVIEW

☑ Final check of your goals: audience needs and purpose

☑ Appearance of the document (see <u>layout and design</u>, Tab 7)

☑ Review by a trusted colleague, especially for crucial documents (see <u>collaborative writing</u>)

See also Tab 11, "Grammar," and Tab 12, "Punctuation and Mechanics."

MARK/SYMBOL	MEANING	EXAMPLE	CORRECTED TYPE
✄	Delete	the ~~manager's~~ report	the report
^	Insert	the report	the manager's report
dots (stet)	Let stand	the ~~manager's~~ report	the manager's report
≡ (cap)	Capitalize	the monday meeting	the Monday meeting
/ (lc)	Lowercase	the Monday Meeting	the Monday meeting
∿ (tr)	Transpose	the cover lettre	the cover letter
⌒	Close space	a loud speaker	a loudspeaker
#	Insert space	a loudspeaker	a loud speaker
¶	Paragraph	...report. The meeting...	...report. The meeting...
⌐	Run in with previous line or paragraph	...report. The meeting...	...report. The meeting...
— (ital)	Italicize	the New York Times	the *New York Times*
∿ (bf)	Boldface	Use boldface sparingly.	Use **boldface** sparingly.
⊙	Insert period	I wrote the e-mail	I wrote the e-mail.
⌃	Insert comma	However we cannot...	However, we cannot...
⸗	Insert hyphen	clearcut decision	clear-cut decision
$\frac{1}{m}$	Insert em dash	Our goal productivity	Our goal—productivity
⌃ or :/	Insert colon	We need the following	We need the following:
⌃ or ;/	Insert semicolon	we finished we achieved	we finished; we achieved
⌄ ⌄	Insert quotation marks	He said, I agree.	He said, "I agree."
⌄	Insert apostrophe	the managers report	the manager's report

FIGURE 1–6. Proofreader's Marks

1

DIGITAL TIP

Proofreading for Format Consistency

To check your documents for consistency, use both a "macro" and a "micro" approach. Zooming out in your word-processing software reveals the general appearance of your document and helps you spot any problems with layout or structure. Printing your document and examining it carefully will help you notice inconsistencies in such details as typography, line spacing, and indentation.

purpose

What do you want your readers to know, to believe, or to do when they have read your document? When you answer that question about your audience, you have determined the primary purpose, or objective, of your document. Be careful not to state a purpose too broadly. A statement of purpose such as "to explain continuing-education standards" is too general to be helpful during the writing process. In contrast, "to explain to American Association of Critical-Care Nurses (AACN) members how to determine if a continuing-education course meets AACN professional standards" is a specific purpose that will help you focus on what you need your document to accomplish. Often the context will help you focus your purpose.

The writer's primary purpose is often more complex than simply "to explain" something, as shown in the previous paragraph. To fully understand this complexity, you need to ask yourself not only *why* you are writing the document but also *what* you want to influence your reader to believe or to do after reading it. Suppose a writer for a newsletter has been assigned to write an article about cardiopulmonary resuscitation (CPR). In answer to the question *what?* the writer could state the purpose as "to emphasize the importance of CPR." To the question *why?* the writer might respond, "to encourage employees to sign up for evening CPR classes." Putting the answers to the two questions together, the writer's purpose might be stated as, "To write an article that will emphasize the importance of CPR and encourage employees to sign up for evening CPR classes." Note that the primary purpose of this document is to persuade the readers of the importance of CPR, and the secondary goal is to motivate them to register for a class. Secondary goals often involve such abstract notions as to motivate, to persuade, to reassure, or to inspire your reader. See also persuasion.

If you answer the questions *what?* and *why?* and put the answers into writing as a stated purpose that includes both primary and secondary goals, you will simplify your writing task and more likely achieve your purpose. For a <u>collaborative writing</u> project, it is especially important to collectively write a statement of your purpose to ensure that the document achieves its goals. Do not lose sight of that purpose as you become engrossed in the other steps of the writing process. See also "Five Steps to Successful Writing" (page xxvii).

readers

The first rule of effective writing is *to help your readers*. If you overlook this commitment, your writing will not achieve its <u>purpose</u>, either for you or for your business or organization. For meeting the needs of both individual and multiple readers, see <u>audience</u>.

revision

When you revise your draft, read and evaluate it primarily from the point of view of your <u>audience</u>. In fact, revising requires a different frame of mind than <u>writing a draft</u>. To achieve that frame of mind, experienced writers have developed the following tactics:

- Allow a "cooling period" between writing the draft and revision in order to evaluate the draft objectively.
- Print your draft and mark up the paper copy; it is often difficult to revise on-screen.
- Read your draft aloud—often, hearing the text will enable you to spot problems that need improvement.
- Revise in passes by reading through your draft several times, each time searching for and correcting a different set of problems.

When you can no longer spot improvements, you may wish to give the draft to a colleague for review—especially for projects that are crucial for you or your organization as well as for collaborative projects, as described in <u>collaborative writing</u>.

Writer's Checklist: Revising Your Draft

☑ *Completeness.* Does the document achieve its primary **purpose**? Will it fulfill the readers' needs? Your writing should give readers exactly what they need but not overwhelm them.

☑ *Appropriate introduction and conclusion.* Check to see that your **introduction** frames the rest of the document and that your **conclusion** ties the main ideas together. Both should account for revisions to the content of the document.

☑ *Accuracy.* Look for any factual inaccuracies that may have crept into your draft.

☑ *Unity and coherence.* Check to see that sentences and ideas are closely tied together (coherence) and contribute directly to the main idea expressed in the topic sentence of each paragraph (unity). Provide transitions where they are missing and strengthen those that are weak. See Tab 10, "Style and Clarity."

☑ *Consistency.* Make sure that design and visuals are consistent. (See Tab 7, "Design and Visuals.") Refer to the same items with the same terms throughout a document.

☑ *Conciseness.* Trim unnecessary words, phrases, sentences, and even paragraphs. See **conciseness** (Tab 10). Use the search-and-replace command to find and revise wordy phrases, such as *that is*, *there are*, *the fact that*, and *to be*, and unnecessary helping **verbs** (Tab 11), such as *will*.

☑ *Awkwardness.* Look for **awkwardness** (Tab 10) in sentence construction—especially any **garbled sentences** (Tab 10).

☑ *Ethical writing.* Check for **ethics in writing** and eliminate **biased language** (Tab 10).

☑ *Active voice.* Use the active **voice** (Tab 11) unless the passive voice is more appropriate.

☑ *Word choice.* Check **word choice** (Tab 10) and eliminate **affectation** (Tab 10), **clichés** (Tab 10), **vague words** (Tab 10), and unnecessary **intensifiers** (Tab 10). Check for unclear **pronoun references** (Tab 11).

☑ *Jargon.* If you have any doubt that all your readers will understand any **jargon** (Tab 10) or special terms you have used, eliminate or define those words or phrases.

☑ *Grammar.* Check your draft for grammatical errors. Because grammar checkers are not always accurate, treat their recommendations only as suggestions.

☑ *Typographical errors.* Check your final draft for typographical errors both with your spell checker and with thorough **proofreading** because spell checkers do not catch all errors.

DIGITAL TIP

Incorporating Tracked Changes

When colleagues review your document, they can "track" changes and insert comments within the document itself. Tracking and commenting vary with types and versions of word-processing programs, but in most programs you can view the document with all reviewers' edits and comments highlighted, or see the document as it would look if you accepted any changes made.

scope

Scope is the depth and breadth of detail you include in a document as defined by your audience's needs, your <u>purpose</u>, and the <u>context</u>. (See also <u>audience</u>.) For example, if you write a trip report about a routine visit to a company facility, your readers may need to know only the basic details and any unusual findings. However, if you prepare a trip report about a visit to a division that has experienced problems and your purpose is to suggest ways to solve those problems, your report will contain many more details, observations, and even recommendations.

You should determine the scope of a document during the <u>preparation</u> stage of the writing process, even though you may refine it later. Defining your scope will expedite your <u>research</u> (Tab 5) and can help determine team members' responsibilities in <u>collaborative writing</u>.

Your scope will also be affected by the type of document you are writing and the medium you select for your message. For example, funding organizations often prescribe the general content and length for proposals, and some organizations set limits for the length of memos, e-mails, and digital postings. See <u>selecting the medium</u> (Tab 2) and "Five Steps to Successful Writing" (page xxvii).

writing a draft

You are well prepared to write a rough draft when you have established your <u>purpose</u> and reader's needs, considered the <u>context</u>, defined your <u>scope</u>, completed adequate <u>research</u> (Tab 5), and prepared an outline (whether rough or developed). (See also <u>audience</u> and <u>outlining</u>.) Writing a draft is simply transcribing and expanding the notes from your outline into paragraphs, without worrying about grammar, refinements of language, or spelling. Refinement will come with <u>revision</u> and <u>proofreading</u>. See also "Five Steps to Successful Writing" (page xxvii).

Writing and revising are different activities. Do not let worrying about a good opening slow you down. Instead, concentrate on getting your ideas on paper—now is not the time to polish or revise. Do not wait for inspiration—treat writing a draft as you would any other on-the-job task.

Writer's Checklist: Writing a Rough Draft

- ☑ Resist the temptation of writing first drafts without planning.
- ☑ Use an outline (rough or developed) as a springboard to start and to write quickly.
- ☑ Give yourself a set time in which you write continuously, regardless of how good or bad your writing seems to be. But don't stop if you are rolling along easily—keep your momentum.
- ☑ Start with the section that seems easiest. Your readers will neither know nor care that the middle section of the document was the first section you wrote.
- ☑ Keep in mind your readers' needs, expectations, and knowledge of the subject. Doing so will help you write directly to your readers and suggest which ideas need further development.
- ☑ When you come to something difficult to explain, try to relate the new concept to something with which the readers are familiar, as discussed in <u>figures of speech</u> (Tab 10).
- ☑ Routinely save your draft to your local drive, company network, external hard drive, or the cloud.
- ☑ Give yourself a small reward—a short walk, a soft drink, a brief chat with a friend, an easy task—after you have finished a section.
- ☑ When you return to your writing, reread what you have written. Seeing what you have already written can return you to a productive frame of mind

2

Workplace Technology

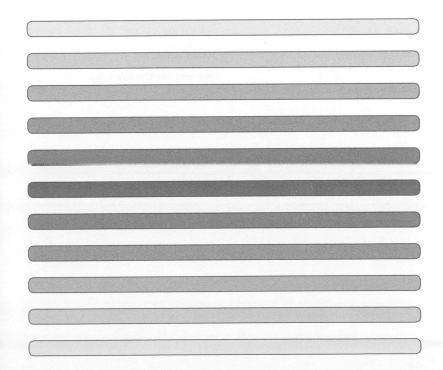

Preview

This section presents an overview of the technologies that are integral to workplace writing and offers guidelines for using them effectively. The first entry, **adapting to new technologies**, covers how to learn and make the best use of technologies as they evolve. The entry **selecting the medium** covers how to evaluate and choose from among communication technologies in a way that best suits your message.

The **e-mail**, **text messaging**, and **instant messaging** entries focus on techniques for managing these applications, the evolving set of online manners (netiquette), and privacy and confidentiality issues to consider before sending a message.

The **social media** entry provides an overview of ways to use these platforms to promote your organization and to present yourself professionally. The entries **blogs and forums**, **FAQs (frequently asked questions)**, **repurposing**, and **writing for the Web** will help you further develop and adapt online content.

adapting to new technologies

In the classroom or in the workplace, hardware, software, and other technologies quickly become out of date. This entry is designed to help you cope with such changes by providing useful approaches to working with new technologies. See also <u>selecting the medium</u>.

Technology You Need to Know

When faced with a new technology, ask "How much do I *need* to know about the specific technology to do my work?" What you need to learn will depend on your workplace <u>context</u> (Tab 1). Sometimes you may need only basic knowledge to accomplish specific and limited tasks. Other times, you may need much more in-depth knowledge—even expert knowledge—to serve as an adviser or a resource for your colleagues. The checklist that follows provides suggestions for navigating the functions and operations of devices and programs with which you are unfamiliar.

Writer's Checklist: Strategies for Learning a New Technology

☑ *Experiment.* Acquaint yourself with a new technology simply by using it. This approach, in which you "play" with a new tool until it becomes familiar, will help you develop greater confidence with new technologies and will rarely have negative consequences.

☑ *Conduct careful Internet searches.* Search for an issue using precise terminology; include the name of the tool and keywords that describe your specific problem. Consider as well browsing relevant Internet message boards and the Web site of the company that developed the tool.

☑ *Consult IT staff and trusted colleagues.* Seek help from your organization's technology specialists and trainers as you begin to use a new tool. If such specialists are not available, tech-savvy colleagues on your team may be willing to help.

☑ *Use built-in help and official help manuals.* Use built-in tutorials, digital or printed instructional materials, and links to searchable online help sites. Many help documents are written in plain, easy-to-understand language.

☑ *Take product workshops and online tutorials.* Enroll in a workshop; those offered face-to-face or online teach everything from the basics to advanced functions of devices and software, and they offer the benefit of other users' experience. Check for workshops and tutorials provided by the product vendor before also looking for paid and free tutorials from sites such as Lynda.com, PCWorld, and YouTube.

☑ *Refer to third-party help manuals.* Look for how-to guides for computer software and hardware. With full-color printing, plenty of photos, and a casual, friendly tone, these books often simplify information.

blogs and forums

A *blog* (from *Web log*) is a Web-based journal in which an individual or a blogger team post entries (displayed from the most recent to the earliest posting) that document experiences, express opinions, provide information, and respond to other bloggers on subjects of mutual interest. A blog should have a well-defined focus (or subject), <u>audience</u> (Tab 1), and <u>purpose</u> (Tab 1). You will also need to establish and maintain a regular posting schedule. As you plan a blog, survey such popular blogging platforms as WordPress (www.wordpress.com) or Tumblr (www.tumblr.com) and consult with your information technology (IT) and marketing staff on how a blog might contribute to your organization.

Although blogs may allow readers to post comments, a *forum* typically fosters a wider "conversation" in which site visitors can not only respond to the posts of others but also begin new topics or discussion threads. Organizations often use forums for customer or technical support. If your Web site features a forum, you must promote it, contribute content, and solicit content from users or the forum will quickly lose its usefulness and fade. See also <u>social media</u> and <u>writing for the Web</u>.

Organizational Uses

Organizations create blogs and forums to help meet such goals as attracting and retaining clients or customers, promoting goodwill, obtaining valuable feedback on their products and services, and developing a sense of community among their customers and employees. Blogs and forums can be both external and internal.

External sites are publicly available on the Internet both for an organization's customers or clients and for executives, spokespeople, or employees to share their views. Blogs and forums can help to build loyalty for a company because customers can make a direct connection with an organization's representatives and with other customers. They can also exchange current information that may not be available in published documents and elsewhere online. *Internal sites* are usually created for an organization's employees and can be accessed only through its intranet. Internal blogs may serve as interactive newsletters that help build a sense of community within an organization or to share "breaking news" about product development, employee benefits, or new team members.

Writing Style

Write blog or forum entries in an informal, conversational style that uses contractions, first person, and active voice. (See Tab 10, "Style and Clarity.")

BLOG POSTING	Check out the latest concept for our new Toyota Camry dashboards—we've added enough space to hold your coffee and a digital device by moving the air ducts. Tell us what you think.
FORUM POSTING	I'm new to this thread, but I'm surprised no one's discussed the issue of confidentiality. My experience has been that Facebook's recent changes in privacy settings are just confusing. Have I missed something?

Keep your sentences and paragraphs concise. Use bulleted lists, italics, and other layout-and-design elements, such as boldface and white space if possible. (See Tab 7, "Design and Visuals.") Doing so can help readers scan the postings or text to find information that is interesting or relevant to them. Keep headlines short and direct to catch attention and increase the visual appeal and readability. Where helpful, provide links to other sites and resources that participants might find useful. When blogs expand or forums become popular, you may need to organize them using *categories* (links to discussion topics) or *tags* (keywords for searching the site's postings).

❖ ETHICS NOTE Because organizations expect employees to assume full responsibility for the content they post on a company blog or forum, you must maintain high ethical standards. See also ethics in writing (Tab 1).

- Do not post information that is confidential, proprietary, or sensitive to your employer.
- Do not attack competitors or use abusive language toward other participants while making strong points on topics.
- Do not post content that is profane, libelous, or harassing, or that violates the privacy of others. See also biased language (Tab 10).
- Be aware that everything you post becomes permanently accessible to a wide public audience, especially for external sites.
- Obtain permission before using any material that is protected by copyright (Tab 5), and identify sources for quotations (Tab 5). See also plagiarism (Tab 5). ❖

e-mail

2

Workplace Technology

E-mail (or *email*) functions in the workplace as a primary medium to exchange information and share electronic files with colleagues, clients, and customers. E-mail messages range from short, informal notes to longer, more formal communications with clients and professionals. You may also attach memos, letters, and other files to e-mails. For general writing strategy and appropriate professional style, see correspondence (Tab 3). See also selecting the medium.

Review and Confidentiality

Avoid the temptation to send the first draft of a message without rereading it for clarity and appropriateness. As with all correspondence, your message should include all crucial details and be free of grammatical and factual errors, ambiguities, and unintended implications. See proofreading (Tab 1) and spelling (Tab 12).

Keep in mind that e-mails are easily forwarded and are never truly deleted. Most companies back up and save all their e-mail messages and are legally entitled to monitor e-mail use. Companies can be compelled, depending on circumstances, to provide e-mail and digital messaging logs in response to legal requests. Consider the content of all your messages in the light of these possibilities, and carefully review your message before you click "Send."

▶ PROFESSIONALISM NOTE Be especially careful when sending messages to superiors in your organization or to people outside the organization. Spending extra time reviewing your e-mail can save you the embarrassment caused by a carelessly written message. One helpful strategy is to write the draft and revise your e-mail before filling in the "To" line with the address of your recipient. ▶

Writer's Checklist: Maintaining Professionalism

☑   Review your organization's policy regarding the appropriate use of e-mail.

☑   Do not forward jokes or *spam*, discuss office gossip, or use biased language (Tab 10).

Writer's Checklist: Maintaining Professionalism (continued)

☑ Do not send *flames* (e-mails that contain abusive, obscene, or derogatory language) to attack someone. See also <u>blogs and forums</u>.

☑ Avoid abbreviations (BTW for *by the way*, for example) and emoticons used in personal e-mail, discussion forums, <u>text messaging</u>, and <u>instant messaging</u>.

☑ Do not write in all lowercase letters or in ALL UPPERCASE LETTERS.

☑ Base your e-mail username on your personal name (msmith@domain .com), if possible, and avoid clever or hobby-related names (sushilover @domain.com).

☑ Write a cover message when including attachments ("Attached is a copy of . . ."), and double-check that it is indeed attached. See <u>cover letters</u> (Tab 3).

☑ Always sign the e-mail or use a signature block (see Figure 2–1 on page 51) or both; doing so is not only polite but also avoids possible confusion.

☑ Send a "courtesy response" informing the sender when you need additional time to reply or when you need to confirm that you have received a message or an attachment.

DIGITAL TIP

Sharing Electronic Files

When you need to send large attachments or a collection of several attachments, consider an alternative: Use one of the many free online services designed for archiving and sharing files. After uploading a file to a specialized Web site, you will be given a URL that you can share via e-mail, allowing your recipients to download the file at their convenience. Although these tools shouldn't be used for sensitive documents, they work well in most situations.

Writing and Design

Make the main point early and use short paragraphs to avoid dense blocks of text. For longer and more detailed messages, provide a brief paragraph overview at the beginning. Adapt forwarded messages by revising the subject line to reflect the current content and cut irrelevant previous text or highlight key text, based on your purpose and context.

Provide a specific subject line, as described on page 84, after composing the message so that your topic is precise and clear to the reader. An empty subject line is unprofessional and may be interpreted as spam, thus routed to junk mail.

Most e-mail programs allow you to provide emphasis with typographical features, such as various fonts and bullets. For systems that do not, consider using a "plain text" setting with alternative highlighting devices, such as asterisks for emphasis, or attaching a highly formatted document to an e-mail. Place your response to someone else's message at the beginning (or top) of the e-mail window so that recipients can see your response immediately.

Adapt your salutation and complimentary closing to your audience and the context.

- When e-mail functions as a traditional business letter, consider the standard salutation (*Dear Ms. Tucker:* or *Dear Docuform Customer:*) and closing (*Sincerely,* or *Best wishes,*).
- When you send e-mail to individuals or small groups inside an organization, you may wish to adopt a more personal greeting (*Dear Andy,* or *Dear Project Colleagues,*) and closing (*Regards,* or *Good luck,*).
- When e-mail functions as a personal note to a friend or close colleague, you can use an informal greeting or only a first name (*Hi Mike,* or *Hello Jenny,* or *Bill,*) and a closing (*Take care,* or *Best,*).

Be aware that in some cultures, professionals do not refer to recipients or colleagues by their first names. See <u>international correspondence</u> (Tab 3).

Many companies and professionals include signature blocks (also called *signatures*) at the bottom of their messages. Signatures, which are set to appear at the end of every e-mail, supply information traditionally provided on company letterhead. Many organizations provide graphic signature forms or formatting standards. If yours does not, consider the following guidelines for formatting text-based signatures:

- Keep line length to 60 characters or fewer to avoid unpredictable line wraps.
- Test your signature block in plain-text e-mail systems to verify your format.
- Avoid using quotations, aphorisms, proverbs, or other sayings from popular culture, religion, or poetry in professional signatures.

The pattern shown in Figure 2–1 is typical.

▶ PROFESSIONALISM NOTE Double-check your "To" box addressees carefully before hitting the "Send" button. The auto-fill feature in e-mail programs automatically fills in the names of recipients and other information in your "To" box based on the first few letters you type. Although it is a convenient feature, be aware that your e-mail can easily wind up in the wrong in-box when the names of people in your address book are similar (Donna/Donnie) or when two people share the same last name. The result can lead to embarrassing misunderstandings or to confidential information being sent to the wrong people. ▶

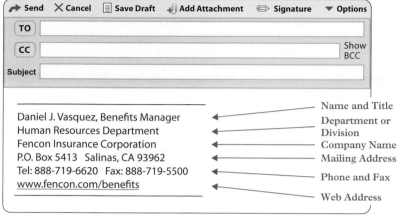

FIGURE 2–1. E-mail Signature Block

*Writer's Checklist: Managing Your E-mail and Reducing Overload**

☑ Avoid becoming involved in an e-mail exchange if a phone call or meeting would be more efficient.

☑ Consider whether an e-mail message could prompt an unnecessary response from the recipient, and make clear to the recipient whether you expect a response.

☑ Send a copy ("cc:") of an e-mail only when the person copied needs or wants the information.

☑ Review all messages on a subject before responding to avoid dealing with issues that are no longer relevant.

☑ Set priorities for reading e-mail by skimming sender names and subject lines as well as where you appear in a "cc:" address line.

☑ Check the e-mail address before sending an e-mail to make sure it is correct.

☑ Create e-mail folders using key topics and personal names to file messages.

☑ Check your in-box regularly and try to clear it or categorize it and file new messages by the end of each day.

☑ Use the search command to find particular subjects and personal names.

*Based in part on Gail Fann Thomas and Cynthia L. King, "Reconceptualizing E-mail Overload," *Journal of Business and Technical Communication* 20, no. 3 (July 2006): 252–87.

❖ ETHICS NOTE The blind-copy (*bcc:*) function allows writers to send copies of a message to someone without the primary receiver's knowledge. Use the bcc: notation with great care. Sending sensitive or confidential information to a third party as a blind copy without the original recipient's knowledge is unethical when used to play office politics. The blind-copy function is both ethical and useful, however, when used to protect the privacy of the e-mail addresses of a large group of recipients. ❖

FAQs (frequently asked questions)

An FAQ section is a list (Tab 7) of questions, paired with their answers, that readers will likely ask about products, services, or other information presented on a Web site or in customer-oriented documents. By presenting commonly sought information in one place, FAQs save readers from searching through an entire Web site or document to find what they need.

A well-planned FAQ list can create a positive impression with customers and clients because the writer acknowledges that the readers' time is valuable. An FAQ list also helps a company spend less time answering phone calls and responding to questions on e-mail. However, an FAQ list is not a substitute for solving problems with a product or service.

❖ ETHICS NOTE If customers are experiencing numerous problems because of a product design or programming flaw, you need to work with your company's product developers to correct the problem rather than attempting to avoid the issue by burying it within an FAQ. ❖

Questions to Include

Develop the list of questions and their answers by brainstorming with colleagues who regularly are in contact with customers. If customers frequently ask about company stock information and request annual reports, for example, your FAQ list could include the question "How do I obtain a copy of your latest annual report?" This question can be followed with a brief answer that includes the Web address from which the annual report can be downloaded or the name, phone number, and e-mail address of the person who distributes the annual reports. See also writing for the Web.

Organization

Organize the list so that readers can find the information they need quickly and easily. List your questions in decreasing order of importance for your readers so that they can obtain the most important information first. If you have a number of questions that are related to a specific topic, such as investor relations, product returns, or completing forms, group them into categories and identify each category with a heading, such as "Investor Relations," "Shipping," and "Forms." You may also want to create a table of contents at the top of the FAQ page so that readers can quickly find the topics relevant to their interests. See organization (Tab 1).

Study other FAQ lists for products or services similar to yours. Analyze them for their approach and organization: Can you find answers quickly, or do you need to scroll through many pages to find them? Are the questions with their answers separated into logical categories or listed in random order? Is it easy to differentiate the question from the answer? Do the answers provide too little or too much information? Does the FAQ list offer specialized search tools to help readers find information for longer FAQs?

Placement

The location of your FAQ list should enable readers to find answers quickly. On Web sites, an FAQ page is usually linked from the homepage. In small printed documents, such as brochures, FAQs are usually highlighted and placed after the body of the document.

Writer's Checklist: Developing FAQs

☑ *Focus on your reader.* Write your questions and answers from a "you" viewpoint (Tab 10) and with a positive, conversational tone.

☑ *Separate long FAQ lists into groups.* Group related questions under topic headings (Tab 7). For long online FAQs, consider listing only questions and include links to separate pages, each containing an individual question and answer.

☑ *Distinguish questions from answers.* Use boldface type for questions and use white space to separate questions from answers. Use sparingly multiple colors, italics, or other formatting styles that can make the list difficult to read.

☑ *Keep questions and answers concise.* If a question has a long answer, add a link to a separate Web page or refer to an appropriate page number in a printed document.

☑ *Keep the list updated.* Review and update FAQs at least monthly—or more frequently if your content changes often.

☑ *Give readers the opportunity to respond.* Provide an e-mail link for existing and possible customers to submit questions they would like to see added to the FAQ list.

☑ *Consider available tools for automating the process.* Many content-management systems, for example, have built-in FAQ-writing software.

instant messaging

Instant messaging (IM) is a communications medium that allows both real-time text communications and the transfer of text or other files, such as an image or a document. (See also <u>text messaging</u>.) Instant messaging is especially useful to those who are working in an environment that demands near-instant, brief, written exchanges between two or more participants. See also <u>e-mail</u> and <u>selecting the medium</u>.

When writing instant messages, keep them simple and to the point, covering only one subject in each message to prevent confusion and inappropriate responses. Because screen space is often limited and speed is essential, many who send instant messages use abbreviations and shortened spellings ("u" for "you"). Be sure that your reader will understand such abbreviations; when in doubt, avoid them. In Figure 2–2, the manager of a software development company in Maine ("Diane") is exchanging instant messages with a business partner in the Netherlands ("Andre"). Notice that the correspondents use an informal style that includes personal and professional abbreviations with which both are familiar ("NP" for *no problem* and "QSG" for *Quick Start Guide*). These messages demonstrate how IM can not only help people exchange information quickly but also build rapport among distant colleagues and team members.

2

Workplace Technology

✳ instant message with Andre	**Last message received at 09:04 AM**
8:58 AM	Andre: Hi Diane! me: good morning
9:00 AM	Andre: Time for a quick question? me: NP! Andre: How is it going with the QSG?
9:01 AM	Andre: Will you be finished soon? me: I am working on it. me: I am targeting Friday
9:02 AM	Andre: If you are not quite finished, send me what you have. me: I would recommend finishing the QSG before we focus on user guide.
9:03 AM	Andre: good idea Andre: ok, I won't keep you any longer Andre: bye
9:04 AM	me: Talk to you later.

FIGURE 2–2. Instant-Message Exchange (U.S. Eastern Time Shown)

❖ ETHICS NOTE Be sure to follow your employer's IM policies, such as any limitations on sending personal messages during work hours or requirements concerning confidentiality. If no specific policy exists, check with your management before using this medium. ❖

Writer's Checklist: Instant Messaging Privacy and Security

☑ Set up distinct business and professional contact lists (or accounts) to avoid inadvertently sending a personal message to a business associate.

☑ Learn the options (such as "away" messages) and security limitations of your IM system and set the preferences that best suit your needs.

☑ Save significant IM exchanges (or logs) for your future reference.

☑ Be aware that instant messages can be saved by your recipients and may be archived by your employer.

☑ Do not use professional IM for office gossip or inappropriate exchanges.

repurposing

Repurposing is the copying or converting of existing content, such as written text and visuals, from one document or medium into another for a different <u>purpose</u> (Tab 1).* For example, if you are preparing a promotional brochure, you may be able to reuse material from a product description that is currently published on your organization's Web site. The brochure might then be printed or placed on the Web site for downloading. See also <u>selecting the medium</u>.

In the workplace, this process saves time because content that often requires substantial effort to develop need not be re-created for each new application. The process of repurposing may be as simple as copying and pasting content from one document into another or as complex as distributing content and updates through a content-management system.

Content can be repurposed exactly as it is written only if it fits the <u>scope</u> (Tab 1), <u>audience</u> (Tab 1), and purpose of the new document. If the content alters these areas, you must adapt that content to fit its new <u>context</u> (Tab 1), as described in the following sections.

---

*The reuse of standard texts or content in technical publications is often referred to as "single-source publishing" or simply "single sourcing." Traditionally, such reuse of standard texts has been referred to as "boilerplate."

Repurpose for the Context

Staying focused on the purpose of your new document is critical, especially when repurposing content between different media. If you are writing a sales proposal, for example, and you only need to describe the specifications for a product, it may be useful to repurpose the specification list from your organization's Web site. However, the purpose of the Web-site content may be *to inform* customers about your products, whereas the purpose of a proposal is *to persuade* customers to buy your products. To effectively use the repurposed content in your proposal, you may need to adapt the tense, voice, tone, grammar, and point of view (Tab 1) to make the repurposed content more persuasive and fit within the context of a sales proposal. See Tab 10, "Style and Clarity," and Tab 11, "Grammar."

Repurpose for the Medium

The proper style and format of content written for a specific medium, such as a brochure or fact sheet, may not work as effectively when repurposed for a different medium, such as a Web site. Adapt the layout and design of the repurposed content as appropriate to accommodate your readers' needs for the medium. See also writing for the Web and Tab 7, "Design and Visuals."

❖ ETHICS NOTE In the workplace, repurposing content within an organization does not violate copyright (Tab 5) because an organization owns the information it creates and can share it across the company. Likewise, a writer in an organization may use and repurpose material in the public domain and, with some limitations, content that is licensed under Creative Commons (see *http://creativecommons.org/about*).

In the classroom, of course, the use of content or someone else's unique ideas without acknowledgment or the use of someone else's exact words without quotation marks (Tab 12) and appropriate credit is plagiarism (Tab 5). ❖

selecting the medium

Selecting the most appropriate medium (or *channel*) for communicating in the workplace depends on a wide range of factors related to your audience (Tab 1), purpose (Tab 1), and context (Tab 1). Those factors include the following:

- The audience's preferences and expectations
- The organization's practices and policies

- How widely information needs to be distributed
- The urgency of the communication
- The sensitivity or confidentiality required
- Your own most effective communication style

As this list suggests, choosing the best medium may involve personal considerations as well as the essential functions of the medium. If you need to collaborate with someone to solve a problem, for example, you may find e-mail exchanges less effective than a phone call or face-to-face meeting. If you need precise wording or a record of a complex or sensitive message, however, a written medium is often essential.

Many of the following media and forms of communication overlap and evolve as technology develops. Understanding their basic functions will help you select the most appropriate medium for your needs. See Figure 2–3 for a table summarizing the media discussed in this entry. See also adapting to new technologies.

E-mail

E-mail (or *email*) functions in the workplace as a primary medium to communicate and share files with colleagues, clients, and customers. Although e-mail may function as informal notes, e-mail messages should follow the writing strategy and style described in correspondence (Tab 3). All e-mail requires special review because recipients can easily forward messages and attachments to others and because e-mail messages are subject to legal disclosure.

Memos

Memos (Tab 3) are appropriate for internal communication among members of the same organization; they use a standard header and are sent on paper or as attachments to e-mails. Memos can be used to instruct employees, announce policies, report results, disseminate information, and delegate responsibilities. Printed memos may be used in manufacturing or service industries, for example, where employees do not have easy access to e-mail.

Letters

Business letters (Tab 3) with handwritten signatures are often appropriate for formal communications with professional associates or customers outside an organization. Letters printed on organizational letterhead stationery communicate formality, respect, and authority. Letters are often used for job applications, for recommendations, and in other official and social contexts.

Medium	Use
E-mail	Primary informal or formal medium for communicating and file sharing with colleagues, clients, and customers.
Memos	Internal correspondence for announcements, instructions, reports within an organization.
Letters	Letterhead correspondence for formal communications with professional associates outside an organization.
Text and Instant Messages	*Text messages* for exchanges between people on the move or in nontraditional workspaces; *instant messages* for real-time exchanges among coworkers, customers, and suppliers.
Phone Calls and Voice Messages	*Phone calls* for substantial interaction on complex or sensitive issues; *voice-mail messages* for clear and brief notes.
Faxes	Faxed documents, often with handwritten additions, for viewing in their original form.
Meetings and Conference Calls	*Individual and group meetings* for establishing rapport, solving problems, and reaching decisions; *conference calls* for saving travel costs.
Web Conferences and Videoconferences	*Web conferences* for multiple participants through their computers, often using Web video applications; *formal videoconferences* with high-end equipment for participants at multiple locations using shared visuals or demonstrations.
Web Networking and Promotion	*Intranet sites* for file and idea sharing within organizations; *public Web sites* for providing product and client access; *social-media sites* for enhancing individual and organization brand identity.

FIGURE 2–3. Choosing the Appropriate Medium

Text and Instant Messages

Text messaging, or *texting*, refers to the exchange of brief written messages between mobile phones. Text messaging is effective for simple messages communicated between people on the move or in nontraditional work spaces.

2

Workplace Technology

Instant messaging (IM) on a computer or handheld device may be an efficient way to communicate in real time with coworkers, suppliers, and customers who need near-instant, brief written exchanges between two or more participants. Instant messaging requires that recipients are ready and available to participate in an immediate exchange of messages.

Phone Calls and Voice Messages

Phone calls are best used for exchanges that require substantial interaction and the ability of participants to interpret each other's tone of voice. They are useful for discussing sensitive issues and resolving misunderstandings, although they do not provide the visual cues possible during face-to-face meetings. Be careful when using a cell phone in public places, and follow appropriate etiquette and organizational policies. See "Web Conferences and Videoconferences" on page 60.

Should you need to leave a voice-mail message, it should be clear and brief. ("I got your package, so you don't need to call the distributor" or "I'd like to discuss options for the new system, so call when you get a chance.") For complicated messages, use another medium, such as e-mail.

Faxes

A fax is used when a document like a drawing or signed contract must be viewed in its original form. Faxing is used when scanning is not an option or when a faxed document is requested. Fax machines can be located in shared areas, so let the intended recipient know before you send confidential or sensitive information. Use a cover sheet that includes at least the name of the recipient and the number of pages in the document to ensure full receipt. Although faxes can be replaced with scanned documents sent as e-mail attachments, faxing is often more convenient for submitting forms and for sending sensitive material over the Internet without encryption. In some countries, faxes are legally required for documents and contracts with signatures.

Meetings and Conference Calls

In-person meetings (Tab 8) with individuals are most appropriate with an associate or a client with whom you intend to develop an important, long-term relationship. A face-to-face meeting may also be useful to help establish rapport, interview someone on a complex topic, solve a technical problem, or handle a controversial issue.

Group or committee meetings may be best for brainstorming, collaborating with various experts on a complex topic, and reaching decisions. A teleconference (or *conference call*) among three or more participants is an inexpensive alternative to face-to-face meetings requiring travel. Conference calls work best when the person coordinating the call works

2

Workplace Technology

from an agenda shared by all the participants and directs the discussion as if chairing an in-person meeting. For advice on how to record discussions and decisions, see minutes of meetings (Tab 8).

Web Conferences and Videoconferences

These conferences may be used for committee meetings when participants are geographically separated, for small groups working on a specific problem, for numerous participants in training, or for educational seminars (referred to as *webinars*). Participants can be connected through downloaded applications. Web conferences may be enhanced with phone connections and video applications, like Skype, GoToMeeting, or Webex.

More formal videoconferences with high-end equipment often require professional services. They work best with participants who are at ease in front of the camera, and such conferences should be carefully planned with technical support staff available.

Web Networking and Promotion

A company intranet Web site is ideal for sharing documents and files—including announcements and policies and procedures—within an organization. An intranet site can serve not only as a home base for resources like company directories and newsletters but also as a place where ideas can be developed through, for example, discussion boards and wikis.

A company public Web site can provide sales and product information as well as information about an organization and opportunities to foster contacts with customers and clients. Such sites may include new-product announcements, press releases, FAQs, manuals, product or service reviews, blogs and forums, employment opportunities, and requests for proposals. See also writing for the Web.

Using social media sites can help individuals and organizations cultivate professional contacts and promote products and services. Networks for professionals, such as LinkedIn, aim to connect individuals and groups with common interests. Organizations may use social-networking sites like Facebook to market their products and services as well as to enhance their brand identity. See also job search (Tab 9).

social media

Social media refers to Web sites or applications—such as Facebook, LinkedIn, Twitter, and Instagram—that allow the creation of online communities through which individuals and organizations can create content, interact, and share information. Accessed through Web browsers or mobile devices, social-media platforms often incorporate instant messaging and e-mail components, and many have blogs and forums that allow for comments, links to other Web sites, and the collection of information that is of interest to its community.

Social media plays several vital roles in professional communication. It can help job seekers establish a professional presence and network and help companies communicate more easily with stakeholders.

On an individual level, you can use accounts on sites such as LinkedIn and Twitter to develop your presence within your field to connect with colleagues. When you create accounts on these sites, your profile, including your profile picture, should be consistent to make it easier for potential employers and colleagues to find you. Your profile and postings should also be professional in tone; if you have primarily used social media for personal purposes, you may wish to create separate accounts that are focused on your work. You can also use social media for active networking. Many industries and professional organizations have established conversations around Twitter hashtags (such as #SmallBizChat, #IMCchat, or #womenintech, among others), and meet at regularly scheduled times to discuss current events and mentoring needs. Figure 2–4 shows a résumé for a job seeker who has developed an effective social-media profile.

The candidate in the sample résumé in Figure 2–4 currently works as a social-media manager for a small business. Many organizations now employ writers to maintain their social-media accounts, recognizing that their efforts in this area are vital in the current business culture. Organizations use social media to connect with their clients, share information about their products, and reach new customers. Social media can help organizations promote goodwill, resolve problems, and obtain near-instant feedback on their products and services through conversations with their online communities.

Choosing the Appropriate Platform

When you or your organization chooses which social-media platform to join, consider both what you hope to accomplish and which platform reaches more of the organization's target customers or contacts. (See also selecting the medium.) For example, a manufacturing company might choose a platform that focuses on users of products similar to its own, whereas a service-oriented company might select a platform that allows users to request and receive immediate assistance. A small shop might choose several platforms for different purposes, such as advertising images of its products on a platform that is heavily image-based while participating in another platform that allows the store's owner to build a professional network.

Two social-media characteristics — status updates and networks — are particularly useful in the workplace. Status updates, which include posts on Facebook and tweets on Twitter, allow individuals or

SAM THORNTON

Mobile: (555)-555-5555 • E-mail: samtsocial@gmail.com
Twitter: @samtmarketing

EDUCATION:

West Chester University of Pennsylvania   **May 2015**
B.S., Marketing
Minor, Business and Technical Writing

EXPERIENCE:

Charming Vintage (@charmvintagepa)   **Philadelphia, PA**
Social Media Manager   *May 2015–present*

- Maintain and review social media content strategy for local chain of four vintage stores
- Draft and edit content for posts on Instagram and Twitter
- Photograph products for social media posts
- Schedule daily Instagram and Twitter posts using Tweetdeck
- Respond to customer queries and concerns on all social media accounts
- Communicate with sales staff to ensure social media sales are handled efficiently
- Monitor status of social media sales orders
- Interact with local media as required

Burger Shack   **Philadelphia, PA**
Marketing Intern   *June 2013–May 2015*

- Promoted products through door-to-door advertising and daily social media posts using Hootsuite
- Encouraged managers to open and use Instagram for marketing products
- Increased dessert sales by 20% over a one-month period

Smith's Bakery and Coffee Shop   **Bryn Mawr, PA**
Barista   *September 2010–May 2013*

- Promoted products through daily Instagram and Facebook posts
- Evaluated and calculated inventory lists
- Assisted in decorating for special events

References available on request.

FIGURE 2–4. Sample Résumé (Social Media Specialist)

organizations to post brief announcements or responses to questions. Once these status updates are published, other accounts can immediately respond to them. Networks allow one individual or organization to link its company and products to another individual or organization. By doing so, the two entities become "connected" in the social-media community, allowing their posts to be intertwined into a type of ongoing conversation. Figure 2–5 provides an overview of three popular social-media platforms of interest to businesses and professionals and shows how each uses status updates and networks to support its community.

Before selecting a specific social-media platform, consider the following:

- Conversations within social media are impossible to control or pause. You must be willing to respond to the inquiries and comments, positive and negative, of other community members.
- Social-media platforms may demand significant time from account holders. Users of many platforms expect quick, ongoing responses and updates. If a crisis occurs, you must be willing and able to monitor the account outside of normal business hours.
- Communications within a social-media platform might have a wider audience than you intend, even though most platforms allow accounts to limit their audiences.

Writing Style and Privacy Considerations

For writing style, follow both the practices of your organization and the requirements of the selected social-media platform. Some organizations have strict guidelines regarding who can contribute to social-media–based conversations and how those contributions must be designed and worded. Pay close attention to the <u>context</u> (Tab 1), <u>purpose</u> (Tab 1), and <u>audience</u> (Tab 1) of your message, ensuring that your message is clear, precise, and free of grammatical errors. See <u>proofreading</u> (Tab 1).

Posts in a social-media platform are immediately and often widely shared among other community participants and potentially on other, unassociated Web sites. For this reason, consider both the benefit of your post to your immediate audience and the potential implications of that post to those outside your social media network. Although many platforms are considered "informal" and used primarily for personal communication, the ability of writing to be shared throughout a given network demands that you consider how your contributions represent you professionally. Organizations often review the social-media profiles of their applicants as part of the employment process. Other organizations employ services to monitor what is said about them online. Many organizations have policies that prohibit employees from discussing the workplace, even within a personal social-media account.

LinkedIn	Offers individuals opportunities to connect with others and to create a professional network or community.
	Provides a profile page that acts much like a **résumé** (Tab 9) by highlighting an individual's work, education, skills, and experiences.
	Allows community members to participate in profession-specific discussion boards, as well as post and respond to employment ads.
	Allows people to "follow" specific businesses and organizations.
Facebook	Enables businesses to broaden their brand recognition and to interact with current and new customers.
	Provides insight about potential employees, vendors, and business associates.
	Assigns each individual or business a "wall" that can be used to post status updates, pictures, videos, or links to other Web sites.
	Allows users to "friend" or "like" other users, connecting the accounts and allowing interaction between each user.
Twitter	Allows users to "follow" a company or an individual who can keep clients and others aware of an organization's or individual's activities.
	Limits every message or "status update" to 140 characters; businesses and individuals can post timely updates or critical announcements.
	Allows organizations to enter near synchronous conversations with their clients and customers.

FIGURE 2–5. Comparison of Social-Media Platforms

Writer's Checklist: Judicious Use of Social Media

☑   Always consider the purpose and suitability of your contributions. Avoid contributions that publicly discuss topics better suited for one-on-one communication or that are considered divisive.

☑   Understand the availability of your social-media contributions. Consider your posts to be available to everyone, and take into account how someone, such as your employer or school, might view your status update or shared picture.

☑   Follow your employer's policies regarding social media. Attempting to circumvent policies, by using a mobile device to access a blocked site, for example, could result in severe penalties or even termination.

☑   Never comment about a job, an employer, or an instructor. Consider everything that you contribute to a social-media platform as available to the organization or individuals that you might be writing about. Avoid comments on workplace relationships.

Writer's Checklist: Judicious Use of Social Media (continued)

☑ Carefully consider "friend" requests. Before establishing a connection, consider your organization's policy, your professional relationship, and any potential current or future conflicts of interest.

☑ Have at least one public, professional social-media account, especially if you are searching for jobs. Many employers now search job candidates' social-media accounts before hiring them. Given the prevalence of social media, employers may be suspicious that you are hiding something if they cannot find you online.

☑ Consider also the information in the Ethics Note on page 47 as you compose your message.

text messaging

Text messaging, or *texting*, refers to the delivery or exchange of brief written messages between mobile phones over cellular networks. Text messaging is effective for simple messages communicated between people on the move or in nontraditional workplaces. ("Client backup servers down.") Some text messages can include photographs, video, and other digital files. As with your workplace e-mail, consider carefully the content of your messages before sending them. For the real-time exchange of brief messages, the phone or instant messaging may be a better choice. See also selecting the medium.

writing for the Web

This entry is intended to help you contribute content for your company's or organization's Web site. For questions about the appropriateness of content you plan to post, check with your webmaster or manager to determine if your content complies with your organization's Web policy. On campus, consult your instructor or campus computer support staff about standards for posting Web content. See also blogs and forums and FAQs.

Crafting Content for Your Site

Most readers scan Web pages for specific information, so state your important points first, before providing detailed supporting information. Keep your writing style straightforward and concise, and use plain language (Tab 10) as much as possible. Use the following techniques to make your content more accessible to your audience. See also conciseness (Tab 10).

Text Content.   Break up dense blocks of text by dividing them into short <u>paragraphs</u> (Tab 1) so that they stand out and can be quickly scanned and absorbed. Focus each passage on one facet of your topic. Where necessary, include links to more detailed secondary information.

Headings.   Use informative topic <u>headings</u> (Tab 7) for paragraphs or sections to help readers decide at a glance whether to read a passage. Headings also clarify text by highlighting structure and organization. They signal breaks in coverage from one topic to the next as well as mark <u>transitions</u> (Tab 10) between topics. Set off headings in boldface or another text style, such as a different color, on a separate line directly above the text they describe, or in the left margin directly across from the text. See also <u>layout and design</u> (Tab 7).

Lists.   Use bulleted and numbered <u>lists</u> (Tab 7) to break up dense paragraphs, reduce text length, and highlight important content. Do not overuse lists, however. Lists without supporting explanatory text lack <u>coherence</u> (Tab 10).

Keywords.   To help search engines and your audience find your site, use terms that highlight content in the first 50 or so words of text for each new topic.

WITHOUT KEYWORDS	We are proud to introduce a new commemorative coin honoring our bank's founder and president. The item will be available on this Web site after December 3, 2017, which is the 100th anniversary of our first deposit.
WITH KEYWORDS	The new *Reynolds* commemorative coin features a portrait of *George G. Reynolds*, the founder and president of *Reynolds Bank*. The coin can be purchased after December 3, 2017, in honor of the 100th anniversary of *Reynolds*'s first deposit.

To learn more about search engine optimization (SEO), Google Adwords, and Internet marketing tools, visit *http://moz.com/beginners -guide-to-seo.*

Directional Cues.   Avoid navigational cues, such as "on the next page," that make sense on the printed page but not on a Web screen. Instead, position links so that they are tied directly to the content to which they pertain, such as the ***Back to Top*** links on pages that are several screens long.

Graphics.   Graphics provide information that text alone cannot; they also provide visual relief. Use only <u>visuals</u> (Tab 7) that are appropriate for your audience and <u>purpose</u> (Tab 1), however. Avoid overusing complex graphs and animation that can clutter or slow access to your site. Work with the site webmaster to optimize all graphics for speed of access. Ask about the preferred file-compression format for your visuals. Also consider giving visitors a graphics-free option for quicker access to your content.

Fonts.   Font sizes and styles affect screen legibility. Because screens display fonts at lower resolutions compared to printed text, sans serif fonts often work better for online text passages. Do not use ALL CAPITAL LETTERS or **boldface type** for blocks of text because they slow the reader. For content that contains special characters (such as mathematical or chemical content), consult your webmaster about the best way to submit the files for HTML (hypertext markup language) coding or post them as portable document format (PDF) files.

Using Links

Use *internal links* to help readers navigate the information at your site. If text is longer than two or three screens, create a <u>table of contents</u> (Tab 6) of links for it at the top of the Web page and link each item to the relevant content further down the page. Use *external links* to enrich coverage of your topic with information outside your site and to help reduce content on your page. When you do, consider placing an icon or a text label next to the link to inform users that they are leaving the host site. Avoid too many links within text paragraphs because they can distract readers, make scanning the text difficult, and tempt readers to leave your site before reaching the end of your page.

Links to outside sites can expand your content. However, *review such sites carefully before linking to them.* Is the site's author or sponsoring organization reputable? Is its content accurate, current, and unbiased? Does the site date-stamp its content with notices such as, "This page was last updated on January 1, 2017"? Link directly to the page or specific area of an outside site that is relevant to your users, and be sure that you provide a clear <u>context</u> (Tab 1) for why you are sending your readers there. For more advice on evaluating Web sites, see pages 173–74.

Posting an Existing Document

If you post existing documents to a Web site, try to retain the original sequence and layout of the documents. If, for example, you shorten or revise an existing document for posting to the Web, add a notice informing readers how it differs from the original.

Before posting the document publicly, review it offline to ensure that it is the correct version and that all links work and go to the right places. Consider creating a "single-file version" of the content (a version formatted as a single, long Web page) for readers who will print the content to read offline. See also <u>proofreading</u> (Tab 1) and <u>repurposing</u>.

❖ ETHICS NOTE Keep a record of how and where you find content online, be it text, images, tables, streaming video, or other material. Seek approval from the holder of the <u>copyright</u> (Tab 5) before using any such information. Documenting your sources not only is required legally and ethically but also bolsters the credibility of your site. To document your sources, either provide links to your source or use a citation, as described in <u>documenting sources</u> (Tab 5). See also <u>plagiarism</u> (Tab 5). ❖

Protecting User Privacy

Ensure that your content is consistent with your site's privacy policies for site users. A site's privacy statement informs visitors about how the site sponsor handles solicited and unsolicited information, its policy on the use of cookies,* and its policy on handling security breaches.

Writing for a Global Audience

When you write for a site aimed at an international audience, eliminate expressions and references that make sense only to someone familiar with American English. Express <u>dates</u> (Tab 12), clock times, and measurements consistent with international practices. For visuals, choose symbols and icons, colors, representations of human beings, and captions that can be easily understood, as described in <u>global communication</u> (Tab 1) and <u>global graphics</u> (Tab 7). See also <u>biased language</u> (Tab 10), <u>English as a second language</u> (Tab 11), and <u>idioms</u> (Tab 10).

DIGITAL TIP

Digitally Enhancing Repurposed Content

Convert documents such as reports, flyers, and brochures to PDF files to make sure your electronic documents look identical to your printed documents. Readers can view a PDF file online, download it, or print it in whole or in part. By taking advantage of these digital media, you can add functionality to the content. Using specialized PDF software, you can create sophisticated forms, add signatures and watermarks to documents, and password-protect sensitive files. Digital versions of reports, for example, offer tables of contents that link directly to the individual sections within a report. You can add hyperlinks or mouse-over elements that add links to supplemental information or definitions of specialized terms. Further enhancements could include interactive components, such as forms and graphics, that readers can manipulate.

---

*"Cookies" are small files that are downloaded to your computer when you browse certain Web pages. Cookies hold information, such as language and selections that you've made, so you do not need to render those selections each time you visit the site.

3

Correspondence

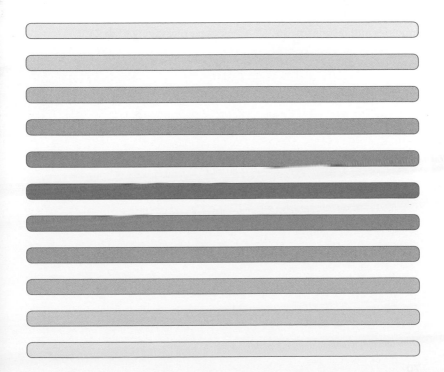

Preview

The process of writing business messages involves many of the same steps that go into most other on-the-job writing tasks, as described in "Five Steps to Successful Writing" (page xxvii). This section contains entries on the general principles of **correspondence** that will help you get the most out of specific entries on such forms as **e-mail** (Tab 2), **letters**, and **memos**. Other entries in this section cover specific situations, such as **complaints** and **adjustments** as well as **international correspondence**. For choosing the best medium for corresponding, see **selecting the medium** (Tab 2).

3

Correspondence

acknowledgments

When a colleague or client sends you something or makes a request, you should acknowledge what was sent, respond to the request, or explain that you cannot respond to the request immediately in a short, polite note. Send a message, like the one shown in Figure 3–1, in the medium used or preferred by your reader, whether a letter, an e-mail (Tab 2), or a text message (Tab 2). See also correspondence.

Send | Cancel | Save Draft | Add Attachment | Signature | Options

SENT: Mon 2/6/17 9:50 AM

TO: Marsha Stein <stein39@macrofoods.com>

CC:

Show BCC

Subject: Checkout Reporting System

Dear Ms. Stein:

Your comprehensive report arrived today. When I finish studying it in detail, I'll send you our cost estimate for the installation of the Checkout Reporting System.

Thank you for preparing such a thorough analysis.

Regards,

Wilbur Kohn

FIGURE 3–1. Acknowledgment

adjustments

An adjustment letter or e-mail (Tab 2) is written in response to a complaint and tells a customer or client what your organization intends to do about the complaint. Although sent in response to a problem, an adjustment letter actually provides an excellent opportunity to build goodwill for your organization. An effective adjustment letter, such as the examples shown in Figures 3–2 and 3–3, can not only repair any damage done but also restore the customer's confidence in your company. See also complaints.

No matter how unreasonable the complaint, the tone (Tab 10) of your response should be positive and respectful. Avoid emphasizing the problem, but do take responsibility for it when appropriate. Focus your response on what you are doing to correct the problem. Settle such matters quickly and courteously, and lean toward giving the customer or client the benefit of the doubt at a reasonable cost to your organization. See also **refusals** and **"you" viewpoint** (Tab 10).

Full Adjustments

Before granting an adjustment to a claim for which your company is at fault, first determine what happened and what you can do to satisfy the customer. Be certain that you are familiar with your company's adjustment policy—and be careful with **word choice** (Tab 10).

▶ We have just received your letter of May 7 about our defective gas grill.

Saying something is "defective" could be ruled in a court of law as an admission that the product is in fact defective. When you are in doubt, seek legal advice.

Grant adjustments graciously: A settlement made grudgingly will do more harm than good. Not only must you be gracious, but you must also acknowledge the error in such a way that the customer will not lose confidence in your company. Emphasize early what the reader will consider good news.

▶ Enclosed is a replacement for the damaged part.

▶ Yes, you were incorrectly billed for the delivery.

▶ Please accept our apologies for the error in your account.

▶ **PROFESSIONALISM NOTE** If an explanation will help restore your reader's confidence, explain what caused the problem. You might point out any steps you are taking to prevent a recurrence of the problem. Explain that customer feedback helps your firm keep the quality of its product or service high. Close pleasantly, looking toward the future, and avoid recalling the problem in your closing (do not write, "Again, we apologize . . ."). ▶

The adjustment letter in Figure 3–2, for example, begins by accepting responsibility and offers an apology for the customer's inconvenience (note the use of the pronouns *we* and *our*). The message also states that the customer will receive complimentary Internet service. The second paragraph expresses a desire to restore goodwill and describes specifically how the writer intends to make the adjustment. The third paragraph expresses appreciation to the customer for calling attention to the problem and assures him that his complaint has been taken seriously.

INTERNET SERVICES CORPORATION
10876 Crispen Way
Chicago, Illinois 60601

May 12, 2017

Mr. Jason Brandon
4319 Anglewood Street
Tacoma, WA 98402

Dear Mr. Brandon:

We are sorry that your experience with our customer support help line did not go smoothly. We are eager to restore your confidence in our ability to provide dependable, high-quality service. Your next three months of Internet access will be complimentary as our sincere apology.

Providing dependable service is what is expected of us, and when our staff doesn't provide quality service, it is easy to understand our customers' disappointment. I truly wish we had performed better in our guidance for setup and log-in procedures and that your experience had been a positive one. To prevent similar problems in the future, we plan to use your letter, anonymized, in training sessions with customer support personnel.

We appreciate your taking the time to write us. It helps to receive comments such as yours, and we conscientiously follow through to be sure that proper procedures are being met.

Yours truly,

Inez Carlson

Inez Carlson, Vice President
Customer Support Services

3

Correspondence

www.isc.com

FIGURE 3–2. Adjustment Letter (Company Takes Responsibility)

Partial Adjustments

You may sometimes need to grant a partial adjustment—even if a claim is not really justified—to regain the lost goodwill of a customer or client. If, for example, a customer incorrectly uses a product or service, you may need to help that person better understand the correct use of that product or service. In such a circumstance, remember that your customer or client believes that his or her claim is justified. Therefore, you should give the explanation before granting the claim—otherwise, your reader may never get to the explanation. If your explanation establishes customer responsibility, do so tactfully. Figure 3–3 is an example of a partial adjustment message. See also <u>correspondence</u>.

> Dear Mr. Sanchez:
>
> Thank you for your letter requesting the replacement of your CS7 laptop computer.
>
> You said in your letter that you used the unit on an open patio. As our service representative and the CS7 instruction manual states, exposure to heat and direct sunlight can produce irreparable damage. Because your unit was used in such conditions, we cannot honor the warranty.
>
> However, we are enclosing a certificate entitling you to a trade-in allowance equal to your local CS dealer's markup for the unit. This means you can purchase a new unit at wholesale, provided you return your original unit to your local dealer.
>
> Sincerely,
>
> Linda Rae, Customer Service

FIGURE 3–3. Partial Adjustment (Accompanying a Product)

complaints

A complaint, sent by <u>e-mail</u> (Tab 2) or <u>letter</u>, describes a problem that the writer requests the recipient to solve. The <u>tone</u> (Tab 10) of the message is important: If your message is angry and belligerent, you may not be taken seriously. Likewise, immediately posting a complaint to a company's <u>social media</u> (Tab 2) site or to a public forum might be seen as an "attack" and not as an honest attempt to work out a problem and reach a resolution. Assume that the recipient will be conscientious in correcting the problem. However, anticipate reader reactions or rebuttals. See <u>audience</u> (Tab 1).

▶ I reviewed my user manual's "safe operating guidelines" carefully before I installed the device.
[This assures readers you followed instructions.]

Without such explanations, readers may be tempted to dismiss your complaint. Figure 3–4 shows a complaint that details a billing problem. Although the circumstances and severity of the problem may vary, effective complaint letters generally follow this pattern:

1. Identify the problem or faulty item(s) and include relevant invoice numbers, part names, and dates.
2. Include or attach a copy of the receipt, bill, contract, or perhaps a photo of a damaged part and keep the original for your records.
3. Explain logically, clearly, and specifically what went wrong, especially for a problem with a service. (Avoid guessing why you *think* some problem occurred.)
4. State what you expect the reader to do to solve the problem.

➤ Send ✕ Cancel ▤ Save Draft ᶙ Add Attachment ▱ Signature ▼ Options

SENT: Thurs 8/17/17 9:24 AM

TO | customerservice@ST3.com

CC | | Show BCC

Subject | ST3 Diagnostic Scanners

🗋 MKeller_ST3-1179R.pdf   Download

On July 13, I ordered nine ST3 Diagnostic Scanners (order # ST3-1179R). The scanners were ordered from your customer Web site.

On August 3, I received seven HL monitors from your parts warehouse in Newark, New Jersey. I immediately returned those monitors with a note indicating that a mistake had been made. However, not only have I failed to receive the ST3 scanners that I ordered, but I have also been billed repeatedly for the seven monitors.

I have attached a copy of my confirmation e‑mail, the shipping form, and the most recent bill. If you cannot send me the scanners I ordered by September 15, please cancel my order.

Sincerely,

Marissa Keller

FIGURE 3–4. Complaint Message

Be sure to check the company's Web site for any instructions for submitting a complaint. When you cannot find specific instructions, you may address your complaint to Customer Service for large organizations. In smaller organizations, you might write to a vice president in charge of sales or service, or directly to the owner. Often, a well-written e-mail, followed, if necessary, by a letter sent through standard mail will solicit the best response. If you do not receive a timely response to your complaint, try sending it to a different person in the company. See also adjustments and refusals.

correspondence

3

Correspondence

Correspondence in the workplace—whether through e-mail (Tab 2), letters, memos, or another medium—requires many of the steps described in "Five Steps to Successful Writing" (page xxvii). As you prepare even a simple e-mail, for example, you might study previous messages (research) and then list or arrange the points you wish to cover (organization) in an order that is logical for your readers. See also selecting the medium (Tab 2).

Corresponding with others in the workplace also requires that you focus on both establishing or maintaining a positive working relationship with your readers and conveying a professional image of yourself and your organization. See also audience (Tab 1).

Audience and Writing Style

Effective correspondence uses an appropriate conversational style. To achieve that style, imagine your reader sitting across from you and write to the reader as if you were talking face to face. Take into account your reader's needs and feelings. Ask yourself, "How might I feel if I received this letter or e-mail?" and then tailor your message accordingly. Remember, an impersonal and unfriendly message to a customer or client can tarnish the image of you and your business, but a thoughtful and sincere one can enhance it.

Whether you use a formal or an informal writing style depends entirely on your reader and your purpose (Tab 1). You might use an informal (or casual) style, for example, with a colleague you know well and a formal (or restrained) style with a client you do not know.

CASUAL   It worked! The new process is better than we had dreamed.

RESTRAINED   You will be pleased to know that the new process is more effective than we had expected.

You will probably find yourself using the restrained style more frequently than the casual style. Remember that an overdone attempt to sound casual or friendly can sound insincere. However, do not adopt so formal a style that your writing reads like a legal contract. Affectation (Tab 10) not only will irritate and baffle readers but also can waste time and produce costly errors.

AFFECTED   Per yesterday's discussion, we no longer possess an original copy of the brochure requested. Please be advised that a PDF copy is attached herewith to this e-mail.

IMPROVED   We are out of printed copies of the brochure we discussed yesterday, so I am attaching a PDF copy to this e-mail.

The improved version is not only clearer and less stuffy but also more concise. See also business writing style (Tab 10) and conciseness (Tab 10).

Openings and Closings

The opening of any correspondence should identify the subject and often the main point of the message.

▶ Attached is the final installation report, which I hope you can review by Monday, December 11. You will notice that the report includes . . .

When your reader is not familiar with the subject or with the background of a problem, you may provide an introductory paragraph before stating the main point of the message. Doing so is especially important in correspondence that will serve as a record of crucial information. Generally, longer or complex subjects benefit most from more thorough introductions (Tab 1). However, even when you are writing a short message about a familiar subject, remind readers of the context (Tab 1). In the following example, words that provide context are shown in *italics*.

▶ *As Maria recommended,* I reviewed the office reorganization plan. I like most of the features; however, the location of the receptionist and the assistant . . .

3

Correspondence

Do not state the main point first when (1) readers are likely to be highly skeptical or (2) key readers, such as managers or clients, may disagree with your position. In those cases, a more persuasive tactic is to state the problem or issue first, then present the specific points supporting your final recommendation, as discussed later under the *indirect pattern* on page 81. See also <u>persuasion</u> (Tab 1).

Your closing can accomplish many important tasks, such as building positive relationships with readers, encouraging colleagues and employees, letting recipients know what you will do or what you expect of them, and stating any assignment deadlines.

▶ I will discuss the problem with the marketing consultant and let you know by Wednesday (August 2) what we are able to change.

Routine statements are sometimes unavoidable. ("If you have further questions, please let me know.") However, try to make your closing work for you by providing specific prompts to which the reader can respond. See also <u>conclusions</u> (Tab 1).

▶ Thanks again for the report, and let me know if you want me to send you a copy of the test results.

Goodwill and the "You" Viewpoint

Write concisely, but do not be so blunt that you risk losing the reader's goodwill. Responding to a vague written request with "Your request was unclear" or "I don't understand" could offend your reader. Instead, establish goodwill to encourage your reader to provide the information you need.

▶ I will be glad to help, but I need additional information to locate the report you requested. Specifically, can you give me the report's title, release date, or number?

Although this version is a bit longer, it is more tactful and will elicit a helpful response. See also <u>telegraphic style</u> (Tab 10).

You can also build goodwill by emphasizing the reader's needs or benefits. Suppose you received a refund request from a customer who forgot to include the receipt with the request. In a response to that customer, you might write the following:

WEAK   We must receive the sales receipt before we can process a refund. [The writer's needs are emphasized: "*We* must receive."]

If you consider how to keep the customer's goodwill, you could word the request this way:

IMPROVED   Please send the sales receipt so that we can process your refund. [Although polite, the sentence still focuses on the writer's needs: "so that *we* can process."]

You can put the reader's needs and interests foremost by writing from the reader's perspective. Often, doing so means using the words *you* and *your* rather than *we, our, I,* and *mine*—a technique called the "you" viewpoint (Tab 10). Consider the following revision:

> EFFECTIVE   So that you can receive your refund promptly, please mail or fax the sales receipt. [The reader's needs are emphasized with *you* and *your*.]

This revision stresses the reader's benefit and interest. By emphasizing the reader's needs, the writer will be more likely to accomplish the purpose: to get the reader to act. See also positive writing (Tab 10).

If overdone, however, goodwill and the "you" viewpoint can produce writing that is fawning and insincere. Messages that are full of excessive praise and inflated language may be ignored—or even resented—by the reader.

> EXCESSIVE   You are just the kind of astute client that deserves
> PRAISE   the finest service that we can offer—and you
>   deserve our best deal. Understanding how
>   carefully you make decisions, I know you'll think
>   about the advantages of using our consulting
>   service.

> REASONABLE   From our earlier correspondence, I understand
>   your need for reliable service. We strive to give
>   all our priority clients our full attention, and after
>   you have reviewed our proposal I am confident
>   you will appreciate our "five-star" consulting
>   option.

Writer's Checklist: Using Tone to Build Goodwill

Use the following guidelines to achieve a **tone** (Tab 10) that builds goodwill with your recipients.

☑ Be respectful, not demanding.

> DEMANDING   Submit your answer in one week.
> RESPECTFUL   I would appreciate your answer within one week.

☑ Be modest, not arrogant.

> ARROGANT   My attached report is thorough, and I'm sure that
>   you won't be able to continue without it.
> MODEST   The attached report contains details of the refi-
>   nancing options that I hope you will find useful.

(continued)

3

Correspondence

Writer's Checklist: Using Tone to Build Goodwill (continued)

☑ Be polite, not sarcastic.

SARCASTIC	I just now received the shipment we ordered six months ago. I'm sending it back—we can't use it now. Thanks a lot!
POLITE	I am returning the shipment we ordered on March 12. Unfortunately, it arrived too late for us to be able to use it.

☑ Be positive and tactful, not negative and condescending.

NEGATIVE	Your complaint about our prices is way off target. Our prices are definitely not any higher than those of our competitors.
TACTFUL	Thank you for your suggestion concerning our prices. We believe, however, that our prices are comparable to those of our competitors.

Direct and Indirect Patterns

Direct Pattern.   The direct pattern is effective in workplace correspondence because readers appreciate messages that get to the main point quickly. The direct pattern shown in the following list also accomplishes the goals described on page 76.

1. Main point of message
2. Explanation of details or facts
3. Goodwill closing

The direct pattern is especially appropriate for presenting good news, as shown in Figure 3–5. This message presents the good news in the opening (the main point), follows with an explanation of the facts, and closes by looking toward the future (goodwill). The direct pattern may also be appropriate for negative messages in situations where little is at stake for the writer or reader and the reasons for the negative message are relatively unimportant.

▶ Dear Mr. Coleman:

We do not have the part you requested currently in stock, but we hope to have it within the next month. Our supplier, who has been reliable in the past, assures us that the manufacturer that produces those parts will be able . . . [Continues with details and goodwill closing.]

Dear Ms. Mauer:

Good news	We are pleased to offer you the position of Records Administrator at Southtown Dental Center at the salary of $54,300. Your qualifications fit our needs precisely, and we hope you will accept our offer.
Explanation	If the terms we discussed in the interview are acceptable to you, please come to the main office at 9:30 a.m. on November 17. At that time, we will ask you to complete our benefits form, in addition to . . .
Goodwill	Our entire office looks forward to working with you. Everyone was favorably impressed with you during your interview.

Sincerely,

FIGURE 3–5. Good-News Message

Indirect Pattern. The indirect pattern may be effective when you need to present especially sensitive or negative messages in correspondence. Research has shown that people form their impressions and attitudes very early when reading correspondence. For this reason, presenting bad news, refusals, or sensitive messages *indirectly* is often more effective than presenting negative information directly, especially if the stakes are high.* See also refusals.

As with any type of writing, imagine how your audience will react to your message. Consider the thoughtlessness in the job rejection that follows:

▶ Dear Ms. Mauer:

Your application for the position of Records Administrator at Southtown Dental Center has been rejected. We have found someone more qualified than you.
Sincerely,

Although the letter is concise and uses the pronouns *you* and *your,* the writer has not considered how the recipient will feel as she reads the

---

*Gerald J. Alred, "'We Regret to Inform You': Toward a New Theory of Negative Messages," in *Studies in Technical Communication,* ed. Brenda R. Sims (Denton: University of North Texas and NCTE, 1993), 17–36.

letter. The letter is, in short, rude. The pattern of this letter is (1) bad news, (2) curt explanation, (3) close.

The indirect pattern for such bad-news correspondence allows the explanation or details to lead logically and tactfully to the negative message, as in the following pattern:

1. Context of message
2. Explanation or details
3. Bad news or negative message
4. Goodwill closing

The opening (traditionally called a "buffer") should provide a context for the subject and establish a professional tone. However, it must not mislead the reader to believe that good news may follow, and it must not contain irrelevant information.*

The body should provide an explanation by reviewing the details or facts that lead to a negative decision or refusal. Give the negative message simply, based on the facts; do not belabor the bad news or provide an inappropriate apology. Neither the details nor an overdone apology can turn bad news into something positive. Your goal should be to establish for the reader that the writer or organization has been *reasonable* given the circumstances. To accomplish this goal, you need to organize the explanation carefully and logically.

The closing should establish or reestablish a positive relationship through goodwill or helpful information. Consider, for example, the revised bad-news letter, shown in Figure 3–6. This letter carries the same disappointing news as the message above, but the writer of this letter begins by not only introducing the subject but also thanking the reader for her time and effort. Then the writer explains why Ms. Mauer was not accepted for the job and offers her encouragement by looking toward a potential future opportunity. Bad news is never pleasant; however, information that either puts the bad news in perspective or makes the bad news reasonable maintains respect between the writer and the reader. The goodwill closing reestablishes an amicable professional relationship.

The indirect pattern can also be used in relatively short e-mail messages and memos. Consider the unintended secondary message a manager conveys in the following notice:

WEAK   It has been decided that the office will be open the day after Thanksgiving.

---

*Kitty O. Locker, "Factors in Reader Responses to Negative Letters: Experimental Evidence for Changing What We Teach," *Journal of Business and Technical Communication* 13, no. 1 (January 1999): 29.

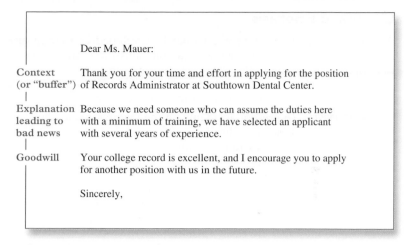

Dear Ms. Mauer:

Context
(or "buffer") — Thank you for your time and effort in applying for the position of Records Administrator at Southtown Dental Center.

Explanation leading to bad news — Because we need someone who can assume the duties here with a minimum of training, we have selected an applicant with several years of experience.

Goodwill — Your college record is excellent, and I encourage you to apply for another position with us in the future.

Sincerely,

FIGURE 3–6. Courteous Bad-News Message

"It has been decided" not only sounds impersonal but also communicates an authoritarian, management-versus-employee tone. The passive voice also suggests that the decision maker does not want to say "I have decided" and thus accept responsibility for the decision. One solution is to remove the first part of the sentence.

IMPROVED   The office will be open the day after Thanksgiving.

The best solution, however, would be to suggest both that there is a good reason for the decision and that employees are privy to (if not a part of) the decision-making process.

EFFECTIVE   Because we must meet the December 15 deadline for submitting the Bradley Foundation proposal, the office will be open the day after Thanksgiving.

By describing the context of the bad news first (the need to meet the deadline), the writer focuses on the reasoning behind the decision to work. Employees may not necessarily like the message, but they will at least understand that the decision is not arbitrary and is tied to an important deadline.

3

Correspondence

Clarity and Emphasis

A clear message is one that is adequately developed and emphasizes your main points. The following example illustrates how adequate development is crucial to the clarity of your message.

> VAGUE   Be more careful on the loading dock.
>
> DEVELOPED   To prevent accidents on the loading dock, follow
>   these procedures:
>   1. Check to make sure . . .
>   2. Load only items that are rated . . .
>   3. Replace any defective parts . . .

Although the first version is concise, it is not as clear and specific as the "developed" revision. Do not assume your readers will know what you mean: Vague messages are easily misinterpreted.

Lists.   Vertically stacked words, phrases, and other items with numbers or bullets can effectively highlight such information as steps in a sequence, materials or parts needed, key or concluding points, and recommendations. As described in lists (Tab 7), provide context and be careful not to overuse lists. A message that consists almost entirely of lists is difficult to understand because it forces readers to connect separate and disjointed items. Further, lists lose their impact when they are overused.

Headings.   Headings (Tab 7) are particularly useful because they call attention to main topics, divide material into manageable segments, and signal a shift in subject. Readers can scan the headings and read only the section or sections appropriate to their needs.

Subject Lines.   Subject lines for e-mails, memos, and some letters announce the topic and focus of the correspondence. Because they also aid filing and later retrieval, they must be specific and accurate.

> VAGUE   Subject: Tuition Reimbursement
>
> VAGUE   Subject: Time-Management Seminar
>
> SPECIFIC   Subject: Tuition Reimbursement for
>   Time-Management Seminar

Capitalize all major words in a subject line except articles, prepositions, and conjunctions with fewer than five letters (unless they are the first or last words). Remember that the subject line should not substitute for an opening that provides context for the message. See also titles (Tab 4).

Writer's Checklist: Correspondence and Accuracy

☑ Begin by establishing your purpose, analyzing your reader's needs, determining your **scope** (Tab 1), and considering the context.

☑ Prepare an outline, even if it is only a list of points to be covered in the order you want to cover them. (See **outlining**, Tab 1.)

☑ Write the first draft. (See **writing a draft**, Tab 1.)

☑ Allow for a cooling-off period prior to **revision** (Tab 1) or seek a colleague's advice, especially for correspondence that addresses a problem.

☑ Revise the draft, checking for key problems in clarity and **coherence** (Tab 10).

☑ Use the appropriate or standard format, for example, as in **letters** and **memos**.

☑ Check for accuracy: Make sure that all facts, figures, and dates are correct.

☑ Use effective **proofreading** (Tab 1) techniques to check your punctuation and usage (see the Appendix, "Usage"). See also Tab 12, "Punctuation and Mechanics."

☑ Consider who should receive a copy of the message and in what order the names or e-mail addresses should be listed (alphabetize if rank does not apply).

☑ Remember that when you sign a letter or send a message, you are accepting responsibility for it.

3

Correspondence

cover letters

A cover **letter**, a **memo**, or an **e-mail** (Tab 2) accompanies a document, a digital file, or other material. It identifies an item that is being sent, the person to whom it is being sent, the reason that it is being sent, and any content that should be highlighted for readers. A cover letter (or *transmittal*) provides a permanent record for both the writer and the reader. For cover letters to résumés, see **application cover letters** (Tab 9).

The cover message in Figure 3–7 is concise, but it also includes details such as how the information for the report was gathered.

Send	✕ Cancel	🗐 Save Draft	🔊 Add Attachment	✉ Signature	▼ Options

SENT: Fri 9/8/17 1:17 PM

TO AHammersmith@IDC.com

CC   Show BCC

Subject Annual Energy Estimate Report

📄 AnnualEnergyEstimate.sc.pdf   Download

Dear Mr. Hammersmith:

Attached is the report estimating our energy needs for the year as requested by John Brenan, Vice President, on September 5.

The report is a result of several meetings with the manager of plant operations and her staff and an extensive survey of all our employees. The survey was delayed by the transfer of key staff in Building A. However, the report should provide the information you need in order to furnish us with a cost estimate for the installation of your Mark II Energy Saving System.

We would like to thank Diana Biel of ESI for her assistance in preparing the survey. If you need any more information, please let me know.

Best wishes,

Sophia Crane

FIGURE 3–7. Cover Message

inquiries and responses

The purpose of writing inquiry messages is to obtain responses to requests or to specific questions, as in Figure 3–8, which shows a college student's request for information from an official at a power company. Inquiries may benefit either the reader (as in requests for information about a product that a company sells) or the writer (as in the student's inquiry in Figure 3–8). Inquiries that primarily benefit the writer require the use of persuasion (Tab 1) and special consideration of the needs of your audience (Tab 1). See also correspondence.

```
↪ Send   ✕ Cancel   ▤ Save Draft   ┅ Add Attachment   ✏ Signature   ▼ Options
```

SENT: Fri 10/13/17 12:11 PM

| TO | SMetcalf@MillerAssociates.com |
| CC | |

Show BCC

| Subject | Info Request: Heating Systems |

Dear Ms. Metcalf:

As an architecture student at the University of Dayton, I am working with a team of students to design an energy-efficient house for a class project. We need information on heating systems based on the specifications of our design. To meet our deadline, we would appreciate any information you could provide by November 17.

The house we are designing contains 2,000 square feet of living space (17,600 cubic feet) and meets all the requirements in your brochure "Insulating for Efficiency." We need the following information, based on the southern Ohio climate:

- The proper-size heat pump for our design.
- The wattage of the supplemental electrical heating units required.
- The estimated power consumption and rates for those units for one year.

We will be happy to send you our preliminary design report. If you have questions or suggestions, contact me at kparsons@fly.ud.edu or call 513-229-4598.

Thank you for your help.

Kenneth Parsons

FIGURE 3–8. Inquiry

3

Correspondence

Respond to an inquiry by answering promptly, and be sure to answer every inquiry or question asked, as shown in Figure 3–9. How long and how detailed your response should be depends on the nature of the question and the information the writer provides. If you have received an inquiry that you feel you cannot answer, find out who can and forward the inquiry to that person. The person who replies to a forwarded inquiry should state in the first paragraph of the response who has forwarded the original inquiry, as shown in Figure 3–9.

FIGURE 3–9. Response to an Inquiry

Writer's Checklist: Writing Inquiries and Responding

☑   Make your questions specific, clear, and concise to receive a prompt, helpful reply.

☑   Phrase your request so that the reader will know immediately the type of information you are seeking, why you need it, and how you will use it.

☑   Present questions in a numbered or bulleted <u>list</u> (Tab 7), if possible, to make it easy for your reader to respond.

☑   Keep the number of questions to a minimum to improve your chances of receiving a prompt response.

Writer's Checklist: Writing Inquiries and Responding (continued)

☑ Offer some inducement for the reader to respond, if possible, such as promising to share the results of your research. See also <u>"you" view-point</u> (Tab 10).

☑ Promise to keep responses confidential, when appropriate.

☑ Provide a date by which you need a response.

☑ Close by thanking the reader for taking the time to respond and provide your contact information, as shown in Figure 3–8.

☑ Respond to an inquiry promptly if you have the information and authority.

☑ Check your organization's policy and any special issues related to your response.

☑ Notify the writer if you need to forward the inquiry to someone else for response.

international correspondence

Business <u>correspondence</u> varies among national cultures. Organizational patterns, persuasive strategies, forms of courtesy, levels of comfort with uncertainty, and ideas about efficiency differ from country to country. For example, in the United States, direct, concise correspondence usually demonstrates courtesy by not wasting the reader's time. In many other countries, however, such directness and brevity may suggest to readers that the writer is dismissive or lacking in manners. (See <u>audience</u>, Tab 1, and <u>tone</u>, Tab 10.) Similarly, a U.S. writer might consider one brief <u>letter</u> or <u>e-mail</u> (Tab 2) sufficient to communicate a request, while a writer in another country might expect an exchange of three or four e-mails to pave the way for action.

Cultural Differences in Correspondence

When you read correspondence from businesspeople in other cultures or countries, be alert to variations in such features as customary expressions, openings, and closings. For example, business writers in some cultures, for example, traditionally use indirect openings that may express good wishes about the recipient's family or compliment the reader's success or prosperity. Consider deeper issues as well, such as how writers from other cultures express bad news. Some cultures

3

Correspondence

traditionally express negative messages, such as <u>refusals</u>, indirectly to avoid embarrassing the recipient. Such differences in correspondence are often based on cultural perceptions of time, face-saving, and other traditions. The features and communication styles of specific national cultures are complex; the entries <u>global communication</u> (Tab 1) and <u>global graphics</u> (Tab 7) provide information and resources for cross-cultural study.

Cross-Cultural Examples

Figures 3–10 and 3–11 show a draft and a final version of a letter written by an American businessperson to a Japanese businessperson. The opening and closing of the draft in Figure 3–10 do not include enough of the politeness strategies that are important in Japanese culture, and the informal salutation inappropriately uses the recipient's first name (*Dear Ichiro:*). This draft also contains idioms (*looking forward, company family*), jargon (*transport will be holding*), contractions (*I'm, don't*), informal language (*just e-mail or fax, Cheers*), and humor and allusion (*"ptomaine palace" across from our main offices*). See Tab 10, "Style and Clarity" and Tab 12, "Punctuation and Mechanics."

Compare that letter to the one in Figure 3–11, which is written in language that is courteous, literal, and specific. This revised letter begins with concern about the recipient's family and prosperity because that opening honors traditional Japanese patterns in business correspondence. The letter is free of slang, idioms, and jargon. The sentences are shorter than in the draft; in addition, the writer uses bulleted lists to break up the paragraphs, avoids contractions, spells out months, and uses 24-hour-clock time.

When writing for international readers, rethink the ingrained habits that define how you express yourself, learn as much as you can about the cultural expectations of others, and focus on politeness strategies that demonstrate your respect for readers. Doing so will help you achieve clarity and mutual understanding with international readers.

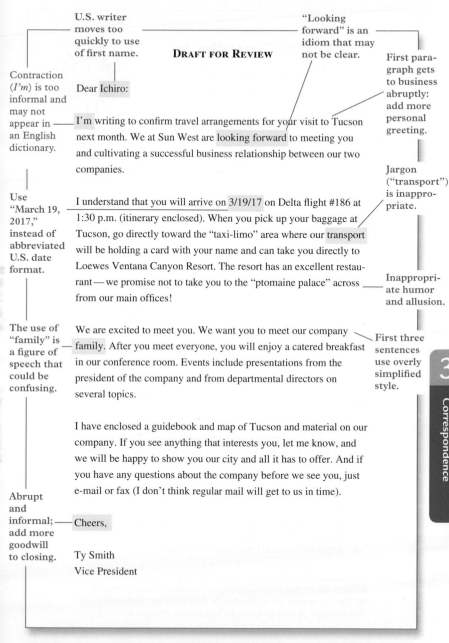

U.S. writer moves too quickly to use of first name.

"Looking forward" is an idiom that may not be clear.

First paragraph gets to business abruptly: add more personal greeting.

Contraction (*I'm*) is too informal and may not appear in an English dictionary.

Use "March 19, 2017," instead of abbreviated U.S. date format.

The use of "family" is a figure of speech that could be confusing.

Jargon ("transport") is inappropriate.

Inappropriate humor and allusion.

First three sentences use overly simplified style.

Abrupt and informal; add more goodwill to closing.

DRAFT FOR REVIEW

Dear Ichiro:

I'm writing to confirm travel arrangements for your visit to Tucson next month. We at Sun West are looking forward to meeting you and cultivating a successful business relationship between our two companies.

I understand that you will arrive on 3/19/17 on Delta flight #186 at 1:30 p.m. (itinerary enclosed). When you pick up your baggage at Tucson, go directly toward the "taxi-limo" area where our transport will be holding a card with your name and can take you directly to Loewes Ventana Canyon Resort. The resort has an excellent restaurant—we promise not to take you to the "ptomaine palace" across from our main offices!

We are excited to meet you. We want you to meet our company family. After you meet everyone, you will enjoy a catered breakfast in our conference room. Events include presentations from the president of the company and from departmental directors on several topics.

I have enclosed a guidebook and map of Tucson and material on our company. If you see anything that interests you, let me know, and we will be happy to show you our city and all it has to offer. And if you have any questions about the company before we see you, just e-mail or fax (I don't think regular mail will get to us in time).

Cheers,

Ty Smith
Vice President

3

Correspondence

FIGURE 3–10. Inappropriate International Correspondence (Draft Marked for Revision)

Sun West Corporation, Inc.

2565 North Armadillo

Tucson, AZ 85719

Phone: (602) 555-6677

Fax: (602) 555-6678   sunwest.com

March 5, 2017

Ichiro Katsumi
Investment Director
Toshiba Investment Company
1-29-10 Ichiban-cho
Tokyo 105, Japan

Dear Mr. Katsumi:

I hope that you and your family are well and prospering in the new year. We at Sun West Corporation are very pleased that you will be coming to visit us in Tucson this month. It will be a pleasure to meet you, and we are very gratified and honored that you are interested in investing in our company.

So that we can ensure that your stay will be pleasurable, we have taken care of all of your travel arrangements. You will

- Depart Narita–New Tokyo International Airport on Delta Airlines flight #75 at 1700 on March 19, 2017.
- Arrive at Los Angeles International Airport at 1050 local time and depart for Tucson on Delta flight #186 at 1205.
- Arrive at Tucson International Airport at 1330 local time on March 19.
- Depart Tucson International Airport on Delta flight #123 at 1845 on March 26.
- Arrive in Salt Lake City, Utah, at 1040 and depart on Delta flight #34 at 1115.
- Arrive in Portland, Oregon, at 1210 local time and depart on Delta flight #254 at 1305.
- Arrive in Tokyo at 1505 local time on March 27.

If you need additional information about your travel plans or information on Sun West Corporation, please call, fax, or e-mail me directly at tsmith@sunwest.com. That way, we will receive your message in time to make the appropriate changes or additions.

FIGURE 3–11. Appropriate International Correspondence

Mr. Ichiro Katsumi   2   March 5, 2017

After you arrive in Tucson, a chauffeur from Skyline Limousines
will be waiting for you at Gate 12. He or she will be carrying a
card with your name, will help you collect your luggage from the
baggage claim area, and will then drive you to the Loewes Ventana
Canyon Resort. This resort is one of the most prestigious in Tucson,
with spectacular desert views, high-quality amenities, and one of
the best golf courses in the city. The next day, the chauffeur will be
back at the Ventana at 0900 to drive you to Sun West Corporation.

We at Sun West Corporation are very excited to meet you and
introduce you to all the staff members of our hardworking and
growing company. After you meet everyone, you will enjoy a
catered breakfast in our conference room. At that time, you will
receive a schedule of events planned for the remainder of your trip.
Events include presentations from the president of the company and
from departmental directors on

- The history of Sun West Corporation
- The uniqueness of our products and current success in the
  marketplace
- Demographic information and the benefits of being located in
  Tucson
- The potential for considerable profits for both our companies
  with your company's investment

We encourage you to read through the enclosed guidebook and map
of Tucson. In addition to events planned at Sun West Corporation,
you will find many natural wonders and historical sites to see in
Tucson and in Arizona in general. If you see any particular event
or place that you would like to visit, please let us know. We will be
happy to show you our city and all it has to offer.

Again, we are very honored that you will be visiting us, and we
look forward to a successful business relationship between our two
companies.

Sincerely,

Ty Smith

Ty Smith
Vice President

Enclosures (2)

3

Correspondence

FIGURE 3–11. Appropriate International Correspondence (*continued*)

Writer's Checklist: Writing International Correspondence

☑ Observe the guidelines for courtesy, such as those in the *Writer's Checklist: Using Tone to Build Goodwill* on page 79.

☑ Write clear and complete sentences: Unusual word order or rambling sentences will frustrate and confuse readers. See **garbled sentences** (Tab 10).

☑ Avoid an overly simplified style that may offend or any **affectation** (Tab 10) that may confuse the reader. See also **English as a second language** (Tab 11).

☑ Avoid humor, irony, and sarcasm; they are easily misunderstood outside their cultural **context** (Tab 1).

☑ Do not use idioms, jargon, slang expressions, unusual figures of speech, or allusions to events or attitudes particular to life in the United States. See Tab 10, "Style and Clarity."

☑ Consider whether necessary technical terminology can be found in abbreviated English-language dictionaries; if it cannot, carefully define such terminology.

☑ Do not use contractions or abbreviations that may not be clear to international readers.

☑ Avoid inappropriate informality, such as using first names too quickly.

☑ Write out **dates** (Tab 12), whether in the month-day-year style (*June 11, 2017* not *6/11/17*) used in the United States or the day-month-year style (*11 June 2017* not *11/6/17*) used in many other parts of the world.

☑ Specify time zones or refer to international standards, such as Greenwich Mean Time (GMT) or Universal Time Coordinated (UTC).

☑ Use international measurement standards, such as the metric system (*18°C, 14 cm, 45 kg*) where possible.

☑ Consult local laws concerning e-mail to ensure that you are in compliance with those regulations. Many countries have different regulations for business e-mail correspondence, particularly marketing messages. For example, some countries require businesses to have an individual's express consent before sending that person any e-mail messages.

☑ Ask someone from your intended audience's culture or with appropriate expertise to review your draft before you complete your final **proofreading** (Tab 1).

letters

Business letters—normally written for those outside an organization—are often the most appropriate choice for formal communications with professional associates or customers. Letters may be especially effective for those people who receive a high volume of e-mail and other electronic messages. Letters printed on organizational letterhead communicate formality, respect, and authority. See correspondence for advice on writing strategy and style. See also selecting the medium (Tab 2).

Although word-processing software includes templates for formatting business letters, the templates may not provide the appropriate dimensions and elements you need. The following sections offer specific advice on formatting and related etiquette for business letters.*

Letter Format

If your employer requires a particular letter format, use it. Otherwise, follow the design guidelines shown in Figure 3–12. Figure 3–12 illustrates the popular *full-block style* in which the entire letter is aligned at the left margin. To achieve a professional appearance, center the letter on the page vertically and horizontally. Regardless of the default margin provided in a word-processing program, it is more important to establish a picture frame of blank space surrounding the text of the letter. When you use organizational stationery with letterhead at the top of the page, consider the bottom of the letterhead as the top edge of the paper. The right margin should be approximately as wide as the left margin. To give a fuller appearance to very short letters, increase both margins to about an inch and a half from the typical one-inch margins. Use your full-page or print-preview feature to check for proportion.

Heading

Unless you are using letterhead stationery, place your full return address and the date in the heading. Because your name appears at the end of the letter, it need not be included in the heading. Spell out words such as *street, avenue, first,* and *west* rather than abbreviating them. You may either spell out the name of the state in full or use the standard Postal Service abbreviation available at *www.usps.com.* The date usually goes directly beneath the last line of the return address. Do not abbreviate the name of the month. Begin the heading about two inches from

*For additional details on letter formats and design, you may wish to consult a guide such as *The Gregg Reference Manual,* 11th ed., by William A. Sabin (New York: McGraw-Hill, 2010).

Letterhead	520 Niagara Street Braintree, MA 02184 Phone: (781) 787-1175 Fax: (781) 787-1213 EvansTE.com

Date

May 15, 2017

Inside
address

Mr. George W. Nagel
Director of Operations
Boston Transit Authority
57 West City Avenue
Boston, MA 02210

Salutation

Dear Mr. Nagel:

Enclosed is our final report evaluating the safety measures for
the Boston Intercity Transit System.

Body

We believe that the report covers the issues you raised in our last
meeting and that you will be pleased with the results. However,
if you have any further questions, we would be happy to meet
with you again at your convenience.

We would also like to express our appreciation to Mr. L. K.
Sullivan of your committee for his generous help during our
trips to Boston.

Compli-
mentary
closing

Sincerely,

Signature

Carolyn Brown

Writer's
signature
block

Carolyn Brown, Ph.D.
Director of Research
cbrown@EvansTE.com

End
notations

CB/ls
Enclosure: Final Safety Report
cc: ITS Safety Committee Members

FIGURE 3–12. Full-Block-Style Letter (with Letterhead)

the top of the page. If you are using letterhead that gives the company address, enter only the date, three lines below the last line of the letterhead.

Inside Address

The inside address includes the recipient's full name, title, and address. Place the inside address two to six lines below the date, depending on the length of the letter. The inside address should be aligned with the left margin.

Salutation

Place the salutation, or *greeting*, two lines below the inside address and align it with the left margin. In most business letters, the salutation contains the recipient's personal title (such as *Mr.*, *Ms.*, *Dr.*) and last name, followed by a colon. If you are on a first-name basis with the recipient, use only the first name in the salutation.

Address women as *Ms.* unless they have expressed a preference for *Miss* or *Mrs.* However, professional titles (such as *Professor*, *Senator*, *Major*) take precedence over *Ms.* and similar courtesy titles.

When a person's first name could refer to either a woman or a man, one solution is to use both the first and last names in the salutation (*Dear Pat Smith:*).

For multiple recipients, the following salutations are appropriate:

▶ Dear Professor Allen and Dr. Rivera: [two recipients]

▶ Dear Ms. Becham, Ms. Moore, and Mr. Stein: [three recipients]

▶ Dear Colleagues: [*Members*, or other suitable collective term]

Subject Line

An optional element in a letter is a subject line, which should follow the salutation. Insert one blank line above and one blank line below the subject line. The subject line in a letter functions as it does for e-mail and other correspondence as an aid in focusing the topic and filing the letter. (For information on creating subject lines, see page 84 of **correspondence**.)

Subject lines are especially useful if you are writing to a large company and do not know the name or title of the recipient. In such cases, you may address a letter to an appropriate department or identify the subject in a subject line and use no salutation.

► National Medical Supply Group
501 West National Avenue
Minneapolis, MN 55407

Attention: Customer Service Department

Subject: Defective Cardio-100 Stethoscopes

I am returning six stethoscopes with damaged diaphragms
that . . .

In other circumstances in which you do not know the recipient's name,
use a title appropriate to the <u>context</u> (Tab 1) of the letter, such as *Dear
Customer* or *Dear IT Professional*.

Body

The body of the letter should begin two lines below the salutation (or any
element that precedes the body, such as a subject or an attention line).
Single-space within and double-space between paragraphs, as shown in
Figure 3–12. To provide a fuller appearance to a very short letter, you
can increase the side margins or increase the font size. You can also
insert extra space above the inside address, the writer's signature block,
and the initials of the person typing the letter—but do not exceed twice
the recommended space for each of these elements.

Complimentary Closing

Type the complimentary closing two spaces below the body. Use a standard
expression such as *Sincerely*, *Sincerely yours*, or *Yours truly*. (If the recipient
is a friend as well as a business associate, you can use a less-formal closing such as *Best wishes* or *Best regards* or, simply, *Best*.) Capitalize only the
initial letter of the first word, and follow the expression with a comma.

Writer's Signature Block

Type your full name four lines below and aligned with the complimentary closing. On the next line include your business title, if appropriate.
The following lines may contain your individual contact information,
such as a telephone number or an e-mail address, if not included in the
letterhead or the body of your letter. Sign the letter in the space between
the complimentary closing and your name.

End Notations

Business letters sometimes require additional information that is placed
at the left margin, two spaces below the typed name and title of the
writer in a long letter, four spaces below in a short letter.

Reference initials show the letter writer's initials in capital letters, followed by a slash mark (or colon), and then the initials of the person typing the letter in lowercase letters, as shown in Figure 3–12. When the writer is also the person typing the letter, no initials are needed.

Enclosure notations indicate that the writer is sending material (such as an invoice or an article) along with the letter. Note that you should mention the enclosure in the body of the letter. Enclosure notations may take several forms:

▶ Enclosure: Final Safety Report

▶ Enclosures (2)

▶ Enc. *or* Encs.

Copy notation ("cc:") tells the reader that a copy of the letter is being sent to the named recipient(s) (see Figure 3–12). Use a blind-copy notation ("bcc:") when you do not want the addressee to know that a copy is being sent to someone else. A blind-copy notation appears only on the copy, not on the original ("bcc: Dr. Brenda Shelton"). See the Ethics Note in <u>e-mail</u> (Tab 2) on page 52.

Continuing Pages

If a letter requires a second page (or, in rare cases, more), always carry at least two lines of the body text over to that page. Use plain (nonletterhead) paper of quality equivalent to that of the letterhead stationery for the second page. It should have a header with the recipient's name, the page number, and the date. Place the header information in the upper left-hand corner or across the page, as shown in Figure 3–13.

3

Correspondence

memos

Memos are used within organizations for routine correspondence, short reports, proposals, and other internal documents. Memos use a standard form (*To:*, *From:*, *Date:*, *Subject:*) whether sent on paper or attached to an <u>e-mail</u> (Tab 2).

Even for organizations where e-mail messages have largely taken the function of memos, a printed or an attached memo with organizational letterhead can communicate with formality and authority in addition to offering the full range of word-processing features. Paper memos are also useful in manufacturing and service industries, as well as in other businesses where employees do not have easy access to e-mail.

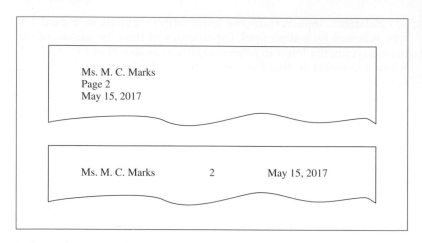

FIGURE 3–13. Alternative Headers for the Second Page of a Letter

For a discussion of writing strategies for memos, see <u>correspondence</u>. See also <u>selecting the medium</u> (Tab 2).

Memo Format

The memo shown in Figure 3–14 illustrates a typical memo format. As this example illustrates, the use of <u>headings</u> (Tab 7) and <u>lists</u> (Tab 7) fosters clarity by providing <u>emphasis</u> (Tab 10) and highlighting organization. See also <u>letters</u>. For a discussion of subject lines, see page 84.

▶ PROFESSIONALISM NOTE As with e-mail, be alert to the practices of addressing and distributing memos in your organization. Consider who should receive or needs to be copied on a memo and in what order—senior managers, for example, take precedence over junior managers. If rank does not apply, alphabetizing recipients by last name is safe. ▶

Some organizations ask writers to initial or sign formal memos that are printed (*hard copy*) to verify that the writer accepts responsibility for a memo's content.

Additional Pages

When memos require more than one page, use a second-page header and always carry at least two lines of the body text over to that page. The header should include either the recipient's name or (if there are too many names to fit) an abbreviated subject line, the page number, and the date. Place the header in the upper left-hand corner or across the page, as shown in Figure 3–15.

Professional Publishing Services

MEMORANDUM

TO: Barbara Smith, Publications Manager

FROM: Hannah Kaufman, Vice President *HK*

DATE: April 11, 2017

SUBJECT: Schedule for ACM Electronics Brochures

Handwritten initials may be used with printed formal memos.

ACM Electronics has asked us to prepare a comprehensive set of brochures for its Milwaukee office by August 11, 2017. We have worked with similar firms in the past, so this job should be relatively easy to prepare. I estimate that the job will take nearly two months. Ted Harris has requested time and cost estimates for the project. Fred Moore in production will prepare the cost estimates, and I would like you to prepare a tentative schedule for the project.

Additional Personnel
In preparing the schedule, check the status of the following:
- Production schedule for all staff writers
- Availability of freelance writers
- Availability of dependable graphic designers

Ordinarily, we would not need to depend on outside personnel; however, because our bid for the *Wall Street Journal* special project is still under consideration, we could be short of staff in June and July. Further, we have to consider vacations that have already been approved.

Time Estimates
Please give me time estimates by April 17. A successful job done on time will give us a good chance to obtain the contract to do ACM Electronics' annual report for its stockholders' meeting this fall.

I am mailing separately several brochures that may be helpful.

cc: Ted Harris, President
    Fred Moore, Production Editor

Copy notation may be placed at top with memo heading.

3

Correspondence

FIGURE 3–14. Typical Memo Format

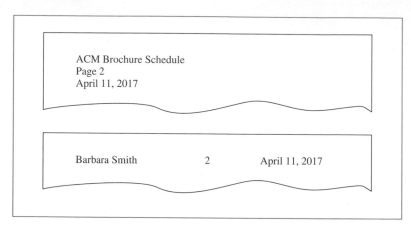

FIGURE 3–15. Alternative Headers for the Second Page of a Memo

refusals

A refusal delivers a negative message (or bad news) in the form of a <u>letter</u>, a <u>memo</u>, or an <u>e-mail</u> (Tab 2). The ideal refusal says "no" in such a way that you not only avoid antagonizing your reader but also maintain goodwill. See also <u>audience</u> (Tab 1) and <u>"you" viewpoint</u> (Tab 10).

The refusal in Figure 3–16 declines an invitation to speak at a meeting, and the stakes for the writer are relatively low; however, the writer wishes to acknowledge the honor of being asked.

When the stakes are high, you must convince your reader that the bad news is *based on reasons that are logical or at least understandable* (see also <u>correspondence</u>). Stating a negative message in your opening may cause readers to react too quickly and dismiss your explanation. The following pattern, used in Figure 3–17, is an effective way to handle this problem:

1. *Context.* In the opening, introduce the subject, but do not provide irrelevant information or mislead the reader that good news may follow.
2. *Explanation.* Review the facts or details that lead logically to the bad news, trying to see things from your reader's point of view.
3. *Bad news.* State your refusal or negative message, based on the facts, concisely and without apology.
4. *Goodwill.* In the closing, establish or reestablish a positive relationship by providing an alternative if possible, assure the reader of your high opinion of his or her product or service, offer a friendly remark, or simply wish the reader success.

FIGURE 3–16. Refusal with Low Stakes

Your opening should provide an appropriate <u>context</u> (Tab 1) and establish a professional <u>tone</u> (Tab 10) by, for example, expressing appreciation for a reader's time, effort, or interest

> ▶ The Safety Procedures Committee appreciates the time and effort you spent on your proposal for a new security-clearance procedure.

Next, review the circumstances of the situation sympathetically by placing yourself in the reader's position. Clearly detail the reasons you cannot do what the reader wants—even though you have not yet said you cannot do it. A good explanation should ideally detail the reasons for your refusal so thoroughly that the reader will accept the negative message as a logical conclusion, as shown in the following example.

Send | Cancel | Save Draft | Add Attachment | Signature | Options

SENT: Thurs 3/2/17 4:22 PM

TO: Marsha Coleman <mc2@ntr.com>

CC: Show BCC

Subject: NTR Check Sorter

Dear Ms. Coleman:

Context — Thank you for your cooperation and your patience with us as we struggled to reach a decision. We believe our long involvement with your company reflects our confidence in your products.

Review of facts — Based on our research, we found that the Winton Check Sorter has all the features that your sorter offers and, in fact, has two additional features that your sorter does not. Most important is a backup function that retains totals in its memory, even if the power fails. The second additional feature is stacked pockets, which are less space-consuming than the linear pockets on your **Refusal** — sorter. For these reasons, we have decided to purchase the Winton Check Sorter.

Goodwill close — We were generally impressed with your proposal and your staff. We will certainly consider other NTR products in the future.

Sincerely,

Nancy Nygaard

FIGURE 3–17. Refusal with High Stakes

► We reviewed the potential effects of implementing your proposed security-clearance procedure companywide. We not only asked the Security Systems Department to review the data but also surveyed industry practices, sought the views of senior management, and submitted the idea to our legal staff. As a result of this process, we have reached the following conclusions:

- The cost savings you project are correct only if the procedure could be required throughout the company.
- The components of your procedure are legal, but most are not widely accepted by our industry.
- Based on our survey, some components could alienate employees who would perceive them as violating an individual's rights.
- Enforcing companywide use would prove costly and impractical.

Do not belabor the negative message — state your refusal quickly, clearly, and as positively as possible.

▶ For those reasons, the committee recommends that divisions continue their current security-screening procedures.

Close your message in a way that reestablishes goodwill — do not repeat the bad news. (Avoid writing "Again, we are sorry we cannot use your idea.") Ideally, provide an alternative, as in the following:

▶ Because some components of your procedure may apply in certain circumstances, we would like to feature your ideas in the next issue of *The Guardian*. I have asked the editor to contact you next week. On behalf of the committee, thank you for the thoughtful proposal.

For responding to a complaint, see <u>adjustments</u>. For refusing a job offer, see <u>acceptance / refusals (for employment)</u> (Tab 9).

sales letters

A sales letter — a printed or an electronic message that promotes a product, service, or business — requires both a thorough knowledge of the product or service and an understanding of the potential customer's needs.

An effective sales (or *pitch*) letter (1) catches readers' attention, (2) engages their interest, (3) convinces them that your product or service will fulfill a need or desire, and (4) confidently asks them to take the course of action you suggest. See also <u>correspondence</u>, <u>persuasion</u> (Tab 1), <u>promotional writing</u> (Tab 1), and <u>tone</u> (Tab 10).

Your first task in writing a sales letter is to determine to whom your message should be sent. One good source of names is a list of your customers; people who have at some time purchased a product or service from you may do so again. Other sources are lists of people who may be interested in similar products or services. Companies that specialize in marketing techniques compile such lists from the membership rolls of professional associations, lists of trade-show attendees, and the like. Because outside lists may be expensive, select them with care.

Sales letters sent by e-mail are often more economical than print options, especially for large groups of potential and existing customers. If you choose e-mail as a medium, consider laws related to e-mail marketing, such as the CAN-SPAM Act (*www.business.ftc.gov/documents /bus61-can-spam-act-compliance-guide-business*). Consider as well how e-mail offers the ability to include multimedia (such as video and purchase links) and the need to keep content targeted and short. See also selecting the medium (Tab 2).

Once you determine who is to receive your sales letter, learn as much as you can about your readers so that you can effectively tell them how your product or service will satisfy their needs. Knowledge of your audience (Tab 1)—their gender, age, vocation, geographic location, educational level, financial status, and interests—will help determine your approach.

Analyze your product or service carefully to determine your strongest psychological sales points. Psychological selling involves stressing a product's benefits, which may be intangible, rather than its physical features. Select the most important psychological selling point about your product or service and build your sales message around it. Show how your product or service will make your readers' jobs easier, increase their status, make their personal lives more pleasant, and so on. Show how your product or service can satisfy your readers' needs or desires, which you identified in your opening. Then describe the physical features of your product in terms of their benefit to your readers. Help your readers with photos and Web links to imagine themselves using your product or service—and enjoying the benefits of doing so. See also "you" viewpoint (Tab 10).

❖ ETHICS NOTE Be certain that any claim you make in a sales message is valid. To claim that a product is safe guarantees its absolute safety; therefore, say that the product is safe "provided that normal safety precautions are taken." Further, while you can highlight differences, do not exaggerate or speak negatively about a competitor. For further ethical and legal guidelines, visit the Direct Marketing Association Web site at *https://thedma.org*. See also ethics in writing (Tab 1). ❖

Writer's Checklist: Writing Sales Letters

☑ Attract your readers' attention and pique their interest in the opening, for example, by describing a product's feature that would appeal strongly to their needs. See also **introductions** (Tab 1).

☑ Convince readers that your product or service is everything you say it is through case histories, free-trial use, money-back guarantee, or testimonials and endorsements.*

☑ Suggest ways readers can make immediate use of the product or service. Include a brochure or a Web link with photos or videos.

Writer's Checklist: Writing Sales Letters (continued)

☑ Minimize the negative effect price can have on readers.

- Mention the price along with a reminder of the benefits of the product.
- State the price in terms of units rather than sets ($20 per item, not $600 per set).
- Identify the daily, monthly, or even yearly cost based on the estimated life of the product.
- Suggest a series of payments rather than one total payment, if possible.
- Compare the cost of your product with that of something readers accept readily. ("This entire package costs no more than a dinner and a concert.")

☑ Make it easy and worthwhile for customers to respond: Include instructions for ordering online or by phone, information about free delivery, or special discount codes.

☑ Include links to **social media** (Tab 2) and invite readers to become part of the conversation and community surrounding the product, service, or brand. Doing so also fosters the organization's Web presence.

*For detailed advice, see the Federal Trade Commission Advertising Guidance Web site at *www.ftc.gov/tips-advice/business-center/advertising-and-marketing*, and explore the section on endorsements and testimonials.

3

Correspondence

Business Writing Documents and Elements

Preview

This section contains entries on various forms of business documents, including **proposals** and such frequently written **reports** as **progress and activity reports**, **trip reports**, and **incident reports**. Because of their size and complexity, **formal reports** and related parts are covered separately in Tab 6, "Formal Reports," which includes a sample formal report (pages 185–201).

4

Documents
and Elements

feasibility reports

When organizations consider a new project—developing a new product or service, expanding a customer base, purchasing equipment, or moving operations—they first try to determine the project's chances for success. A feasibility report presents evidence about the practicality of a proposed project based on specific criteria (Figure 4–1). It answers such questions as the following: Is new construction or development necessary? Is sufficient staff available? What are the costs? Is funding available? What are the legal or regulatory ramifications? Based on the findings of this analysis, the report offers logical conclusions and recommends whether the project should be carried out. When feasibility reports stress specific steps that should be taken as a result of a study of a problem or an issue, they are often referred to as *recommendation reports*.

Before beginning to write a feasibility report, analyze the needs of the audience (Tab 1) as well as the context (Tab 1) and purpose (Tab 1) of the study. Then write a purpose statement, such as "The purpose of this study is to determine the feasibility of expanding our Pacific Rim operations," to guide you or a collaborative writing team. See also collaborative writing (Tab 1).

Report Sections

Every feasibility report should contain an introduction, a body, a conclusion, and a recommendation. See also proposals and formal reports (Tab 6).

Introduction. The introduction states the purpose of the report, describes the circumstances that led to the report, and includes any pertinent background information. It may also discuss the scope of the report, any procedures or methods used in the analysis of alternatives, and any limitations of the study. See also introductions (Tab 1).

Body. The body presents a detailed review of the alternatives for achieving the goals of the project. Examine each option according to specific criteria, such as cost and financing, availability of staff, and other relevant requirements, identifying the subsections with topic headings (Tab 7) to guide readers.

Conclusion. The conclusion interprets the available options and leads to one option as the best or most feasible. See also conclusions (Tab 1).

4

Documents
and Elements

Introduction

The purpose of this report is to determine which of two proposed options would best enable Darnell Business Forms Corporation to upgrade its file servers and its Internet capacity to meet its increasing data and communication needs. . . .

Background.   In October 2014, the Information Development Group put the MACRON System into operation. Since then, the volume of processing transactions has increased fivefold (from 1,000 to 5,000 updates per day). This increase has severely impaired system response time; in fact, average response time has increased from 10 seconds to 120 seconds. Further, our new Web-based client-services system has increased exponentially the demand for processing speed and access capacity.

Scope.   We have investigated two alternative solutions to provide increased processing capacity: (1) purchase of an additional Aurora processor to supplement the one in operation and (2) purchase of an Icardo 60 with expandable peripherals to replace the Aurora processor currently in operation. The two alternatives are evaluated here, according to both cost and expanded capacity for future operations.

Additional Aurora Processor

Purchasing a second Aurora processor would require increased annual maintenance costs, salary for a second computer specialist, increased energy costs, and a one-time construction cost for necessary remodeling and installing Internet connections.

Annual maintenance costs	$35,000
Annual costs for computer specialist	75,000
Annual increased energy costs	7,500
Total annual operating costs	$117,500
Construction cost (one-time)	50,000
Total first-year costs	$167,500

The installation and operation of another Aurora processor are expected to produce savings in system reliability and readiness.

FIGURE 4–1. Feasibility Report

4

Recommendation.   The recommendation section clearly presents the writer's (or team's) opinion on which alternative best meets the criteria as summarized in the conclusion.

System Reliability.   An additional Aurora would reduce current downtime periods from four to two per week. Downtime recovery averages 30 minutes and affects 40 users. Assuming that 50 percent of users require system access at a given time, we determined that the following reliability savings would result:

2 downtimes × 0.5 hours × 40 users × 50% × $50/hour overtime × 52 weeks = $52,000 annual savings.

[*The feasibility report would also discuss the second option— purchase of the Icardo 60 and its long-term savings.*]

Conclusion
A comparison of costs for both systems indicates that the Icardo 60 would cost $2,200 more in first-year costs.

	Aurora	Icardo 60
Net additional operating costs	$56,300	$84,000
One-time construction costs	50,000	24,500
First-year total	$106,300	$108,500

Installation of an additional Aurora processor would permit the present information-processing systems to operate relatively smoothly and efficiently. It would not, however, provide the expanded processing capacity that the Icardo 60 processor would for implementing new subsystems required to increase processing speed and Internet access.

Recommendation
The Icardo 60 processor should be purchased because of the long-term savings and because its additional capacity and flexibility will allow for greater expansion in the future.

3

FIGURE 4–1. Feasibility Report (*continued*)

4

incident reports

The incident report is used to analyze such events as accidents, equipment failures, or health emergencies. For example, the report shown in Figure 4–2 describes an accident involving personal injury. The report

Consolidated Energy, Inc.

To: Marvin Lundquist, Vice President
                Administrative Services

From: Kalo Katarlan, Safety Officer   *KK*
                Field Service Operations

Date: August 21, 2017

Subject: Field Service Employee Accident on August 7, 2017

The following is an initial report of an accident that occurred on Monday, August 7, 2017, involving John Markley, and that resulted in two days of lost time.

Accident Summary
John Markley stopped by a rewiring job on German Road. Chico Ruiz was working there, stringing new wire, and John was checking with Chico about the materials he wanted for framing a pole. Some tree trimming had been done in the area, and John offered to help remove some of the debris by loading it into the pickup truck he was driving. While John was loading branches into the bed of the truck, a piece broke off in his right hand and struck his right eye.

Accident Details
1. John's right eye was struck by a piece of tree branch. John had just undergone laser surgery on his right eye on Friday, August 4, to reattach his retina.
2. John immediately covered his right eye with his hand, and Chico Ruiz gave him a paper towel with ice to cover his eye and help ease the pain.

7. On Thursday, August 10, John returned to his eye surgeon. Although bruised, his eye was not damaged, and the surgically reattached retina was still in place.

Recommendations
To prevent a recurrence of such an accident, the Safety Department will require the following actions in the future:

- When working around and moving debris, such as tree limbs or branches, all service crew employees must wear safety eyewear with side shields.
- All service crew employees must always consider the possibility of shock for an injured employee. If crew members cannot leave the job site to care for the injured employee, someone on the crew must call for assistance from the Service Center. The Service Center phone number is printed in each service crew member's handbook.

4

Documents and Elements

FIGURE 4–2. Incident Report (Using Memo Format)

assesses the causes of a problem and suggests changes necessary to prevent its recurrence. Because it is usually an internal document, an incident report normally follows the <u>memo</u> (Tab 3) format unless your organization has a standard incident report form.

In the subject line of the memo, state the precise event you are reporting. Then, in the body of the report, provide a detailed, precise description of the event. What happened? Where and when did it occur? Was anybody hurt? Was there any property damage? Was there a work stoppage?

In your conclusion, state what has been or will be done to correct the conditions that led to the event. That may include, for example, recommendations for training in safety practices, using improved equipment, and wearing protective clothing. See also <u>reports</u>.

❖ ETHICS NOTE Because insurance claims, workers' compensation awards, and even lawsuits may hinge on the information contained in an incident report, be sure to include precise times, dates, locations, treatment of injuries, names of any witnesses, and any other crucial information. (Notice the careful use of language and factual detail in Figure 4–2.) Be thorough and accurate in your analysis of the event and support any judgments or conclusions with facts. Be objective: Always use a neutral <u>tone</u> (Tab 10) and avoid assigning blame. If you speculate about the cause of an incident, make it clear to your readers that you are speculating. See also <u>ethics in writing</u> (Tab 1). ❖

investigative reports

An investigative <u>report</u> offers a precise analysis of a workplace problem or an issue in response to a need for information. The investigative report shown in Figure 4–3, for example, evaluates whether a company should adopt a program called "Basic English" to prepare documentation for and train non-English-speaking readers.

Open an investigative report with a statement of its primary and any secondary purposes, then define the scope of your investigation. (See also <u>purpose</u>, Tab 1, and <u>scope</u>, Tab 1.) If the report includes a survey of opinions, for example, indicate the number of people surveyed and other identifying information, such as income categories and occupations. Include any information that is pertinent in defining the extent of the investigation. Then report your findings and discuss their significance with your <u>conclusions</u> (Tab 1).

Sometimes the person requesting the investigative report may need to make recommendations based on your findings. In that case, the report may be referred to as a *recommendation report*. See also <u>feasibility reports</u> and <u>incident reports</u>.

4

Documents and Elements

Memo

To: Noreen Rinaldo, Training Manager
From: Charles Lapinski, Senior Instructor
Date: February 6, 2017
Subject: Adler's Basic English Program

As requested, I have investigated Adler Medical Instruments' (AMI's) Basic English Program to determine whether we might adopt a similar program.

AMI's program teaches medical technologists outside the United States who do not speak or read English to understand procedures written in a special 800-word vocabulary called *Basic English*. This program eliminates the need for AMI to translate its documentation into a number of different languages. The Basic English Program does not attempt to teach the medical technologists to be fluent in English but, rather, to recognize the 800 basic words that appear in Adler's documentation.

Course Analysis

The course teaches technologists a basic medical vocabulary in English; it does not provide training in medical terminology. Students must already know, in their own language, the meaning of medical vocabulary (e.g., the meaning of the word *hemostat*). Students must also have basic knowledge of their specialty, must be able to identify a part in an illustrated parts book, must have used AMI products for at least one year, and must be able to read and write in their own language.

Students receive an instruction manual, an illustrated book of equipment with parts and their English names, and pocket references containing the 800 words of the Basic English vocabulary plus the English names of parts. Students can write the corresponding word in their language beside the English word and then use the pocket reference as a bilingual dictionary. The course consists of 30 two-hour lessons, each lesson introducing approximately 27 words. No effort is made to teach pronunciation; the course teaches only recognition of the 800 words.

Course Success

The 800-word vocabulary enables the writers of documentation to provide medical technologists with any information that might be required because the subject areas are strictly limited to usage, troubleshooting, safety, and operation of AMI medical equipment. All nonessential words (*apple*, *father*, *mountain*, and so on) are eliminated, as are most synonyms (for example, *under* appears, but *beneath* does not).

Conclusions and Recommendations

AMI's program appears to be quite successful, and a similar approach could also be appropriate for us. I see two possible ways in which we could use some or all of the elements of AMI's program: (1) in the preparation of our student manuals or (2) as AMI uses the program.

I think it would be unnecessary to use the Basic English methods in the preparation of manuals for all of our students. Most of our students are English speakers to whom an unrestricted vocabulary presents no problem.

As for our initiating a program similar to AMI's, we could create our own version of the Basic English vocabulary and write our instructional materials in it. Because our product lines are much broader than AMI's, however, we would need to create illustrated parts books for each of the different product lines.

FIGURE 4–3. Investigative Report (Using Memo Format)

progress and activity reports

Progress reports provide details on the tasks completed for major workplace projects, whereas *activity reports* focus on the ongoing work of individual employees. Both are sometimes called *status reports*. Although some organizations use standardized templates and others use Web-based report forms, the content and structure shown in Figures 4–4 and 4–5 are typical.

Progress Reports

A progress report provides information to decision makers about the status of a project—whether it is on schedule and within budget. Progress reports are often submitted by a contracting company to a client company, as shown in Figure 4–4. They are used mainly for projects that involve many steps over a period of time and are issued at regular intervals to describe what has been done and what remains to be done. Progress reports help projects run smoothly by helping managers assign work, adjust schedules, allocate budgets, and order supplies and equipment. All progress reports for a particular project should have the same format.

The introduction to the first progress report should identify the project, methods used, necessary materials, expenditures, and completion date. Subsequent reports summarize the progress achieved since the preceding report and list the steps that remain to be taken. The body of the progress report should describe the project's status, including details such as schedules and costs, a statement of the work completed, and perhaps an estimate of future progress. The report ends with conclusions and recommendations about changes in the schedule, materials, techniques, and other information important to the project.

Activity Reports

Within an organization, employees often submit activity reports to managers on the status of ongoing projects. Managers may combine the activity reports of several individuals or teams into larger activity reports and, in turn, submit those larger reports to their own managers. The activity report shown in Figure 4–5 on page 119 was submitted by a manager (Wayne Tribinski) who supervises 11 employees; the reader of the report (Kathryn Hunter) is Tribinski's manager.

Because the activity report is issued periodically (usually monthly) and contains material familiar to its readers, it normally needs no introduction or conclusion, but it may need a brief opening to provide <u>context</u> (Tab 1). Although the format varies from company to company, the following sections are typical: Current Projects, Current Problems, Plans for the Next Period, and Current Staffing Level (for managers).

4

Documents
and Elements

Hobard Construction Company
9032 Salem Avenue
Lubbock, TX 79409

www.hobardcc.com
(808) 769-0832
Fax: (808) 769-5327

August 15, 2017

Walter M. Wazuski
County Administrator
109 Grand Avenue
Manchester, NH 03103

Dear Mr. Wazuski:

Subject: Progress Report 8 for July 31, 2017

The renovation of the County Courthouse is progressing on schedule and within budget. Although the cost of certain materials is higher than our original bid indicated, we expect to complete the project without exceeding the estimated costs because the speed with which the project is being completed will reduce overall labor expenses.

Costs
Materials used to date have cost $178,600, and labor costs have been $293,000 (including some subcontracted plumbing). Our estimate for the remainder of the materials is $159,000; remaining labor costs should not exceed $400,000.

Work Completed
As of July 31, we finished the installation of the circuit-breaker panels and meters, the level-one service outlets, and all the subfloor wiring. The upgrading of the courtroom, the upgrading of the records-storage room, and the replacement of the air-conditioning units are in the preliminary stages.

Work Scheduled
We have scheduled the upgrading of the courtroom to take place from August 29 to October 9, the upgrading of the records-storage room from October 13 to November 17, and the replacement of the air-conditioning units from November 24 to December 15. We see no difficulty in having the job finished by the scheduled date of December 22.

Sincerely yours,

Tran Nuguélen

Tran Nuguélen
ntran@hobardcc.com

4

FIGURE 4–4. Progress Report (Using Letter Format)

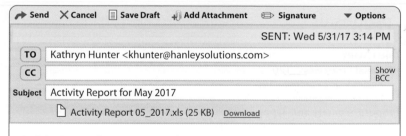

Activity Report for May 2017

We are dealing with the following projects and problems, as of May 31.

Projects

1. For the *Software Training Mailing Campaign*, we anticipate producing a set of labels for mailing software training information to customers by June 13.
2. The *Search Project* is on hold until the PL/I training has been completed, probably by the end of June.
3. The project to provide a database for the *Information Management System* has been expanded in scope to provide a database for all training activities. We are rescheduling the project to take the new scope into account.

Problems

The *Information Management System* has been delayed. The original schedule was based on the assumption that a systems analyst who was familiar with the system would work on this project. Instead, the project was assigned to a newly hired systems analyst who was inexperienced and required much more learning time than expected.

Bill Michaels, whose activity report is attached, is correcting a problem in the *CNG Software*. This correction may take a week.

Plans for Next Month

- Complete the *Software Training Mailing Campaign*.
- Resume the *Search Project*.
- Restart the project to provide a database on information management with a schedule that reflects its new scope.
- Write a report to justify the addition of two software developers.
- Congratulate publicly the recipients of Meritorious Achievement Awards: Bill Thomasson and Nancy O'Rourke.

Current Staffing Level

Current staff: 11
Open requisitions: 0

Please direct questions to ITsupport@hanleysolutions.com.

FIGURE 4–5. Activity Report (Using E-mail Format)

4

Documents
and Elements

proposals

A proposal is a document written to persuade readers that what is proposed will benefit them by solving a problem or fulfilling a need. When you write a proposal, therefore, you must convince readers that they need what you are proposing, that it is practical and appropriate, and that you are the right person or organization to provide the proposed product or service. See also persuasion (Tab 1) and "you" viewpoint (Tab 10).

Proposal Strategies

For any proposal, support your assertions with relevant facts, statistics, and examples. Your supporting evidence must lead logically to your proposed plan of action or solution. Cite relevant sources of information that provide strong credibility to your argument. Avoid ambiguity, do not wander from your main point, and never make false claims. See ethics in writing (Tab 1).

Audience and Purpose.   Proposals often require more than one level of approval, so take into account all the readers in your audience (Tab 1). Consider especially their levels of technical knowledge of the subject. For example, if your primary reader is an expert on your subject but a supervisor who must also approve the proposal is not, provide an executive summary (Tab 6) written in nontechnical language for the supervisor. You might also include a glossary (Tab 6) of terms used in the body of the proposal or an appendix (Tab 6) that explains highly detailed information in nontechnical language. If your primary reader is not an expert but a supervisor is, write the proposal with the nonexpert in mind and include an appendix that contains the technical details for experts.

Writing a persuasive proposal can be simplified by composing a concise statement of <u>purpose</u> (Tab 1)—the exact problem or opportunity that your proposal is designed to address and how you plan to persuade your readers to accept what you propose. Composing a purpose statement before outlining and writing your proposal will also help you and any collaborators understand the direction, scope, and goals of your proposal.

Project Management.   Proposal writers are often faced with writing high-quality, persuasive proposals under tight organizational deadlines. Dividing the task into manageable parts is the key to accomplishing your goals, especially when proposals involve substantial <u>collaborative writing</u> (Tab 1). For example, you might set deadlines for completing various proposal sections or stages of the writing process. Proposal-management software is popular for companies that manage frequent and extensive proposal-writing projects. Such software allows businesses to automate the more routine tasks while easily tracking multiple versions.

Proposal Context and Types

Proposals are written within a specific <u>context</u> (Tab 1). As that entry describes, understanding the context will help you determine the most appropriate writing strategy. In general, to persuade those within your organization to make a change or an improvement or perhaps to fund a project, you would write an *internal proposal*. To persuade those outside your company to agree to a plan or take a course of action, you would write an *external proposal*.

Writer's Checklist: Writing Persuasive Proposals

☑ Analyze your audience carefully to determine how to best meet your readers' needs or requirements.

☑ Write a concise purpose statement at the outset to clarify your proposal's goals

☑ Divide the writing task into manageable segments and develop a timeline for completing tasks.

☑ Review the descriptions of proposal contexts, structure, and types in this entry.

☑ Focus on the proposal's benefits to readers and anticipate their questions or objections.

(*continued*)

4

Documents
and Elements

Writer's Checklist: Writing Persuasive Proposals (continued)

☑ Incorporate evidence to support the claims of your proposal.

☑ Select an appropriate, visually appealing format (unless one is defined by the request for proposals). See <u>layout and design</u> (Tab 7).

☑ Use a confident, positive <u>tone</u> (Tab 10) throughout the proposal.

Internal Proposals

The purpose of an internal proposal is to suggest a change or an improvement within the writer's organization. It is addressed to a superior within the organization who has the authority to accept or reject the proposal. Internal proposals are typically reviewed by one or more departments for cost, practicality, and potential benefits, so take account of all relevant audience members. Two common types of internal proposals—informal and formal—are often distinguished from each other by the frequency with which they are written and by the degree of change they propose.

Informal Internal Proposals.   Informal internal proposals are the most common type of proposal and typically include small spending requests, requests for permission to hire new employees or increase salaries, and requests to attend conferences or purchase new equipment. In writing informal or routine proposals, highlight any key benefits to be realized.

Formal Internal Proposals.   Formal internal proposals usually involve requests to commit large sums of money or to recommend large-scale reorganizations. They are usually organized into sections that describe a problem, propose a solution, and offer to implement the suggested recommendation. The body, in turn, is further divided into sections to reflect the subject matter. The proposal may begin with a section describing the background or history of an issue and go on to discuss options for addressing the issue in separate sections.

The *introduction* of your internal proposal should establish that a problem exists and needs a solution. If the audience is not convinced there is a problem, your proposal will not succeed. After you identify the problem, summarize your proposed solution and indicate its benefits and estimated total cost. Notice how the introduction in Figure 4–6 states the problem directly and then summarizes the writer's proposed solution. See also <u>introductions</u> (Tab 1).

The *body* of your internal proposal should offer a practical solution to the problem and provide the details necessary to inform and persuade your readers. In the body, describe the problem for which

ABO, Inc.
Interoffice Memo

To: Joan Marlow, Director, Human Resources Division

From: Leslie Galusha, Chief   *LG*
               Employee Benefits Department

Date: June 16, 2017

Subject: Proposal to Reduce Employee Health-Care Costs

Health-care and workers' compensation insurance costs at ABO, Inc., have risen 100 percent over the last six years. In 2011, costs were $5,675 per employee per year; in 2017, they have reached $11,560 per employee per year. This doubling of costs mirrors a national trend, with health-care costs anticipated to continue to rise at the same rate for the next ten years. Controlling these escalating expenses will be essential. They are reducing ABO's profit margin because the company currently pays 70 percent of the costs for employee coverage.

Healthy employees bring direct financial benefits to companies in the form of lower employee insurance costs, lower absenteeism rates, and reduced turnover. Regular physical exercise promotes fit, healthy people by reducing the risk of coronary heart disease, diabetes, osteoporosis, hypertension, and stress-related problems. I propose that to promote regular, vigorous physical exercise for our employees, ABO implement a health-care program that focuses on employee fitness. . . .

Problem of Health-Care Costs
The U.S. Department of Health and Human Services (HHS) recently estimated that health-care costs in the United States will triple by the year 2024. Corporate expenses for health care are rising at such a fast rate that, if unchecked, in seven years they will significantly erode corporate profits.

According to HHS, people who do not participate in a regular and vigorous exercise program incur double the health-care costs and are hospitalized 30 percent more days than people who exercise regularly. Nonexercisers are also 41 percent more likely to submit medical claims over $10,000 at some point during their careers than are those who exercise regularly.

These figures are further supported by data from independent studies. A model created by the National Institutes of Health (NIH) . . .

4

Documents
and Elements

FIGURE 4–6. Special-Purpose Internal Proposal (*continued*) (Introduction and Body)

Joan Marlow   2   June 16, 2017

Proposed Solutions for ABO
The benefits of regular, vigorous physical activity for employees and
companies are compelling. To achieve these benefits at ABO, I propose that
we choose from one of two possible options: Build in-house fitness centers
at our warehouse facilities, or offer employees several options for
membership at a national fitness club. The following analysis compares . . .

Recommendation and Conclusion
I recommend that ABO, Inc., participate in the corporate membership
program at AeroFitness Clubs, Inc., by subsidizing employee memberships.
This program will show ABO's commitment to the importance of a fit
workforce. Club membership allows employees at all five ABO warehouses
to participate in the program. The more employees who participate, the
greater the long-term savings. . . .

Enrolling employees in the corporate program at AeroFitness would
allow them to receive a one-month free trial membership. Those interested
in continuing could then join the club and pay half of the one-time
membership fee. . . .

Implementing this program will help ABO, Inc., reduce its health-care
costs while building stronger employee relations by offering employees a
desirable benefit. If this proposal is adopted, I have some additional thoughts
about publicizing the program to encourage employee participation. I look
forward to discussing the details of this proposal with you and answering
any questions you may have.

FIGURE 4–6. Special-Purpose Internal Proposal (*continued*) (Conclusion)

you are offering a solution; the methodology of your proposed solution;
details about equipment, materials, and staff; cost breakdowns; and a
comprehensive schedule. Figure 4–6 provides a section from the body
of an internal proposal.

The *conclusion* of your internal proposal should tie everything together, restate your recommendation, and close with a spirit of cooperation (offering to set up a meeting, supply additional information, or
provide any other assistance that might be needed). Keep your conclusion brief, as in Figure 4–6. See also <u>conclusions</u> (Tab 1).

If your proposal cites information that you obtained through
<u>research</u> (Tab 5), such as published reports, government statistics, or
interviews, follow the conclusion with a list of works cited that provides
complete publication information for each source.

External Proposals

External proposals are prepared for clients and customers outside your company. They are either submitted in response to a request for goods and services from another organization (a solicited proposal) or sent to them without a prior request (an unsolicited proposal). Grant proposals, a type of external proposal, are usually submitted to nonprofit organizations to request funding to support research that could benefit the funding organization. (See the grant-proposal section on page 128.)

Solicited Proposals. To find the best method of meeting their needs and the most-qualified company to help reach that goal, procuring organizations commonly issue a request for proposals (RFP) or an invitation for bids (IFB) that asks competing companies such as yours to bid for a job.

An RFP often defines a need or problem and allows those who respond to propose possible solutions. The procuring organization generally distributes an RFP to several predetermined vendors. The RFP usually outlines the specific requirements for the ideal solution. For example, if an organization needs a new accounting system, it may require the proposed system to create customized reports. The RFP also may define specific formatting requirements for the proposal, such as page length, font type and size, margin widths, headings (Tab 7), sections, and appendix items. Some large organizations require that proposals be submitted entirely online with specific requirements. When responding to RFPs, follow their requirements exactly—proposals that do not provide the required information, do not follow the required format or submission protocols, or miss the submittal deadline are usually considered "noncompliant" and immediately rejected.

In contrast to an RFP, an IFB is commonly issued by federal, state, and local government agencies to solicit bids on clearly defined products or services. An IFB is restrictive, binding the bidder to produce an item or a service that meets the exact requirements of the organization issuing the IFB. The goods or services are defined in the IFB by references to performance standards stated in technical specifications. Bidders must be prepared to prove that their product will meet all requirements of the specifications. The procuring organization generally publishes its IFB online, either on its own Web site or on others such as Federal Business Opportunities at *www.fbo.gov*. Like RFPs, IFBs usually define specific format requirements; proposals that do not follow the required format can be rejected without review.

Unsolicited Proposals. Unsolicited proposals are those submitted to a company without a prior request for a proposal. Companies often operate for years with a problem they have never recognized (unnecessarily high maintenance costs, for example, or poor inventory-control methods). Many unsolicited proposals are preceded by a letter of inquiry that specifies the problem or unmet need to determine whether there is any potential interest. If you receive a positive response, you would conduct a detailed study of the prospective client's needs to determine whether you can be of help and, if so, exactly how. You would then prepare a formal proposal on the basis of your study.

Sales Proposals.   The sales proposal, a major marketing tool for business and industry, is a company's offer to provide specific goods or services to a potential buyer within a specified period of time and for a specified price. The primary purpose of a sales proposal is to demonstrate that the prospective customer's purchase of the seller's products or services will solve a problem, improve operations, or offer other benefits.

Sales proposals vary greatly in length and sophistication. Some are a page or two written by one person; others are many pages written collaboratively by several people; and still others are hundreds of pages written by a proposal-writing team. Many sales proposals note that the offer is valid for a limited period (often 90 days). See also <u>collaborative writing</u> (Tab 1).

❖ ETHICS NOTE Once submitted, a sales proposal is a legally binding document that promises to offer goods or services within a specified time and for a specified price. ❖

Simple sales proposals typically follow the introduction-body-conclusion pattern. Long sales proposals must accommodate a greater variety of information and are organized to include some or all of the following sections specified in the RFP:

- Cover letter
- Title page
- Executive or project summary
- General description of products
- Detailed solution or rationale
- Cost analysis
- Delivery schedule or work plan
- Site-preparation description
- Training requirements
- Statement of responsibilities
- Description of vendor
- Organizational sales pitch
- Conclusion
- Appendixes

COVER LETTER.   A long sales proposal begins with a <u>cover letter</u> (Tab 3) that expresses your appreciation for the opportunity to submit your proposal and for any assistance you may have received in studying the customer's requirements. The letter should acknowledge any previous positive association with the customer. Then it should summarize the recommendations offered in the proposal and express your confidence that they will satisfy the customer's needs. Cover letters often list the documents attached or enclosed to help readers keep the associated documents together.

TITLE PAGE. The title page contains the title of the proposal, the date of submission, the company to which it is being submitted, your company's name, and any symbol or logo that identifies your company.

EXECUTIVE SUMMARY. An <u>executive summary</u> (Tab 6)—sometimes called a *project summary*—follows the title page. The executive summary is intended for the decision maker who will ultimately accept or reject the proposal and should summarize in nontechnical language how you plan to approach the work.

DESCRIPTION. If your proposal offers products as well as services, it should include a general description of the products. In many cases, product descriptions will already exist as company boilerplate; be sure to check your company's files or server for such information before drafting a description from scratch.

❖ **ETHICS NOTE** In the workplace, employees often borrow material freely from in-house manuals, reports, and other company documents. Using such "boilerplate" is neither <u>plagiarism</u> (Tab 5) nor a violation of <u>copyright</u> (Tab 5). See also <u>repurposing</u> (Tab 2). ❖

RATIONALE. Following the executive summary and general description of products, explain exactly how you plan to do what you are proposing. This section, called the *detailed solution* or *rationale*, will be read by specialists who can understand and evaluate your plan. It usually begins with a statement of the customer's problem, follows with a statement of the solution, and concludes with a statement of the benefits to the customer. In some proposals, the headings "Problem" and "Solution" are used for this section.

COST ANALYSIS. A cost analysis itemizes the estimated cost of all the products and services that you are offering.

DELIVERY SCHEDULE. The delivery schedule—also called a *work plan*—commits you to a specific timetable for providing those products and services.

SITE PREPARATION. If your recommendations include modifying your customer's physical facilities by moving walls, adding increased electrical capacity, and the like, include a site-preparation description that details the modifications required. In some proposals, the headings "Facilities" and "Equipment" are used for this section.

TRAINING. If the products and services you are proposing require training the customer's employees, specify the required training and its cost.

4

Documents
and Elements

RESPONSIBILITIES. To prevent misunderstandings about what your and the customer's responsibilities will be, draw up a statement of responsibilities that explains in detail the tasks that are solely your responsibility and those that are solely the customer's responsibility.

VENDOR DESCRIPTION. The description-of-vendor section gives a profile of your company, its history, and its present position in the industry. The description-of-vendor section typically includes a list of people or subcontractors and the duties they will perform. The résumés (Tab 9) of key personnel may also be placed here or in an appendix.

SALES PITCH. An organizational sales pitch usually follows the description-of-vendor section and is designed to sell the company and its general capability in the field. The sales pitch promotes the company and concludes the proposal on an upbeat note.

CONCLUSION. Some long sales proposals include a conclusion (Tab 1) section that summarizes the proposal's salient points, stresses your company's strengths, and includes information about whom the potential client can contact for further information. It may also end with a request for the date the work will begin should the proposal be accepted.

APPENDIXES. Some proposals include appendixes (Tab 6) made up of statistical analyses, maps, charts, tables, and résumés of the principal staff assigned to the project. Appendixes to proposals should contain only supplemental information; the primary information should appear in the body of the proposal.

Grant Proposals. Grant proposals are written to nonprofit and government organizations to request the approval of and funding for projects that solve a problem or fulfill a need. A scientist, for example, may write a grant proposal to the National Institutes of Health requesting a specific sum of money to study a new cancer therapy, or the executive director of Habitat for Humanity may write a grant proposal to a local government requesting funding to purchase supplies to construct new housing for disadvantaged families in the area.

Granting organizations typically post opportunities, along with detailed application guidelines, on their Web sites and specify their requirements for the format and content of proposals. Most federal and state government grants are now submitted electronically, and various sections may have imposed word, character, or content limits that are enforced electronically. When preparing a nonelectronic proposal, always organize its elements in the exact order described or required in the request for proposals (RFP) or in the grant maker's guidelines. Although application guidelines and processes may differ from one organization to another, grant proposals generally require the following sections at a minimum:

- Cover letter
- Title page
- Application form
- Introduction/summary
- Literature review (if needed)
- Project narrative
  - *Project description*
- *Project outcomes*
- *Budget narrative*
- *Task schedule*
- Organization description
- Conclusion
- Attachments

COVER LETTER. Usually one page long, the cover letter should identify who you are and your professional affiliation. It should specify the grant that you are applying for, summarize the proposed project, and include the amount of funding you are requesting.

TITLE PAGE. On a single page, show the title of the project, names of project staff and their affiliations, the date submitted, and the name of the recipient's organization. This page serves as the cover of the grant proposal.

APPLICATION FORM. Especially in online grant applications, an application form may replace the cover letter and title page. This form may be one or more pages and may require you to check boxes, fill in blanks, or insert brief descriptions or other information into text boxes or blank spaces. A word or character limit (typically 250–400 words) may be imposed or enforced. An official signature (or its electronic equivalent) is often required. This section may request detailed information about the applicant organization, such as staff or board of directors' demographic composition or its human resources policies.

INTRODUCTION. The introduction or summary is your proposal at a glance—it briefly describes (within a given limit) the problem to be solved and projects the expected outcomes of your grant proposal. If substantial research is involved, you may also describe your proposed research methods (interviews, questionnaires, videos, observations, etc.) in a separate paragraph. See also <u>abstracts</u> (Tab 6).

LITERATURE REVIEW. The literature review lists the relevant research sources you consulted in preparing your proposal. Also called a *References* or *Works Cited* section, it allows reviewers of your proposal to assess your familiarity with current research in the field. Is your research up to date? Thorough? Pertinent? Be selective: Include only relevant journal articles, books, interviews, broadcasts, <u>blogs and forums</u> (Tab 2), and other sources. In nonresearch proposals (those not based on secondary or formal research), a limited number of citations are frequently included in text within the project narrative or as footnotes or endnotes.

PROJECT NARRATIVE. The heart of the proposal, the project narrative describes in detail the scope of the work, expected outcomes, list of tasks, project activity schedule from start to finish, and estimated cost. Be specific and thorough.

Project Description The project description includes an overview of the project and details of how the research project or program will be conducted (its methodology). In nonresearch proposals, include a succinct *statement of need*—also called a *case statement*—which presents the facts and evidence that support the need for the project. The information presented can come from authorities in the field, as well as from your agency's own experience or research. A logical and persuasive statement of need demonstrates that your company or nonprofit organization sufficiently understands the situation and is therefore capable of addressing it satisfactorily. Clearly indicate why or how your solution improves on existing or previous ones, and cite evidence to support this. Emphasize the benefits of the proposed activities for the grant maker's intended constituency or target population and why your solution to the problem or plan to fulfill the need should be approved. Most RFPs and grant-maker guidelines provide a list of specific questions for applicants to answer or required topics that must be persuasively addressed in this section.

Project Outcomes Having described the preparations and justification for the program, the grant writer must describe the outcomes or deliverables of the proposal—what the funding organization can expect as a result of the time, labor, and financial support it has invested in the program. Outcomes are stated as quantifiable objectives—improvements in reading scores, volume of carbon emission reductions, aerobic fitness measures, and so on. Grant proposals, especially those solicited by government agencies, also must provide detailed plans for collecting, analyzing, and interpreting data to evaluate the success or failure of the research or program in achieving the stated outcomes.*

Budget Narrative Next, include a budget-narrative section that provides a detailed listing of costs for personnel, equipment, building renovations, and other grant-related expenses. This information must be clear, accurate, and arranged in an easily understood format for those evaluating the data (usually in a table, Tab 7). Many granting organizations, including government agencies, require that specified budget forms be used. If your proposal is approved, you will be entrusted with funds belonging to

*Many grant writers find the system called SMART useful. The SMART system assists writers in setting feasible performance goals and means of measuring success. It is described at *www.yale.edu/hronline/yaleperformancemanagement/goal.html*.

someone else and you will be accountable for them. Your cost estimates may also be subject to changes over which you have no control, such as price increases for equipment, software, or consulting assistance. The project may also require ongoing funding following completion of the grant's tasks. Either provide an estimate of such costs or note that they will appear in a Future Funding or Sustainability section.

Task Schedule   Next, prepare a schedule of tasks that need to be performed to implement the program or complete the project. Arrange them as bulleted points in sequence from first to last with due dates for each, or present them in a table or perhaps in a Gantt chart as described in <u>graphs</u> (Tab 7).

ORGANIZATION DESCRIPTION.   The organization description may follow the Introduction or it may be placed just prior to the Conclusion, depending on RFP requirements or the granting organization's guidelines. Describe the applicant organization briefly in terms of mission, history, qualifications, and credibility (significant, related accomplishments), taking care to include all information requested in the RFP or grant guidelines. Granting organizations consider not only the merits of the proposed program or research but also your organization's standing in the community and similar advantages.

CONCLUSION.   This brief wrap-up section emphasizes the benefits or advantages of your project. This section affords you one more opportunity to give the funding organization a reason why your proposal merits its support. Emphasize the benefits of the research, program, or other activities for the grant maker's intended constituency or target population. Finally, express your appreciation for the opportunity to submit the proposal and close with a statement of your willingness to provide further information.

ATTACHMENTS.   Funding organizations request supporting information, such as nonprofit-status documentation, copies of legal documents (for example, articles of incorporation or bylaws), or lists of information that you may need to design and compose yourself. Provide a comprehensive list of attachments and clearly label each item to guide the grant reviewer in evaluating the proposal package. See also <u>appendixes</u> (Tab 6).

Writer's Checklist: Writing Grant Proposals

☑ Analyze the granting organization's RFP or guidelines carefully to best formulate your request to match its funding interests and priorities.

☑ Review the descriptions of proposal contexts, strategies, and types in this entry.

(continued)

4

Documents and Elements

Writer's Checklist: Writing Grant Proposals (continued)

- ☑ Respond to every question or address every topic requested.
- ☑ Strive for **conciseness** (Tab 10) in the narrative without sacrificing clarity—make every word count.
- ☑ Emphasize the benefits of your proposal to the granting organization and its constituents.
- ☑ Follow all instructions meticulously because failure to include requested information or to observe format requirements may be grounds for rejection or lack of review.
- ☑ Review the final grant proposal carefully. Because many online submission systems do not have a spell check function, draft sections in a word-processing program and then paste them into the electronic form.

Requests for Proposals.   Organizations seeking help with a task or service usually announce their requirements by issuing a request for proposals (RFP) for vendors to evaluate and decide whether to bid on the project. Potential vendors prepare **proposals** to describe their solutions for meeting an RFP's requirements. RFPs vary in length and structure; the following sections are typical.

ORGANIZATIONAL INFORMATION. Organization information describes the requesting organization's mission, goals, size, facility locations, position in the marketplace, and contact information. It parallels the "Description of Vendor" section in proposals (see page 128).

PROJECT DESCRIPTION. Sometimes called "Scope of Work," the project description describes the project or service needed in detail. It may also indicate whether a deliverable, like software, must be created new or obtained commercially and adapted to the project.

DELIVERY SCHEDULE. The delivery schedule specifies the time allotted for the project and a proposed schedule of tasks.

PROPOSAL DESCRIPTION. The proposal description provides the RFP format requirements; number of copies expected; due date; where, to whom, and how the RFP should be sent; and electronic file requirement.

VENDOR QUALIFICATIONS. Vendor qualifications typically request a summary of vendor experience, references from recent customers, professional certifications, number of employees, years in business, quality-control procedures, awards and honors, and the résumés of principal employees assigned to the project.

4

Documents and Elements

PROPOSAL-EVALUATION CRITERIA. Proposal-evaluation criteria inform vendors of the organization's selection criteria: solely on cost, cost and vendor past performance, or technical expertise. Some firms grade proposals on a scale of 100 or 1,000.

APPENDIXES. Some RFPs include appendixes for essentials too detailed for the RFP body, such as sample forms and questionnaires, a sample contract, an organization's server and workstation configurations, workflow-analysis diagrams, and dates and times for vendor site visits.

❖ ETHICS NOTE To protect organization confidential information, include a legally binding nondisclosure statement for vendors to sign before you send the full RFP. Many organizations also include a guarantee not to open proposals before the due date and never to disclose information in one vendor's proposal to a competing vendor. ❖

DIGITAL TIP

RFP Site Search Software

The federal government lists RFPs at Federal Business Opportunities (*www.fbo.gov*); many state, county, and municipal governments list their RFPs at BidNet (*www.bidnet.com*). Businesses and nonprofit organizations often distribute RFPs directly to approved vendor lists, so they are less likely to appear at aggregator sites or to be posted on their Web sites.

---

reports

A report is an organized presentation of factual information, often aimed at multiple <u>audiences</u> (Tab 1), that may present the results of an investigation, a trip, or a research project. For any report, assessing the readers' needs is essential. Following is a list of report entries in this book:

Formal reports often present the results of long-term projects or those that involve multiple participants. (See also <u>collaborative writing</u>, Tab 1.)

4

Documents
and Elements

Formal reports generally follow a precise format and include such elements as <u>abstracts</u> (Tab 6) and <u>executive summaries</u> (Tab 6). Such projects may be done either for your own organization or as a contractual requirement for another organization. See also <u>proposals</u>.

Informal and short reports normally run from a few paragraphs to a few pages and ordinarily include only an <u>introduction</u> (Tab 1), a body, a <u>conclusion</u> (Tab 1), and (if necessary) recommendations. Because of their brevity, informal reports are customarily written as <u>correspondence</u> (Tab 3), including <u>e-mails</u> (Tab 2), <u>letters</u> (Tab 3), and <u>memos</u> (Tab 3).

The introduction of any report announces the subject of the report, states its <u>purpose</u> (Tab 1), and gives any essential background information. The body presents a clearly organized account of the report's subject—the results of a test, the status of a project, and other details readers may need. The amount of detail to include depends on your reader's knowledge, your <u>scope</u> (Tab 1), and the complexity of the subject.

The conclusion summarizes your findings and interprets their significance for readers. In some reports, a final, separate section gives recommendations; in others, the conclusions and the recommendations are combined into one section. This final section makes suggestions for a course of action based on the data you have presented. See also <u>persuasion</u> (Tab 1).

titles

Titles of documents are important because many readers decide whether to read a <u>report</u> or message, for example, based on its title. Titles are also crucial for filing and retrieving documents. For advice on creating and using titles for figures and tables, see <u>visuals</u> (Tab 7).

Reports and Long Documents

Titles for reports, <u>proposals</u>, articles, and similar documents should identify the document's topic, reflect its <u>tone</u> (Tab 10), and indicate its <u>scope</u> (Tab 1) and <u>purpose</u> (Tab 1), as in the following:

▶ "Using Chaos Theory to Evaluate Small-Business Growth Management"

Such titles should be concise but not so short that they are not specific. For example, the title "Chaos Theory and Small Businesses" announces the topic and might be appropriate for a book, but it does not answer important questions that readers of an article would expect, such as "What does the article say about the relationship between chaos theory and small businesses?" and "What aspect of small businesses is related to chaos theory?"

Avoid titles with such redundancies as "Notes on," "Studies on," or "A Report on." However, works like annual reports or feasibility reports should be identified as such in the title because this information specifies the purpose and scope of the report. For titles of progress and activity reports, indicate the dates in a subtitle ("Quarterly Report on Hospital Admission Rates: January–March 2017"). Avoid using technical shorthand, such as chemical formulas, and other abbreviations (Tab 12) in your title unless the work is addressed exclusively to specialists in the field. For multivolume publications, repeat the title on each volume and include the subtitle and number of each volume.

Do not write titles in sentence form, except for titles of articles in newsletters, magazines, and similar publications that ask a rhetorical question, as in the following:

▶ "Is Online Learning Right for You?"

E-mail, Memos, and Online Postings

Subject lines of e-mail messages, memos (Tab 3), and online postings function as titles and should concisely and accurately describe the topic of the message. Because recipients often use subject-line titles to prioritize and sort their correspondence (Tab 3), such titles must be specific.

VAGUE	Subject: Tuition Reimbursement
SPECIFIC	Subject: Tuition Reimbursement for Time-Management Seminar

Although the title in the subject line announces your topic, you should still develop an opening that provides context (Tab 1) for the message. (See blogs and forums, Tab 2.)

Formatting Titles

Use the standards in this section for formatting titles, unless you are following a style that recommends otherwise.

Capitalization. Capitalize the initial letters of the first and last words of a title as well as all major words in the title. Do not capitalize articles (*a, an, the*), coordinating conjunctions (*and, but*), or short prepositions (*at, in, on, of*) unless they begin or end the title (*The Lives of a Cell*). Capitalize prepositions in titles if they contain five or more letters (*Between, Since, Until, After*).

Italics. Use italics (Tab 12) or underlining when referring to titles of separately published works, such as a book, periodical, newspaper, blog (but *not* the URL), pamphlet, brochure, legal case, movie, television series, and Web site based on a periodical.

▶ *Turning Workplace Conflict into Collaboration* [book] by Joyce Richards was reviewed in the *New York Times* [newspaper, online or print].

▶ We will include links to the blog *Gizmodo* (http://gizmodo.com/) and to *Consumer Reports Online* (www.consumerreports.org).

Abbreviations of such titles are italicized if their spelled-out forms would be italicized.

▶ *NEJM* stands for the *New England Journal of Medicine*.

Italicize the titles of CDs, DVDs, plays, long poems, paintings, sculptures, and long musical works.

Quotation Marks.   Use <u>quotation marks</u> (Tab 12) when referring to parts of publications, such as chapters of books and articles or sections within periodicals or blogs.

▶ Her chapter titled "Effects of Government Regulations on Motorcycle Safety" in the book *Government Regulation and the Economy* was cited in a recent article, "No-Fault Insurance and Motorcycles?" published on the blog *AmericanCycle*.

Titles of reports, essays, short poems, short musical works (including songs), short stories, and single episodes of radio and television programs are also enclosed in quotation marks.

Special Cases.   Some titles, by convention, are not set off by quotation marks, underlining, or italics. Such titles follow standard practice for capitalization and the practice of the organization.

▶ Microsoft.com [Web site], Business Writing [college course title], Old Testament, Magna Carta, the Constitution, Lincoln's Gettysburg Address, the Lands' End Catalog

The treatment for Internet content, such as individual YouTube videos, varies among documentation styles. See <u>documenting sources</u> (Tab 5).

trip reports

A trip report provides a permanent record of a business trip and its accomplishments. It provides managers with essential information about the results of the trip and can enable other staff members to benefit from the information. See also <u>reports</u>.

A trip report is normally written as a <u>memo</u> (Tab 3) or an <u>e-mail</u> (Tab 2) and addressed to an immediate superior, as shown in Figure 4–7. The subject line identifies the destination and dates of the trip. The body of the report explains why you made the trip, whom you visited, and what you accomplished. The report should devote a brief section to

---

↗ Send   ✕ Cancel   📄 Save Draft   📎 Add Attachment   ✉ Signature   ▾ Options

SENT: Mon 1/9/17 11:44 AM

TO | Roberto Camacho <rcamacho@psys.com>

CC | Show BCC

Subject | Trip to Smith Electric Co., Huntington, West Virginia, January 6–7, 2017

📄 Expense Report.xls (25 KB) Download

I visited the Smith Electric Company in Huntington, West Virginia, to determine the cause of a recurring failure in a Model 247 printer. Attached is my expense report.

Problem
The printer stopped printing periodically for no apparent reason. Repeated efforts to bring it back online eventually succeeded, but the problem recurred at irregular intervals. Neither customer personnel operating the printer nor the local maintenance specialist was able to solve the problem.

Action
On January 6, I met with Ms. Ruth Bernardi, the office manager, who explained the problem. My troubleshooting did not reveal the cause of the problem then or on January 7.

Only when I tested the logic cable did I find that it contained a broken wire. I replaced the logic cable and then ran all the normal printer test patterns to make sure no other problems existed. All patterns were positive, so I turned the printer over to the customer.

Conclusion
There are more than 12,000 of these printers in the field, and to my knowledge this is the first occurrence of a bad cable. I conclude that the logic cable problem at Smith Electric Company reflects the recurring failures during 2016.

James D. Kerson, Product Analyst
Printer Systems, Inc.
1366 Federal St., Allentown, PA 18101
(610) 747-9955   Fax: (610) 747-9956
jdkerson@psys.com
www.psys.com

FIGURE 4–7. Trip Report Sent as E-mail (with Attachment)

each major activity and may include a <u>heading</u> (Tab 7) for each section. You need not give equal space to each activity—instead, elaborate on the more important ones. Follow the body of the report with the appropriate conclusions and recommendations. Finally, if required, attach a record of expenses to the trip report.

trouble reports (see <u>incident reports</u>)

5

Research and Documentation

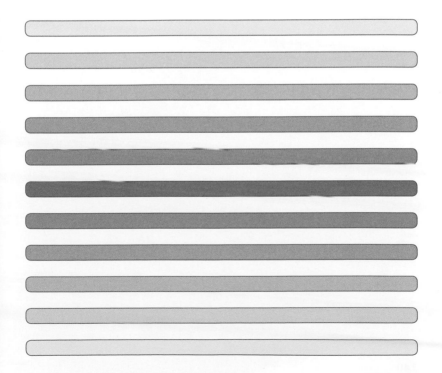

Preview

This section contains entries related to the process of <u>research</u> using both library and Internet sources, <u>**interviewing for information**</u>, and <u>**note-taking**</u>. Entries in this section provide help for incorporating research material into your document, as well as using <u>quotations</u>, <u>**paraphrasing**</u>, and avoiding <u>plagiarism</u>. The entry <u>documenting sources</u> provides not only examples of bibliographic citations in the two major systems — American Psychological Association (APA) and Modern Language Association (MLA) — but also sample pages using those styles.

bibliographies

A bibliography is an alphabetical list of books, articles, online sources, and other works that have been consulted in preparing a document or that are useful for reference purposes. A bibliography provides a convenient list of sources in a standardized form for readers interested in getting further information on the topic or in assessing the scope of the research.

A list of references or works cited refers to works actually cited in the text; a bibliography also includes works consulted for general background information. For information on using various citation styles, see documenting sources.

Entries in a bibliography are listed alphabetically by the author's last name. If an author is unknown, the entry is alphabetized by the first word in the title (not including *A*, *An*, or *The*). Entries also can be arranged by subject and then ordered alphabetically within those categories.

An annotated bibliography includes complete bibliographic information about a work (author, title, place of publication, publisher, and publication date), followed by a brief description or evaluation of what the work contains.

copyright

Copyright establishes legal protection for original works of authorship, including literary, dramatic, musical, artistic, and other intellectual works in printed or electronic form; it gives the copyright owner exclusive rights to reproduce, distribute, perform, or display a work. Copyright protects all original works from the moment of their creation, regardless of whether they are published or contain a notice of copyright (©).

❖ ETHICS NOTE If you plan to reproduce copyrighted material in your own publication or on your Web site, you must obtain permission from the copyright holder. To do otherwise is a violation of U.S. law. ❖

Permissions. To seek permission to reproduce copyrighted material, you must write to the copyright holder. In some cases, it is the author; in other cases, it is the editor or publisher of the work. For Web sites, read the site's "terms-of-use" information (if available) and e-mail your request to the appropriate party. State specifically which portion of the work you wish to reproduce and how you plan to use it. The copyright holder has the right to charge a fee and specify conditions and limits of use.

Exceptions.   Some print and Web material—including text, <u>visuals</u> (Tab 7), and other digital forms—may be reproduced without permission. The rules governing copyright can be complex, so it is prudent to carefully check the copyright status of anything you plan to reproduce.

- *Fair use.* A small amount of material from a copyrighted source may be used for educational purposes (such as classroom handouts), commentary, criticism, news reporting, and scholarly reports without permission or payment as long as the use satisfies the "fair-use" criteria, as described at the U.S. Copyright Office Web site, *www.copyright.gov.* Whether a particular use qualifies as fair use depends on all the circumstances.
- *Company boilerplate.* Employees often borrow material freely from in-house manuals and reports, as well as other company documents in doing work for the company to save time and ensure consistency. Using such "boilerplate," or "repurposed," material is not a copyright violation because the company is considered the author of works prepared by its employees on the job. See also <u>repurposing</u> (Tab 2).
- *Public domain material.* Works created by or for the U.S. government and not classified or otherwise protected are in the public domain—that is, they are not copyrighted. The same is true for older written works when their copyright has lapsed or never existed. Be aware that some works in the public domain may include "value-added" features—such as introductions, visuals, and indexes—that may be copyrighted separately from the original work and may require permission even if the main work is in the public domain.
- *Copyleft Web material.* Some public access Web sites, such as Wikipedia, follow the "copyleft" principle and grant permission to freely copy, distribute, or modify material, but the modified material is also required to be made freely available on the same basis.*

❖ ETHICS NOTE The Internet has changed the face of copyright, creating an illusion of universal access to online material, when in fact permission is often required to alter or use it in any way. Alternative forms of permissions—like those offered by Creative Commons—allow users to freely incorporate specific content into their documents and to license their own original content. Still, even when you use material that may be reproduced or published without permission, you must nonetheless give appropriate credit to the source from which the material is taken, as described in <u>documenting sources</u> and <u>plagiarism</u>. ❖

---

*"Copyleft" is a play on the word *copyright* and is the effort to free materials from many of the restrictions of copyright. See *http://en.wikipedia.org/wiki/Copyleft.*

documenting sources

Documenting sources achieves three important purposes:

- It allows readers to locate and consult the sources used and to find further information on the subject.
- It enables writers to support their assertions and arguments in such documents as proposals, reports, and trade journal articles.
- It helps writers to give proper credit to others and thus avoid plagiarism by identifying the sources of facts, ideas, visuals (Tab 7), quotations, and paraphrases. See also paraphrasing.

This entry shows citation models and sample pages for two principal documentation systems: American Psychological Association (APA) and Modern Language Association (MLA). The following examples compare these two styles for citing a book by one author: *Leading Change* by John P. Kotter, which was published in 2012 by Harvard Business Review Press in Boston, Massachusetts.

- The APA system of citation is often used in the social sciences. It is referred to as an author-date method of documentation because parenthetical in-text citations and a reference list (at the end of the paper) in APA style emphasize the author(s) and date of publication so that the currency of the research is clear.

APA IN-TEXT CITATION

(Author's Last Name, Year)

(Kotter, 2012)

APA REFERENCES ENTRY

Author's Last Name, Initials. (Year). *Title in italics*. Place of Publication: Publisher.

Kotter, J. P. (2012). *Leading change*. Boston, MA: Harvard Business Review Press.

- The MLA system is used in literature and the humanities. MLA style uses parenthetical in-text citations and a list of works cited and places greater importance on the pages on which cited information can be found than on the publication date.

MLA IN-TEXT CITATION

(Author's Last Name Page Number)

(Kotter 141)

MLA WORKS-CITED ENTRY

Author's Last Name, First Name. *Title Italicized*. Publisher, Date of Publication.

Kotter, John P. *Leading Change*. Harvard Business Review Press, 2012.

These systems are described in full detail in the following style manuals:

American Psychological Association. *Publication Manual of the American Psychological Association*. 10th ed. American Psychological Association, 2010. See also *www.apastyle.org*.

Modern Language Association. *MLA Handbook*. 8th ed. Modern Language Association, 2016. See also *www.mla.org/style*.

APA Documentation

APA In-Text Citations. Within the text of a paper, APA parenthetical documentation gives a brief citation—in parentheses—of the author, year of publication, and a relevant page number if it helps locate a passage in a lengthy document.

▶ Technology that once remedied loneliness may now lead to feelings of seclusion and sadness (Slade, 2012).

▶ According to Slade (2012), "We look to machines to perform human functions: They provide communications, calculations, care, and company" (p. 9).

When APA parenthetical citations are needed midsentence, place them after the closing quotation marks and continue with the rest of the sentence.

▶ In short, these "prosthetic substitutes" (Slade, 2012, p. 13) replace the flesh-and-blood friends in our lives.

If the APA parenthetical citation follows a block quotation, place it after the final punctuation mark.

▶ . . . a close collaboration with the marketing staff and the development group is essential. (Thompson, 2010)

When a work has two authors, cite both names joined by an ampersand: (Bartlett & Steele, 2012). For the first citation of a work with three, four, or five authors, include all names. For subsequent citations and for works with more than five authors, include only the last name of the first author followed by "et al." (not italicized and with a period after "al."). When two or more works by different authors are cited in the same parentheses, list the citations alphabetically and use semicolons to separate them: (Bartlett & Steele, 2012; Dauch, 2012).

APA Documentation Models. In reference lists, APA requires that the first word of book and article titles be capitalized and all subsequent words be lowercased. Exceptions include the first word after a colon or dash and proper nouns.

BOOKS

Single Author

Black, A. (2015). *How business works: A graphic guide to business success.* London, UK: Dorling Kindersley.

Multiple Authors

Jain, P., & Sharma, P. (2014). *Behind every good decision: How anyone can use business analytics to turn data into profitable insight.* New York, NY: AMACOM.

Corporate Author

DK Publishing. (2014). *The business book (big ideas simply explained).* London, UK: Dorling Kindersley.

Edition Other Than First

FitzGerald, J., Dennis, A., & Durcikova, A. (2014). *Business data communications and networking* (12th ed.). Hoboken, NJ: Wiley.

Multivolume Work

Standard and Poor's. (2013). *Standard and Poor's 500 guide, 2013 edition.* New York, NY: McGraw-Hill.

Work in an Edited Collection

Judah, B. (2014). London's laundry business. In D. Starkman, M. M. Hamilton, & R. Chittum (Eds.), *The best business writing, 2014 edition* (pp. 78–99). New York, NY: Columbia University Press.

Encyclopedia or Dictionary Entry

Brewer, D. J., & Picus, L. O. (Eds.). (2014). Access to education. In *Encyclopedia of education economics and finance.* Thousands Oaks, CA: Sage.

ARTICLES IN PERIODICALS

Magazine Article

Kuttner, R. (2015, Spring). The wealth problem. *The American Prospect,
26*(2), 33–37.

Journal Article

Wales, W., Wiklund, J., & McKelvie, A. (2015). What about new entry?
Examining the theorized role of new entry in the entrepreneurial
orientation-performance relationship. *International Small Business
Journal, 33*(4), 351–373.

Newspaper Article

Hiltzik, M. (2015, June 12). Emissions cap-and-trade program is working well in California. *Los Angeles Times*, p. 17.

Article with Unknown Author

Put up the firewalls. (2015, June 11). *The Economist*, 23–24.

ELECTRONIC SOURCES

The APA recommends that, at minimum, references to online
sources should provide an author (whenever possible), the date of
publication or update (use "(n.d.)" if no date is available), the title
of the article, and retrieval information, such as an address (URL
or DOI) that links directly to the document or section. Include the
retrieval date only if the content could change. (The retrieval date
is not necessary for content with a fixed publication date, such as a
journal article.) On the rare occasion that you need to cite multiple
pages of a Web site (or the entire site), provide a URL that links to
the site's homepage. No periods follow URLs.

Document on a Web Site with an Author

Harvey, C. (2015, March). *We are killing the environment one hamburger at
a time*. Retrieved from http://www.businessinsider.com
/one-hamburger-environment-resources-2015-2

Document on a Web Site with a Corporate or an Organizational Author

Centers for Disease Control and Prevention. (2015). Healthy food
service guidelines. Retrieved from http://www.cdc.gov/obesity
/strategies/food-serv-guide.html

Document on a Web Site with an Unknown Author

Facebook news feed algorithm now considers time spent looking at a post. (2015).
Retrieved from http://www.forbes.com/sites/amitchowdhry/2015
/06/13/facebook-news-feed-algorithm-now-considers-time
-spent-looking-at-a-post

Article with a Digital Object Identifier (DOI)

Lukason, O., & Hoffman, R. C. (2014). Firm bankruptcy probability
and causes: An integrated study. *International Journal of Business and
Management, 9*(11), 72–79. doi:10.5539/ijbm.v9n11p80

Article or Other Work from a Database

Velinov, A., & Chen, W. (2015). Do stock prices reflect their fundamen-
tals? New evidence in the aftermath of the financial crisis. *Journal of
Economics and Business, 80*, 1–20. Retrieved from http://www
.sciencedirect.com/science/article/pii/S0148619515000119

Article in an Online Periodical

Goldman, D., & Pagliery, J. (2015, June 13). Net neutrality is here. What
it means for you. *CNNMoney*. Retrieved from http://money.cnn
.com/2015/06/12/technology/net-neutrality

Online Book

World Bank, Development Research Center of the State Council, & the
People's Republic of China. (2014). *Urban China: Toward efficient,
inclusive, and sustainable urbanization*. Retrieved from https://
openknowledge.worldbank.org/handle/10986/18865

E-Mail

Personal communications (including e-mail and messages from
discussion groups and electronic bulletin boards) are not cited in
an APA references list. They can be cited in the text as follows:
"According to J. D. Kahl (personal communication, October 2,
2014), Web pages need to reflect. . . ."

Entry in a Wiki

Pedagogical scenarios. (n.d.). Retrieved December 9, 2014, from http://
edutechwiki.unige.ch/en/Category:Pedagogical_scenarios

Message Posted to a Newsgroup, an Online Forum, or a Discussion Board

Electronic discussion sources, including postings to electronic mailing lists, online forums, or discussion groups, are seldom cited in
formal publications because they are difficult to retrieve and not
considered scholarly material. If you do include one of these sources,
provide the real name of an author if given; otherwise, provide the
screen name. Follow the name with the date of the posting, the
subject line of the message, and any identifiers for the message in
brackets after the title.

myrc60. (2014, May 5). Re: Independent Contractors [Online forum].
Retrieved from https://www.smallbusinessforums.org/showthread
.php?850-Independent-Contractors

Blog Post

Zumbrun, J. (2015, May 29). Today's graduates may have the strongest
first decade in the job market of all millennials. [Web log post].
Retrieved from http://blogs.wsj.com/economics/2015/05/29
/todays-graduates-may-have-the-strongest-first-decade-in-the-job
-market-of-all-millennials/

Publication on CD-ROM

Malkin, M. (2015). *Who built that: awe-inspiring stories of American tinkerpreneurs* [CD-ROM]. New York, NY: Mercury Ink.

MULTIMEDIA SOURCES
Map or Chart

Bhutan Transportation. (2012). [Map]. Retrieved from https://www
.cia.gov/library/publications/resources/cia-maps-publications
/map-downloads/bhutan_transportation.jpg/image.jpg

Colorado. (2016). [Map]. Chicago, IL: Rand.

Film or Video

McNeal, D. [Host]. (2014). *Entrepreneurial thinking* [DVD]. Waterford,
MI: Seminars on DVD.

McDonald, M. [Host]. (2015, June 9). Blue satellite in Decatur. [Video
files]. *Illinois stories*. Retrieved from https://www.networkknowledge
.tv/service/illinois-stories

Radio or Television Program

Siegel, R. (Host). (2015). Often employees, rarely CEOs: Challenges
Asian Americans face in tech. *All things considered* [Radio broadcast].
Philadelphia, PA: WHYY.

Alfonsi, S. (Host). (2015, June 7). The storm after the storm [Television
series episode]. In J. Fager (Executive producer), *60 minutes*. Boston,
MA: WBZ.

Podcast or Webcast

Tyson, N. D. (2013, January 23). House science & national labs caucus:
Neil deGrasse Tyson [Video webcast]. *The Library of Congress literature webcasts*. Retrieved from http://www.loc.gov/today/cyberlc
/feature_wdesc.php?rec=5790

Glass, I. (Host). (2014, November 7). The leap [Audio podcast]. *This
American life*. Retrieved from http://www.thisamericanlife.org
/radio-archives/episode/539/the-leap

OTHER SOURCES

Published Interview

Dadich, S. (2014, August 22). The most wanted man in the world: Behind the scenes with Edward Snowden [Interview]. *Wired, 22*(9), 29–35.

Personal Interview and Letters

Personal communications (including telephone conversations) are not cited in a references list. They can be cited in the text as follows: "According to J. D. Kahl (personal communication, October 2, 2014), Web pages need to reflect. . . ."

Brochure or Pamphlet

American Cancer Society. (2015). Colorectal cancer screening [Brochure]. Atlanta, GA: Author.

Government Document

U.S. Department of Labor, Bureau of Labor Statistics. (2014, October). *Female self-employment in the United States: An update to 2012.* Washington, DC: Government Printing Office.

Report Published in a Collection

Cady, L. E., & Fessenden, T. (2013). Gendering the divide: Religion, the secular, and the politics of sexual difference. In L. E. Cady & T. Fessenden (Eds.), *Religion, the secular, and the politics of sexual difference* (pp. 3–24). New York, NY: Columbia University Press.

Report Published Separately

Mitchell, A. (2015). *State of the news media 2015.* Washington, DC: Pew Research Center.

Unpublished Data

Kavsan, G., & Hersom, P. (2014). [Oregon small-business statistics, by county]. Unpublished raw data.

APA Sample Pages

ETHICS CASES   14 Shortened
                                                   title and page
                                                   number.

This report examines the nature and disposition of the 3,458
ethics cases handled companywide by CGF's ethics officers and
managers during 2014. The purpose of such reports is to provide
the Ethics and Business Conduct Committee with the information   One-inch
necessary for assessing the effectiveness of the first year of CGF's   margins. Text
Ethics Program (Davis, Marks, & Tegge, 2004). According to   double-spaced.
Matthias Jonas (2004), recommendations are given for consideration
"in planning for the second year of the Ethics Program" (p. 152).

The Office of Ethics and Business Conduct was created to
administer the Ethics Program. The director of the Office of Ethics
and Business Conduct, along with seven ethics officers throughout
CGF, was given the responsibility for the following objectives, as
described by Rossouw (2000):

> Communicate the values, standards, and goals of CGF's   Long quote
> Program to employees. Provide companywide channels   indented
> for employee education and guidance in resolving ethics   one-half inch,
> concerns. Implement companywide programs in ethics   double-spaced,
> awareness and recognition. Employee accessibility to   without
>   quotation
> ethics information and guidance is the immediate goal of   marks.
> the Office of Business Conduct in its first year. (p. 1543)

The purpose of the Ethics Program, established by the Committee,
is to "promote ethical business conduct through open communica-   In-text
tion and compliance with company ethics standards" (Jonas, 2006,   citation gives
p. 89). To accomplish this purpose, any ethics policy must ensure   name, date,
                                                                   and page
confidentiality and anonymity for employees who raise genuine   number.
ethics concerns. The procedure developed at CGF guarantees that
employees can . . .

FIGURE 5–1. APA Sample Page (from a Report)

ETHICS CASES   21

Heading centered.

References

Davis, W. C., Marks, R., & Tegge, D. (2004). *Working in the system: Five new management principles.* New York, NY: St. Martin's Press.

International Business Ethics Institute. (2008). Retrieved from http://business-ethics.org

First word of title capitalized and subsequent words lowercased.

Jonas, M. (2004). The Internet and ethical communication: Toward a new paradigm. *Journal of Ethics and Communication, 32,* 147–177.

Jonas, M. (2006). Ethics in organizational communication: A review of the literature. *Journal of Ethics and Communication, 29,* 79–99.

List alphabetized by authors' last names and double-spaced.

National Science Foundation. (2007). *Conflicts of interest and standards of ethical conduct.* Arlington, VA: National Science Foundation.

Rossouw, G. J. (2000). Business ethics in South Africa. *Journal of Business Ethics, 16,* 1539–1547.

Hanging-indent style used for entries.

Schipper, F. (2007). Transparency and integrity: Contrary concepts? In K. Homann, P. Koslowski, & C. Luetge (Eds.), *Globalisation and business ethics* (pp. 101–118). Burlington, VT: Ashgate.

Smith, T. (Reporter), & Lehrer, J. (Host). (2006). *NewsHour business ethics anthology* [DVD]. Encino, CA: Business Training Media.

FIGURE 5–2. **APA Sample List of References**

5

MLA Documentation

MLA In-Text Citations.   The MLA parenthetical citation within the text of a paper gives a brief citation—in parentheses—of the author and relevant page number(s), separated only by a space. When citing Web sites where no author or page reference is available, provide a short title of the work in parentheses. If you are citing time-based media, such as an audio or film clip, cite the relevant time or range of times as hours, minutes, and seconds, separated by colons instead of a page number.

▶ Achieving results is one thing while maintaining results is another because "like marathon runners, companies hit a performance wall" (Studer 3).

▶ As Studer writes, the poor performance of a few employees will ultimately affect the performance—and the morale—of all of the employees (8).
  [If the author is cited in the text, include only the page number(s) in parentheses.]

▶ In 1810, Peter Durand invented the can, which was later used to provide soldiers and explorers canned rations and ultimately "saved legions from sure starvation" ("Forgotten Inventors").

If the parenthetical citation refers to a long, indented quotation, place it outside the punctuation of the last sentence.

▶ . . . a close collaboration with the marketing staff and the development group is essential. (Thompson 37)

If no author is named or if you are using more than one work by the same author, give a shortened version of the title in the parenthetical citation, unless you name the title in the text (a "signal phrase"). A citation for Quint Studer's book *Results That Last: Hardwiring Behaviors That Will Take Your Company to the Top* would appear as (Studer, *Results* 93).

MLA Documentation Models

BOOKS

Single Author

Black, Alexandra. *How Business Works: A Graphic Guide to Business Success.* Dorling Kindersley, 2015.

Multiple Authors

Jain, Piyanka, and Puneet Sharma. *Behind Every Good Decision: How Anyone Can Use Business Analytics to Turn Data into Profitable Insight.* AMACOM, 2014.

Corporate Author

DK. *The Business Book (Big Ideas Simply Explained)*. Dorling Kindersley, 2014.

Edition Other Than First

FitzGerald, Jerry, et al. *Business Data Communications and Networking*. 12th ed., Wiley, 2014.

Multivolume Work

Dubofsky, Melvyn, and Paul S. Boyer, editors. *The Oxford Encyclopedia of American Business, Labor, and Economic History*. Oxford UP, 2013. 2 vols.

Work in an Edited Collection

Judah, Ben. "London's Laundry Business." *The Best Business Writing 2014*, edited by Dean Starkman, et al., Columbia UP, 2014, pp. 78–99.

Encyclopedia or Dictionary Entry

"Access to Education." *Encyclopedia of Education Economics and Finance*. Edited by Dominic J. Brewer and Lawrence O. Picus, SAGE Publications, 2014.

ARTICLES IN PERIODICALS
Magazine Article

Kuttner, Robert. "The Wealth Problem." *The American Prospect*, 15 Mar. 2015, pp. 33–37.

Journal Article

Wales, William, et al. "What About New Entry? Examining the Theorized Role of New Entry in the Entrepreneurial Orientation-Performance Relationship." *International Small Business Journal*, vol. 33, no. 4, June 2015, pp. 351–73.

Newspaper Article

Hiltzik, Michael. "Emissions Cap-and-Trade Program Is Working Well in California." *Los Angeles Times*, 12 June 2015, p. B2.

Article with Unknown Author

"Put Up the Firewalls." *The Economist*, 11 June 2015, pp. 23–24.

ELECTRONIC SOURCES
Entire Web Site

GreenpeaceBlogs.org. Greenpeace, 26 Sept. 2016, www.greenpeace.org /usa/blog/.

Short Work from a Web Site, with an Author

Harvey, Chelsea. "We Are Killing the Environment One Hamburger at a
     Time." *Business Insider*, 5 Mar. 2015, www.businessinsider.com
     /one-hamburger-environment-resources-2015-2.

Short Work from a Web Site, with a Corporate Author

Centers for Disease Control and Prevention. "Healthy Food Service
     Guidelines." *CDC.gov*, 25 July 2016, www.cdc.gov/obesity/strategies
     /food-serv-guide.html.

Short Work from a Web Site, with an Unknown Author

"Chapter 2: What Can Be Patented?" *Lemelson-MIT*. Massachusetts
     Institute of Technology, lemelson.mit.edu/resources/chapter-2
     -what-can-be-patented. Accessed 11 Oct. 2016.

Article from a Database (Subscription)

Rosen, Christine Meisner. "What Is Business History?" *Enterprise &
     Society*, vol. 3, no. 13, Sept. 2013, pp. 475–85. *Project Muse*,
     muse.jhu.edu/article/519885.

Article in an Online Journal

McGowan, Pauric, et al. "The Influence of Social and Human Capital in
     Developing Young Women as Entrepreneurial Business Leaders."
     Journal of Small Business Management, vol. 53, no. 3, Apr. 2015,
     pp. 645–61. *Wiley Online Library*, doi:10.1111/jsbm.12176.

Article in an Online Magazine

Thomsen, Jacqueline. "'Less Soda Means More Adderall': What Happens
     When a College Campus Bans Sugary Drinks?" *Slate*, 19 June 2015,
     www.slate.com/articles/life/inside_higher_ed/2015/06/university
     _of_california_at_san_francisco_soda_ban_the_health_and
     _science.html.

Article in an Online Newspaper

Vanderkam, Laura. "Working Mothers Who Make It All Work." *Wall
     Street Journal*, 19 June 2015, www.wsj.com/articles/working
     -mothers-who-make-it-all-work-1434712370.

Online Book

World Bank, Development Research Center of the State Council, & the
     People's Republic of China. *Urban China: Toward Efficient, Inclusive,
     and Sustainable Urbanization*. World Bank, 2014. *Open Knowledge
     Repository*, 2014, openknowledge.worldbank.org/handle
     /10986/18865.

Publication on CD-ROM

Malkin, Michelle. *Who Built That: Awe-Inspiring Stories of American Tinkerpreneurs*. Simon & Schuster Audio/Mercury Ink, 2015.

E-Mail Message

Kahl, Jonathan D. "Re: Web page." Received by Shelby Young, 2 Oct. 2016.

Blog

Ng, Amy. *Pikaland*. Pikaland Media, 2015, www.pikaland.com/.

Entry or Comment on a Blog

Zumbrun, Josh. "Today's Graduates May Have the Strongest First Decade in the Job Market of All Millennials." *Real Time Economics*, 29 May 2015, blogs.wsj.com/economics/2015/05/29/todays -graduates-may-have-the-strongest-first-decade-in-the-job-market -of-all-millennials/.

Posting to a Social Networking Site

kevincannon. "Portrait of Norris Hall in #Savannah, GA—home (for a few more months, anyway) of #SCAD's sequential art department." *Instagram*, Mar. 2014, www.instagram.com/p/lgmqk4i6DC/.

@grammarphobia (Patricia T. O'Conner and Steward Kellerman). "Is 'if you will,' like, a verbal tic? http://goo.gl/oYrTYP #English #language #grammar #etymology #usage #linguistics #WOTD." *Twitter*, 14 Mar. 2016, 9:12 a.m., twitter.com/grammarphobia.

MULTIMEDIA SOURCES

Map or Chart

Colorado. Rand McNally, 2016. Map.

"San Francisco." *Google Maps*, 2017, www.google.com/maps/place /California/.

Film or Video

McNeal, Delatorro. *Entrepreneurial Thinking*. Directed by Michael Jeffreys, Seminars on DVD, 2014.

Nayar, Vineet. "Employees First, Customers Second." *YouTube*, 9 June 2015, www.youtube.com/watch?v=cCdu67s_C5E.

Radio or Television Program

"Massive Cyberattack on Federal Government." *The Situation Room*, hosted by Wolf Blitzer, CNN, 4 June 2015.

5

Research and
Documentation

MLA

Glinton, Sonari. "How a Tax on Chicken Changed the Playing Field for U.S. Automakers." *Morning Edition*, hosted by Steve Inskeep and David Greene, National Public Radio, 19 June 2015.

Television Interview

Brokaw, Tom. Interview by Charlie Rose. *The Charlie Rose Show*, PBS, 11 May 2015.

Podcast

Green, Sarah. "Why Leadership Feels Awkward." *HBR IdeaCast*, Harvard Business Review, 12 Feb. 2015, hbr.org/ideacast/2015/02/why -leadership-feels-awkward.html.

OTHER SOURCES

Published Interview

Snowden, Edward. "The Most Wanted Man in the World." Interview by Scott Dadich. *Wired*, 22 Aug. 2014, www.wired.com/2014/08 /edward-snowden/.

Personal Interview

Sariolgholam, Mahmood. Personal interview, 29 Nov. 2016.

Personal Letter

Pascatore, Monica. Letter to the author, 10 Apr. 2017.

Brochure or Pamphlet

American Cancer Society. *Colorectal Cancer Screening*. American Cancer Society, Inc., 2015.

Government Document

United States, Department of Labor. *Female Self-Employment in the United States: An Update to 2012*. GPO, 2014.

Lecture or Speech

Morehead, Shellee. "Sex, DNA, and Family History." Local and Family History Lecture Series, Boston Public Library, Boston, MA, 29 May 2015.

MLA Sample Pages

Author's
last name
and page
number.

Litzinger 14

One-inch
margins.
Text
double-
spaced.

This report examines the nature and disposition of the 3,458 ethics cases handled companywide by CGF's ethics officers and managers during 2014. The purpose of such reports is to provide the Ethics and Business Conduct Committee with the information necessary for assessing the effectiveness of the first year of CGF's Ethics Program (Davis et al. 142). According to Matthias Jonas, recommendations are given for consideration "in planning for the second year of the Ethics Program" ("Internet" 152).

The Office of Ethics and Business Conduct was created to administer the Ethics Program. The director of the Office of Ethics and Business Conduct, along with seven ethics officers throughout CGF, was given the responsibility for the following objectives, as described by Rossouw:

Long quote
indented
one-half
inch,
double-
spaced,
without
quotation
marks.

Communicate the values, standards, and goals of CGF's Program to employees. Provide companywide channels for employee education and guidance in resolving ethics concerns. Implement companywide programs in ethics awareness and recognition. Employee accessibility to ethics information and guidance is the immediate goal of the Office of Business Conduct in its first year. (1543)

In-text
citations
give author
name
and page
number.
Title used
when
multiple
works
by same
author
cited.

The purpose of the Ethics Program, according to Jonas, is to "promote ethical business conduct through open communication and compliance with company ethics standards" ("Ethics" 89). To accomplish this purpose, any ethics policy must ensure confidentiality for anyone . . .

FIGURE 5–3. MLA Sample Page (from a Report)

5

Works Cited

Brevard, Jacqueline E., chairman. International Business Ethics Institute 2016, business-ethics.org/.

Davis, W. C., et al. *Working in the System: Five New Management Principles*. St. Martin's, 2004.

Jonas, Matthias. "Ethics in Organizational Communication: A Review of the Literature." *Journal of Ethics and Communication* vol. 29, no. 2, Spring 2006, pp. 79–99.

---. "The Internet and Ethical Communication: Toward a New Paradigm." *Journal of Ethics and Communication* vol. 27, no. 1, Fall 2004, pp. 147–77.

Rossouw, George J. "Business Ethics in South Africa." *Journal of Business Ethics* vol. 16, no. 14, Jan. 2000, pp. 1539–47.

Sariolghalam, Mahmood. Personal interview. 29 Jan. 2016.

Schipper, Fritz. "Transparency and Integrity: Contrary Concepts?" *Globalisation and Business Ethics,* edited by Karl Homann, et al., Ashgate, 2007, pp. 101–18.

Smith, Terrence. "Legislating Ethics." *NewsHour Business Ethics Anthology,* hosted by Jim Lehrer, Business Training Media, 2006.

United States. National Science Foundation. *Conflicts of Interest and Standards of Ethical Conduct*. NSF Manual No. 15, National Science Foundation, 2007.

Heading centered.

List alphabetized by authors' last names and double-spaced.

Hanging-indent style used for entries.

FIGURE 5-4. MLA Sample List of Works Cited

❖ ETHICS NOTE Visuals under copyright require permission from copyright owners before they can be reproduced. Contact the publisher to find out what needs permission, how best to obtain it, and what information copyright owners require in source lines and reference entries. Source lines almost always require mention of permission from the copyright owner to reproduce. ❖

interviewing for information

Interviewing others who have knowledge of your subject is often an essential method of <u>research</u> in business writing.

Determining the Proper Person to Interview

Many times, your subject or <u>purpose</u> (Tab 1) logically points to the proper person to interview for information. For example, if you were writing a feasibility report about marketing consumer products in India, you would want to interview someone with extensive experience in that area. The following sources can help you determine the appropriate person to interview: (1) workplace colleagues or faculty in appropriate academic departments, (2) local chapters of professional societies, (3) "Contact" and "About" sections on organizational Web sites, and (4) targeted Internet searches.

Preparing for the Interview

Before the interview, learn as much as possible about the person you are going to interview and the organization for which he or she works.

▶ PROFESSIONALISM NOTE When you contact the prospective interviewee, explain who you are, why you would like an interview, the subject and purpose of the interview, the best setting or medium for the interview (in person or by phone, video conference, or e-mail), and approximately how much time it will take. You should also ask permission if you plan to record the interview and let your interviewee know that you will allow him or her to review your draft. ▶

After you have made the appointment, prepare a list of questions to ask your interviewee. Avoid vague, general questions. A question such as "Do you think the Web would be useful for you?" is too general to elicit useful information. It is better to ask specific but open-ended questions, such as the following: "Many physicians in your specialty are using the Web to answer routine patient questions. How might providing such information on your Web site affect your relationship with your patients?"

Conducting the Interview

Arrive promptly or connect on time if videoconferencing and be prepared to guide the discussion. During the interview, take only memory-jogging notes that will help you recall the conversation later; do not ask your interviewee to slow down so that you can take detailed notes. As the interview is reaching a close, take a few minutes to skim your notes and ask the interviewee to clarify anything that is ambiguous.

▶ PROFESSIONALISM NOTE If you plan to conduct an interview using videoconferencing, find an environment that is quiet and allows you to focus on the interview. Be mindful of your surroundings, personal appearance, and the appearance of your videoconferencing platform because all will be conveyed to the person you are interviewing. Make sure that you can take notes in a way that allows you to maintain your focus on your subject, as described in listening (Tab 8). Finally, ensure you are using high-quality software and connections. ▶

Expanding Your Notes Soon After the Interview

Immediately after leaving the interview, use your memory-jogging notes to help you mentally review the interview and expand those notes. Do not postpone this step; otherwise, you risk forgetting important points. See also note-taking.

Interviewing by Phone or E-mail

When an interviewee is not available for a face-to-face meeting or video-conference, consider a phone interview. Most of the principles for conducting face-to-face interviews apply to phone interviews; be aware, however, that phone calls do not offer the important nonverbal cues of face-to-face or video meetings. Further, taking notes can be challenging while holding a phone, so consider using a high-quality headset or speakerphone to alleviate that problem.

Another alternative is to consider an e-mail interview in which you exchange a number of back-and-forth messages. (See also e-mail, Tab 2.) Such an interview, however, lacks the spontaneity and the immediacy of an in-person, a video, or a phone conversation. But the interviewing principles in this entry can still help you obtain useful responses. Before you send any questions, make sure that your contact is willing to participate and respond to follow-up clarifications. As a courtesy, give the respondent a general idea of the number of questions you plan to ask and the level of detail you expect. When you send the questions, ask for a reasonable deadline from the interviewee ("Would you be able to send your response by . . . ?").

Writer's Checklist: Interviewing Successfully

☑ Be pleasant but purposeful. You are there to get information, so don't be timid about asking leading questions on the subject.

☑ Use the list of questions you have prepared, starting with the less-complex topics to get the conversation started and moving toward the more-challenging aspects.

☑ Let your interviewee do most of the talking. Remember that the interviewee is the expert.

☑ Be objective. Do not offer your opinions on the subject. You are there to get information, not to debate.

☑ Ask additional questions as they arise.

☑ Do not get sidetracked. If the interviewee strays too far from the subject, ask a specific question to direct the conversation back on track.

☑ If you use audio or video recording, do not let it lure you into relaxing so that you neglect to ask crucial questions.

☑ After thanking the interviewee, ask permission to contact him or her again to clarify a point or two as you complete your interview notes.

☑ A day or two after the interview, send a thank-you note to the interviewee.

note-taking

The purpose of note-taking is to summarize and record information you extract during <u>research</u>. The challenge in taking notes is to condense someone else's thoughts into your own words without distorting the original thinking. As you extract information, let your knowledge of the <u>audience</u> (Tab 1) and the <u>purpose</u> (Tab 1) of your writing guide you.

❖ ETHICS NOTE Resist copying your source word for word as you take notes; instead, paraphrase the author's idea or concept. If you change even a few words from a source and incorporate that text into your document without giving credit to your source, you will be guilty of <u>plagiarism</u>. See also <u>paraphrasing</u>. ❖

On occasion, when an expert source states something that is especially precise, striking, or noteworthy, or that reinforces your point, you can justifiably quote the source directly and incorporate it into your document. If you use a direct quotation, enclose the material in quotation marks in your notes. In your finished writing, document the source of your quotation. Normally, you will rarely need to quote anything longer than a paragraph. See also <u>documenting sources</u> and <u>quotations</u>.

When taking notes on abstract ideas, as opposed to factual data, do not sacrifice clarity for brevity—notes expressing concepts can lose their meaning if they are too brief. The critical test is whether you can understand the note a week later and recall the significant ideas of the passage.

Writer's Checklist: Taking Notes

☑ Ask yourself the following questions: What information do I need to fulfill my purpose? What are the needs of my audience?

☑ Record only the most important ideas and concepts. Be sure to record all vital names, dates, and definitions.

☑ When in doubt about whether to take a note, consider the difficulty of finding the source again should you want it later.

☑ Use direct or indirect quotations when sources state something that is precise, striking, or noteworthy or that succinctly reinforces a point you are making.

☑ Photocopy or download pages and highlight passages that you intend to quote.

☑ Give proper credit: Record the author; title; publisher; place; page number; URL; and date of publication, posting, or retrieval. (On subsequent notes from the same source, include only the author and page number or URL.)

☑ Record notes in a way that you find efficient and useful for <u>outlining</u> (Tab 1), whether using the latest note-taking software or traditional index cards.

☑ Check your notes for accuracy against the original material before moving on to another source.

paraphrasing

Paraphrasing is restating or rewriting the essential ideas of another writer in your own words. The following example is an original passage and a paraphrased version that restates accurately the essential information in a form appropriate for a report.

ORIGINAL   Generally, the goals of workplace profes-
                sionals demand that they think in specific,
                practical, and immediately applicable ways;

those of us in the academy must think in terms that are more abstract, conceptual, and long-term. It is understandable, then, that works that might be highly valued by either practitioners or academics can seem entirely irrelevant to the other.

—Gerald J. Alred, "Bridging Cultures: The Academy and the Workplace," *Journal of Business Communication.*

PARAPHRASE   Practitioners who value specific, practical goals and academics who need to think in abstract, long-term ways understandably value different works (Alred, 2006).

❖ ETHICS NOTE Because paraphrasing does not quote a source word for word, quotation marks are not used. However, paraphrased material should be credited because the *ideas* are taken from someone else. See also note-taking, plagiarism, and quotations. ❖

plagiarism

Plagiarism is the use of someone else's unique ideas without acknowledgment or the use of someone else's exact words without quotation marks and appropriate credit. Plagiarism is considered to be the theft of someone else's creative and intellectual property and can result in legal action, academic sanctions, and serious professional consequences. See also ethics in writing (Tab 1) and research.

Citing Sources

Quoting a passage—including cutting and pasting a passage from an Internet source into your work—is permissible only if you enclose the passage in quotation marks and properly cite the source. For detailed guidance on quoting correctly, see quotations. If you intend to publish, reproduce, or distribute material that includes quotations from published works, including Web sites, you may need to obtain written permission from the copyright holders of those works.

Even Web sites that grant permission to copy, distribute, or modify material under the "copyleft" principle, such as Wikipedia, nonetheless caution that you must give appropriate credit to the source from which material is taken (see *http://en.wikipedia.org/wiki/Wikipedia:Citing _Wikipedia*).

Paraphrasing the words and ideas of another *also requires that you cite your source,* even though you do not enclose paraphrased ideas or materials in quotation marks. (See also documenting sources.) Paraphrasing a passage without citing the source is permissible only when the information paraphrased is common knowledge.

Common Knowledge

Common knowledge generally refers to information that is widely known and readily available in handbooks, manuals, atlases, and other references. For example, the "law of supply and demand" is common knowledge and is found in virtually every economics and business textbook.

Common knowledge also refers to information within a specific field that is generally known and understood by most others in that field—even though it is not widely known by those outside the field.

An indication that something is common knowledge is its appearance in multiple sources without citation. However, when in doubt, cite the source.

❖ ETHICS NOTE In the workplace, employees often borrow material freely from in-house manuals, reports, and other company documents. Using or repurposing (Tab 2) such material is neither plagiarism nor a violation of copyright. For information on the use of public domain and government material, see copyright. ❖

---

quotations

Using direct and indirect quotations is an effective way to support a point and strengthen the credibility of your writing. But do not rely too heavily on the use of quotations, and avoid quoting anything that is longer than one paragraph.

❖ ETHICS NOTE When you use a quotation (or an idea of another writer), cite your source properly. If you do not, you will be guilty of plagiarism. See also note-taking and research. ❖

Direct Quotations

A direct quotation is a word-for-word copy of the text of an original source. Choose direct quotations (which can be of a word, a phrase, a sentence, or, occasionally, a paragraph) carefully and use them sparingly. Enclose direct quotations in quotation marks (Tab 12) and separate them from the rest of the sentence by a comma (Tab 12) or colon (Tab 12). Use the initial capital letter of a quotation if the quoted material originally began with a capital letter.

▶ The economist stated, "Regulation cannot supply the dynamic stimulus that in other industries is supplied by competition."

When dividing a quotation, set off the material that interrupts the quotation with commas, and use quotation marks around each part of the quotation.

▶ "Regulation," the economist said in a recent interview, "cannot supply the dynamic stimulus that in other industries is supplied by competition."

Indirect Quotations

An indirect quotation is a paraphrased version of an original text. It is usually introduced by the word *that* and is not set off from the rest of the sentence by punctuation marks. See also paraphrasing.

▶ In a recent interview, he said *that* regulation does not stimulate the industry as well as competition does.

Deletions or Omissions

Deletions or omissions from quoted material are indicated by three ellipsis points (. . .) within a sentence and a period plus three ellipsis points (. . . .) at the end of a sentence. See ellipses (Tab 12).

▶ "If monopolies could be made to respond . . . we would be able to enjoy the benefits of . . . large-scale efficiency. . . ."

When a quoted passage begins in the middle of a sentence rather than at the beginning, ellipsis points are not necessary; the fact that the first letter of the quoted material is not capitalized tells the reader that the quotation begins in midsentence.

▶ Rivero goes on to conclude that "coordination may lessen competition within a region."

In omitting material, be careful to not change the author's original meaning, which would be unethical as well as inaccurate.

Inserting Material into Quotations

When it is necessary to insert a clarifying comment within quoted material, use brackets (Tab 12).

▶ "The industry is an integrated system that serves an extensive [geographic] area, with divisions existing as islands within the larger system's sphere of influence."

When quoted material contains an obvious error or might be questioned in some other way, insert the expression *sic* (Latin for "thus") in italic type and enclose it in brackets ([*sic*]) following the questionable material to indicate that the writer has quoted the material *exactly as it appeared in the original.*

▶ The contract states, "Tinted windows will be installed to protect against son [*sic*] damage."

Incorporating Quotations into Text

Quote word for word only when a source with particular expertise states something that is especially precise, striking, or noteworthy, or that may reinforce a point you are making. Quotations must also logically, grammatically, and syntactically match the rest of the sentence and surrounding text. Notice in Figure 5–5 that the quotation blends with the content of the surrounding text, which uses <u>transition</u> (Tab 10) to introduce and comment on the quotation.

Depending on the citation system, the style of incorporating quotations varies. For examples of two different styles, see <u>documenting sources</u>. Figure 5–5 shows APA style for a long quotation.

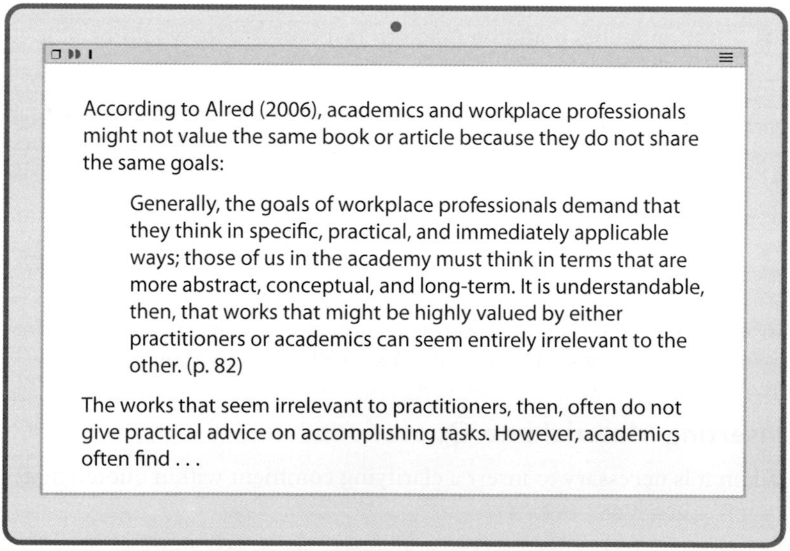

According to Alred (2006), academics and workplace professionals might not value the same book or article because they do not share the same goals:

> Generally, the goals of workplace professionals demand that they think in specific, practical, and immediately applicable ways; those of us in the academy must think in terms that are more abstract, conceptual, and long-term. It is understandable, then, that works that might be highly valued by either practitioners or academics can seem entirely irrelevant to the other. (p. 82)

The works that seem irrelevant to practitioners, then, often do not give practical advice on accomplishing tasks. However, academics often find . . .

FIGURE 5–5. Long Quotation (APA Style)

research

Research is the process of investigation—the discovery of information. To be focused, research must be preceded by <u>preparation</u> (Tab 1), especially consideration of your <u>audience</u> (Tab 1), <u>purpose</u> (Tab 1), and <u>scope</u> (Tab 1). Effective <u>note-taking</u> is essential for a coherent <u>organization</u> (Tab 1) that strategically integrates your own ideas, supporting facts, and any well-selected <u>quotations</u> into an effective draft and final document. See also <u>documenting sources</u>, <u>outlining</u> (Tab 1), and "Five Steps to Successful Writing" (page xxvii).

In an academic setting, your preparatory resources include conversations with your fellow students, instructors, and reference librarians, as well as searches on the Internet. On the job, your main resources are your own knowledge and experience and that of your colleagues. In business, the most important sources of information may also include market research, questionnaires and surveys, focus groups, shareholder meetings, and the like. In this setting, begin by brainstorming with colleagues about what sources will be most useful to your topic and how you can find them.

Primary Research

Primary research is the gathering of raw data from such sources as firsthand experience, interviews, direct observation, surveys and questionnaires, focus groups, <u>meetings</u> (Tab 8), and the like. In fact, direct observation and interaction are often the only ways to obtain certain kinds of information on such topics as human behavior and the functioning of organizations, as in ethnographic research. You can also conduct primary online research by participating in discussion groups and online forums and by e-mailing requests for information to specific audiences. When conducting primary research, focus on keeping accurate, complete records that indicate date, time of day, observation duration, and so on, saving interpretations for a later time. See also <u>blogs and forums</u> (Tab 2), <u>interviewing for information</u>, and <u>listening</u> (Tab 8).

❖ ETHICS NOTE If you conduct research that involves observation or a questionnaire at your university or college, ask your instructor whether your methods or questions are appropriate, whether you may need to file an application with your school's Institutional Review Board (IRB), and the best way to obtain permission from your study subjects. ❖

Secondary Research

Secondary research is the gathering of information that has been previously analyzed, assessed, evaluated, compiled, or otherwise organized into accessible form. Sources include books, articles, online documents, audio and video recordings, podcasts, <u>correspondence</u> (Tab 3), <u>minutes of meetings</u> (Tab 8), brochures, and various <u>reports</u> (Tab 4). The following two sections—Library Research Strategies and Web Research Strategies—provide methods for finding secondary sources.

As you seek information, keep in mind that in most cases the more recent the information, the better. Recent periodicals and newspapers—as well as academic (.edu in the U.S.), government (.gov), and frequently updated corporate Web sites—can be good sources of current information and can include the latest published interviews, articles, papers, and conference proceedings. See *Writer's Checklist: Evaluating Print and Online Sources* (page 173).

When a resource seems useful, read it carefully and take notes that include additional questions about your topic. Some of your questions may eventually be answered in other sources; those that remain unanswered can guide you to further research, both primary and secondary. See <u>paraphrasing</u> and <u>plagiarism</u>.

Library Research Strategies

The library provides organized paths into scholarship and specialized resources—such as subscription-only databases, indexes, catalogs, and directories—that are not accessible through standard Web searches. The first step in using library resources, either in an academic institution or in a workplace, is to develop a search strategy appropriate to the information needed for your topic. Begin by asking a reference librarian for help (in person or by phone, live chat, or e-mail) to find the best print or online resources for your topic—a brief conversation can focus your research and save you time. In addition, use your library's homepage for access to its catalogs and various databases.

Your search strategy depends on the kind of information you are seeking. For example, if you need the latest data offered by government research, check the Web, as described later in this entry. Likewise, if you need a current scholarly article on a topic, search an online database (such as EBSCOhost's Academic Search Premier) subscribed to by your library. For an overview of a subject, you might turn to an encyclopedia; for historical background, your best resources are books, journals, and primary documents (such as a labor contract).

DIGITAL TIP

Storing Search Results

Databases offer various ways to save your results. You may be able to save your searches and note-taking within the database itself by creating a personal account, by sending selected references and full-text articles to an e-mail account, or by exporting them to citation-management software, such as RefWorks, Evernote, or Zotero. These programs allow you to build your own database of references from multiple sources, sort them into folders, and generate <u>bibliographies</u> in the format of your choice. Database search tools will vary from library to library, so contact a reference librarian for usage guidance at your library.

Online Catalogs (Locating Library Holdings). An online catalog allows you to search a library's licensed holdings, indicates an item's location and availability, and may allow you to arrange an interlibrary loan.

You can search a library's online catalog by author, title, keyword, or subject. The most common ways of searching for a specific topic are by subject or by keyword. If your search turns up too many results, you can usually narrow it by using the "limit search" or "advanced search" option.

Online Databases and Indexes (Locating Articles). Most libraries subscribe to online databases that are available only through a login to the library's Web site:

- *EBSCOhost's Academic Search Premier:* a large multidisciplinary database, providing full text for nearly 4,500 periodicals, including more than 7,400 abstracted and indexed peer-reviewed journals
- *Gale's Expanded Academic ASAP:* a large database covering general-interest and scholarly journals plus business, law, and health-care publications (many in full text)
- *ERIC (Educational Resources Information Center):* a U.S. Department of Education database providing access to journals and reports in education
- *JSTOR:* a full-text, archival collection of journals in humanities, social sciences, and sciences
- *LexisNexis Academic:* a collection of databases that is particularly strong for news, business, legal, and corporate and financial information (most articles in full text) as well as congressional, statistical, and government resources

These databases, sometimes called *periodical indexes*, are excellent resources for articles published within the last 10 to 20 years. Many include descriptive abstracts and full texts of articles. To find older articles, you may need to consult a print index, such as the *Readers' Guide to Periodical Literature* and the *New York Times Article Archive*, both of which have been digitized and may be available in some libraries.

Reference Works.   In addition to articles, books, and online sources, you may want to consult reference works such as encyclopedias, dictionaries, and manuals for a brief overview of your subject. Ask your reference librarian to recommend works and bibliographies that are most relevant to your topic. Many are available online and can be accessed through your library's homepage.

ENCYCLOPEDIAS.   Encyclopedias are comprehensive collections of articles arranged alphabetically. Some cover a wide range of subjects, while others—such as *The Encyclopedia of Careers and Vocational Guidance*, 15th ed. (Chicago: Ferguson, 2010)—focus on specific areas. The free online encyclopedia Wikipedia is a useful starting point for your research, but keep in mind that users continually update entries (with varying degrees of expert oversight).

DICTIONARIES.   Specialized dictionaries define terms used in a particular field, such as computer science, architecture, or consumer affairs, and they offer detailed definitions of field-specific terms, usually written in straightforward language.

HANDBOOKS AND MANUALS.   Handbooks and manuals are typically one-volume compilations of frequently used information in a particular field. They offer brief definitions of terms or concepts, standards for presenting information, procedures for documenting sources, and visuals (Tab 7) to illustrate principles.

BIBLIOGRAPHIES.   Bibliographies list books, periodicals, and other research materials published in areas such as business, medicine, the humanities, and the social sciences.

OTHER LIBRARY RESOURCES.   Many libraries offer special kinds of research information. For example, a library may provide access to data that can be downloaded into statistical packages, such as SPSS (Statistical Package for the Social Sciences) for manipulation. Others offer GIS (geographic information systems) software that links data to spatial information, allowing the researcher to create detailed maps that show factors such as income, ethnicity, or purchasing habits.

Web Research Strategies

The Web varies widely in its completeness and accuracy, so you need to evaluate Internet sources critically by following the advice in *Writer's Checklist: Evaluating Print and Online Sources* (page 173).

Search Engines.   Search engines use words or combinations of words that you specify to locate the documents or files that contain one or more of these words in their titles, descriptions, or text. Common search engines include Google, Bing, and Yahoo! Some search engines have specialized interfaces for searching academic texts (*http://scholar .google.com*).

As comprehensive as search engines and directories may seem, none is complete or objective, and they carry only a preselected range of content. Some, for example, may not index PDF files or Usenet newsgroups, and many cannot index databases and other non–HTML-based content. Search engines rank the sites they believe will be relevant to your search based on a number of different criteria. Although search engines vary in what and how they search, you can navigate them all with some basic strategies, described in the following *Writer's Checklist*.

Writer's Checklist: Using Search Engines and Keywords

☑   Check any search tips available in the engine you use and consider any additional search phrases the search engine may suggest.

☑   Enter precise keywords and phrases that are specific to your topic, such as *nuclear power* rather than only the term *nuclear*, which would also yield listings for *nuclear family*, *nuclear medicine*, and hundreds of other unrelated topics.

☑   Try several search engines to get more varied results. Remember that search engines may sell high rankings to advertisers and therefore may not rank as highly the pages most relevant to your search.

☑   Consider using a metasearch engine, such as Dogpile (*www.dogpile .com*), which displays results from multiple search engines.

☑   Refine and narrow your terms as you evaluate the results of each search.

Web Subject Directories.   A subject directory organizes information by broad subject categories (business, entertainment, health, sports) and related subtopics (marketing, finance, investing). A subject-directory search eventually produces a list of specific sites that contain information about the topics you request. Other directories can help you to conduct selective, scholarly research on the Web:

Infomine	*http://infomine.ucr.edu*
IPL2	*www.ipl.org*
The WWW Virtual Library	*www.vlib.org*

Some directories and sites are devoted to specific subject areas, such as the following resources for researching a business topic:

CIO's Resource Centers	*www.cio.com* (use search function)
globalEDGE	*http://globaledge.msu.edu*
Inc.com Articles by Topic	*www.inc.com* (use search function)
LSU Libraries Federal Agency Directory	*www.lib.lsu.edu/gov/index.html*
FedStats	*https://fedstats.sites.usa.gov*

AOL operates a special contributor-generated directory referred to as an "Open Directory" (*http://dmoz.org*).

Evaluating Sources

The easiest way to ensure that information is valid is to obtain it from a reputable source. For online sources, be especially concerned about the validity of the information provided. Because anyone can publish on the Web, it is sometimes difficult to determine authorship of a document, and frequently a person's qualifications for speaking on a topic are absent or questionable. The online versions of established, reputable journals in medicine, management, engineering, computer software, and the like, merit the same level of trust as the printed versions. The following domain abbreviations may help you determine an Internet site sponsor, but only a few (such as .edu and .gov) restrict who can register a Web site with a given domain:

.aero	aerospace industry	.pro	professionals
.biz	business	.mil	U.S. military
.com	company or individual	.name	individual
.coop	business cooperative	.net	company or individual
.edu	educational institution	.org	general organization
.gov	U.S. government	.info	general use

As you move away from established, reputable sites, exercise more caution. Be especially wary of unmoderated Web sites where the author or source cannot be determined. Collectively generated Web sites, such as Wikipedia, often make no guarantee of the validity of information on their sites.

Writer's Checklist: Evaluating Print and Online Sources

Keep in mind the following four criteria when evaluating sources: authority, accuracy, bias, and currency.

FOR ALL SOURCES

☑ Is the resource up to date and relevant to your topic? Is it readily available?

☑ Who is the intended audience? Is it the mainstream public? A small group of professionals?

☑ Who is the author(s)? Is the author(s) an authority on the subject?

☑ Does the author(s) provide enough supporting evidence and document sources so that you can verify the information's accuracy?

☑ Is the information presented in an objective, unbiased way? Are any biases made clear? Are opinions clearly labeled? Are viewpoints balanced, or are opposing opinions acknowledged?

☑ Are the language, tone, and style appropriate and cogent?

FOR A BOOK

☑ Does the preface or introduction indicate the author's or book's purpose?

☑ Does the table of contents relate to your topic? Does the index contain terms related to your topic?

☑ Are the chapters useful? Skim through one chapter that seems related to your topic — notice especially the introduction, headings, and closing.

FOR AN ARTICLE

☑ Is the publisher of the magazine or other periodical well known?

☑ What is the article's purpose? For an academic article, read the abstract; for a newspaper article, read the headline and opening sentences.

☑ Does the article contain informative diagrams or other visuals that indicate its scope?

(continued)

5

Writer's Checklist: Evaluating Print and Online Sources (continued)

FOR A WEB SITE

☑ Does a reputable individual, group, or organization sponsor or maintain the site?

☑ Are the purpose and scope of the site clearly stated? Check the "Mission Statement" or "About Us" pages. Does the site carry any disclaimers?

☑ Is the site updated and current? Are the links functional and up to date?

☑ Is the documentation authoritative and credible? Check the links to other sources and cross-check facts at other reputable Web sites, such as academic ones.

☑ Is the site well designed? Is the material well written and error free?

6

Formal Reports

Preview

This section includes entries about the formal report and its components. Although the number and arrangement of elements in formal reports vary, the guidelines given in the **formal reports** entry follow the most common pattern. The other entries in this section provide more-detailed guidance for preparing key sections often included in formal reports. A sample formal report begins on page 185. For specific types of reports and other documents that may be presented in formal-report format, see Tab 4, "Business Writing Documents and Elements."

DIGITAL TIP

Digitally Enhancing Formal Reports

Many organizations publish formal reports as PDF files or Web documents. Digital versions of formal reports can offer tables of contents that link directly to the individual sections within a report. You can add hyperlinks or mouseover elements that provide definitions of specialized terms or links to supplemental information.

abstracts

An abstract summarizes and highlights the major points of a <u>formal report</u>, journal article, dissertation, or other long work. Its primary purpose is to enable readers to decide whether to read the work in full. For a discussion of how summaries differ from abstracts, see <u>executive summaries</u>.

Although abstracts, typically 200 to 250 words long, are published with the longer works they condense, they can also be published separately in periodical indexes, by abstracting services, and in introductory sections of online journals (see <u>research</u>, Tab 5). For this reason, an abstract must be readable apart from the original document and contain appropriate key search terms for researchers using online databases.

Types of Abstracts

Depending on the kind of information they contain, abstracts are often classified as descriptive or informative (see Figure 6–1). A *descriptive abstract* summarizes the purpose, scope, and methods used to arrive at the reported findings. It is a slightly expanded <u>table of contents</u> in sentence and paragraph form. A descriptive abstract need not be longer than several sentences. An *informative abstract* is an expanded version of the descriptive abstract, including a summary of any results, conclusions, and recommendations. The informative abstract retains the tone and essential scope of the original work, while omitting its details. The first two paragraphs of the abstract shown in Figure 6–1 alone would be descriptive; with the addition of the paragraphs that detail the findings and conclusions of the report, the abstract becomes informative.

The type of abstract you should write depends on your <u>audience</u> (Tab 1) and the organization or publication for which you are writing. Informative abstracts work best for wide audiences that need to know conclusions and recommendations; descriptive abstracts work best for compilations, such as proceedings and progress reports, that do not contain conclusions or recommendations.

Writing Strategies

Write the abstract *after* finishing the report or document. Otherwise, the abstract may not accurately reflect the longer work. Begin with a topic sentence that announces the subject and scope of your original document. Then, using the major and minor headings of your outline or table of contents to distinguish primary ideas from secondary ones, decide what material is relevant to your abstract. (See <u>outlining</u>, Tab 1.) Write with clarity and <u>conciseness</u> (Tab 10), eliminating unnecessary

6

Formal Reports

ABSTRACT

Purpose

This report investigates the long-term effects of long-distance running on the bones, joints, and general health of runners aged 50 to 72. The Sports Medicine Institute of Columbia Hospital sponsored this investigation, first to decide whether to add a geriatric unit to the Institute, and second to determine whether physicians should recommend long-distance running for their older patients.

Methods and scope

The investigation is based on recent studies conducted at Stanford University and the University of Florida. The Stanford study tested and compared male and female long-distance runners aged 50 to 72 with a control group of runners and nonrunners. The groups were matched by sex, race, education, and occupation. The Florida study used only male runners who had run at least 20 miles a week for five years and compared them with a group of runners and nonrunners. Both studies based findings on medical histories and on physical and X-ray examinations.

Findings

Both studies conclude that long-distance running is not associated with increased degenerative joint disease. Control groups were more prone to spur formation, sclerosis, and joint-space narrowing and showed more joint degeneration than runners. Female long-distance runners exhibited somewhat more sclerosis in knee joints and the lumbar spine area than matched control subjects. Both studies support the role of exercise in retarding bone loss with aging. The investigation concludes that the health risk factors are fewer for long-distance runners than for those less active aged 50 to 72.

The investigation recommends that the Sports Medicine Institute of Columbia Hospital consider the development of a geriatric unit a priority and that it inform physicians that an exercise program that includes long-distance running can be beneficial to their aging patients' health.

Descriptive section

Conclusions

Recommendations

iii

FIGURE 6–1. Informative Abstract (from a Report)

words and ideas. Do not, however, become so terse that you omit articles (*a, an, the*) and important transitional words and phrases (*however, therefore, but, next*). Write complete sentences, but avoid stringing together a group of short sentences end to end; instead, combine ideas by using <u>subordination</u> (Tab 10) and <u>parallel structure</u> (Tab 10). Spell out all but the most common <u>abbreviations</u> (Tab 12). In a report, an abstract follows the title page and is numbered page iii.

appendixes

An appendix, located at the end of a <u>formal report</u>, a <u>proposal</u> (Tab 4), or another long document, supplements or clarifies the information in the body of the document. Appendixes (or *appendices*) can provide information that is too detailed or lengthy for the primary <u>audience</u> (Tab 1) of the document. For example, an appendix could contain such material as maps, statistical analyses, <u>résumés</u> (Tab 9) of key personnel involved in a proposed project, or other documents needed by secondary readers.

A document may have more than one appendix, with each providing only one type of information. When you include more than one appendix, arrange them in the order they are mentioned in the body of the document. List the titles and beginning page numbers of the appendixes in the document's <u>table of contents</u>. Begin each appendix on a new page, and identify each with a letter, starting with the letter *A* (*Appendix A: Sample Questionnaire*). If you have only one appendix, title it simply "Appendix."

executive summaries

An executive summary consolidates the principal points of a <u>formal report</u> or other long document. Executive summaries differ from <u>abstracts</u> in that readers scan abstracts to decide whether to read the work in full. However, an executive summary may be the only section of a longer work read by many readers, so it must accurately and concisely represent the original document. It should restate the document's purpose, scope, methods, findings, conclusions, and recommendations, as well as summarize how results were obtained or the reasons for the recommendations. Executive summaries tend to be about 10 percent of the length and generally follow the same sequence of the documents they summarize.

Write the executive summary so that it can be read independently of the report or proposal. Executive summaries may occasionally include a figure, table, or footnote—if that information is essential to the summary. However, do not refer by number to figures, tables, or references contained elsewhere in the document. See the sample executive summary in Figure 6–2 (page 185).

Writer's Checklist: Writing Executive Summaries

☑ Write the executive summary after you have completed the original document.

☑ Avoid or define terminology that may not be familiar to your intended <u>audience</u> (Tab 1).

(*continued*)

Writer's Checklist: Writing Executive Summaries (continued)

☑ Spell out all uncommon symbols and <u>abbreviations</u> (Tab 12).

☑ Make the summary concise, but do not omit transitional words and phrases (*however, moreover, therefore, for example, next*).

☑ Include only information discussed in the original document.

☑ Place the executive summary at the very beginning of the body of the report, as described in <u>formal reports</u>.

6 | formal reports

Formal Reports

Formal reports are usually written accounts of major projects that require substantial <u>research</u> (Tab 5), and they often involve more than one writer. See also <u>collaborative writing</u> (Tab 1).

Most formal reports are divided into three primary parts—front matter, body, and back matter—each of which contains a number of elements. The number and arrangement of the elements vary depending on the subject, the length of the report, and the kinds of material covered. Many organizations have a preferred style for formal reports and furnish guidelines for report writers. If you are not required to follow a specific style, use the <u>format</u> recommended in this entry. The following list includes most of the elements a formal report might contain, in the order they typically appear. (The items shown with page numbers appear in the sample formal report on pages 185–201.) Often, a <u>cover letter</u> (Tab 3) or <u>memo</u> (Tab 3) precedes the front matter and identifies the report by title, the person or persons to whom it is sent, the reason it was written, the <u>scope</u> (Tab 1), and any information that the <u>audience</u> (Tab 1) considers important, as shown on page 185.

FRONT MATTER

Title Page (186)
Abstract (187)
Table of Contents (188)
List of Figures
List of Tables
Foreword
Preface
List of Abbreviations and Symbols

BODY

Executive Summary (189)
Introduction (191)
Text (including headings) (194)
Conclusions (199)

Front Matter

The front matter serves several functions: It explains the writer's <u>purpose</u> (Tab 1), describes the scope and type of information in the report, and lists where specific information is covered in the report. Not all formal reports include every element of front matter described here. A title page and table of contents are usually mandatory. But the scope of the report and its <u>context</u> (Tab 1), as well as the intended audience, determine whether the other elements are included.

Title Page.   Although the formats of title pages may vary, they often include the following:

- *The full title of the report.* The title describes the topic, scope, and purpose of the report, as discussed in <u>titles</u> (Tab 4).
- *The name of the writer(s), principal investigator(s), or compiler(s).* Sometimes contributors identify themselves by their job title or role on the project (*Olivia Jones, Principal Investigator*).
- *The date(s) of the report.* For one-time reports, use the date the report is distributed. For reports issued periodically (monthly, quarterly, or yearly), the subtitle shows the period that the report covers and the distribution date is shown elsewhere on the title page, as shown in Figure 6–2 on page 186.
- *The name of the organization for which the writer(s) works.*
- *The name of the organization to which the report is being submitted.* Include this information if the report is written for a customer or client.

Front-matter pages are numbered with Roman numerals. The title page should not be numbered, as in the example on page 186, but it is considered page i for subsequent pagination. The back of the title page, which is left blank and unnumbered, is considered page ii, so the abstract falls on page iii. The body of the report begins with Arabic number 1, and a new chapter or large section typically begins on a new right-hand (odd-numbered) page. Reports with printing on only one side of each sheet can be numbered consecutively regardless of where new sections begin. Center page numbers at the bottom of each page throughout the report.

Abstract.   An <u>abstract</u>, which normally follows the title page, highlights the major points of the report, as shown on page 187, enabling readers to decide whether to read the report.

Table of Contents.   A <u>table of contents</u> lists all the major sections or <u>headings</u> (Tab 7) of the report in their order of appearance, as shown on page 188, along with their page numbers.

List of Figures.   All <u>visuals</u> (Tab 7) contained in the report—<u>drawings</u>, <u>photographs</u>, <u>maps</u>, charts, and <u>graphs</u>—are labeled as figures. When a report contains more than five figures, list them, along with their page numbers, in a separate section, beginning on a new page immediately following the table of contents. Number figures consecutively with Arabic numbers.

List of Tables.   When a report contains more than five <u>tables</u> (Tab 7), list them, along with their titles and page numbers, in a separate section immediately following the list of figures (if there is one). Number tables consecutively with Arabic numbers.

Foreword.   A foreword is an optional introductory statement about a formal report or publication that is written by someone other than the author(s). The foreword author is usually an authority in the field or an executive of the organization sponsoring the report. That author's name and affiliation appear at the end of the foreword, along with the date it was written. The foreword generally provides background information about the publication's significance and places it in the context of other works in the field. The foreword precedes the preface when a work has both.

Preface.   The preface, another type of optional introductory statement, is written by the author(s) of the formal report. It may announce the work's purpose, scope, and context (including any special circumstances leading to the work). A preface may also specify the audience for a work, those who helped in its preparation, and permissions obtained for the use of copyrighted works. See also <u>copyrights</u> (Tab 5).

List of Abbreviations and Symbols.   When the report uses numerous <u>abbreviations</u> (Tab 12) and symbols that readers may not be able to interpret, the front matter may include a section that lists symbols and abbreviations with their meanings.

Body

The body is the section of the report that provides context for the report, describes in detail the methods and procedures used to generate the report, demonstrates how results were obtained, describes the results, draws conclusions, and, if appropriate, makes recommendations.

Executive Summary.   The body of the report begins with the <u>exec-utive summary</u>, which provides a more complete overview of the report than an abstract does. See an example on pages 189–90 and review the entry cross-referenced above.

Introduction.   The <u>introduction</u> (Tab 1) gives readers any general information—such as the report's purpose, scope, and context—necessary to understand the detailed information in the rest of the report (see pages 191–93).

Text.   The text of the body presents, as appropriate, the details of how the topic was investigated, how a problem was solved, what alternatives were explored, and how the best choice among them was selected. This information is enhanced by the use of visuals, tables, <u>headings</u>, and references that both clarify the text and persuade the reader. See also <u>persuasion</u> (Tab 1).

Conclusions.   The <u>conclusions</u> (Tab 1) section pulls together the results of the research and interprets the findings of the report, as shown on pages 199–200.

Recommendations.   Recommendations, which are sometimes combined with the conclusions, state what course of action should be taken based on the earlier arguments and conclusions of the study, as are shown on pages 199–200.

Explanatory Notes.   Occasionally, reports contain notes that amplify terms or points that might otherwise interrupt the text of the report. Such notes may be included as footnotes on the page where the term or point appears, or they may appear in a "Notes" section at the end of the report.

References (or Works Cited).   A list of references or works cited appears in a separate section if the report refers to or quotes directly from research sources. If your employer has a preferred reference style, follow it; otherwise, use one of the guidelines provided in the entry <u>documenting sources</u> (Tab 5). For a relatively short report, place a reference or works-cited section at the end of the body of the report, as shown on page 201. For a report with a number of sections or chapters, place a reference or works-cited section at the end of each major section or chapter. In either case, begin the reference or works-cited section on a new page. If a particular reference appears in more than one section or chapter, repeat it in full in each appropriate reference section.

❖ ETHICS NOTE Always identify the sources of any facts, ideas, <u>quotations</u> (Tab 5), and paraphrases you include in a report. Even if unintentional, <u>plagiarism</u> (Tab 5) is unethical and may result in formal academic misconduct charges in a college course. On the job, it can result in legal action or even dismissal. Repurposed in-house material ("boilerplate") may not require a citation—see <u>repurposing</u> (Tab 2). ❖

Back Matter

The back matter of a formal report contains supplementary material, such as where to find additional information about the topic (bibliography), and expands on certain subjects (appendixes). Other back-matter elements define special terms (glossary) and provide information on how to easily locate information in the report (index). For very large formal reports, back-matter sections may be individually numbered or labeled (Appendix A, Appendix B).

Appendixes.   An <u>appendix</u> clarifies or supplements the report with information that is too detailed or lengthy for the primary audience but is relevant to secondary audiences.

Bibliography.   A <u>bibliography</u> (Tab 5) lists alphabetically all the sources that were consulted to prepare the report—not just those cited in the report—and suggests additional resources that readers might want to consult.

Glossary.   A <u>glossary</u> is an alphabetical list of specialized terms used in the report and their definitions.

Index.   An index is an alphabetical list of all the major topics and subtopics discussed in the report. It cites the page numbers where discussion of each topic can be found and allows readers to find information on topics quickly and easily. The index is always the final section of a report.

DIGITAL TIP

Creating an Index

Most word-processing programs can save you time by creating an index automatically based on keywords that you mark while composing the report.

Sample Formal Report

Figure 6–2 shows the typical sections of a formal report. Keep in mind that the number and arrangement of the elements vary, depending on the context, especially on requirements of an organization or a client.

CGF Aircraft Corporation *CGF*

MEMO

To: Members of the Ethics and Business Conduct
          Committee
From: Susan Litzinger, Director of Ethics and Business
          Conduct
Date: March 6, 2017   *SL*
Subject: Reported Ethics Cases, 2016

Enclosed is "Reported Ethics Cases: Annual Report, 2016."
This report, required by CGF Policy CGF-EP-01, contains a   Identifies
review of the ethics cases handled by CGF ethics officers and   topic
managers during 2016, the first year of our Ethics Program.

The ethics cases reported are analyzed according to two
categories: (1) major ethics cases, or those potentially involving
serious violations of company policy or illegal conduct, and   Briefly
(2) minor ethics cases, or those that do not involve serious   summarizes
policy violations or illegal conduct. The report also examines   content
the mode of contact in all of the reported cases and the
disposition of the substantiated major ethics cases.

I hope that this report will provide the Committee with the
information needed to assess the effectiveness of the first year
of CGF's Ethics Program and to plan for the coming year.   Offers
Please let me know if you have any questions about this report   contact
or if you need any further information. I may be reached at   information
(555) 211-2121 and at sl@cgf.com.

                                                                    Enclosure
Enc.   notation

FIGURE 6–2. Formal Report (*continued*) (Cover Memo)

Full title

REPORTED ETHICS CASES
Annual Report, 2016

**Author's
name and
job title**

Prepared by Susan Litzinger
Director of Ethics and Business Conduct

Report Distributed March 6, 2017

**Company
name**

Prepared for
The Ethics and Business Conduct Committee
CGF Aircraft Corporation

**No page
number**

FIGURE 6–2. Formal Report (*continued*) (Title Page)

Reported Ethics Cases—2016

ABSTRACT

This report examines the nature and disposition of 3,458 ethics cases handled companywide by CGF Aircraft Corporation's ethics officers and managers during 2016. The purpose of this annual report is to provide the Ethics and Business Conduct Committee with the information necessary for assessing the effectiveness of the Ethics Program's first year of operation. Records maintained by ethics officers and managers of all contacts were compiled and categorized into two main types: (1) major ethics cases, or cases involving serious violations of company policies or illegal conduct, and (2) minor ethics cases, or cases not involving serious policy violations or illegal conduct. This report provides examples of the types of cases handled in each category and analyzes the disposition of 30 substantiated major ethics cases. Recommendations for planning for the second year of the Ethics Program are (1) continuing the channels of communication now available in the Ethics Program, (2) increasing financial and technical support for the Ethics Hotline, (3) disseminating the annual ethics report in some form to employees to ensure employee awareness of the company's commitment to uphold its Ethics Policies and Procedures, and (4) implementing some measure of recognition for ethical behavior to promote and reward ethical conduct.

Adapted from MLA style to fit context

Summarizes purpose

Methods and scope

Conclusions and recommendations

6

Formal Reports

Lowercase Roman numerals used on front-matter pages

iii

FIGURE 6-2. Formal Report (*continued*) (Abstract)

Uniform
heading
styles

Reported Ethics Cases — 2016

CONTENTS

Indented
subheads

Page
number
for each
entry

iv

FIGURE 6–2. Formal Report (*continued*) (Table of Contents)

Reported Ethics Cases—2016

EXECUTIVE SUMMARY

This report examines the nature and disposition of the 3,458 ethics cases handled by the CGF Aircraft Corporation's ethics officers and managers during 2016. The purpose of this report is to provide CGF's Ethics and Business Conduct Committee with the information necessary for assessing the effectiveness of the first year of the company's Ethics Program.

States purpose

Effective January 1, 2016, the Ethics and Business Conduct Committee (the Committee) implemented a policy and procedures for the administration of CGF's new Ethics Program. The purpose of the Ethics Program, established by the Committee, is to "promote ethical business conduct through open communication and compliance with company ethics standards." The Office of Ethics and Business Conduct was created to administer the Ethics Program. The director of the Office of Ethics and Business Conduct, along with seven ethics officers throughout the corporation, was given the responsibility for the following objectives:

Provides background information

- Communicate the values and standards for CGF's Ethics Program to employees.

- Inform employees about company policies regarding ethical business conduct.

- Establish companywide channels for employees to obtain information and guidance in resolving ethics concerns.

- Implement companywide ethics-awareness and education programs.

Employee accessibility to ethics information and guidance was available through managers, ethics officers, and an ethics hotline.

Major ethics cases were defined as those situations potentially involving serious violations of company policies or illegal conduct. Examples of major ethics cases included cover-up of defective workmanship or use of defective parts in products; discrimination in hiring and promotion; involvement in monetary or other kickbacks; sexual harassment; disclosure of proprietary or company information; theft; and use of corporate Internet resources for inappropriate purposes, such as conducting personal business, gambling, or access to pornography.

Describes scope

1

FIGURE 6–2. Formal Report (*continued*) (Executive Summary)

6

Formal Reports

Reported Ethics Cases—2016

Minor ethics cases were defined as including all reported
concerns not classified as major ethics cases. Minor ethics
cases were classified as informational queries from employees,
situations involving coworkers, and situations involving
management.

**Summarizes
conclusions**

The effectiveness of CGF's Ethics Program during the first
year of implementation is most evidenced by (1) the active
participation of employees in the program and the 3,458
contacts employees made regarding ethics concerns through
the various channels available to them and (2) the action taken
in the cases reported by employees, particularly the disposition
of the 30 substantiated major ethics cases. Disseminating
information about the disposition of ethics cases, particularly
information about the severe disciplinary actions taken in
major ethics violations, sends a message to employees that
unethical or illegal conduct will not be tolerated.

**Includes
recommen-
dations**

Based on these conclusions, recommendations for planning
the second year of the Ethics Program are (1) continuing the
channels of communication now available in the Ethics
Program, (2) increasing financial and technical support for the
Ethics Hotline, the most highly used mode of contact in the
ethics cases reported in 2016, (3) disseminating this report in
some form to employees to ensure their awareness of CGF's
commitment to uphold its Ethics Policies and Procedures, and
(4) implementing some measure of recognition for ethical
behavior, such as an "Ethics Employee of the Month" award to
promote and reward ethical conduct.

**Executive
summary
is about 10
percent of
report length**

2

FIGURE 6-2. Formal Report (Executive Summary) (*continued*)

Reported Ethics Cases — 2016

INTRODUCTION

This report examines the nature and disposition of the 3,458 ethics cases handled companywide by CGF's ethics officers and managers during 2016. The purpose of this report is to provide the Ethics and Business Conduct Committee with the information necessary for assessing the effectiveness of the first year of CGF's Ethics Program. Recommendations are given for the Committee's consideration in planning for the second year of the Ethics Program.

Opening states purpose

Ethics and Business Conduct Policies and Procedures
Effective January 1, 2016, the Ethics and Business Conduct Committee (the Committee) implemented Policy CGF-EP-01 and Procedure CGF-EP-02 for the administration of CGF's new Ethics Program. The purpose of the Ethics Program, established by the Committee, is to "promote ethical business conduct through open communication and compliance with company ethics standards" (CGF, "Ethics and Conduct").

Subheads signal shifts in topic

The Office of Ethics and Business Conduct was created to administer the Ethics Program. The director of the Office of Ethics and Business Conduct, along with seven ethics officers throughout CGF, was given the responsibility for the following objectives:

- Communicate the values, standards, and goals of CGF's Ethics Program to employees.

- Inform employees about company ethics policies.

- Provide companywide channels for employee education and guidance in resolving ethics concerns.

- Implement companywide programs in ethics awareness, education, and recognition.

- Ensure confidentiality in all ethics matters.

List identifies key points

Employee accessibility to ethics information and guidance became the immediate and key goal of the Office of Ethics and Business Conduct in its first year of operation. The following channels for contact were set in motion during 2016:

3

6

Formal Reports

FIGURE 6–2. Formal Report (*continued*) (Introduction)

Reported Ethics Cases—2016

- Managers throughout CGF received intensive ethics training; in all ethics situations, employees were encouraged to go to their managers as the first point of contact.

- Ethics officers were available directly to employees through face-to-face or telephone contact, to managers, to callers using the Ethics Hotline, and by e-mail.

- The Ethics Hotline was available to all employees, 24 hours a day, seven days a week, to anonymously report ethics concerns.

Confidentiality Issues
CGF's Ethics Policy ensures confidentiality and anonymity for employees who raise genuine ethics concerns. Procedure CGF-EP-02 guarantees appropriate discipline, up to and including dismissal, for retaliation or retribution against any employee who properly reports any genuine ethics concern.

Documentation of Ethics Cases
The following requirements were established by the director of the Office of Ethics and Business Conduct as uniform guidelines for the documentation by managers and ethics officers of all reported ethics cases:

- Name, position, and department of individual initiating contact, if available

- Date and time of contact

Includes
detailed
methods

- Name, position, and department of contact person

- Category of ethics case

- Mode of contact

- Resolution

Managers and ethics officers entered the required information in each reported ethics case into an ACCESS database file, enabling efficient retrieval and analysis of the data.

4

FIGURE 6–2. Formal Report (Introduction) (*continued*)

Reported Ethics Cases—2016

Major/Minor Category Definition and Examples
Major ethics cases were defined as those situations potentially
involving serious violations of company policies or illegal
conduct. Procedure CGF-EP-02 requires notification of the
Internal Audit and the Law departments in serious ethics cases.
The staffs of the Internal Audit and the Law departments
assume primary responsibility for managing major ethics cases
and for working with the employees, ethics officers, and
managers involved in each case.

Examples of situations categorized as major ethics cases:

- Cover-up of defective workmanship or use of defective
  parts in products

- Discrimination in hiring and promotion

- Involvement in monetary or other kickbacks from
  customers for preferred orders

- Sexual harassment

- Disclosure of proprietary customer or company
  information

- Theft

- Use of corporate Internet resources for inappropriate
  purposes, such as conducting private business, gambling,
  or gaining access to pornography

Minor ethics cases were defined as including all reported
concerns not classified as major ethics cases. Minor ethics
cases were classified as follows:

- Informational queries from employees

- Situations involving coworkers

- Situations involving management

Organized by
decreasing
order of
importance

6

Formal Reports

5

FIGURE 6–2. Formal Report (Introduction) (*continued*)

Reported Ethics Cases — 2016

ANALYSIS OF REPORTED ETHICS CASES

Reported Ethics Cases, by Major/Minor Category

Text introduces figure

CGF ethics officers and managers companywide handled a total of 3,458 ethics situations during 2016. Of these cases, only 172, or 5 percent, involved reported concerns of a serious enough nature to be classified as major ethics cases (see Fig. 1). Major ethics cases were defined as those situations potentially involving serious violations of company policy or illegal conduct.

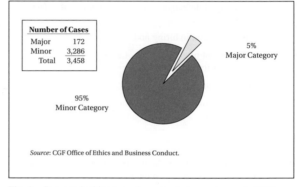

Number of Cases	
Major	172
Minor	3,286
Total	3,458

5%
Major Category

95%
Minor Category

Source: CGF Office of Ethics and Business Conduct.

Number and title identify figure

Fig. 1.   Reported ethics cases by major/minor category in 2016.

Major Ethics Cases

Of the 172 major ethics cases reported during 2016, 57 percent, upon investigation, were found to involve unsubstantiated concerns. Incomplete information or misinformation most frequently was discovered to be the cause of the unfounded concerns of misconduct in 98 cases. Forty-four cases, or 26 percent of the total cases reported, involved incidents partly substantiated by ethics officers as serious misconduct;

6

FIGURE 6–2. Formal Report (*continued*) (Body Text)

Reported Ethics Cases — 2016

however, these cases were discovered to also involve inaccurate information or unfounded issues of misconduct.

Only 17 percent of the total number of major ethics cases, or 30 cases, were substantiated as major ethics situations involving serious ethical misconduct or illegal conduct (CGF, "2016 Ethics Hotline Results") (see Fig. 2).

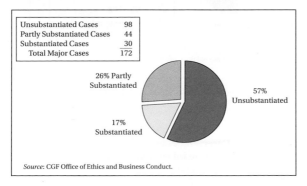

Unsubstantiated Cases	98
Partly Substantiated Cases	44
Substantiated Cases	30
Total Major Cases	172

26% Partly Substantiated

57% Unsubstantiated

17% Substantiated

Source: CGF Office of Ethics and Business Conduct.

Fig. 2.   Major ethics cases in 2016.

Of the 30 substantiated major ethics cases, seven remain under investigation at this time, and two cases are currently in litigation. Disposition of the remainder of the 30 substantiated reported ethics cases included severe disciplinary action in five cases: the dismissal of two employees and the demotion of three employees. Seven employees were given written warnings, and nine employees received verbal warnings (see Fig. 3).

Identifies source of information

6

Formal Reports

7

FIGURE 6–2. Formal Report (Body Text) (*continued*)

Reported Ethics Cases — 2016

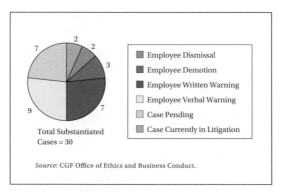

Total Substantiated
Cases = 30

Source: CGF Office of Ethics and Business Conduct.

Fig. 3.   Disposition of substantiated major ethics cases in 2016.

Minor Ethics Cases

Minor ethics cases included those that did not involve serious
violations of company policy or illegal conduct. During 2016,
ethics officers and company managers handled 3,286 such
cases. Minor ethics cases were further classified as follows:

Presents
findings
in detail

- Informational queries from employees

- Situations involving coworkers

- Situations involving management

As might be expected during the initial year of the Ethics
Program implementation, the majority of contacts made by
employees were informational, involving questions about the
new policies and procedures. These informational contacts
comprised 65 percent of all contacts of a minor nature and
numbered 2,148. Employees made 989 contacts regarding
ethics concerns involving coworkers and 149 contacts
regarding ethics concerns involving management (see
Fig. 4).

8

FIGURE 6-2. Formal Report (Body Text) (*continued*)

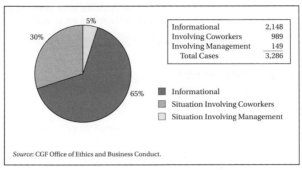

Reported Ethics Cases — 2016

Informational	2,148
Involving Coworkers	989
Involving Management	149
Total Cases	3,286

■ Informational
▨ Situation Involving Coworkers
□ Situation Involving Management

Source: CGF Office of Ethics and Business Conduct.

Fig. 4.   Minor ethics cases in 2016.

Mode of Contact
The effectiveness of the Ethics Program rested on the dissemination of information to employees and the provision of accessible channels through which employees could gain information, report concerns, and obtain guidance. Employees were encouraged to first go to their managers with any ethical concerns, because those managers would have the most direct knowledge of the immediate circumstances and individuals involved.

Assesses findings

Other channels were put into operation, however, for any instance in which an employee did not feel able to go to his or her manager. The ethics officers companywide were available to employees through telephone conversations, face-to-face meetings, and e-mail contact. Ethics officers also served as contact points for managers in need of support and assistance in handling the ethics concerns reported to them by their subordinates.

The Ethics Hotline became operational in mid-January 2016 and offered employees assurance of anonymity and confidentiality. The Ethics Hotline was accessible to all employees on a 24-hour, 7-day basis. Ethics officers companywide took responsibility on a rotational basis for handling calls reported through the hotline.

9

6

Formal Reports

FIGURE 6–2. Formal Report (Body Text) (*continued*)

Reported Ethics Cases—2016

In summary, ethics information and guidance were available to all employees during 2016 through the following channels:

- Employee to manager
- Employee telephone, face-to-face, and e-mail contact with ethics officer
- Manager to ethics officer
- Employee Hotline

The mode of contact in the 3,458 reported ethics cases was as follows (see Fig. 5):

- In 19 percent of the reported cases, or 657, employees went to managers with concerns.
- In 9 percent of the reported cases, or 311, employees contacted an ethics officer.
- In 5 percent of the reported cases, or 173, managers sought assistance from ethics officers.
- In 67 percent of the reported cases, or 2,317, contacts were made through the Ethics Hotline.

Bulleted lists help organize and summarize information

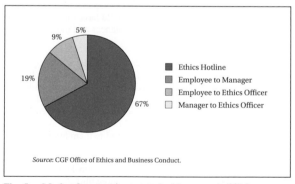

Source: CGF Office of Ethics and Business Conduct.

Fig. 5.   Mode of contact in reported ethics cases in 2016.

10

FIGURE 6-2. Formal Report (Body Text) (*continued*)

Reported Ethics Cases—2016

CONCLUSIONS AND RECOMMENDATIONS

The effectiveness of CGF's Ethics Program during the first year of implementation is most evidenced by (1) the active participation of employees in the program and the 3,458 contacts employees made regarding ethics concerns through the various channels available to them, and (2) the action taken in the cases reported by employees, particularly the disposition of the 30 substantiated major ethics cases.

Pulls together findings

One of the 12 steps to building a successful Ethics Program identified by Frank Navran in *Workforce* magazine is an ethics communication strategy. Navran explains that such a strategy is crucial in ensuring

Uses sources for support

> that employees have the information they need in a timely and usable fashion and that the organization is encouraging employee communication regarding the values, standards and the conduct of the organization and its members. (119)

The 3,458 contacts by employees during 2016 attest to the accessibility and effectiveness of the communication channels that exist in CGF's Ethics Program.

An equally important step in building a successful ethics program is listed by Navran as "Measurements and Rewards," which he explains as follows:

> In most organizations, employees know what's important by virtue of what the organization measures and rewards. If ethical conduct is assessed and rewarded, and if unethical conduct is identified and dissuaded, employees will believe that the organization's principals mean it when they say the values and code of ethics are important. (121)

Long quotation in MLA style

Disseminating information about the disposition of ethics cases, particularly information about the severe disciplinary actions taken in major ethics violations, sends a message to employees that unethical or illegal conduct will not be tolerated. Making public such actions taken in cases of ethical misconduct provides "a golden opportunity to make other employees aware that the behavior is unacceptable and why" (Ferrell, Fraedrich, and Ferrell 129).

Interprets findings

11

6

Formal Reports

FIGURE 6-2. Formal Report (*continued*) (Conclusions and Recommendations)

Reported Ethics Cases—2016

With these two points in mind, I offer the following recommendations for consideration for plans for the Ethics Program's second year:

- Maintain the channels of communication now available in the Ethics Program

Recommends specific steps

- Increase financial and technical support for the Ethics Hotline, the most highly used mode of contact in the reported ethics cases in 2016

- Disseminate this report in some form to employees to ensure employees' awareness of CGF's commitment to uphold its Ethics Policy and Procedures

- Implement some measure of recognition for ethical behavior, such as an "Ethics Employee of the Month," to promote and reward ethical conduct

To ensure that employees see the value of their continued participation in the Ethics Program, feedback is essential. The information in this annual review, in some form, should be provided to employees. Knowing that the concerns they reported were taken seriously and resulted in appropriate action by Ethics Program administrators would reinforce employee involvement in the program.

Although the negative consequences of ethical misconduct contained in this report send a powerful message, a means of communicating the *positive* rewards of ethical conduct at CGF should be implemented. Various options for recognition of employees exemplifying ethical conduct should be considered and approved. See MLogs, "Create and Evaluate a Code of Conduct," *Business Ethics Forum*. Management Logs, September 12, 2009.

Links recommendations to company goal

Continuation of the Ethics Program's successful 2016 operations, with the implementation of the above recommendations, should ensure the continued pursuit of the Ethics Program's purpose: "to promote a positive work environment that encourages open communication regarding ethics and compliance issues and concerns."

12

FIGURE 6–2. Formal Report (Conclusions and Recommendations) (*continued*)

Header provides report title

REFERENCES

CGF. (2014). Ethical business conduct program. Retrieved from CGF.com/About CGF

References listing follows APA format

Ferrell, O. C., & Gardiner, G. (2001). *In pursuit of ethics: Tough choices in the world of work.* Springfield, IL: Smith Collins.

Kelley, T. (2011, February 8). Corporate prophets, Charting a course to ethical profits. *New York Times*, p. BU 12.

Navran, F. (2010, September). 12 steps to building a best-practices ethics program. *Workforce*, 117–122.

6

Formal Reports

Footer provides page number

FIGURE 6–2. Formal Report (*continued*) (References)

DIGITAL TIP

Creating Styles and Templates

You can use a word-processing program to create time-saving templates that automate the design of text elements such as headings, paragraphs, lists, and visuals throughout an individual report or multiple reports. Once you specify your styles, save the template and use it each time you create a report. Keep in mind that many organizations may already provide such templates for reports, so check before you create your own.

glossaries

A glossary is an alphabetical list of definitions of specialized terms used in a <u>formal report</u>, a manual, or other long document. You may want to include a glossary if some readers in your <u>audience</u> (Tab 1) are not familiar with specialized or technical terms you use.

Keep glossary entries concise and be sure they are written in language that all your readers can understand.

▶ **Amortize:** To write off an expenditure by prorating it over a specific period of time.

Arrange the terms alphabetically, with each entry beginning on a new line. The definitions then follow the terms, dictionary style. In a formal report, the glossary begins on a new page and appears after the appendix(es) and bibliography.

Including a glossary does not relieve you of the responsibility of <u>defining terms</u> (Tab 1) that your reader will not know when those terms are first mentioned in the text.

tables of contents

A table of contents lists all the major sections of a long document or Web site in their order of appearance. Tables of contents allow <u>readers</u> (Tab 1) to locate specific information quickly and easily by referencing section page numbers in printed documents or portable document format (PDF) files or by clicking hyperlinks in Web content.

When creating a table of contents, use the major <u>headings</u> (Tab 7) and subheadings of your document exactly as they appear in the text, as shown in the entry <u>formal reports</u>. (See the table of contents in Figure 6–2 and related Digital Tip on page 176.) In print documents, the table of contents is placed in the front matter following the title page and <u>abstract</u>, and it precedes the list of tables or figures, the foreword, and the preface. On large or complex Web sites, the table of contents typically appears at the top of the first page.

6

Formal Reports

Design and Visuals

Preview

This section includes entries related to the physical appearance of a document, as discussed in **layout and design**, and entries concerning specific types of **visuals**, such as **drawings**, **flowcharts**, **graphs**, and **tables**. The section also covers design elements within documents, such as bulleted **lists** and headers and footers (page 224). For a quick overview of using and integrating workplace visuals into documents, see the "Chart for Choosing Appropriate Visuals" (page 233). To create effective documents and visuals, begin with the basic *design principles* discussed on page 221. By understanding these principles, you can make the best use of the abundant tools, programs, and applications that help with creating professional flowcharts, drawings, and various graphics.

7

Design and Visuals

drawings

A drawing can depict an object's appearance and illustrate the steps in procedures or instructions. It can emphasize the significant parts or functions of a device or product, omit what is not significant, and focus on details or relationships that a photograph cannot reveal. Think about your need for drawings during your <u>preparation</u> (Tab 1) and <u>research</u> (Tab 5). Include the drawings in your outline, indicating approximately where each should be placed ("drawing of . . ." enclosed in brackets). For advice on integrating drawings into your text, see <u>outlining</u> (Tab 1) and <u>visuals</u>.

Consider your medium, as well as your purpose and audience, when choosing the type of drawing to include. For example, publishing to an online digital format (such as a Web page) could allow you to include a line drawing that can be enlarged, automatically breaking into labeled cutaway parts. See also <u>selecting the medium</u> (Tab 2).

The types of drawings discussed in this entry are conventional line drawings and cutaway drawings. A conventional line drawing is appropriate if your <u>audience</u> (Tab 1) needs an overview of a series of steps or an understanding of an object's appearance or construction, as in Figure 7–1. A cutaway drawing, like the one in Figure 7–2, can be useful when you need to show the internal parts of a device or structure and illustrate their relationship to the whole.

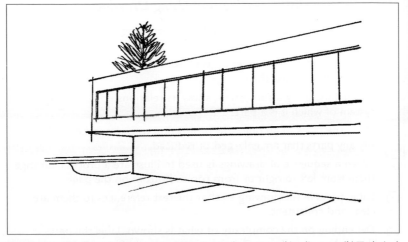

FIGURE 7–1. Conventional Line Drawing. *Source:* http://en.wikipedia.org/wiki/Technical_drawing#mediaviewerFile:Architekturskizze_Verwaltungsgeb%C3%A4ude_Biel.jpg.

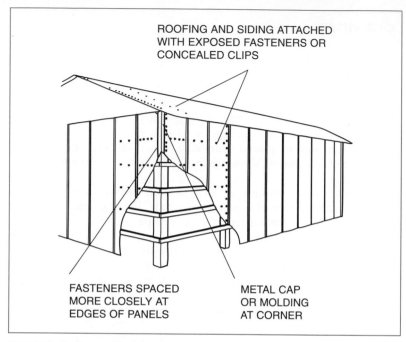

ROOFING AND SIDING ATTACHED
WITH EXPOSED FASTENERS OR
CONCEALED CLIPS

FASTENERS SPACED
MORE CLOSELY AT
EDGES OF PANELS

METAL CAP
OR MOLDING
AT CORNER

FIGURE 7–2. Cutaway Drawing

7

Design and Visuals

Writer's Checklist: Creating and Using Drawings

☑ Seek the help of graphics specialists for drawings that require a high degree of accuracy and precision.

☑ Show equipment and other objects from the point of view of the person who will use them.

☑ When illustrating a subsystem, show its relationship to the larger system of which it is a part.

☑ Draw the parts of an object in proportion to one another and identify any parts that are enlarged or reduced.

☑ When a sequence of drawings is used to illustrate a process, arrange them from left to right or from top to bottom on the page.

☑ Label parts in the drawing so that the text references to them are clear and consistent.

☑ Depending on the complexity of what is shown, label the parts themselves, as in Figure 7–2, or use a key, as in Figure 7–13 on page 216.

❖ ETHICS NOTE Do not use drawings from the Web or other copyrighted sources without proper documentation; if you intend to publish your work, seek permission from the copyright holder. See also <u>copyright</u> (Tab 5), <u>documenting sources</u> (Tab 5), and <u>plagiarism</u> (Tab 5). ❖

flowcharts

A flowchart is a diagram using symbols, words, or pictures to show the stages of a process in sequence from beginning to end. A flowchart provides an overview of a process and allows the reader to identify its essential steps quickly and easily. Flowcharts can take several forms. The steps might be represented by labeled blocks, as shown in Figure 7–3; pictorial symbols, as shown in Figure 7–4; or ISO (International Organization for Standardization) symbols, as shown in Figure 7–5. Useful tools for constructing flowcharts include Microsoft PowerPoint, Visio, SmartDraw, and LucidCharts.

Writer's Checklist: Creating Flowcharts

☑ Label each step in the process or identify each step with labeled blocks, pictorial representations, or standardized symbols.

☑ Follow the standard flow directions: left to right and top to bottom. Indicate any nonstandard flow directions with arrows.

☑ Include a key (or callouts) to define symbols your audience may not understand.

☑ Use standardized symbols for flowcharts that document computer programs and other information-processing procedures, as detailed in *Information Processing — Documentation Symbols and Conventions for Data, Program and System Flowcharts, Program Network Charts, and System Resources Charts*, ISO 5807-1985 (E) (publication available at *www.iso.org*).

For advice on integrating flowcharts into your text, see <u>visuals</u>. See also <u>global graphics</u>.

FIGURE 7–3. Flowchart Using Labeled Blocks

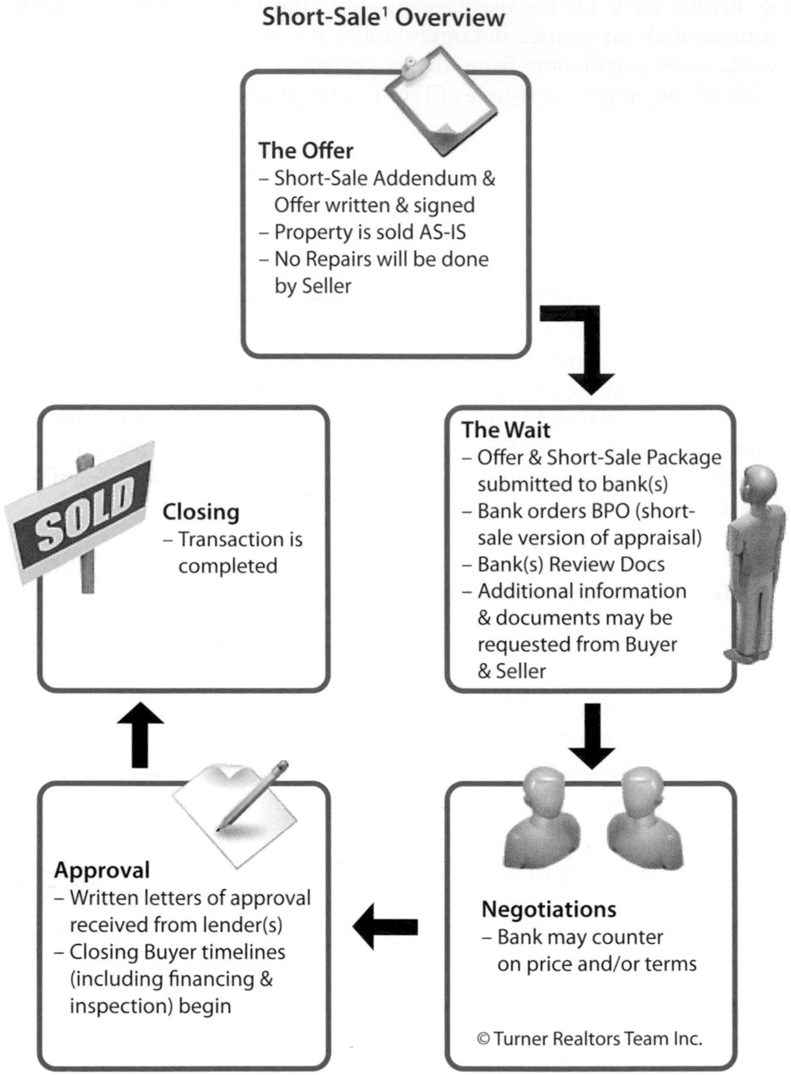

Short-Sale[1] Overview

The Offer
- Short-Sale Addendum &
  Offer written & signed
- Property is sold AS-IS
- No Repairs will be done
  by Seller

The Wait
- Offer & Short-Sale Package
  submitted to bank(s)
- Bank orders BPO (short-
  sale version of appraisal)
- Bank(s) Review Docs
- Additional information
  & documents may be
  requested from Buyer
  & Seller

Closing
- Transaction is
  completed

SOLD

Approval
- Written letters of approval
  received from lender(s)
- Closing Buyer timelines
  (including financing &
  inspection) begin

Negotiations
- Bank may counter
  on price and/or terms

© Turner Realtors Team Inc.

[1] A "short sale" refers to the sale of real estate on which money is owed
(e.g., a mortgage) by a seller with a documented financial hardship even
when the sale price will not pay off the mortgage or other debt.

FIGURE 7–4. Flowchart Using Pictorial Symbols. *Source:* http://portlandrealestateblog
.com/realestate/2011/05/short-sale-flow-chart-for-sellers/

7

Design and Visuals

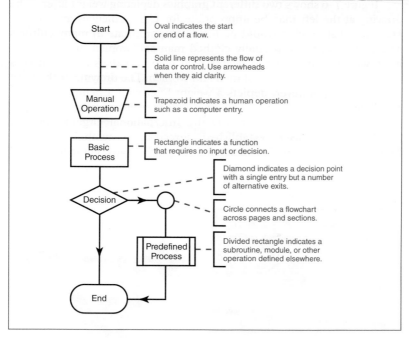

FIGURE 7–5. Common ISO Flowchart Symbols (with Annotations)

global graphics

In a global business and technology environment, <u>graphs</u> and other <u>visuals</u> require the same careful attention given to other aspects of <u>global communication</u> (Tab 1). The complex cultural connotations of visuals challenge writers to think beyond their own experience when they are aiming for audiences outside their own culture.

Symbols, images, and even colors are not free from cultural associations—they depend on <u>context</u> (Tab 1), and context is culturally determined. For instance, in North America, a red cross is commonly used as a symbol for first aid or a hospital. In Muslim countries, however, a cross (red or otherwise) represents Christianity, whereas a crescent (usually green) signifies first aid or a hospital. A manual for use in Honduras could indicate "caution" by using a picture of a person touching a finger below the eye. In France, however, that gesture means "You can't fool me."

Figure 7–6 shows two different graphics depicting weight lifters. The drawing at the left may be appropriate for U.S. audiences and others. However, that graphic would be highly inappropriate in many cultures where the image of a partially clothed man and woman in close proximity would be contrary to deeply held cultural beliefs and even laws about the public depiction of men and women. The drawing at the right in Figure 7–6, however, depicts a weight lifter with a neutral icon that avoids the connotations associated with more realistic images of people.

These examples suggest why the International Organization for Standardization (ISO) established agreed-upon symbols, such as those shown in Figure 7–7, designed for public signs, guidebooks, and manuals.*

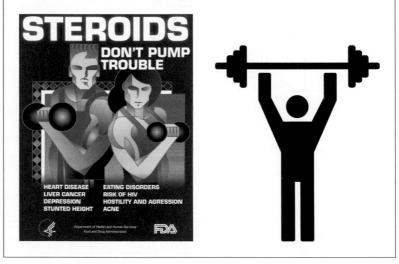

FIGURE 7–6. Graphics for U.S. (left) and Global (right) Audiences

FIGURE 7–7. International Organization for Standardization (ISO) Symbols

*Learn more through the useful illustrations in "The International Language of ISO Graphical Symbols" at www.iso.org/iso/graphical-symbols_booklet.pdf.

Writer's Checklist: Using Appropriate Global Graphics

☑ Consult with an expert or test your use of graphics with individuals from your intended audience's country who understand the effect that visuals may have on an <u>audience</u> (Tab 1). See also <u>presentations</u> (Tab 8).

☑ Organize visual information for the intended audience. Some culture groups read visuals from left to right in clockwise rotation; others read visuals from right to left in counterclockwise rotation.

☑ Be sure that your graphics have no unintended political or religious implications.

☑ Carefully consider how you depict people in visuals — body exposure, positions, and clothing (see Figure 7–6).

☑ Use outlines or neutral abstractions to represent human beings. Consider stick figures as in Figure 7–7.

☑ Choose neutral colors (or those you know are appropriate) or grayscale, which carries no connotation, for your graphics. In some cultures, red symbolizes good fortune or joy; in others, red indicates danger.

☑ Check your use of punctuation marks, which are as language specific as symbols. For example, in North America, the question mark generally represents the need for information or help. In many countries, that symbol has no meaning at all.

☑ Create simple visuals with universal shapes, as illustrated in Figure 7–7.

☑ Explain the meaning of icons or symbols that cannot be changed, such as a company logo.

graphs

A graph presents numerical or quantitative data in visual form and offers several advantages over presenting data within the text or in <u>tables</u>. Trends, movements, distributions, comparisons, and cycles are more readily apparent in graphs than they are in tables. However, although graphs present data in a more comprehensible form than tables do, they are less precise. For that reason, some <u>audiences</u> (Tab 1) may need graphs to be accompanied by tables that give exact data. The types of graphs described in this entry include line graphs, bar graphs, pie graphs, and picture graphs. For advice on integrating graphs within text, see <u>visuals</u>; for information about using presentation graphics, see <u>presentations</u> (Tab 8).

Line Graphs

A line graph shows the relationship between two variables or sets of numbers by plotting points in relation to two axes drawn at right angles (Figure 7–8). The vertical axis usually represents amounts, and the

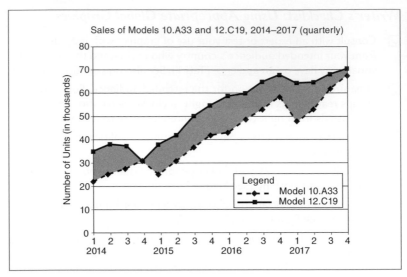

FIGURE 7–8. Double-Line Graph (with Shading)

horizontal axis usually represents increments of time. Line graphs that portray more than one set of variables (double-line graphs) allow for comparisons between two sets of data for the same period of time. You can emphasize the difference between the two lines by shading the space between them, as shown in Figure 7–8.

❖ ETHICS NOTE Be especially careful to proportion the vertical and horizontal scales so that they present the data precisely and free of visual distortion. To do otherwise is not only inaccurate but potentially unethical. (See ethics in writing, Tab 1.) In Figure 7–9, the graph at the left gives the appearance of a slight decline followed by a steady increase in investment returns because the scale is compressed, with some of the years selectively omitted. The graph on the right represents the trend more accurately because the years are evenly distributed without omissions. ❖

Bar Graphs

Bar graphs consist of horizontal or vertical bars of equal width, scaled in length to represent some quantity. They are commonly used to show (1) quantities of the same item at different times, (2) quantities of different items at the same time, and (3) quantities of the different parts of an item that make up a whole (in which case, the segments of the bar graph must total 100 percent). The horizontal bar graph in Figure 7–10 shows the quantities of different items for the same period of time.

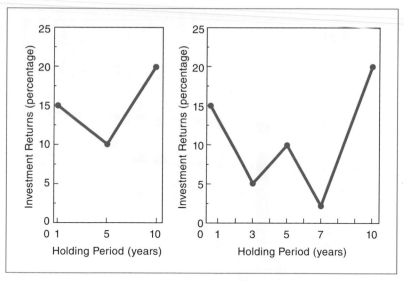

FIGURE 7–9. Distorted (left) and Distortion-Free (right) Expressions of Data

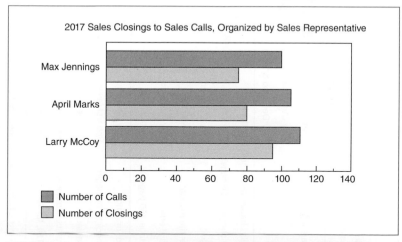

FIGURE 7–10. Bar Graph (Quantities of Different Items During a Fixed Period)

7

Design and Visuals

A Gantt chart is a type of horizontal bar graph designed to plan and track the status of projects from beginning to end. As shown in Figure 7–11, the horizontal axis represents the length of a project divided into time increments—days, weeks, or months. The timeline usually runs across the top of the chart. The vertical axis represents

7

Design and Visuals

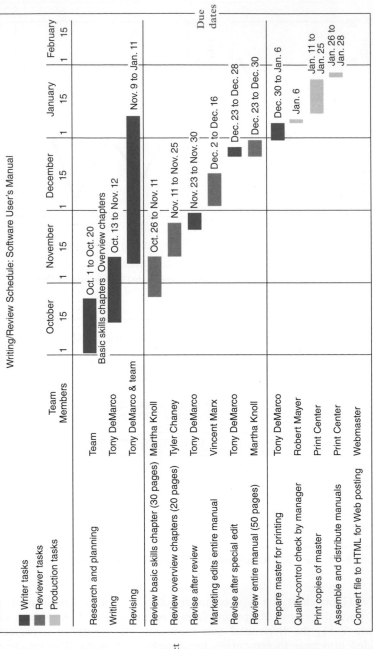

FIGURE 7–11. Gantt Chart Showing Project Schedule

the individual tasks that make up the project and can include a second column listing the staff responsible for each task. The horizontal bars in the body of the chart identify each task and show its beginning and end dates. Gantt charts are often prepared with spreadsheet or project-management software. See also <u>collaborative writing</u> (Tab 1).

Pie Graphs

A pie graph presents data as wedge-shaped sections of a circle. The circle equals 100 percent, or the whole, of some quantity, and the wedges represent how the whole is divided. Figure 7–12 shows wedge-shaped sections that represent percentages of "Your Municipal Tax Dollar." Pie graphs provide a quicker way of presenting information that can be shown in a table; in fact, a table with a more-detailed breakdown of the same information often accompanies a pie graph.

Picture Graphs

Picture graphs are modified bar graphs that use pictorial symbols of the item portrayed. Each symbol corresponds to a specified quantity of the item, as shown in Figure 7–13. Note that, for precision and clarity, the picture graph includes the total quantity following the symbols.

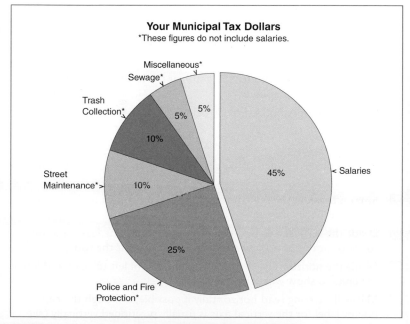

FIGURE 7–12. Pie Graph (Showing Percentages of the Whole)

7

Design and Visuals

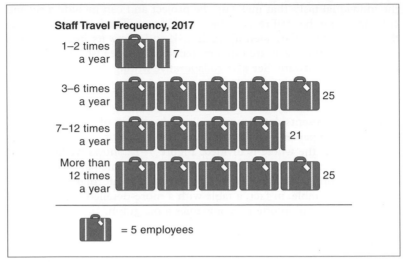

FIGURE 7–13. Picture Graph

Writer's Checklist: Creating Graphs

FOR ALL GRAPHS

☑ Give your graph a descriptive title that is accurate and concise.

☑ Use, as needed, a key or legend that lists and defines symbols (see Figure 7–8).

☑ Include a source line under the graph at the lower left when you use data from another source.

☑ Place explanatory notes directly below the figure caption or label (see Figure 7–12).

FOR LINE GRAPHS

☑ Indicate the zero point of the graph (the point where the two axes intersect).

☑ Insert a break in the scale if the range of data shown makes it inconvenient to begin at zero.

☑ Divide the vertical axis into equal portions, from the least amount (or zero) at the bottom to the greatest amount at the top.

☑ Divide the horizontal axis into equal units from left to right and label the units to show what they represent.

☑ Make all lettering read horizontally if possible, although the caption or label for the vertical axis is usually positioned vertically (see Figure 7–8).

7

Design and Visuals

Writer's Checklist: Creating Graphs (continued)

FOR BAR GRAPHS

☑ Differentiate among the types of data each bar or part of a bar represents by color, shading, or crosshatching.

☑ Avoid three-dimensional graphs when they make bars seem larger than the amounts they represent.

FOR PIE GRAPHS

☑ Make sure that the complete circle is equivalent to 100 percent.

☑ Sequence the wedges clockwise from largest to smallest, beginning at the 12 o'clock position, whenever possible.

☑ Limit the number of items in the pie graph to avoid clutter and to ensure that the wedges are thick enough to be clear. (Some software allows users to open and examine wedges in greater detail.)

☑ Give each wedge a distinctive color, pattern, shade, or texture.

☑ Label each wedge with its percentage value and keep all callouts (labels that identify the wedges) horizontal.

☑ Detach a wedge as shown in Figure 7-12, if you wish to draw attention to a particular segment of the pie graph.

FOR PICTURE GRAPHS

☑ Use picture graphs to add general interest to presentations and documents.

☑ Choose symbols that are easily recognizable. See also **global graphics**.

☑ Let each symbol represent the same number of units.

☑ Indicate larger quantities by using more symbols, instead of larger symbols, because relative sizes are difficult to judge accurately.

☑ Indicate the total quantity following the symbols, as shown in Figure 7-13.

☑ Indicate the zero point of the graph when appropriate.

7

Design and Visuals

headings

Headings (also called *heads*) are titles or subtitles that highlight the main topics and signal topic changes within the body of a document, whether an e-mail, a memo, a report, or a Web page. (See also **writing for the Web**, Tab 2.) Headings help readers find and divide the material into comprehensible segments. Some documents, such as formal reports and proposals, may need several levels of headings

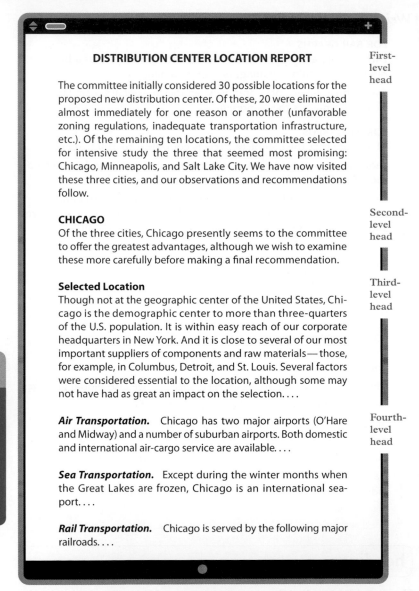

FIGURE 7–14. Headings Used in a Document

(as shown in Figure 7–14) to indicate major divisions, subdivisions, and even smaller units. If possible, avoid using more than four levels of headings. See also <u>layout and design</u>.

Headings typically represent the major topics of a document. In a short document, you can use the major divisions of your outline as headings; in a longer document, you may need to use both major and minor divisions.

No one format for headings is correct. Often an organization settles on a standard format, which everyone in that organization follows. Sometimes a client for whom a report or proposal is being prepared requires a particular format. In the absence of specific guidelines, follow the system illustrated in Figure 7–14. For an example of the decimal system of headings, see <u>outlining</u> (Tab 1).

Writer's Checklist: Using Headings

☑ Use headings to signal a new topic. Use a lower-level heading to indicate a new subtopic within the larger topic.

☑ Make headings concise but specific enough to be informative, as in Figure 7–14.

☑ Avoid too many or too few headings or levels of headings; too many clutter a document, and too few fail to provide recognizable structure.

☑ Ensure that headings at the same level are of relatively equal importance and have **parallel structure** (Tab 10).

☑ Subdivide sections only as needed; when you do, try to subdivide them into at least two lower-level headings.

☑ Do not allow a heading to substitute for discussion; the text should read as if the heading were not there.

☑ Do not leave a heading as the final line of a page. If two lines of text cannot fit below a heading, start the section at the top of the next page.

infographics

Infographics are visual forms of communication that make complex information understandable by combining text, numbers, icons, <u>graphs</u>, <u>flowcharts</u>, <u>drawings</u>, and other <u>visuals</u> into a unified whole, as shown in Figure 7–15. They are often used to educate wide audiences and can be especially useful for <u>instructions</u> and <u>presentations</u>. Infographics might be used to show an overview of a process (how to take out a personal loan), a natural phenomenon (the evolution of an animal species), an accident (the anatomy of a train wreck), or a project plan (public transportation options in a city and projected passenger usage). Each of these subjects might prove difficult to illustrate concisely with text or with images alone. See also <u>tables</u>.

Infographics can be static, noninteractive visuals intended for public display, print publication, or high-resolution online download. They

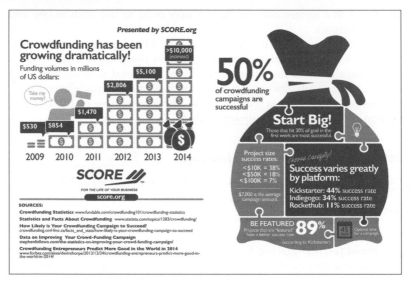

FIGURE 7–15. Infographic Describing a Process. *Source:* www.score.org/resources /infographic-crowd-funding.

can also take digital, interactive forms, including such tools as mouse-over pop-ups that reveal additional details or animated elements that showcase multiple cause-and-effect scenarios.

They are frequently created by graphic designers who collaborate with subject-area experts on the content. However, professionals without a formal design background can also create infographics for the workplace using a range of free online tools. Search for "tools for creating infographics" or visit such sites as piktochart.com, infogr.am, and creately.com. See the *Writer's Checklist: Creating Infographics.*

Note the infographic in Figure 7–15 depicting how crowdfunding for small businesses in the United States has grown recently. It combines explanatory text, typographic devices, images, and data, all organized into a unified overview of this growing trend. It also cites the source information for the infographic and identifies its designers. This process could have been described in a text-dense article, but its impact and explanatory power in the graph are striking and memorable.

Writer's Checklist: Creating Infographics

☑ Use images appropriate to the topic, **purpose**, and **audience**.

☑ Select images (illustrations and icons), where possible, that are self-explanatory.

Writer's Checklist: Creating Infographics (continued)

- ☑ Arrange text and images in the appropriate sequence to illustrate a process.
- ☑ Do not use dated or obsolete images or icons (rotary telephones, modems).
- ☑ Use culturally neutral images for international audiences (see global graphics).
- ☑ Use design elements—logo, typeface, colors—consistent with your organization's branding practices.
- ☑ Ensure that all types of data, graphics, and illustrations are uniform in color and design (see layout and design).
- ☑ Check the text for conciseness (Tab 10), clarity (Tab 10), and accuracy.
- ☑ Cite your sources of information appropriately (see plagiarism, Tab 5).

layout and design

Thoughtful layout and design of a document can make even the most complex information accessible and give readers a favorable impression of the writer and the organization. To accomplish those goals, a design should help readers find information easily; offer a simple and uncluttered presentation; and highlight structure, hierarchy, and order. The design must also fit the purpose (Tab 1) of the document and its context (Tab 1). For example, clients paying a high price for consulting services might expect a more-sophisticated, polished design, while employees aware of pressing deadlines and budgets are likely to accept—or even expect—a standard, functional design for internal documents.

Design Principles

Readers are quick to make inferences based on the pattern, form, and organization of document elements. When creating documents and visuals, use those instincts to your advantage by keeping in mind three major principles of design: grouping, contrast, and repetition.

Grouping.   Grouping helps readers see relationships among items on a page or screen, which in turn helps them grasp how information is organized and what is most important. Grouping can occur in several different ways.

- *Proximity.* Items that are close together seem like part of a group, while items that are far apart seem dissimilar. Related items (for example, a heading and the paragraph that follows it) should be closer together than less closely related items (a heading and the paragraph above the heading).

- *Similarity.* Items that share qualities (such as size, shape, color) are viewed as similar and tend to be associated as part of a group.
- *Alignment.* Items that are aligned tend to be seen as part of a group. If the items in a bulleted list are aligned with one another and indented from the rest of the text, for example, readers immediately recognize them as related.

Contrast.   Contrast sets items apart and helps readers quickly grasp which items are different from one another. For example, to emphasize one data bar in a graph, you might give it a different color or pattern from the other bars. To give readers an easy way to navigate a long document, you might contrast the headings from the body text by making them larger or a different color from the surrounding text.

Repetition.   Repetition communicates consistency and predictability through repeated patterns of design elements, whether on a page, screen, or visual. Inconsistencies in these patterns are confusing and distracting. If like items on a page (headings, footers, bulleted lists) vary slightly from one another in their design, readers do not know whether the items are supposed to be a related group. Consistency ensures that the patterns in a document or visual are clear and unambiguous. Repetition thus allows the users of a document to focus on the things they should pay attention to (the things that you, as the author, want them to pay attention to) instead of spending time trying to interpret the design.

Typography

Typography refers to the style and arrangement of type on a page. A complete set of all the letters, numbers, and symbols available in one typeface (or style) is called a *font*. The letters in a typeface have a number of distinctive characteristics, as shown in Figure 7–16.

Typeface and Type Size.   For most on-the-job writing, select a typeface primarily for its legibility. Avoid typefaces that make text difficult to read or that may distract readers. Instead, choose popular typefaces with which readers are familiar, such as Times New Roman or Arial. Avoid using more than two typefaces in the text of a document. For certain documents, however, such as newsletters, you may wish to use distinctively different typefaces for contrast among various elements such as headlines, headings, inset quotations (Tab 5), and sidebars. Experiment before making final decisions, keeping in mind your audience (Tab 1).

One way typefaces are characterized is by the presence or absence of serifs. Serif typefaces have projections, as shown in Figure 7–16; sans

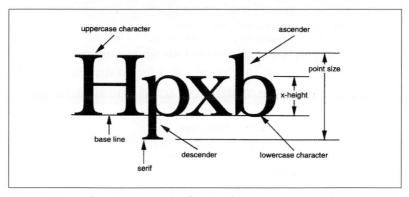

FIGURE 7–16. Primary Components of Letter Characters

serif styles do not. (*Sans* is French for "without.") The text of this book is set in Plantin, a serif typeface. Although sans serif type has a clean and uncluttered look, serif type is easier to read in print, especially in the smaller sizes. Sans serif, however, works well for headings (like the entry titles in this book) and for Web sites and documents read on-screen.

Ideal font sizes for the main text of paper documents range from 10 to 12 points.* However, for some elements or documents, you may wish to select typeface sizes that are smaller (as in footnotes) or larger (as in headlines for brochures). See Figure 7–17 for a comparison of type sizes in a serif typeface.

Your readers and the distance from which they will read a document should help determine type size. For example, instructions that will rest on a table at which the reader stands require a larger typeface than a document that will be read up close. For <u>presentations</u> (Tab 8) and <u>writing for the Web</u> (Tab 2), preview your document to see the effectiveness of your choice of point sizes and typefaces.

Type Style and Emphasis.   One method of achieving emphasis through typography is to use capital or "uppercase" letters. HOWEVER, LONG STRETCHES OF ALL UPPERCASE LETTERS ARE DIFFICULT TO READ. (See also <u>e-mail</u>, Tab 2.) Use all uppercase letters only in short spans, such as in headings. Likewise, use italics sparingly because *continuous italic type reduces legibility and thus slows readers.* Of course, italics are useful if your aim is to slow readers, as in cautions and warnings. Highlighting in color may be useful to call attention to small sections or words in a document. **Boldface**, used in moderation, may be the best cuing device because it is visually different yet retains the customary shapes of letters and numbers.

*A point is a unit of type size equal to 0.01384 inch, or approximately ¹⁄₇₂ of an inch.

6 pt. This size might be used for dating a source.
8 pt. This size might be used for footnotes.
10 pt. This size might be used for figure captions.
12 pt. This size might be used for main text.
14 pt. This size might be used for headings.

FIGURE 7–17. Type Sizes (6- to 14-Point Type)

Page-Design Elements

Thoughtfully used design elements can provide not only emphasis but also visual logic within a document by highlighting organization. The following typical elements can be used to make your document accessible and effective: justification, headings, headers and footers, lists, columns, white space, and color. Some of these elements are illustrated in the formal report (Tab 6) on pages 185–201.

Justification.   Left-justified (ragged-right) margins are generally easier to read than full-justified margins, especially for text using wide margins on 8½ × 11" pages. Left justification is also better if full justification causes your word-processing or document software to insert irregular spaces between words, producing unwanted white space or unevenness in blocks of text. Full-justified text is more appropriate for publications aimed at a broad audience that expects a more-formal, polished appearance. Full justification is also useful with narrow, multiple-column formats because the spaces between the columns (called *alleys*) need the definition that full justification provides. The body text of this book is full-justified.

Headings.   Headings reveal the organization of a document and help readers decide which sections they need to read. Provide typographic contrast between headings and the body text with either a different typeface or a different style (**bold**, *italic*, CAPS, and so on). Headings are often effective in boldface or in a sans serif typeface that contrasts with a body text in a serif typeface.

Headers and Footers.   A header in a report, letter, or other document appears at the top of each page (as in this book), and a footer appears at the bottom of each page. Document pages may have headers or footers (or both) that include such elements as the topic or subtopic of a section, the date the document was written, the page number, and the document name. Keep your headers and footers concise because too much information in them can create visual clutter. However—at a minimum—a multipage document should include the page number in a header or footer. For headers used in letters and memos, see correspondence (Tab 3).

Lists.   Vertically stacked words, phrases, and other items with numbers or bullets can effectively highlight such information as steps in sequence, materials or parts needed, key or concluding points, and recommendations. For further detail, see lists.

Columns.   As you design pages, consider how columns may improve the readability of your document. A single-column format works well with larger typefaces, double-spacing, and left-justified margins. For smaller typefaces and single-spaced lines, the two-column structure keeps text columns narrow enough so that readers need not scan back and forth across the width of the entire page for every line. Using columns with different formats or sizes can separate main text from secondary material. Avoid a single word or line carried over to the top of the next column or page; likewise, avoid opening a paragraph or stranding a word at the end of a column or page.

White Space.   The area on a page or screen that is free of text or design elements is called "white space." It is an important element of design because it visually frames text and other elements, and breaks pages into manageable chunks. For example, white space between paragraphs or sections can serve as a visual cue to signal the ending or beginning of a topic or section.

Color.   Color and screening (shaded areas on a page) can distinguish one part of a document from another or unify a series of documents. They can set off sections within a document, highlight examples, or emphasize warnings. In tables, screening can highlight column titles or sets of data to which you want to draw the reader's attention.

Visuals

Readers notice visuals before they notice text, and they notice larger visuals before they notice smaller ones. Thus, the size of an illustration suggests its relative importance. For newsletter articles and publications aimed at wide audiences, consider especially the proportion of the visual to the text. Magazine designers have traditionally used the three-fifths rule: Page layout is more dramatic and appealing when the major element (photograph, drawing, or other visual) occupies three-fifths rather than one-half of the available space.

Visuals can be gathered in one place (for example, at the end of a report), but placing them in the text closer to their accompanying explanations makes them more effective. Illustrations in the text also provide visual relief. For advice on the placement of visuals, see the *Writer's Checklist: Creating and Integrating Visuals* (page 235).

Icons.   Icons are simplified pictorial or symbolic representations that are used online as links to programs (as in apps), commands, or files. In a printed document, icons can indicate a recurring feature or quality, such as a special cross-reference. Icons must be simple and easily recognized without accompanying text. For example, on the Web, national flags might symbolize different language versions of a document. For advice on using icons that are culturally appropriate, see <u>global graphics</u>.

Captions.   Captions are titles that highlight or describe visuals. Captions often appear below figures and above tables; they may be aligned with the visual to the left or they may be centered.

Rules.   Rules are vertical or horizontal lines used to enclose material in a box or to divide one area of the page from another. For example, rules and boxes set off visuals from surrounding explanations or highlight warning statements from the steps in instructions.

Page Layout and Thumbnails

Page layout involves combining typography, design elements, and visuals on a page to make a coherent whole. The flexibility of your design is affected by your design software, your method of printing the document, your budget, and whether your employer or client requires you to use a template.

Before you spend time positioning actual text and visuals on a page, especially for visually complex documents such as brochures, you may want to create a thumbnail sketch, in which blocks of simulated text and visuals indicate the placement of elements. You can go further by roughly assembling all the thumbnail pages to show the size, shape, form, and general style of a large document. Such a mock-up, called a *dummy*, allows you to see how a finished printed document will look.

7

Design and Visuals

lists

Vertically stacked lists of words, phrases, and other items are often highlighted with bullets, numbers, or letters to set them apart from surrounding text. Lists can save readers time by allowing them to see at a glance specific items or key points. They also help readers by breaking up complex statements and by focusing on such information as steps in a sequence, materials or parts needed, questions or concluding points, and recommendations, as shown in Figure 7–18.

> Before we agree to hold the regional sales conference at the Brent Hotel, we need to make sure the hotel can provide the following resources:
>
> - Business center with state-of-the-art digital and printing services
> - Main exhibit area that can accommodate thirty 8-foot-by-15-foot booths
> - Eight meeting rooms, each with a podium or table and seating for 25 people
> - Wi-Fi Internet access and digital projection in each room
> - Ballroom dining facilities for 250 people with a dais for four speakers
>
> To confirm that the Brent Hotel is our best choice, we should tour the facilities during our stay in Kansas City.

FIGURE 7–18. Bulleted List in a Paragraph

As Figure 7–18 also shows, you should provide <u>context</u> (Tab 1) for a list with an introductory sentence followed by a colon (or no punctuation for an incomplete sentence). Ensure <u>coherence</u> (Tab 10) by following the list with some reference to the list or to the statement that introduced it.

Writer's Checklist: Using Lists

Follow the practices of your organization or use these guidelines for consistency and formatting.

CONSISTENCY

- ☑ Do not overuse lists or create extended lists in documents or in **presentation** (Tab 8) slides.
- ☑ List only comparable items, such as tasks or equipment, that are balanced in importance (as in Figure 7–18).
- ☑ Begin each listed item in the same way—whether with nouns, verbs, or other parts of speech—and maintain **parallel structure** (Tab 10) throughout.
- ☑ List bulleted items in a logical order, keeping your **audience** (Tab 1) and **purpose** (Tab 1) in mind. See also **organization** (Tab 1).

(continued)

7

Design and Visuals

Writer's Checklist: Using Lists (continued)

FORMATTING

☑ Capitalize the first word in each listed item, unless doing so is visually awkward.

☑ Use periods or other ending punctuation when the listed items are complete sentences.

☑ Avoid commas or semicolons following items and do not use the conjunction *and* before the last item in a list.

☑ Use numbers to indicate sequence or rank.

☑ Follow each number with a period and start the item with a capital letter.

☑ Use bullets (round, square, arrow) when you do not wish to indicate rank or sequence.

☑ When lists need subdivisions, use letters with numbers (see <u>outlining</u>, Tab 1).

organizational charts

An organizational chart shows how the various divisions or units of an organization are related to one another. This type of <u>visual</u> is useful when you want to give readers an overview of an organization or to display the lines of authority within it, as in Figure 7–19.

The title of each organizational component (office, section, division) is placed in a separate box. The boxes are then linked to a central authority. If readers need the information, include the name of the person and position title in each box.

spreadsheets

A spreadsheet is an interactive computer application for the organization, analysis, and storage of data in tabular form. (See also <u>tables</u>.) A typical spreadsheet in Microsoft Excel contains columns, rows, and cells, as shown in Figure 7–20. The columns from left to right across the top of a spreadsheet are labeled with letters (A, B, C, and so on), and the rows at the far left of a spreadsheet are sequenced from top to bottom numerically (1, 2, 3, and so on). A cell is the point at which one column and one row meet, so it can be identified to match the column and the number in the row (A1, B2, and so on). The data in

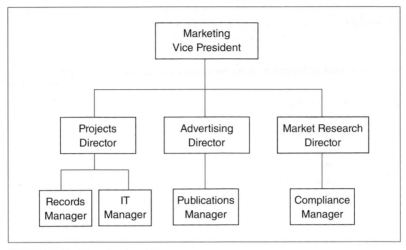

FIGURE 7-19. Organizational Chart

	A	B	C	D	E	F	G
1	Date	Company	State	Name	E-Mail	Source	Units
2	10/21/16	Company 1	NH	Allyson	Allyson@company1.com	Google search	100
3	10/21/16	Company 2	MA	John	John@company2.com	Referral from HR	250
4	10/22/16	Company 3	RI	Akram	Akram@company3.com	Met at convention	700
5	10/23/16	Company 4	CA	Hilary	Hilary@company4.com	Google search	430
6	10/24/16	Company 5	ME	Ming	Ming@company5.com	Contacted me	150
7	10/25/16	Company 6	MD	Sonia	Sonia@company6.com	Met at convention	75
8	10/25/16	Company 7	PA	Toby	Toby@company7.com	Contacted me	380
9						TOTAL	2085

FIGURE 7-20. Spreadsheet

7

Design and Visuals

the columns and rows can be sorted (as in A–Z or Z–A), manipulated with various mathematical operations, and formatted or printed as in a word-processing program.

Spreadsheet programs like Excel offer a wide variety of functions, options, and variations; therefore, you should make use of the tutorials built into the program for learning spreadsheet capabilities. Many colleges offer continuing education courses in the use of spreadsheets, and workplaces often provide courses or experts within the organization to help employees. The Web offers many videos and tutorials, but the Microsoft Office Web site for Excel is a useful starting point to connect with experts and other users via live chat and blogs (*https://products.office.com/en-us/excel*). Spreadsheets, or sections from them, can be printed and integrated into <u>reports</u> (Tab 4) and other documents, as described in <u>visuals</u>. See also <u>graphs</u>.

tables

A table organizes numerical and verbal data, such as statistics, into parallel rows and columns that allow readers to make precise item-to-item comparisons. Overall data trends, however, are more easily conveyed in <u>graphs</u> and other <u>visuals</u>.

Table Elements

Tables typically include the elements shown in Figure 7–21.

Table Number. Table numbers should be placed above tables and assigned sequentially throughout the document.

Table Title. The title (or caption), which is normally placed just above the table, should describe concisely what the table represents.

Box Head. The box head contains the column headings, which should be brief but descriptive. Units of measurement should be either specified as part of the heading or enclosed in parentheses beneath it. Standard abbreviations and symbols are acceptable. Avoid vertical or diagonal lettering.

Stub. The stub, the left vertical column of a table, lists the items about which information is given in the body of the table.

Body. The body comprises the data below the column headings and to the right of the stub. Within the body, arrange columns so that

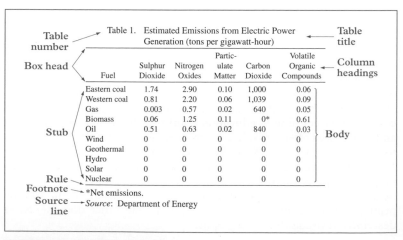

Table 1.   Estimated Emissions from Electric Power Generation (tons per gigawatt-hour)

Fuel	Sulphur Dioxide	Nitrogen Oxides	Particulate Matter	Carbon Dioxide	Volatile Organic Compounds
Eastern coal	1.74	2.90	0.10	1,000	0.06
Western coal	0.81	2.20	0.06	1,039	0.09
Gas	0.003	0.57	0.02	640	0.05
Biomass	0.06	1.25	0.11	0*	0.61
Oil	0.51	0.63	0.02	840	0.03
Wind	0	0	0	0	0
Geothermal	0	0	0	0	0
Hydro	0	0	0	0	0
Solar	0	0	0	0	0
Nuclear	0	0	0	0	0

*Net emissions.

Source: Department of Energy

Labels in figure: Table number, Box head, Stub, Rule, Footnote, Source line, Table title, Column headings, Body

FIGURE 7–21. Elements of a Table

Design and Visuals — 7

the items to be compared appear in adjacent rows and columns. Align the numerical data in columns for ease of comparison, as shown in Figure 7–21. Where no information exists for a specific item, substitute a row of dots or a dash to acknowledge the gap.

Rules.   Rules are the lines (or *borders*) that separate the table into its various parts. Tables should include top and bottom borders. Tables often include right and left borders, although they may be open at the sides, as shown in Figure 7–21. Generally, include a horizontal rule between the column headings and the body of the table. Separate the columns with vertical rules within a table only when they aid clarity.

Footnotes.   Footnotes are used for explanations of individual items in the table. Symbols (such as * and †) or lowercase letters (sometimes in parentheses) rather than numbers are ordinarily used to indicate table footnotes. Otherwise, numbers might be mistaken for numerical data or could be confused with the numbering system for text footnotes. See also <u>documenting sources</u> (Tab 5).

Source Line.   The source line identifies where the data originated. When a source line is appropriate, it appears below the table. Many organizations place the source line below the footnotes. See also <u>copyright</u> (Tab 5) and <u>plagiarism</u> (Tab 5).

Continuing Tables.   When a table must be divided so that it can be continued on another page, repeat the column headings and the table number and title on the new page with a "*continued*" label (for example, "Table 3. [title], *continued*").

Informal Tables

To list relatively few items that would be easier for the reader to grasp in tabular form than in running text, you can use an informal table, as long as you introduce it properly, as shown in Figure 7–22. Although informal tables do not need titles or table numbers to identify them, they do require column headings that accurately describe the information listed.

Dear Customer:
To order replacement parts, use the following part numbers and prices:

Part	*Part Number*	*Price ($)*
Diverter valve	2-912	12.50
Gasket kit	2-776	0.95
Adapter	3-212	0.90

FIGURE 7–22. Informal Table

7

Design and Visuals

visuals

Visuals can express ideas or convey information in ways that words alone cannot by making abstract concepts and relationships concrete. Visuals can show how things look (drawings, photographs, maps), represent numbers and quantities (graphs, tables), depict processes or relationships (flowcharts, Gantt charts), and show hierarchical relationships (organizational charts). They also highlight important information and emphasize key concepts succinctly and clearly.

Many of the qualities of good writing—simplicity, clarity, conciseness, directness—are equally important when creating and using visuals. Presented with clarity and consistency, visuals can help readers focus on key portions of your document, presentation, or Web site. Be aware, though, that even the best visual will not be effective without context (Tab 1)—and most often context is provided by the text that introduces the visual and clarifies its purpose.

The following entries in this book are related to specific visuals and their use in printed and online documents, as well as in presentation software (see page 252).

drawings 205
flowcharts 207
formal reports (Tab 6) 180
global graphics 209
graphs 211

layout and design 221
organizational charts 228
spreadsheets 228
tables 230
writing for the Web (Tab 2) 65

Selecting Visuals

Consider your audience (Tab 1) and your purpose (Tab 1) carefully in selecting visuals. You would need different illustrations for an automobile owner's manual or an auto dealer's Web site, for example, than you would for a technician's diagnostic guide. Figure 7–23 can help you select the most appropriate visuals, based on their purposes and special features. Jot down visual options when you are considering your scope (Tab 1) and organization (Tab 1).

❖ ETHICS NOTE Visuals have the potential of misleading readers when data are selectively omitted or distorted. For example, Figure 7–9 on page 213 shows a graph that gives a misleading impression of investment returns because the scale is compressed, with some years selectively omitted. Visuals that mislead readers call the credibility of you and your organization into question—and they are unethical. The use of misleading visuals can even subject you and your organization to lawsuits. ❖

7

Design and Visuals

Choosing Appropriate Visuals

TO SHOW OBJECTS AND SPATIAL RELATIONSHIPS

Drawings

FASTENERS SPACED
MORE CLOSELY AT
EDGES OF PANELS

METAL CAP
OR MOLDING
AT CORNER

- Depict real objects difficult to photograph
- Depict imaginary objects
- Highlight only parts viewers need to see
- Show internal parts of equipment in cutaway views
- Show how equipment parts fit together in exploded views
- Communicate to international audiences more effectively than text alone

Photographs

Monkey Business Images/
Shutterstock

- Show images of subjects
- Record an event in process
- Record the development of phenomena over time
- Record the as-found condition of a situation for an investigation
- Show the colors essential to the accuracy of information in medical, chemical, forensic, botanical, and other fields

TO DISPLAY GEOGRAPHIC INFORMATION

Maps

- Show specific geographic features of an area
- Show distance, routes, or locations of sites
- Show the geographic distribution of information (e.g., populations by region)

TO SHOW NUMERICAL AND OTHER RELATIONSHIPS

Tables

Divisions	Employees
Research	1,052
Marketing	2,782
Automotive	13,251
Consumer Products	2,227

- Organize information systematically in rows and columns
- Present large numerical quantities concisely
- Facilitate item-to-item comparisons
- Clarify trends and other graphical information with precise data
- Store, analyze, and manipulate data in rows, columns, and cells with a spreadsheet program

Bar & Column Graphs

- Depict data in vertical or horizontal bars and columns for comparison
- Show quantities that make up a whole
- Track status of projects from start to finish
- Visually represent data shown in tables

Line Graphs

- Show trends over time in amounts, sizes, rates, and other measurements
- Give an at-a-glance impression of trends, forecasts, and extrapolations of data
- Compare more than one kind of data over the same time period
- Visually represent data shown in tables

7

Design and Visuals

FIGURE 7–23. Chart for Choosing Appropriate Visuals (*continued*)

Picture Graphs

- Use recognizable images to represent specific quantities
- Help nonexpert readers grasp the information
- Visually represent data shown in tables

Pie Graphs

- Show quantities that make up a whole
- Give an immediate visual impression of the parts and their significance
- Visually represent data shown in tables or lists

TO SHOW STEPS IN A PROCESS OR RELATIONSHIPS IN A SYSTEM

Flowcharts

- Show how the parts or steps in a process or system interact
- Show the stages of an actual or a hypothetical process in the correct direction, including recursive steps

Schematic Diagrams

- Show how the components in electronic, chemical, electrical, and mechanical systems interact and are interrelated
- Use standardized symbolic representations rather than realistic depictions of system components

TO GIVE AN OVERVIEW OF A COMPLEX PROCESS OR EVENT

Infographics

- Integrate text, graphs, images, and numbers to "tell a story"
- Combine the communications advantages of text and graphics to give both an overview and a narrative explanation of a topic
- Organize disparate facts, concepts, images into an understandable whole

TO SHOW RELATIONSHIPS IN A HIERARCHY

Organizational Charts

- Give an overview of an organization's departmental components
- Show how the components relate to one another
- Depict lines of authority within an organization

TO SUPPLEMENT OR REPLACE WORDS

Symbols & Icons

- Convey ideas without words
- Save space and add visual appeal
- Transcend individual languages to communicate ideas effectively for international readers
- Communicate culturally neutral images

FIGURE 7–23. Chart for Choosing Appropriate Visuals (*continued*)

Integrating Visuals with Text

After selecting your visuals, carefully integrate them with your text. The following guidelines will improve the effectiveness of your visuals by describing how to position and identify them consistently and uniformly.

Begin by considering the best locations for visuals during the <u>outlining</u> (Tab 1) stage of your draft. At appropriate points in your outline, either make a rough sketch of the visual, if you can, or write "illustration of . . . ," noting the source of the visual and enclosing each suggestion in a text box. You may also include sketches of visuals in your thumbnail pages, as discussed in <u>layout and design</u>. When <u>writing a draft</u> (Tab 1), place visuals as close as possible to, but following, the text where they are discussed—in fact, no visual should precede its first text mention. Refer to graphics (such as drawings and photographs) as "figures" and to tables as "tables." Clarify for readers why each visual is included in the text. The amount of description you should provide will vary, depending on your readers' backgrounds. For example, non-experts may require lengthier explanations than experts need.

❖ ETHICS NOTE Obtain written permission to use copyrighted visuals in works that you intend to publish in print or on the Web—including images and multimedia material from Web sites. Acknowledge all quoted or borrowed material in a source line below the caption for a figure and in a footnote at the bottom of a table. Use a site's "Contact Us" page to request approval. Acknowledge your use of any material from the public domain (thus uncopyrighted), such as demographic or economic data from government publications and Web sites, with a source line. See also <u>copyright</u> (Tab 5), <u>documenting sources</u> (Tab 5), and <u>plagiarism</u> (Tab 5). ❖

7

Design and Visuals

Writer's Checklist: Creating and Integrating Visuals

CREATING VISUALS

☑ Keep visuals simple. Include only information needed for discussion in the text and eliminate unneeded labels, arrows, boxes, and lines.

☑ Position the lettering of any explanatory text or labels horizontally; allow adequate white space within and around the visual.

☑ Specify the units of measurement used, make sure relative sizes are clear, and indicate distance with a scale when appropriate.

☑ Use consistent terminology; for example, do not refer to the same information as a "proportion" in the text and a "percentage" in the visual.

(continued)

Writer's Checklist: Creating and Integrating Visuals (continued)

☑ Define **abbreviations** (Tab 12) the first time they appear in the text and in figures and tables. If any symbols are not self-explanatory, label them as in Figure 7–13 (page 216).

☑ Give each visual a caption or concise **title** (Tab 4) that clearly describes its content, and assign figure and table numbers if your document contains more than one illustration or table.

INTEGRATING VISUALS

☑ Clarify for readers why each visual is included in the text and provide an appropriate description.

☑ Place visuals as close as possible to the text where they are discussed but always after their first text mention.

☑ Allow adequate white space on the printed or Web page around and within each illustration.

☑ Refer to visuals in the text of your document as "figures" or "tables" and by their figure or table numbers.

☑ Consider placing lengthy or detailed visuals in an **appendix** (Tab 6), which you refer to in the body of your document.

☑ In documents with more than five illustrations or tables, include a section following the table of contents titled "List of Figures" or "List of Tables" that identifies each by number, title, and page number.

☑ Follow the editorial guidelines or recommended style manual when preparing visuals for a publication.

8

Presentations and Meetings

Preview

This section contains entries on **listening** and **presentations**, subjects essential to success in the workplace, as well as entries on conducting **meetings** and recording **minutes of meetings**. Because preparing an oral presentation is much like preparing to write, review Tab 1, "The Writing Process," noting in particular the entries **audience**, **context**, **organization**, and **purpose**.

8

Presentations and Meetings

listening

Effective listening enables the listener to understand the directions of an instructor, the message in a speaker's <u>presentation</u>, the goals of a manager, and the needs and wants of customers. Above all, it lays the foundation for productive communication.

Fallacies About Listening

Most people assume that because they can hear, they know how to listen. In fact, *hearing* is passive, whereas *listening* is active. Hearing voices in a crowd or a ringing telephone requires no analysis and no active involvement—we have no choice but to hear such sounds. Listening, however, requires actively focusing on a speaker, interpreting the message, and assessing its worth. Listening also requires that you consider the <u>context</u> (Tab 1) of messages and the differences in meaning that may be the result of differences in the speaker's and the listener's occupation, education, culture, sex, race, or other factors. See also <u>global communication</u> (Tab 1), <u>biased language</u> (Tab 10), <u>connotation</u> / <u>denotation</u> (Tab 10), and <u>English as a second language</u> (Tab 11).

Active Listening

To become an active listener, take the following steps:

Step 1: Make a Conscious Decision.   The first step to active listening is simply making up your mind to listen. Active listening requires a conscious effort, something that does not come naturally. The well-known precept offers good advice: "Seek first to understand and *then* to be understood."*

Step 2: Define Your Purpose.   Knowing why you are listening can go a long way toward managing the most common listening problems: drifting attention, formulating your response while the speaker is still talking, and interrupting the speaker. To help you define your purpose for listening, ask yourself these questions:

- What kind of information do I hope to get from this exchange, and how will I use it?
- What kind of message do I want to send while I am listening? (Do I want to portray understanding, determination, flexibility, competence, or patience?)

*Stephen R. Covey, *The 7 Habits of Highly Effective People: Powerful Lessons in Personal Change*, 15th ed. (New York: Free Press, 2004).

- What factors—boredom, daydreaming, anger, impatience—might interfere with listening during the interaction? How can I keep these factors from placing a barrier between the speaker and me?

Step 3: Take Specific Actions.   Becoming an active listener requires a willingness to become a responder rather than a reactor. A *reactor* simply says the first thing that comes to mind or draws a conclusion without checking to make sure that he or she accurately understands the message. In contrast, a *responder* waits to be certain that he or she understands the speaker's intended message before responding. Take the following actions to help you become a responder and not a reactor.

- Make a conscious effort to be impartial when evaluating a message. For example, do not dismiss a message because you dislike the speaker or are distracted by the speaker's appearance, mannerisms, or accent.
- Slow down the communication by asking for more information or by paraphrasing (Tab 5) the message received before you offer your thoughts. Paraphrasing lets the speaker know you are listening, gives the speaker an opportunity to clear up any misunderstanding, and keeps you focused.
- Listen with empathy by putting yourself in the speaker's position. When people feel they are being listened to empathetically, they tend to respond with appreciation and cooperation, thereby improving the communication.
- Take notes, when possible, to help you stay focused on what a speaker is saying. Note-taking (Tab 5) not only communicates your attentiveness to the speaker but also reinforces the message and helps you remember it.

Step 4: Adapt to the Situation.   The requirements of active listening differ from one situation to another. For example, when you are listening to a lecture, you may be listening only for specific information. However, if you are on a team project that depends on everyone's contribution, you need to listen at the highest level so that you can gather information as well as pick up on nuances the other speakers may be communicating. See also collaborative writing (Tab 1).

meetings

Meetings enable people to share information and collaborate more productively than exchanges of multiple messages or conversations allow. Like a presentation, a successful meeting requires planning and preparation. See also selecting the medium (Tab 2).

Planning a Meeting

Begin by determining the purpose of the meeting, deciding who should attend, and choosing the best time and place to hold it. Prepare an agenda for the meeting and determine who should take the minutes.

Determine the Purpose of the Meeting.   The first step in planning a meeting is to focus on the desired outcome by asking questions to help you determine the meeting's <u>purpose</u> (Tab 1): What should participants know, believe, do, or be able to do as a result of attending the meeting?

Once you have your desired outcome in focus, use the information to write a purpose statement for the meeting that answers the questions *what* and *why*.

▶ The purpose of this meeting is to gather ideas from the sales force [*what*] in order to create a successful sales campaign for our new Model PN-4 tablet computer [*why*].

Decide Who Should Attend.   Determine first the key people who need to attend the meeting. If a meeting must be held without some key participants, ask those people for their contributions prior to the meeting or invite them to participate by speakerphone, videoconference, or such remote methods as described in *Digital Tip: Conducting Online Meetings* (page 243).

DIGITAL TIP

Scheduling Meetings Online

If you are responsible for scheduling meetings, you can simplify the process by using the advanced features of your organization's calendar application or by using one of several free online scheduling tools.

Choose the Meeting Time.   Schedule a meeting for a time when all or most of the key people can be present. Consider as well other factors, such as time of day and length of the meeting, that can influence its outcome:

• Monday morning is often a time people use to prepare for the coming week's work.
• Friday afternoon is often when people focus on completing the current week's tasks.
• Long meetings may need to include breaks to allow participants to respond to messages and go to the restroom.

- Meetings held during the last 15 minutes of the day will be quick, but few people will remember what happened.
- Remote participants may need consideration for their time zones.

Choose the Meeting Location.   Having a meeting at your own location can give you an advantage: You feel more comfortable than your guests, who are new to the surroundings. Holding the meeting on someone else's premises, however, can signal cooperation. For balance, especially when people are meeting for the first time or are discussing sensitive issues, meet at a neutral site where no one gains an advantage and attendees may feel freer to participate.

Establish the Agenda.   A tool for focusing the group, the agenda is an outline of what the meeting will address. Figure 8–1 shows a typical agenda. Always prepare an agenda for a meeting, even if it is only an informal list of main topics. Ideally, the agenda should be distributed to attendees a day or two before the meeting. For a longer meeting in which participants are required to make a presentation, try to distribute the agenda a week or more in advance.

The agenda should list the attendees, the meeting time and place, and the topics you plan to discuss. If the meeting includes presentations, list the time allotted for each speaker. Finally, indicate an approximate length for the meeting so that participants can plan the rest of their day.

Sales Meeting Agenda

Purpose:	To get input for a sales campaign for the PN-4 Tablet
Date:	Wednesday, May 10, 2017
Place:	Conference Room E
Time:	9:30 a.m.–11:00 a.m.
Attendees:	Advertising Manager, Sales Manager and Reps, Customer Service Manager

Topic	Presenter	Time
PN-4 Tablet	Bob Arbuckle	9:30–9:45
The Campaign	Maria Lopez	9:45–10:00
The Sales Strategy	Mary Winifred	10:00–10:15
Discussion	Led by Dave Grimes	10:15–11:00

FIGURE 8–1. Meeting Agenda

DIGITAL TIP

Conducting Online Meetings

When participants cannot meet face to face, consider holding a video-conference. In such meetings, the participants use an application on their computers or mobile devices to connect with others running compatible applications. Many of these applications are free or inexpensive, but all participants will need high-speed Internet connections and webcams.

If the agenda is distributed in advance of the meeting, it should be accompanied by a memo or an e-mail informing people of the following:

- The purpose of the meeting
- The date and place of the meeting
- The meeting start and stop times
- The names of the people invited
- Instructions on how to prepare for the meeting

Figure 8–2 shows a cover message announcing a meeting with an attached agenda.

Assign the Minute-Taking.   Delegate the minute-taking to someone other than the leader. The minute-taker should record major decisions made and tasks assigned. To avoid misunderstandings, the minute-taker needs to record each assignment, the person responsible for it, and the date on which it is due. Determine as well if the minute-taker will need to follow any legal or organizational rules for recording the minutes. The minute-taker is responsible for distributing the minutes to everyone, including appropriate nonattendees. For a standing committee, it is best to rotate the responsibility of taking minutes. See also minutes of meetings and note-taking (Tab 5).

Conducting the Meeting

Assign someone to write on a board or project an image of information that needs to be viewed by everyone present.

During the meeting, keep to your agenda; however, create a productive environment by allowing room for differing views and fostering an environment in which participants listen respectfully to one another.

- Consider the feelings, thoughts, ideas, and needs of others—do not let your own agenda blind you to other points of view.
- Help other participants feel valued and respected by listening to them and responding to what they say.

8

Presentations and
Meetings

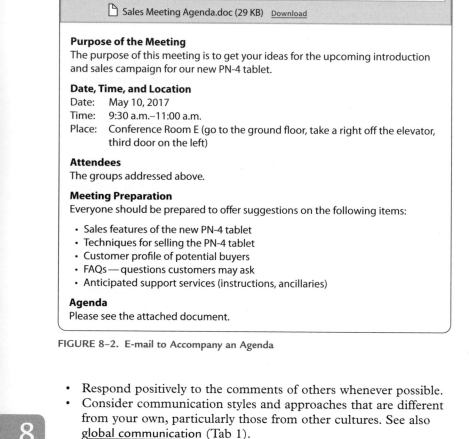

FIGURE 8–2. E-mail to Accompany an Agenda

- Respond positively to the comments of others whenever possible.
- Consider communication styles and approaches that are different from your own, particularly those from other cultures. See also <u>global communication</u> (Tab 1).

Deal with Conflict.   Despite your best efforts, conflict is inevitable. However, conflict is potentially valuable; when managed positively, it can stimulate creative thinking by challenging complacency and showing ways to achieve goals more efficiently or economically. See <u>collaborative writing</u> (Tab 1).

Members of any group are likely to vary in their personalities and attitudes, and you may encounter people who approach meetings differently. Consider the following tactics for the interruptive, negative, rambling, overly quiet, and territorial personality types.

- The *interruptive person* rarely lets anyone finish a sentence and may intimidate the group's quieter members. Tell that person in a firm but nonhostile tone to let the others finish in the interest of getting everyone's input. By addressing the issue directly, you signal to the group the importance of putting common goals first.
- The *negative person* has difficulty accepting change and often considers a new idea or project from a negative point of view. Such negativity, if left unchecked, can demoralize the group and suppress enthusiasm for new ideas. If the negative person brings up a valid point, however, ask for the group's suggestions to remedy the issue being raised. If the negative person's reactions are not valid or are outside the agenda, state the necessity of staying focused on the agenda and perhaps recommend a separate meeting to address those issues.
- The *rambling person* cannot collect his or her thoughts quickly enough to verbalize them succinctly. Restate or clarify this person's ideas. Try to strike a balance between providing your own interpretation and drawing out the person's intended meaning.
- The *overly quiet person* may be timid or may just be deep in thought. Ask for this person's ideas, being careful not to embarrass the person. In some cases, you can have a quiet person jot down his or her thoughts and give them to you later.
- The *territorial person* fiercely defends his or her group against real or perceived threats and may refuse to cooperate with members of other departments, companies, and so on. Point out that although such concerns may be valid, everyone is working toward the same overall goal and that goal should take precedence.

Close the Meeting. Just before closing the meeting, review all decisions and assignments. Paraphrase each to help the group focus on what individual participants have agreed to do and to ensure that the minutes will be complete and accurate. Now is the time to raise questions and clarify any misunderstandings. Set a date by which everyone at the meeting can expect to receive copies of the minutes. Finally, thank everyone for participating, and close the meeting on a positive note.

Writer's Checklist: Planning and Conducting Meetings

- ☑ Develop a purpose statement for the meeting to focus your planning.
- ☑ Invite only those essential to fulfilling the purpose of the meeting.
- ☑ Select a time and place convenient to all those attending.

(continued)

8

Presentations and Meetings

Writer's Checklist: Planning and Conducting Meetings (continued)

☑ Create an agenda and distribute it at least a day or two before the meeting.

☑ Assign someone to take meeting minutes.

☑ Ensure that the minutes record key decisions; assignments; due dates; and the date, time, and location of any follow-up meeting.

☑ Follow the agenda to keep everyone focused.

☑ Respect the views of others and how they are expressed.

☑ Use the strategies in this entry for handling conflict and attendees whose style of expression may prevent getting everyone's best thinking.

☑ Close the meeting by reviewing key decisions and assignments.

minutes of meetings

Organizations and committees refer to official records of their meetings as *minutes*. Because minutes are often used to record decisions and to settle disputes, they must be accurate, complete, and clear. When approved, minutes of meetings are official and can be used as evidence in legal proceedings. A section from the minutes of a meeting is shown in Figure 8–3.

Keep your minutes brief and to the point. Except for recording formally presented motions, which must be transcribed word for word, summarize what occurs and paraphrase discussions. To keep the minutes concise, follow a set format, and use headings for each major point discussed. See also note-taking (Tab 5).

Avoid abstractions and generalities; always be specific. Refer to everyone in the same way—a lack of consistency in titles or names may suggest deference to one person at the expense of another. Avoid adjectives and adverbs that suggest good or bad qualities, as in "Mr. Sturgess's *capable* assistant read the *comprehensive* report to the subcommittee." Minutes should be objective and impartial.

If a member of the committee is to follow up on something and report back to the committee at its next meeting, clearly state the person's name and the responsibility he or she has accepted.

NORTH TAMPA MEDICAL CENTER

Minutes of the Monthly Meeting
Medical Audit Committee

DATE: June 22, 2017

PRESENT: G. Miller (Chair), C. Bloom, J. Dades, K. Gilley,
D. Ingoglia (Secretary), S. Ramirez

ABSENT: D. Rowan, C. Tsien, C. Voronski, R. Fautier, R. Wolf

Dr. Gail Miller called the meeting to order at 12:45 p.m. Dr. David Ingoglia made a motion that the June 1, 2017, minutes be approved as distributed. The motion was seconded and passed.

The committee discussed and took action on the following topics.

(1) TOPIC: Meeting Time

Discussion: The most convenient time for the committee to meet.
Action taken: The committee decided to meet on the fourth Tuesday of every month at 12:30 p.m.

FIGURE 8-3. Meeting Minutes (Partial Section)

Writer's Checklist: Items Included in Minutes of Meetings

☑ The name of the group or committee holding the meeting

☑ The topic of the meeting

☑ The kind of meeting (a regular meeting or a special meeting called to discuss a specific subject or problem)

☑ The number of members present and, for committees or boards of ten or fewer members, the names of those present and absent

☑ The place, time, and date of the meeting

☑ A statement that the chair and the secretary were present or the names of any substitutes

☑ A statement that the minutes of the previous meeting were approved or revised

☑ A list of any reports that were read and approved

☑ All the main motions that were made, with statements as to whether they were carried, defeated, or tabled (vote postponed), and the names of those who made and seconded the motions (motions that were withdrawn are not mentioned)

(continued)

8

Presentations and Meetings

Writer's Checklist: Items Included in Minutes of Meetings (continued)

☑ A full description of resolutions that were adopted and a simple statement of any that were rejected

☑ A record of all ballots with the number of votes cast for and against resolutions

☑ The time the meeting was adjourned (officially ended) and the place, time, and date of the next meeting

☑ The recording secretary's signature and typed name and, if desired, the signature of the chairperson

presentations

DIRECTORY

The steps required to prepare an effective presentation parallel the steps you follow to write a document. As with writing a document, determine your **purpose** (Tab 1) and analyze your **audience** (Tab 1). Then gather the facts that will support your point of view or proposal and logically organize that information. Presentations do, however, differ from written documents because your spoken delivery requires as much attention as your content, and your organization and **visuals** (Tab 7) must be adapted to an audience that will view your presentation.

Determining Your Purpose

Determine the primary purpose of your presentation by asking the following question: What do I want the audience to know, to believe, or to do when I have finished the presentation? Based on the answer to that question, write a purpose statement that answers the *what?* and *why?* questions.

▶ The purpose of my presentation is to convince my company's senior management of the need to hire a full-time social-media marketing coordinator [*what*] so that they will be persuaded to allocate additional funds in the budget for this position in the next fiscal year [*why*].

Analyzing Your Audience

Once you have determined the desired end result of the presentation, ask yourself these questions about your audience so that you can tailor your presentation to their needs.

- What is their level of experience or knowledge about your topic?
- What are their educational levels, ages, and other demographics?
- What is their attitude toward your topic and—based on that attitude—what are their possible concerns, fears, or objections?
- Are there subgroups in the audience with different concerns or needs?
- What questions might audience members ask about this topic?

Gathering Information

Once you have focused the presentation, you need to find the facts and arguments that support your point of view or the action you propose. As you gather information, keep in mind that you should give the audience only what will accomplish your goals; too much detail will overwhelm them and too little will not adequately inform your listeners or support your recommendations. For advice on gathering information, see research (Tab 5).

Structuring the Presentation

When structuring the presentation, focus on your audience as listeners. Listeners are freshest at the outset and refocus their attention near the end. Take advantage of that pattern. Give your audience a brief overview of your presentation at the beginning, use the body to develop your ideas, and end with a summary of what you covered and, if appropriate, a call to action. See also organization (Tab 1).

The Introduction.   Include in the introduction (Tab 1) an opening that focuses your audience's attention, as in the following examples:

▶ [*Definition of a problem*] "You have to write an important report, and you'd like to incorporate lengthy handwritten notes from several meetings. But hand writing all those pages seems an incredible waste of time! Have I got a solution for you."

▶ [*An attention-getting statement*] "As many as 70 million Americans have high blood pressure."

▶ [*A rhetorical question*] "Would you be interested in a full-sized computer keyboard that's waterproof, noiseless, and rolls up like a rubber mat?"

▶ [*A personal experience*] "On a recent business trip, my rental car's navigation system had me on the wrong highway—and thirty miles in the wrong direction! After I managed to head in the right direction, I realized: we need a mobile alert app."

▶ [*An appropriate quotation*] "According to researchers at the Massachusetts Institute of Technology, 'Garlic and its cousin, the onion, confer major health benefits—including fighting cancer, infections, and heart disease.'"

Following your opening, use the introduction to set the stage for your audience by providing an overview of the presentation. Such an overview can include general or background information that will be needed to understand the detailed information in the body of your presentation. It can also preview how you have organized the material.

▶ This presentation analyzes three high-volume, networked on-demand printers for us to consider purchasing. Based on a comparison of all three, I will recommend the one I believe best meets our needs. To do so, I'll discuss the following five points:

1. Why we need a networked high-volume printer [*the problem*]
2. The basics of networked on-demand technology [*general information*]
3. The criteria I used to compare the three printer models [*comparison*]
4. The printer models I compared and why [*possible solutions*]
5. The printer I propose we buy [*proposed solution*]

The Body.   If your goal is to persuade, present the evidence that will persuade the audience to agree with your conclusions and act on them. If you are discussing a problem, demonstrate that it exists and offer a solution or range of possible solutions. For example, if your introduction stated that the problem for a company is low profits, high costs, or outdated technology, you could use the following approach.

1. Prove your point.
   • Strategically organize the facts and data you need.
   • Present the information using easy-to-understand visuals.

2. Offer solutions.
   - Increase profits by lowering production costs.
   - Cut overhead to reduce costs, or abolish specific programs or product lines.
   - Replace outdated technology, or upgrade existing technology.
3. Anticipate questions ("How much will it cost?") and objections ("We're too busy now—when would we have time to learn the new software?") and incorporate the answers into your presentation.

See persuasion (Tab 1).

Transitions. Planned transitions (Tab 10) should appear between the introduction and the body, between major points in the body, and between the body and the closing. Transitions are simply a sentence or two to let the audience know that you are moving from one topic to the next. They also prevent a choppy presentation and provide the audience with assurance that you know where you are going and how to get there.

▶ Before getting into the specifics of each printer I compared, I'd like to present the benefits of networked, on-demand printers in general. That information will provide you with the background you'll need to compare the differences among the printers and their capabilities discussed in this presentation.

It is also a good idea to pause for a moment after you have delivered a transition between topics to let your listeners shift gears with you. Remember, they do not know your plan.

The Closing. Fulfill the goals of your presentation in the closing. If your purpose is to motivate the listeners to take action, ask them to do what you want them to do; if your purpose is to get your audience to think about something, summarize what you want them to think about. Many presenters make the mistake of not actually closing—they simply quit talking, shuffle papers, and then walk away.

Because your closing is what your audience is most likely to remember, use that time to be strong and persuasive. Consider the following typical closing.

▶ Based on all the data, I believe that the Worthington TechLine 5510 Production Printer best suits our needs. It produces 40 pages per minute *more* than its closest competitor and provides modular systems that can be upgraded to support new applications. The Worthington is also compatible with our current network, and staff training at our site is included with our purchase. Although the initial cost is higher than that for the other two models, the additional capabilities, compatibility with most

8

Presentations and
Meetings

standard environments, lower maintenance costs, and strong customer-support services make it a better value.

I recommend we allocate the funds necessary for this printer by the fifteenth of this month in order to be well prepared for the production of next quarter's customer publications.

This closing brings the presentation full circle and asks the audience to fulfill the purpose of the presentation—exactly what a <u>conclusion</u> (Tab 1) should do.

Using Visuals

Well-planned visuals can add interest, focus, and emphasis to your presentation. Charts, graphs, and illustrations can greatly increase audience understanding and retention of information, especially for complex issues and technical information that could otherwise be misunderstood or overlooked.

❖ ETHICS NOTE Be sure to provide credit for any visual taken from a print or an online source. You can include a citation either on an individual visual (such as a slide) or in a list of references or works cited that you distribute to your audience. For information on citing visuals, see <u>documenting sources</u> (Tab 5). ❖

You can create and present the visual components of your presentation by using a variety of media—flip charts, whiteboards or chalkboards, slides, or presentation software. See also <u>layout and design</u> (Tab 7).

▶ PROFESSIONALISM NOTE If your audience needs extensive notes or complex drawings, prepare handouts on which the audience can jot notes and which they can keep for future reference. ▶

Flip Charts. Flip charts, usually on easels, are ideal for use with smaller groups in a conference room or classroom and work well for brainstorming with your audience.

Whiteboards or Chalkboards. The whiteboards or chalkboards common to classrooms are convenient for creating sketches and for jotting notes during your presentation.

Presentation Software. Presentation software, such as Microsoft PowerPoint, Apple Keynote, Prezi, and open-source products, helps you integrate text, audio, images, links, and video content into your presentation. These programs and others that offer various collaborative and file-sharing capabilities constantly evolve and require that you keep current with the latest versions and enhancements. (See <u>adapting to new</u>

technologies, Tab 2.) As you learn the various possibilities of presentation software, keep in mind that you should avoid using too many enhancements, which may distract your audience from your message. Figure 8–4 shows well-balanced slides for a presentation based on the sample formal report in Figure 6–2.

▶ PROFESSIONALISM NOTE Be sure to anticipate and prepare for potential technical difficulties. Should you encounter a technical snag during the presentation, stay calm and give yourself time to solve the problem. If you cannot solve the problem, move on without the technology. As a precaution, always carry a hard-copy printout of your slides and copies for your audience, and save a backup copy of your digital presentation file. ▶

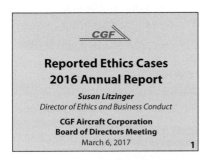

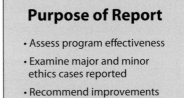

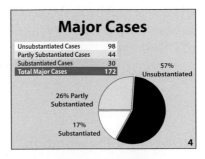

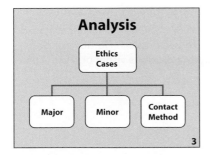

FIGURE 8–4. Presentation Slides

Writer's Checklist: Using Visuals in a Presentation

☑ Limit each visual to a number of words that can be quickly read by your audience.

☑ Use a font size readable to audience members at the back of the room.

☑ Limit the number of bulleted or numbered items in <u>lists</u> (Tab 7) to no more than five or six per visual, and use numbers if sequence is important and bullets if not.

☑ Keep lists in <u>parallel structure</u> (Tab 10) and balanced in content.

☑ Make your visuals consistent in font style, size, and spacing.

☑ Consider the contrast between your text and the background to ensure the text and images are clear to those in the audience.

☑ Use only one or two illustrations per visual (or slide) to avoid clutter and confusion.

☑ Use graphs and charts to show data trends.

☑ Avoid overloading your presentation with so many visuals that you distract or tax the audience's concentration: One visual for every two minutes is a common guideline.

☑ Avoid using sound or visual effects in presentation software that distract from the content or may seem unprofessional.

☑ Do not read the text on your visual word for word. Your audience can read the visuals; they look to you to develop the key points.

☑ Match your delivery of the content to your visuals. Do not put one visual on the screen and talk about the previous visual or, even worse, the next one.

Delivering a Presentation

Once you have outlined and drafted your presentation and prepared your visuals, you are ready to practice your presentation and delivery techniques. See also <u>outlining</u> (Tab 1).

Practice.　Familiarize yourself with the sequence of the material—major topics, notes, and visuals—in your outline. Once you feel comfortable with the content, you are ready to practice the presentation (in front of others if possible).

PRACTICE ON YOUR FEET AND OUT LOUD.　Try to practice in the room where you will give the presentation. Practicing on-site helps you get the feel of the room: the lighting, the equipment, the arrangement of the chairs, the position of electrical outlets and switches, and so forth. Practice out loud to gauge the length of your presentation, to uncover problems such as awkward transitions, and to eliminate verbal tics (for example, "um," "you know," and "like").

PRACTICE WITH YOUR VISUALS AND TEXT. Integrate your visuals into your practice sessions to help your presentation go more smoothly. Operate the equipment (computer or presentation system) until you are comfortable with it. Decide if you want to use a remote control or wireless mouse or if you want to have someone else advance your slides. Even if things go wrong, being prepared and practiced will give you the confidence and poise to continue.

Delivery Techniques That Work. Your delivery is both aural and visual. In addition to your words and message, your nonverbal communication affects your audience. Be animated—your words have impact and staying power when they are delivered with physical and vocal animation. If you want listeners to share your point of view, show enthusiasm for your topic. The most common delivery techniques include making eye contact; using movement and gestures; and varying voice inflection, projection, and pace.

EYE CONTACT. The best way to establish rapport with your audience is through eye contact. In a large audience, directly address those people who seem most responsive to you in different parts of the room. Doing that helps you establish rapport with your listeners by holding their attention and gives you important visual cues that let you know how your message is being received. Do the listeners seem engaged and actively listening? Based on your observations, you may need to adjust the pace of your presentation.

MOVEMENT. Animate the presentation with physical movement. Take a step or two to one side after you have been talking for a minute or so. That type of movement is most effective at transitional points in your presentation between major topics or after pauses or emphases. Too much movement, however, can be distracting, so try not to pace.

Another way to integrate movement into your presentation is to walk to the screen and point to the visual as you discuss it. Touch the screen with the pointer and then turn back to the audience before beginning to speak (remember the three *t*'s: touch, turn, and talk).

GESTURES. Gestures both animate your presentation and help communicate your message. Most people gesture naturally when they talk; nervousness, however, can inhibit gesturing during a presentation. Keep one hand free and use that hand to gesture.

8

Presentations and
Meetings

VOICE. Your voice can be an effective tool in communicating your sincerity, enthusiasm, and command of your topic. Use it to your advantage to project your credibility. *Vocal inflection* is the rise and fall of your voice at different times, such as the way your voice naturally rises at the end of a question ("You want it *when?*"). Conversational delivery and eye contact promote the feeling among audience members that you are addressing them directly. Use vocal inflection to highlight differences between key and subordinate points in your presentation.

PROJECTION.   Most presenters think they are speaking louder than they are. Remember that your presentation is ineffective for anyone in the audience who cannot hear you. If listeners must strain to hear you, they may give up trying to listen. Correct projection problems by practicing out loud with someone listening from the back of the room.

PACE. Be aware of the speed at which you deliver your presentation. If you speak too fast, your words will run together, making it difficult for your audience to follow. If you speak too slowly, your listeners will become impatient and distracted.

Presentation Anxiety.   Everyone experiences nervousness before a presentation. Instead of letting fear inhibit you, focus on channeling your nervous energy into a helpful stimulant. Practice will help you, but the best way to master anxiety is to know your topic thoroughly—knowing what you are going to say and how you are going to say it will help you gain confidence and reduce anxiety as you become immersed in your subject.

Writer's Checklist: Preparing for and Delivering a Presentation

☑ Prepare a set of notes that will trigger your memory during the presentation.

☑ Make as much eye contact as possible with your audience to establish rapport and maximize opportunities for audience feedback.

☑ Animate your delivery by integrating movement, gestures, and vocal inflection into your presentation. However, keep your movements and speech patterns natural.

☑ Speak loudly and slowly enough to be heard and understood.

☑ Review *Writer's Checklist: Using Visuals in a Presentation* (page 254) as well as this entry's advice on presentation delivery.

For information and tips on communicating with cross-cultural audiences, see <u>global communication</u> (Tab 1), <u>global graphics</u> (Tab 7), and <u>international correspondence</u> (Tab 3).

9

Job Search and
Application

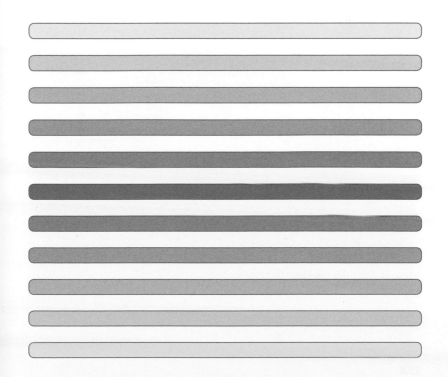

Preview

A successful job search requires diligence and organization as you present yourself in person, online, and in your writing to prospective employers. This section includes entries specifically related to the **job search** — from the crucial **application cover letters** and **résumés** to job **acceptance / refusals**. This section also offers strategies for **interviewing for a job**.

acceptance / refusals (for employment)

When you decide to accept a job offer, you can notify your new employer by telephone or in a meeting—but to make your decision official, you should send your acceptance in writing. What you include in your message and whether you send a letter (Tab 3) or an e-mail (Tab 2) depends on your previous conversations with your new employer. See also correspondence (Tab 3). Figure 9–1 shows an example of a job-acceptance letter written by a graduating student (see his résumé in Figure 9–10 on page 287).

In the first paragraph of Figure 9–1, the writer identifies the job he is accepting and the salary he has been offered—doing so can avoid any misunderstandings about the job or the salary. In the second paragraph, the writer details his plans for relocating and reporting for work. Even if the writer discussed these arrangements during earlier conversations, he needs to confirm them, officially, in this written message. The writer concludes with a brief but enthusiastic statement that he looks forward to working for the new employer.

When you decide to reject a job offer, send a written job refusal to make that decision official, even if you have already notified the

Dear Ms. Castro:

I am pleased to accept your offer of $47,500 per year as a junior graphic designer with the Natural History Museum.

After graduation, I plan to leave Pittsburgh on Tuesday, June 6. I should be able to find living accommodations and be ready to report for work on Monday, June 19. If you need to reach me prior to this date, please call me at 412-555-1212 (cell) or e-mail me at jgoodman@gmail.com.

I look forward to joining the marketing team and working with the excellent support staff I met during the interview.

Sincerely,

Joshua S. Goodman

FIGURE 9–1. Acceptance (for Employment)

9

Dear Mr. Vallone:

I enjoyed talking with you about your opening for a manager of aerospace production at your Rockford facility, and I seriously considered your generous offer.

After giving the offer careful thought, however, I have decided to accept a management position with a research-and-development firm. The job I have chosen is better suited to my long-term goals.

I appreciate your consideration and the time you spent with me. I wish you success in filling the position.

Sincerely,

Robert Mandillo

FIGURE 9–2. Refusal (for Employment)

employer during a meeting or on the phone. Writing to an employer is an important goodwill gesture.

In Figure 9–2, an example of a job refusal, the applicant mentions something positive about his contact with the employer and refers to the specific job offered. He indicates his serious consideration of the offer, provides a logical reason for the refusal, and concludes on a pleasant note. (See his résumé in Figure 9–11 on page 288.) For general advice on handling refusals and negative messages, see <u>refusals</u> (Tab 3).

▶ PROFESSIONALISM NOTE Be especially tactful and courteous—the employer you are refusing has spent time and effort interviewing you and may have counted on your accepting the job. Remember, you may apply for another job at that company in the future. ▶

application cover letters

Job applications require both a <u>résumé</u> and a cover letter, even if it is a relatively short <u>e-mail</u> (Tab 2) with an attached résumé. The application cover letter is essentially a <u>sales letter</u> (Tab 3) in which you demonstrate how your skills, knowledge, and experience will benefit an employer by meeting the requirements of a position. See also cover letters (Tab 3), letters (Tab 3), and persuasion (Tab 1).

The letter must quickly capture the employer's attention, allow readers to easily skim the contents, and point to the attached or enclosed résumé. It should (1) introduce you as a candidate with the skills that can contribute to the particular organization, (2) explain what job interests you and why, (3) highlight the specific qualifications in your résumé that match the position, and (4) provide the opportunity for an interview. See job search and interviewing for a job.

The job ad in Figure 9–3 seeks someone with experience in a professional design environment for a natural history museum. Figure 9–4 shows a cover message for a résumé that responds to the job ad in Figure 9–3. Notice that the applicant (Joshua Goodman) points to his substantial volunteer activities at a local public museum. He also points to his graphic design expertise, which is highlighted in his résumé (shown in Figure 9–10 on page 287).

Position: Junior Graphic Designer
Company: Natural History Museum
Location: Los Angeles, CA 90015

Description
The Natural History Museum of Los Angeles County is an equal-opportunity employer committed to ecological biodiversity, preservation, conservation, and education. The Museum seeks a full-time Junior Graphic Designer to join an in-house Promotions team, conceptualizing and creating digital and print content for exhibits, lectures, concerts, summer festival days, and related events. This position requires a collaborative approach to design, resourcefulness in executing a wide range of projects, an artistic and critical eye, and superior organization and communication skills. Video experience a plus. This position will report to the Creative Services Manager.

Requirements
B.A. or B.F.A. in graphic design or related field
Experience in a professional design environment
Online portfolio demonstrating visual branding solutions

Expert use of Adobe Creative Suite, especially Photoshop and Illustrator
Proficiency in HTML and CSS (hand-coding a plus)
Experience with project management software (Basecamp a plus)

FIGURE 9–3. Partial Job Ad (Description and Requirements)

9

| → Send | ✕ Cancel | ▤ Save Draft | ⏴ Add Attachment | ✉ Signature | ▼ Options |

SENT: Wed 4/5/17 12:23 PM

TO Judith Castro <jcastro@naturalhistoryla.org>

CC   Show BCC

Subject JUNIOR GRAPHIC DESIGNER

📄 jsgoodman-gdesign-resume.pdf   Download

Dear Ms. Castro:

A graphic designer at Dyer/Khan, Jodi Hammel, informed me that you are recruiting for a Junior Graphic Designer in your Marketing Department. Having participated in substantial volunteer activities at a local public museum, I would fit well in this position.

I bring strong, up-to-date academic and practical skills in multimedia tools and graphic arts production, as indicated in my enclosed résumé. Further, I have recent project management experience at Dyer/Khan, where I was responsible for the development of client brochures, newsletters, and posters. As Project Manager, I coordinated the project timelines, budgets, and production with clients, staff, and vendors.

My experience in the Los Angeles area media and entertainment community should help me make use of state-of-the-art design. For example, I helped upgrade the CGI logo for Paramount Pictures and the Director of Marketing commended my work. My work with leading motion picture, television, and music companies should help me develop exciting marketing tools that museum visitors and patrons will find attractive.

Could we schedule a meeting at your convenience? Please e-mail me at jgoodman@gmail.com or call me any weekday morning at 412-555-1212 (cell). Thank you for your consideration.

Sincerely,

Joshua S. Goodman

Portfolio: www.gooddesign.com

FIGURE 9–4. **Application Cover Letter (Graduate Applying for a Graphic Design Job)**

The sample application letters shown in Figures 9–5 and 9–6 also follow the guidelines described in this entry. In each sample, the <u>emphasis</u> (Tab 10), <u>tone</u> (Tab 10), and style are tailored to fit the employer's need and highlight the applicant's qualifications. Note that the letter shown in Figure 9–6 matches the résumé in Figure 9–11 (Robert Mandillo) on pages 288–89.

Send ✕ Cancel 📄 Save Draft 📎 Add Attachment 📧 Signature ▼ Options

SENT: Wed 4/19/17 10:02 AM

TO Patrice Crandall <pcrandall@abels.com>

CC   Show BCC

Subject Application for Summer Internship

📄 Parker_Resume.doc Download

Dear Ms. Crandall:

I learned from your Web site that you are hiring undergraduates for summer internships. An internship with Abel's buyer-training program interests me because your program is one of the best in the industry.

My experiences at Metro University with the Alumni Relations Program and the University Center Committee demonstrate my communication and persuasive abilities as well as my understanding of compromise and negotiation. For example, in the alumni program, I persuaded both uninvolved and active alumni to become more engaged with the direction of the university. On the University Center Committee, I balanced the students' demands with the financial and structural constraints of the administration. With these skills, as outlined in the attached résumé, I can ably assist the members of your department with their summer projects.

I look forward to an interview with you at your convenience. Thank you for your consideration.

Sincerely,

Marsha S. Parker

1251 Pine St.
Providence, RI 02901
(401) 555-9568

FIGURE 9–5. Application Cover Letter Sent as an E-mail (College Student Applying for an Internship)

Writer's Checklist: Tailoring a Cover Letter to a Job Ad

☑ Read the job ad carefully and follow the instructions precisely.

☑ Provide context by referring to the job ad or mentioning how you learned about a possible opening.

☑ Match the tone of your letter to the language of the ad.

☑ Show how the job is appropriate for you with vocabulary from the ad. See **word choice** (Tab 10).

☑ Avoid copying sections of text verbatim from the job ad.

☑ Show that you meet or exceed the employer's minimum requirements.

☑ Describe how you are upgrading skills for any areas in which you fall short.

1234 Everton Lane
Dayton, OH 45424
April 14, 2017

Ms. Angela Smathers, Director
Product Development Division
Aerospace Technologies
1530 East Street NW
Washington, DC 20001

Dear Ms. Smathers:

During the recent NOMAD convention in Washington, Karen
Jarrett, Director of Operations, informed me of an opening at
Aerospace Technologies for a manager of new product development. My extensive background in engineering exhibit design and
management makes me an ideal candidate for this position.

I have been manager of the Exhibit Design Lab at Wright-Patterson
Air Force Base for the past seven years. During that time, I received
two Congressional Commendations for models of a space station
laboratory and a docking/repair port. My experience in advanced
exhibit design would enable me to help develop AT's wind tunnel
and aerospace models. Further, I have just learned this week that
my exhibit design presented at NOMAD received a "Best of Show"
Award.

As described on the enclosed résumé, I not only have workplace
management experience but also have recently received an M.B.A.
from the University of Dayton. As a student in the M.B.A. program,
I won the Luson Scholarship to complete my coursework as well
as the Jonas Outstanding Student Award.

I would be happy to discuss my qualifications in an interview
at your convenience. Please contact me at (937) 255-4137 or at
mand@juno.com. I look forward to speaking with you.

Sincerely,

Robert Mandillo

Enclosure: Résumé

FIGURE 9–6. Application Cover Letter (Applicant with Years of Experience)

Opening

In the opening paragraph, provide <u>context</u> (Tab 1) by indicating how you heard about the position and name the specific job title or area. If you have been referred to a company by an employee, a career counselor, a professor, or someone else, be sure to say so ("I understand from Mr. John Smith, Director of Operations, that your agency . . ."). Show enthusiasm by explaining why you are interested in the job and demonstrate your initiative as well as your knowledge of the organization by relating your interest to some facet of the organization, as in Figure 9–4.

Body

In the middle <u>paragraphs</u> (Tab 1), use specific examples to demonstrate that you are qualified for the job. Aim for <u>conciseness</u> (Tab 10) and limit the content by focusing on one basic point clearly stated in each topic sentence. For example, your second paragraph might focus on educational achievements and your third paragraph might focus on work experience. Do not just tell readers that you are qualified—*show* them by including examples and details. ("Most recently, as an intern at SJX Engineering, I assisted in the infrastructure design for a multi-million-dollar seaside resort.") Highlight a notable achievement that portrays your value and refer the reader to your enclosed résumé. Do not simply list information found in your résumé; rather, indicate how your talents can make valuable contributions to the company.

Closing

In the final paragraph, request an interview. Let the reader know how to reach you by including your phone number and professional e-mail address (see *Writer's Checklist: Maintaining Professionalism* on pages 48–49). End with a statement of goodwill, as shown in the examples in this entry.

Proofreading and Follow-up

Proofread your letter *carefully*. Research shows that many employers eliminate candidates from consideration when they notice even one spelling, grammatical, or mechanical error. Such errors give employers the impression that you are careless in the way you present yourself professionally. See <u>proofreading</u> (Tab 1).

After a reasonable period, consider following up with a reminder. ("I wrote to you a week ago about your graphic design position, and I wonder if that position is still available.") Your initiative will portray your sincere interest in the opportunity. This approach may also provoke a need for action in the reviewer—for example, the need to pass your application to the hiring authority.

interviewing for a job

Job interviews can take place in person, by phone, or by Skype and may last 30 minutes to several hours. Sometimes an initial job interview is followed by a series of additional interviews. Often just one or two people conduct the interview, but on occasion a group or panel of four or more attend. Because it is impossible to know exactly what to expect, it is important to be well prepared. See also <u>job search</u>.

Before the Interview

Before the interview, learn everything you can about the organization, drawing on both internal, company-produced materials including Web sites, annual reports, and corporate advertisements and external sources such as newspaper articles about an organization and industry reports ranking a company alongside its competitors. Ask yourself questions such as the following:

- What kind of organization (profit, nonprofit, government) is it?
- What are the mission, goals, and objectives of the organization?
- What types of services or products does the company provide?
- What is the organization's history, and what sort of reputation has it built over time?
- Does the company operate locally, regionally, or internationally?
- Is the company privately owned or employee owned?
- How many employees are there?
- Is the company a subsidiary of a larger operation?
- How long has the company been in business?
- How does the company differentiate itself from its competitors?
  - How does it advertise its mission, expectations, and benefits to potential employees?
  - What strategies does it employ to market its products and services to clients or consumers?
- Where and how will I fit in? Does there appear to be opportunity for advancement?

You can obtain information from current employees, the company's Web site, press releases, prospectuses, annual reports, business articles about the company, and local news sources. The company's Web site in particular may help you learn about the company's size, sales volume, product line, credit rating, branch locations, subsidiary companies, new products and services, expansion plans, and similar information. Careful Internet <u>research</u> (Tab 5) can provide important background information, but do not hesitate to seek help from a librarian for sources accessible through a library, such as *Dun and Bradstreet, Standard and Poor's,* and *Thomas' Register.*

Try to anticipate the questions an interviewer might ask and think through your answers in advance. Be sure you understand a question before answering it and avoid responding too quickly with a rehearsed reply. The most appealing tone to adopt for interviews is conversational, since you will come across as natural and relaxed as opposed to overly rehearsed. The following are traditional questions that you might expect to be asked during an interview:

- What are your short-term and long-term occupational goals?
- Where do you see yourself five years from now?
- What are your major strengths and weaknesses?
- Do you work better with others or alone?
- What academic or career accomplishment are you particularly proud of? Describe it.
- Why are you leaving your current job?
- May we contact your previous employer?
- Why do you want to work for this organization?
- What will you bring to the organization?
- What salary and benefits do you expect? (see page 270 for salary negotiations)
- What is an example of a mistake from which you learned something valuable?
- What is your greatest accomplishment? Why?

Some employers, however, rather than ask such straightforward questions, use behavioral interviews that focus on asking the candidate to provide examples or respond to hypothetical situations. Interviewers who use behavior-based questions are looking for specific examples from your experience. Prepare for the behavioral interview by recollecting challenging situations or problems that you successfully resolved. Examples of behavior-based questions include the following:

- Tell me about a time when you experienced conflict while on a team.
- If I were your boss and you disagreed with a decision I made, what would you do?
- How have you used your leadership skills to bring about change?
- Tell me about a time when you failed and what you learned from the experience.

Other kinds of interviews are also becoming more common. For example, airline companies have routinely interviewed multiple applicants for onboard positions simultaneously in group settings. Surrounded by other job applicants, individuals are positioned to respond to a crisis with a passenger (played by an actor) or technical failure. As they respond, individuals or groups with the authority to make hiring decisions evaluate applicants' decision-making choices and group dynamics. It is important in such settings to consider which outcomes are most in line with the organization's goals and values.

Organizations are sometimes willing to share information about their interviewing approach when scheduling applicants. Feel free to inquire about the type of interview process you might expect beforehand and ask whether it would be appropriate to bring particular materials with you to the interview (see the following section, During the Interview) or whether you might be better prepared in other ways. Maintain a confident and enthusiastic tone when asking questions about what to expect during the interview since the goal should be to communicate your desire to make a professional impression on the interviewer and other members of the organization.

▶ PROFESSIONALISM NOTE Plan to arrive 10 to 15 minutes early to the interview; never be late. Always bring extra copies of your résumé, a note pad, samples of your work or portfolio (if applicable), and a list of references with contact information. Turn off any electronic devices prior to your arrival. If you are asked to complete an application form, read it carefully before you write and proofread it when you are finished. The form provides a written record for company files and indicates to the company how well you follow directions and complete a task. ▶

During the Interview

The interview enables a potential employer to learn about you, and it allows you to learn how you might fit into that organization. The interview actually begins when you arrive. What you wear and how you act make a first impression. In general, dress professionally and in a manner that is appropriate for working in the particular organization and position to which you are applying. Usually, it is wise to dress simply and conservatively, avoid extremes in fragrance and cosmetics, and be well groomed. Also, be polite to other employees you meet. Think of the interview from start to finish as your first day on the job. First impressions matter. The development of a professional identity begins early—if not when you enter college, then by the time you start taking courses in your major area of study—and continues to take shape as you start your career.

▶ PROFESSIONALISM NOTE Be aware that visible tattoos and body piercings are not acceptable in many white-collar and service-industry positions. Employers are within their legal rights to maintain such a policy if they believe your appearance might negatively affect the image of the organization. Act prudently if you suspect tattoos and piercings are not acceptable—cover tattoos and remove piercings. ❿

Behavior.   After introductions, thank the interviewer for his or her time, express your pleasure at meeting him or her, and remain standing until you are offered a seat. Sit up straight (good posture suggests self-assurance), maintain eye contact with the interviewer, and try to appear relaxed and confident. During the interview, use nervous energy to your advantage by channeling it into the alertness that you will need to listen and respond effectively. Do not attempt to take extensive notes. You can jot down a few facts, but keep your focus on the interviewer. Do not use an electronic device (laptop or tablet), unless you need to showcase a portfolio. See also <u>listening</u> (Tab 8).

Responses.   When you answer questions, stay on topic. Respond directly to the question, and then provide concrete evidence to support your answer. For example, if you reveal to the interviewer that you do not have leadership experience, refer to a specific officer position that you were elected to in an organization or describe your responsibilities as a trainer for other employees at your part-time job during college. Avoid simple yes or no answers—they usually do not allow the interviewer to learn enough about you. Some interviewers allow a silence to fall just to see how you will react. The burden of conducting the interview is the interviewer's, not yours—and he or she may interpret your rush to fill a void in the conversation as a sign of insecurity. If such a silence makes you uncomfortable, be ready to ask an intelligent question about the company, drawing on the research you have done about the organization and the particular position to which you are applying.

If the interviewer overlooks important points, bring them up. Let the interviewer mention salary first. Doing so yourself may indicate that you are more interested in the money than in the work. Make sure, however, that you are aware of prevailing salaries and benefits in your field or geographic region.

Interviewers look for a degree of self-confidence and an applicant's understanding of the field, as well as genuine interest in the field, the company, and the job. Ask questions to communicate your interest in the job and the company. Interviewers respond favorably to applicants who can communicate and present themselves well.

❖ ETHICS NOTE Questions that seem personal, appear to breach legal ethics, or otherwise make you uncomfortable not only can be hard to answer but also can quickly erode the confidence you worked so hard to build during your preparation. Remaining composed and remembering that the employer's objective is simply to determine whether you are the best candidate for the position will help you respond appropriately to difficult questions. Be brief, concise, and truthful in your answers. Common questions that may broach sensitive subjects may include the following:

- Have you ever experienced a layoff or been terminated?
- Why did you stay with previous employers on average for just a year?
- Why do you have such a large gap of employment between these dates? ❖

Salary.   Salary negotiations can take place at the end of a job inter-view, after a formal job offer, or over the course of several conversa-tions. Prepare by determining salary ranges in your field by checking Web sites, such as salary.com, payscale.com, and glassdoor.com. If you are on campus, check with your career-development office, which can advise you on local job salary ranges.

Remember that you are negotiating a package and not just a start-ing salary. Some employers have excellent benefits packages that can balance a lower base salary, as the following possibilities suggest:

- Tuition reimbursement for continued education
- Payment of relocation costs
- Paid personal leave or paid vacations
- Overtime potential and compensation
- Flexible hours and work-from-home options

- Health, dental, optical, and disability coverage
- Retirement and pension plans
- Profit sharing: investment or stock options
- Bonuses or cost-of-living adjustments
- Commuting or parking-cost reimbursement
- Family leave or elder-care benefits

If you do not wish to provide a specific salary requirement during a job interview, you can respond with a wide salary range that you know would be reasonable for someone at your level in your line of work in that region of the country. For example, you could say, "I would hope for a salary somewhere between $35,000 and $45,000, but of course this is negotia-ble." The salary range you provide should be in line with the industry average (see Job Search). Throughout this process, focus on what is most important to you (not others) and on what you would find acceptable.

If you decide to request a salary on the higher end of the average range in the particular industry to which you are applying, be prepared to offer specific, concrete evidence of experiences and skills you have developed that warrant a higher salary. Once you have gained some work experience in the industry, you will be in a better position to make such a request. In the meantime, though, you may refer to projects you have completed in college courses, computer software programs with which you have gained expertise, or internships in the field (see Internships).

Conclusion. At the conclusion of the interview, thank the interviewer for his or her time. Be sure to make note of each interviewer's name or request business cards if convenient. Reiterate your interest in the position and try to get an idea of when the company expects to make a final decision. Reaffirm friendly contact with a firm handshake.

After the Interview

After you leave the interview, jot down the pertinent information you obtained, as it may be helpful in comparing job offers. As soon as possible following a job interview, send the interviewer(s) a thank-you note or e-mail. Many interviewers and other employees you have met will appreciate a handwritten note that mentions a personal detail about your time at the organization, for example, thanking an individual who recommended a particularly good restaurant for lunch. Such messages also often include the following:

- Your thanks for the interview and to individuals or groups that gave you special help or attention during the interview
- The name of the specific job for which you interviewed
- Your impression of the opportunity
- Your confidence that you can perform the job well
- An offer to provide further information or to answer further questions

Figure 9–7 shows a typical example of follow-up correspondence.

If you are offered a job you want, accept the offer verbally and write a brief letter of acceptance as soon as possible—certainly within a week. If you do not want the job, write a refusal letter or e-mail, as described in acceptance / refusal letters.

In some instances, you may be interested in accepting a position but are more enthusiastic about a competing organization with which you have interviewed but that has not yet made you an offer. If you face this situation, it is appropriate to notify the interviewer with whom you spoke at the competing organization to let the individual know that you have been offered a position elsewhere but are still interested in pursuing a position with his or her organization.

222 Morewood Avenue
Pittsburgh, PA 15212
June 2, 2017

Ms. Emily Harrison, Director
Marketing Division
Harper Communications
1201 S. Figueroa Street
Los Angeles, CA 90015

Dear Ms. Harrison:

Thank you for the recent opportunity to interview for the entry-level position in the Marketing Division at Harper Communications. I appreciated learning more about the exciting directions being undertaken at your organization and being introduced to some of the projects I would be involved in if selected for the position.

During my visit, I was especially interested in the innovative branding campaign underway for one of Harper Communications' beverage industry clients. The energy I experienced when speaking with Mr. Joseph Turner, director of marketing, and Ms. Helen Markett, one of Harper Communications' senior marketing professionals, showed me the kind of environment I hope to join as I pursue my career in the field.

I look forward to continuing our conversation about what lies ahead at Harper Communications and how I might contribute to these goals. If I can address any further questions you might have or provide additional evidence of my work, please contact me at (123) 456-7890 or kadwell1234@gmail.com. Thank you again for your consideration.

Sincerely,

Kathleen Adwell

FIGURE 9–7. Follow-up Correspondence

job search

Individuals seek jobs for a number of reasons, including to

- Gain experience in a particular field
- Develop contacts with professionals and strengthen networking skills

- Build concrete evidence of skills and knowledge for inclusion in a professional portfolio
- Diversify skills and knowledge to help set a job seeker apart from the competition
- Explore another career option prior to a career shift or an opportunity that complements current employment (for instance, a freelance career that can be developed on the side)
- Participate in activities that support personal values and character traits

Whether you are applying for your first job or want to change careers entirely, begin by assessing your knowledge, skills, interests, and abilities through brainstorming. Next, consider your career goals and values.* For instance, do you prefer working independently or collaboratively? Do you enjoy public settings? Do you like meeting people? How important are career stability and location? What would you most like to be doing in the immediate future? In two years? In five years? Be honest: What kinds of tasks and responsibilities, big and small, would you like to occupy your days?

Once you have narrowed your goals and identified a professional area that is right for you, consider the following sources to locate the job and kind of work environment you are seeking. It is important to consult both internal sources (documents and other kinds of evidence produced by the organization to which you are applying) and external sources (perspectives on an organization written by an outside party). Some examples of sources from each perspective follow:

Internal Sources:

- Informational interviews with organizational insiders
- Published job ads announcing current position openings
- Organizational Web sites
- Annual reports
- Corporate ads speaking to the identity and reputation of an organization
- Employees currently working for an organization

---

*A good source for stimulating your thinking is the most recent edition of *What Color Is Your Parachute? A Practical Manual for Job-Hunters & Career-Changers* by Richard N. Bolles, published by Ten Speed Press. Also, it is a good idea to head to your university's career services office to ask for current information about industries in which you have interest as well as any positions that have been listed with the office. While you are there, you might inquire about the possibility of signing up to take a personality test like the Myers-Briggs Type Indicator or a career aptitude test; both can provide clues to the types of work and work environments in which you might be most successful.

External Sources:

- Newspaper articles about an organization
- Industry reports that speak to the successes and failures of several organizations, including the one to which you are applying
- Unpaid reviews of an organization's products and services
- Forecasts by investment and workforce experts

Organization is key to a successful job search. Keep files, preferably electronic and hard copy, for potential jobs, and include in each file copies of job ads, <u>application letters</u>, <u>résumés</u>, follow-up correspondence, and contact information. Consider logging your job-search activity on a spreadsheet or other accessible format so that you always know exactly where to find who you have contacted and why. Whatever system you use, keeping track of names and what you have sent to potential employers is crucial.

In an era when multiple communications are sent daily through e-mail, texting, and a variety of social-media outlets, it is crucial to record the names and positions of individuals from an organization with whom you have corresponded in any form. Set up file folders for e-mail exchanges. For example, keep all messages exchanged between an organization's human resources director and any other individuals from the organization in one place for easy reference.

▶ **PROFESSIONALISM NOTE** *Personal branding* is a concept introduced by business guru Tom Peters that has increasingly gained in popularity. Businesses work to establish a positive reputation and image for high-quality products and the successful execution of its services. Personal branding is the idea of marketing a positive image or reputation of yourself. For example, if you are a consultant who sells products or services, the consistently professional and successful execution of service will be remembered as a core part of your brand. By learning how to influence other people's perceptions of your brand, you will gain an immediate advantage over the competition. See *www.fastcompany.com/28905/brand-called-you.* ▶

Many components of the job search discussed in this entry can help you establish a strong personal brand. As you evaluate the opportunities of networking, social media, and internships, for example, keep in mind the core message you would like to send about yourself. Every interaction provides opportunities to enhance your visibility through a full suite of job-search materials. These materials may include a video résumé, business cards, a narrative biography, LinkedIn and other <u>social media</u> (Tab 2) profiles, a personal Web site, a portfolio, reference letters, and testimonials. As you prepare these materials, project a consistent and unified branding message across all media outlets.

To achieve consistency of your brand and to enter a job or career that is personally and professionally satisfying, you must be honest with yourself about what you bring to the workplace and how you self-identify. Avoid trying to maintain a personal brand that sounds like a good fit for a particular organization but that does not genuinely reflect your values, interests, and goals.

Along with "personal branding," consider the way in which you "package" yourself for the job search. Qualified applicants for a position will likely possess many of the same credentials (for instance, an undergraduate degree in a relevant discipline or a required license for entering a particular field) and similar experiences (for example, an internship during college). It is important to consider, then, what unique traits or experiences set you apart from your competitors. Examples can include anything from a meaningful mission trip in which you participated to a passion you have for painting to a significant feature of your upbringing. By combining this unique feature with qualifications that employers expect to see in applicants' materials, you can set yourself apart. For example, each of the following statements reflects effective applicant packaging:

- In addition to bringing knowledge of current marketing theory and practice to this position, my experiences of watching my parents grow their dry cleaning business in our small town taught me much about the importance of building relationships in the community.
- My grades in my civil engineering courses and the leadership roles I played in group projects reveal my commitment to the field. It was my summer work for Habitat for Humanity, though, that taught me the importance of using my training to serve the community.

Networking and Informational Interviews

Career-development experts agree that many open positions are filled through networking. Networking involves communicating with people who might provide useful advice or may know of potential jobs in your interest areas. Your network may include people already working in your chosen field, contacts in professional organizations, professors, family members, or friends. Discussion groups and networking sites, such as LinkedIn, can be helpful in this process. In general, you should always be networking, even when you do not need assistance. Even a simple gesture, such as providing a reference for a recently unemployed colleague, can go a long way toward expanding your network.

Informational interviews are appointments you schedule with working professionals who can give you "insider" views of an occupation or industry. These brief meetings (usually 20 to 30 minutes) also offer you the chance to learn about employment trends as well as leads for employment opportunities. Because you ask the questions,

9

these interviews allow you to participate in an interview situation that is less stressful than the job interview itself. To make the most of informational interviews, prepare carefully and review both interviewing for information (Tab 5) and interviewing for a job.

Campus Career Services

A visit to a college career-development center is another good way to begin your job search. Government, business, and industry recruiters often visit campus career offices to interview prospective employees; recruiters also keep career counselors aware of their companies' current employment needs and submit job descriptions to them. Career counselors not only help you select a career but also put you in touch with the best and most current resources—identifying where to begin your search and saving you time. Career-development centers often hold workshops on résumé preparation and offer other job-finding resources on their Web sites.

Strategic Web Searches

In addition to professional and social-networking sites, you can use the Web in several ways to enhance your job search.

- Consult sites that give advice about careers, job seeking, and résumé preparation like careerbuilder.com.
- Learn about businesses and organizations that may hire employees in your field by visiting their Web sites. Such company sites often describe the company's culture, list job openings, provide instructions for applicants, and offer an overview of employee benefits.
- You can learn about jobs in your field and post your résumé for prospective employers at privately owned or government-sponsored online employment databases. For instance, among the many resources found at CareerOneStop (*www.careeronestop.org*), a job seeker can research salary ranges for a particular region or career field. This tool is particularly valuable when you are moving to a new location, considering a career transition, or determining a valid salary and benefits range for negotiating compensation packages.

Social Media

Social-media sites, such as LinkedIn, allow you to connect with people of like-minded interests both on an individual level and in a broad forum. Social media provides the opportunity to develop a positive image of your work through comments, personal and professional profiles, résumés, the associations to which you belong, and your social-media connections. These components of your social-media presence can help enhance your reputation and personal "brand."

▶ **PROFESSIONALISM NOTE** Surveys show that employers and employment recruiters peruse social media and search engines before recruiting candidates, so carefully consider the material that you post online when using such media as LinkedIn, Facebook, and Twitter. Keep in mind that many software packages allow prospective employers to compile an overview of a job seeker's online presence. Share online only what you would comfortably share at the office, and regularly check the privacy settings on any sites that you use. It is important to remain consistent to your personal "brand" in any communications you share online, which is all the more reason to articulate a brand that is genuine. ▶

Job Advertisements

Many employers advertise job openings on their Web sites, job boards, social-media sites, and newspapers. Because job listings can differ, search in both the printed and Web editions of local and big-city newspapers under *employment* or *job market*. Use the search options they provide or the general strategies for database searches discussed in the entry <u>research</u> (Tab 5).

A human-relations specialist interested in training, for example, might find the specialty listed under "Human Resources" or "Consulting Services." Depending on a company's or government agency's needs, the listing could be even more specific, such as "Software Education Specialist" or "Learning and Development Coordinator."

Set up job alerts on job-aggregator sites, such as indeed.com and simplyhired.com, and scour job boards, company Web sites, and newspaper listings for jobs that meet your criteria and send you e-mail notifications. As you read the ads, take notes on salary ranges, job locations, job duties and responsibilities, and even the terminology used in the ads to describe the work.

Not all organizations publish job ads. Rather, they rely on current employees to spread news of any hiring needs to contacts in their personal and professional networks. It is appropriate to send a "prospecting" application letter and résumé to an organization to let the human resources director or other appropriate representative know that you are interested in working with the organization and in what capacities.

Remember, too, that job ads are often wish lists—descriptions of *ideal* candidates for a position. Not every applicant who submits their materials will meet all of the requirements listed, nor may the individual who is ultimately selected for the position. Pay attention to the language used in an ad to determine which qualifications are "required" as opposed to "desired" or "preferred."

Trade and Professional Journal Listings

Many industry associations publish periodicals of interest to people working in the industry. Such periodicals often contain job listings. To learn about the trade or professional associations for your occupation, consult online resources offered by your library or campus career office. Also, head to the central office for your major to see what kinds of resources are available for students pursuing careers in related fields. Often, those who are on the forefront of the discipline will be in the loop regarding which industries and organizations are seeking employees, are in the process of expanding, or are interested in taking on students for internships or co-ops.

Employment Agencies (Private, Temporary, Government)

Private employment agencies are organizations that are in business to help people find jobs. Be sure you understand who is paying the agency's fee. Often the employer pays the agency's fee; however, if you have to pay, make sure you know exactly how much. As with any written agreement, read the fine print carefully.

A staffing agency or temporary placement agency could match you with an appropriate temporary or permanent job in your field. Temporary work for an organization for which you might want to work permanently is an excellent way to build your network while continuing your job search. Choose an employment or a temporary-placement agency carefully. Some are well established and reputable; others are not. Check with your local Better Business Bureau and your college career office before you sign any agreements.

Recruitment firms (sometimes called *headhunters*) are hired by organizations to fill general needs or specific positions. Especially if you have experience in a field, it is a good idea to make connections with recruiters on networking sites like LinkedIn. You can also search online for recruiters who specialize in your career field, and send your résumé to them through their Web-site form or by e-mail. Even if there is no suitable job opportunity, a résumé submitted to a recruitment firm could turn up in a future database search.

Local, state, and federal government agencies also offer many free or low-cost employment services. Locate local government agencies in Web or telephone directories under the name of your city, county, or state. For information on occupational trends, see the Occupational Outlook Handbook at *www.bls.gov/oco*. For information on jobs with the federal government, see the U.S. Office of Personnel Management at *www.opm.gov*, or USAJOBS, the federal government's official jobs site, at *www.usajobs.gov*. For information on salary negotiations, see page 270.

Internships and Co-ops

As you evaluate job options, consider taking an internship or co-op. Internships typically last from six weeks to an entire semester (if not longer), whereas co-ops (or cooperatives) are often positions that are taken on by a student while in school with the understanding that the position may become full time once the student completes his or her education. An internship or co-op provides you with the chance to gain experience in a field through a variety of career opportunities. It enables you to

- Try a position without making a permanent commitment.
- Explore a field to clarify your career goals.
- Develop skills and gain experience in a new field or industry.
- Evaluate a prospective employer or firm.
- Acquire a mentor in the workplace.
- Establish networking contacts and professional references.
- Position yourself for a future job offer with the employer.

Ask if the internship is paid or unpaid during your interview. If it is not paid, find out how the internship will benefit you based on recent legal criteria for unpaid internships. (See U.S. Department of Labor at *www.dol.gov/whd/regs/compliance/whdfs71.pdf*.) For-profit employers are required to pay interns at least the minimum wage unless the internship experience is designed for the benefit of the intern, such as training that would be given in an educational environment. When this condition is met, the employer is not required to pay the intern for the internship.

To locate internship opportunities, begin with your campus career-development office. Such offices usually post internship opportunities on their Web site, but you can also make appointments with counselors or take advantage of walk-in hours. Finally, try *www.internships.com*, a site that lists internships by type of employer, by location, by means of compensation (paid or unpaid), and by whether the work is full or part time.

Service Internship and "Gap Year" Opportunities

Not all internships involve working for an organization that is in your chosen field. Increasingly, students are choosing to spend a period of time following graduation working in a position sponsored by organizations like Teach for America.

One option that many college graduates consider before pursuing full-time employment in a field that dovetails with their major and career goals is to apply for a position with AmeriCorps or the Peace Corps. These governmental organizations seek volunteers for a limited time period (usually between one and two years) to help to improve the lives of individuals in the United States and abroad.

AmeriCorps offers opportunities for Americans who are interested in contributing their talents to "nonprofits, schools, public agencies, and community and faith-based groups across the country" (*www.national service.gov/programs/americorps*). A specific example of an AmeriCorps program is City Year, which requires selected applicants to work for one year in a school located in an urban environment that lacks sufficient resources.

Working for the Peace Corps can take volunteers to all corners of the world, with missions involving rebuilding structures damaged by tsunamis in places like Thailand or helping farmers in developing countries like Nepal attempt new techniques in agriculture.

There are advantages to spending a gap year (or more) in these kinds of positions. In addition to learning new skills, interacting with people from different locales and backgrounds, and having the opportunity in some cases to acquire another language, governmental programs like those mentioned will often assist in the repayment of student loans.

Direct Inquiries

If you would like to work for a particular firm, peruse the organization's Web site to see if any openings for individuals with your qualifications are advertised. You may also e-mail or call the human resources director or head of a particular division to which you are interested in applying. Remember that all correspondence, even a simple phone call, should be professional because every interaction with an organization reflects your identity. Such contacts work best if you have networked as described earlier in this entry.

A related strategy is to prepare a prospecting letter — a highly targeted letter that outlines why your skills and credentials would be valuable to the employer. Before writing the letter, research the employer to find out about any upcoming plans, goals, and even obstacles to their success. Your prospecting letter can show that you understand the challenges that the employer is facing and you are part of the solution. Describe what you expect to accomplish, both short term and long term, if given the opportunity.

Other Application Genres

Other kinds of documents, print and digital, are used for pursuing positions in the contemporary workplace.

- Application forms: Some organizations ask applicants to complete online or print application forms providing information about work history in an accessible and standard format. When completing these forms, be sure to answer all questions, targeting the word count specified in the instructions. If a specific word count

is not provided, gauge the preferred length for responses according to the amount of space provided.

- LinkedIn profile: LinkedIn is an online site for managing professional profiles and networking with individuals in related fields.
Many employers will check LinkedIn profiles as a first step in the
screening process. Check your LinkedIn profile frequently to see
what comments have been added by those who visit your page
and to ensure that all information is updated.

- Digital (and print) portfolios: Throughout college, it is important
to keep a careful record of your accomplishments, whether academic achievements (for example, being named to the dean's list
or awards earned for work in a particular class) or participation in
campus organizations and clubs. A digital or print (usually bound)
portfolio will offer evidence of the knowledge, skills, and personal
traits that you claim to possess when applying for a position. In
addition to including a résumé and a reflective statement that
unify other materials in the portfolio, you should include items
like samples of your work in classes and jobs, images of events or
programs in which you participated, letters of reference, or other
evaluative statements of your work.

- Video résumés: More applicants are producing more sophisticated,
multimedia résumés in addition to traditional print versions. Like
digital portfolios, video résumés provide extras, for example, short
taped statements by the applicant to further demonstrate an item
listed on the résumé or a link to supporting images.

❖ ETHICS NOTE Providing false information in your job application can
result in a cause for dismissal and will reflect poorly on your character. Be
honest and keep in mind that if you are wrong for a position and lie to
obtain it, the employer can just as easily discover this after you are hired. ❖

Writer's Checklist: Completing Job Applications: Print and Online

☑ Read the entire application and keep your résumé at hand before you
begin.

☑ Copy and paste responses to online applications, as appropriate,
from your current résumé.

☑ Provide all requested information and complete irrelevant entries with
N/A (for "not applicable").

☑ List a specific job title for the "Position Seeking" entry — entries "any"
or "open" receive less consideration.

(continued)

Writer's Checklist: Completing Job Applications: Print and Online (continued)

☑ List salary requirements as "negotiable" or give a range commensurate with the industry and region.

☑ Use positive phrases if asked why you left a previous employer: "relocation," "seeking new challenge," "career advancement," or possibly "will discuss at interview."

☑ List references (with their permission) who can speak to your professionalism, character, or work ethic.

☑ Attach a brief cover letter and résumé with your completed job application, if possible.

☑ Proofread for accuracy and consistency: Review the instructions and check all entries or fields, dates, position titles, links, grammar, and spelling.

☑ Make sure you date, sign (if print), and submit or post the application by the deadline.

☑ Save for your records a copy or screen capture of your completed application.

❖ **ETHICS NOTE** When faced with questions that are sensitive, you must carefully consider your response. If the question does not seem to raise a problem, you can choose to answer it. If you feel the question is inappropriate, you can respond with *N/A* or another response (such as a line through the blank); this will indicate that you have read the content.

Understanding that many employers conduct background checks on candidates to protect their interests will help you determine the validity of a question. For example, a banking institution might be concerned about a candidate's credit history, current debts, or bankruptcy status, or a government organization might be concerned about citizenship or ties to foreign countries. ❖

résumés

DIRECTORY

A résumé is a key component of an effective <u>job search</u> and the foundation for your <u>application cover letter</u>. Prospective employers use the information in the résumé and application cover letter to screen applicants and select candidates for job interviews. During a job interview, the content of your résumé and application cover letter can provide the interviewer with a guideline for developing specific questions. See also <u>interviewing for a job</u>.

Because résumés affect a potential employer's first impression, make sure that yours is well organized, carefully designed, consistently formatted, easy to read, and free of errors. Most important, target your résumé to the specific job so that the employer can easily see that you are a perfect fit. Organize the résumé in a way that highlights your strengths and fits your goals, as suggested by the examples shown in this entry. Your résumé* should be concise, but the length should depend on your credentials, skills, and abilities that are a compelling match to the particular position. <u>Proofreading</u> (Tab 1) is essential—verify the accuracy of the information and have someone else review it.

❖ ETHICS NOTE Be truthful. The consequences of giving false information in your résumé are serious. Many employers use outside agencies to regularly check references and stated experience, automatically rejecting applicants with résumés that are even slightly inaccurate or embellished. If you are hired based on false information, you may later be dismissed or even face a lawsuit for the deception. See also <u>ethics in writing</u> (Tab 1). ❖

Sample Résumés

The sample résumés in this entry provide starting points that you can use to tailor your résumé to your own job search. Before you design and write your résumé, look at as many samples as possible, and then organize and format your own to best highlight your strengths, present your professional goals, and make the most persuasive case to your target employers. See also <u>persuasion</u> (Tab 1).

- Figure 9–8 presents a conventional student résumé in which the student is seeking an entry-level position.
- Figure 9–9 shows a résumé with a variation in the design and placement of conventional headings to highlight professional credentials.
- Figure 9–10 presents a résumé for a recent graduate with a format that is appropriately nonconventional for the purpose of demonstrating the student's skill in graphic design. This résumé matches the application cover letter in Figure 9–4.

*A detailed résumé for someone in an academic or a scientific area is often called a *curriculum vitae* (also *vita* or *c.v.*). It may include education, publications, projects, grants, and awards, as well as a full work history. Outside the United States, the term *curriculum vitae* is often used to mean *résumé*.

- Figure 9–11 depicts a résumé that incorporates a tagline and focuses on the applicant's management experience. A *tagline* is a short quotation or summary of your reasons for seeking a certain position. This résumé matches the application letter in Figure 9–6.
- Figure 9–12 reflects the résumé of a candidate seeking to switch career fields. It uses a job title and immediately states a goal, followed by credentials.
- Figure 9–13 illustrates how an applicant can organize a résumé by combining functional and chronological elements.

Analyzing Your Background

In preparing to write your résumé, determine what kind of job you are seeking. Rarely can you construct a one-size-fits-all résumé: Potential employers will all look for something different, and you will gain increasingly diverse experiences as you progress in your career. You may benefit from preparing a few résumés with different emphases, and you may need to create a unique résumé for a single position, using the language of a particular job description as your guide. Review your credentials and consider the following as you gather information:

- Schools you attended, degrees you hold, your major field of study, academic honors you were awarded, your grade point average, selected academic projects that reflect your best work; continuing education; conferences or seminars you have attended
- Jobs you have held, your principal and secondary duties in each job, when and how long you held each job, promotions you received, skills you developed in your jobs that a potential employer may value and seek in the ideal candidate, and projects or accomplishments that reflect important contributions
- Other experiences and skills you have developed that would be of value in the kind of job you are seeking; extracurricular activities that have contributed to your learning experience; leadership assignments you have accepted; interpersonal and communication skills you have developed; speeches, public presentations, or classes you have given; collaborative work you have performed; publications you have contributed to; computer skills you have acquired or specialized programs you are proficient in using; languages you speak; notable awards or other types of recognition you have received

Use this information to brainstorm further details and personal attributes. Then, based on all the details, decide which to include in your résumé and how you can most effectively present your qualifications.

CAROL ANN WALKER

CAMPUS ADDRESS
148 University Drive
Bloomington, Indiana 47405
(812) 652-4781
caw2@iu.edu

HOME (after June 2017)
Laurel, Pennsylvania 17322
(717) 399-2712
LinkedIn.com/in/cawalker
caw@gmail.com

EDUCATION

Bachelor of Science in Business Administration, expected June 2017
Indiana University

Emphasis: Finance   Minor: Professional Writing
GPA: 3.88/4.0
Senior Honor Society

FINANCIAL EXPERIENCE

FIRST BANK, INC., Bloomington, Indiana, 2016
Research Assistant, Summer and Fall Quarters
    Developed long-range planning models for the manager of corporate
    planning.

MARTIN FINANCIAL RESEARCH SERVICES, Bloomington, Indiana, 2015
Financial Audit Intern
    Created a design concept for in-house financial audits and provided
    research assistance to staff.
Associate Editor, *Martin Client Newsletter*, 2014–2015
    Wrote articles on financial planning with statistical models; developed
    article ideas from survey of business periodicals; edited submissions.

COMPUTER SKILLS

Software: Microsoft Word, Excel, PowerPoint, InDesign, QuarkXPress
Hardware: Macintosh, IBM-PC
Languages: UNIX, JAVA, C++

VOLUNTEER ACTIVITY

Student Affiliate NAPFA: Weekend program to assist low-income elderly
with managing their financial obligations. 2015–2017

FIGURE 9–8. Student Résumé (for an Entry-Level Position)

CHRIS RENAULT, RN, ACLS, BSN

LinkedIn.com/in/chrisrenaultrn
Phoenix, AZ 67903 • (555) 555-5555 • chrisrenault@somedomain.com

---

**Reliable, compassionate, and competent RN seeking
medical-surgical position**

*Dedicated Registered Nurse routinely praised for strengths in patient
relations; clinical knowledge; collaboration with interdisciplinary health-care
teams; chart accuracy; and ability to treat assorted illnesses, injuries, and
medical emergencies.*

Education & Nursing Credentials

UNIVERSITY OF PHOENIX– Phoenix, AZ

Bachelor of Science in Nursing	**Associate Degree in Nursing**
(BSN), 2017 — Graduated	**(AN)**, 2014 — Graduated
summa cum laude (GPA: 3.9)	cum laude (GPA: 3.5)

LICENSURE & CERTIFICATIONS

RN License (AZ), 4/2015 • **ACLS**, 1/2016 • **IV Practice**, 8/2016 • **CPR**, 8/2016

AFFILIATIONS

ANA (Arizona Nurses Association) • **ANA** (American Nursing Association)

Professional Experience–Clinical Rotations

- Earned excellent marks on evaluations throughout clinical rotations
  in diverse practice areas. Participated in activities including patient
  assessment, treatment, medication disbursement, and surgical preparation
  as a member of the health-care team.

- Preceptor Comments: *"Chris has an excellent ability to interact with patients
  and their families, showing a high degree of empathy, medical knowledge,
  and concern for quality and continuity of patient care."*

ROTATIONS SUMMARY

Surgery/Internal Medicine	ABC Hospital: Core Telemetry/Medical-Surgical
Emergency Medicine	ABC Hospital: Emergency Department
Cardiology	GHI Medical Center: Cardiac Telemetry
Oncology	ABC General Hospital: Oncology Department
Long-Term Care	XYZ Skilled-Care Unit
Orthopedics	ABC Hospital: Orthopedic Center
Pediatrics	DEF Hospital: Pediatrics Unit
Rehabilitative Medicine	ABC Hospital: Health Rehabilitation Center

---

Volunteerism

Active Volunteer, The American Cancer Society, Scottsdale, AZ Chapter,
2014 to present
Participant, *Making Strides Against Breast Cancer* walks, 2016, 2017

FIGURE 9–9. Résumé (Highlighting Professional Credentials)

CREATIVE GRAPHIC DESIGNER

Joshua S. Goodman
LinkedIn.com/in
/joshuasgoodman
412-555-1212
jgoodman@gmail.com
www.gooddesign.com

**Digital, Print, and Web skills with
Marketing, Museum, and Client
Experience in Fast-Paced Settings**

PROFESSIONAL EXPERIENCE

**Assistant Designer • Dyer/Khan,
Los Angeles, California
Summer 2015, Summer 2016**
Assistant Designer in a versatile
design studio. Responsible for
design, layout, comps, mechanicals,
and project management.
*Clients: Paramount Pictures, Mattel
Electronics, and Motown Records.*

**Photo Editor • Paramount Pictures
Corporation, Los Angeles, California
Summer 2014**
Photo Editor for merchandising
department. Established art
files for movie and television
properties. Edited images used in
merchandising. Maintained archive
and database.

**Production Assistant • Grafis,
Los Angeles, California
Summer 2013**
Production Assistant at fast-paced
design firm. Assisted with comps,
mechanicals, and miscellaneous
studio work.
*Clients: ABC-TV, A&M Records,
and Ortho Products Division.*

EDUCATION

**RCS School of Design,
Pittsburgh, Pennsylvania
BFA in Graphic Design —
May 2017**

*Graphic Design
Corporate Identity
Industrial Design
Graphic Imaging Processes
Color Theory
Computer Graphics
Typography
Serigraphy
Photography
Video Production*

SKILLS

Adobe Creative Cloud and
Creative Suite (esp. Photoshop,
Illustrator, and InDesign),
JavaScript, QuarkXPress,
MapEdit (Image Mapping),
Micromedia Dreamweaver,
Adobe Flash Professional,
Microsoft Access/Excel, XML,
HTML, iGrafx, CorelDRAW

ACTIVITIES

Museum Docent and Design
  Assistant, Lee Collection
Member, Pittsburgh Graphic
  Design Society

FIGURE 9–10. Recent Graduate Résumé (for Graphic Design Job)

ROBERT MANDILLO
Dayton, OH 45424 • 555.555.1212 • mandillo@somedomain.com
LinkedIn.com/in/robertmandillomba
Design Portfolio: www.robertmandillomba.com

QUALIFICATIONS SUMMARY

Quality-driven mechanical engineering manager whose tenure with
Exhibit Design Lab has been distinguished by exemplary-rated
performance and proven results. Developer of next-generation
exhibit design solutions that have led to increased leads and sales.
Qualifications reinforced by strong aptitudes in reliability engineering,
system troubleshooting, and Lean Six Sigma principles.

EXPERIENCE

MANAGER, EXHIBIT DESIGN LAB   May 2010–Present
Wright-Patterson Air Force Base, Dayton, OH

Managed production of 1,200+ exhibit designs throughout tenure,
supervising a team of 11 technicians in support of engineering exhibit
design and production.

Coordinate all phases of exhibit installations from initial concept and
development of technical drawings to construction, installation, and
fabrication of models.

Ensure the attainment of manufacturing goals and compliance with
safety standards.

Negotiate with vendors and procure materials and supplies for exhibit
design support.

SUPERVISOR, GRAPHICS ILLUSTRATORS   June 2007–April 2010
Henderson Advertising Agency, Cincinnati, OH

Led team to create original design themes, layouts, and graphics for
marketing materials, television commercials, videos, and Web sites.

Recruited, trained, and supervised a team of five illustrators and four
drafting mechanics.

Established strong vendor-partner relationships, competitive rates, and
detailed schedules that elevated quality and increased turnaround time.

EDUCATION

MASTER OF BUSINESS ADMINISTRATION (MBA), 2016
University of Dayton (Dayton, OH)

BACHELOR OF SCIENCE IN MECHANICAL ENGINEERING (BSME), 2007
Edison State College (Wooster, OH)

FIGURE 9–11. Résumé (Applicant with Management Experience)

ROBERT MANDILLO

Résumé • Page Two

Dayton, OH 45424 • 555.555.1212 • mandillo@somedomain.com
LinkedIn.com/in/robertmandillomba
Design Portfolio: www.robertmandillomba.com

AFFILIATIONS

American Society of Mechanical Engineers (ASME)
National Association of Professional Engineers (NSPE)

SKILLS

Rapid Prototyping • SolidWorks • Product Development •
Machining • Product Design • CAD Manufacturing • Engineering •
Simulations • Plastics • Sheet Metal • LabVIEW Procurement &
Supply-Chain Management • Pressure Vessel Internals • R&D

FIGURE 9–11. Résumé (Applicant with Management Experience) (*continued*)

Returning Job Seekers

If you are returning to the workplace after an absence, most career
experts say that it is important to acknowledge the gap in your career.
This is particularly true if, for example, you are re-entering the workforce because you have devoted a full-time period to care for children
or dependent adults. Do not undervalue such work. Although unpaid,
it often provides experience that develops important time-management,
problem-solving, organizational, and interpersonal skills. Although gaps
in employment can be explained in the application cover letter, the following examples illustrate how you might reflect such experiences in a
résumé. These samples would be especially appropriate for an applicant
seeking employment in a field related to child or health care.

▶ **Primary Child-Care Provider, 2014–2016** Provided full-
time care to three preschool children at home. Facilitated
early learning activities; taught basic academic skills, nutrition,
arts, and swimming. Organized schedules and events, managed
the household, and served as Neighborhood-Watch Captain.

▶ **Home Caregiver, 2014–2016** Provided 60 hours per week
in-home care for Alzheimer's patient. Coordinated health-care
and medical appointments, developed and supervised exercise
programs, completed and processed complex medical forms,
administered medications, organized and maintained budgets,
and managed home environment.

LINDA H. GRANGER

lhg.granger@gmail.com
(206) 577-8869 / (206) 656-3324

Sun Valley Heights, VA 20109
LinkedIn.com/in/lhgranger

INFORMATION TECHNOLOGY / SECURITY SPECIALIST

Seeking to build an exciting career in law enforcement with a focus on the application of Information Technology (IT) / Information Security (INFOSEC).

- Application Design / System Analysis
- Testing / Implementation / Integration
- Program / Project Development
- Business Policies / Procedures
- Customer / Client Service
- Dynamic Team Building / Leadership

EDUCATION

BACHELOR OF SCIENCE – INFORMATION TECHNOLOGY
Sun Valley University, VA, May 2016

INTERNSHIP / PROFESSIONAL EXPERIENCE

Federal Law Enforcement Training Center (FLETC), Arlington, VA   *June–Sept. 2016*
Volunteer — Computer, Financial, Intelligence Division

- Accepted into highly selective, competitive FLETC College Intern Summer Program
- Analyzed, evaluated, assessed performance or operating methodology of forensic software
- Assisted law-enforcement staff and instructors with office support in efforts to advance the mission of the FLETC
- Participated in and observed basic-training classes and activities designed to develop and promote the growth of future law-enforcement candidates

Board of Education, Forrest Hills, VA   *Sept. 2014–June 2016*
Instructor / Substitute Teacher

- Provided an educational foundation designed to enable K–12 students to develop confidence, self-direction, and a lifelong interest in learning
- Fostered the development of communication, citizenship, and personal growth

AWARD / RECOGNITION

SUPERB ADMINISTRATIVE SUPPORT – FORENSIC DATA HUB
Federal Law Enforcement Training Center

FIGURE 9–12. Résumé (Experienced Applicant Seeking Career Change)

——————————CAROL ANN WALKER——————————

Sometown, PA 00000 • (555) 555-5555
caw@somedomain.com • LinkedIn.com/in/carolannwalker
Twitter: @carolannwalker

Award-Winning Financial Analyst

- Senior financial analyst offering proven success enhancing P&L scenarios by millions of dollars.
- Excellent analytical capabilities, with an expert foundation in statistics, financial modeling, and complex financial/business/variance analysis.
- Backed by solid credentials, industry honors, and a history of delivering goal-surpassing results.

Financial Analyst of the Year, 2016

Recipient of national award from the Association for Investment Management and Research (AIMR)

Areas of Expertise

- Financial Analysis & Planning
- Forecasting & Trend Projection
- Trend/Variance Analysis
- Comparative Analysis
- Asset-Capacity Planning

- Economic Profit/EVA
- Business Valuation/Due Diligence
- SEC & Financial Reporting
- Risk Assessment
- Auditing/Accounting

Professional Experience

KERFHEIMER CORPORATION, Sometown, PA   2007 to Present

Senior Financial Analyst, 12/2010 to Present
Financial Analyst, 11/2007 to 12/2010

Promoted to lead team of 15 analysts in the management of financial/SEC reporting and analysis for publicly traded, $2.3 billion company and its four subsidiary entities. Develop financial/statistical models used to project and maximize corporate financial performance; provide ad-hoc financial analysis; and support nationwide sales team by providing financial metrics, trends, and forecasts

Key Accomplishments

- Developed long-range funding requirements crucial to firm's subsequent capture of $52 million in government and military contracts.
- Secured more than $100 million through private and government research grants.

FIGURE 9–13. Advanced Résumé (Combining Functional and Chronological Elements) (*continued*)

——————CAROL ANN WALKER——————

Résumé • Page Two

Sometown, PA 00000 • (555) 555-5555
caw@somedomain.com • LinkedIn.com/in/carolannwalker
Twitter: @carolannwalker

Professional Experience (*continued*)

- Facilitated a 15 percent decrease in company's long-term debt during several major building expansions by developing computer models for capital acquisition.
- Designed model that saved 65 percent in proposal-preparation time. Cited by executive VP of sales for efforts that shortened the sales cycle, which helped displace the competition.
- Partnered with department managers to provide budget planning and profitability/cost-per-unit (CPU) analysis, including income, balance sheet, and cash-flow statements.
- Jointly led large-scale systems conversion to Hyperion, including personal upload of database in Essbase. Completed initiative on time and with no interruptions to business operations.

FIRST BANK, INC., Sometown, PA   2002 to 2007

Planning Analyst, 9/2002 to 11/2007
Compiled and distributed weekly, monthly, quarterly, and annual closings/financial reports. Prepared depreciation forecasts, actual-vs.-projected financial statements, key-matrix reports, tax-reporting packages, auditor packages, and balance-sheet reviews.

Key Accomplishments

- Devised strategies to secure $6.2 million credit line at 2 percent below market rate.
- Positioned bank for continued growth by conducting business-unit analysis and cost/benefit studies to determine optimal investment strategies.
- Analyzed financial performance for consistency to plans and forecasts, investigated trends and variances, and alerted senior management to areas requiring action.
- Prepared and presented financial analysis on impacts of foreign currencies, inflationary factors, product-mix changes, merger and acquisition (M&A) activity, and capacity/fixed-cost structures.
- Achieved an average 14 percent return on all investments. Applied critical thinking and sound financial and strategic analysis in all funding options research.

FIGURE 9–13. Advanced Résumé (Combining Functional and Chronological Elements) (*continued*)

—————— CAROL ANN WALKER ——————

Résumé • Page Three

Sometown, PA 00000 • (555) 555-5555
caw@somedomain.com • LinkedIn.com/in/carolannwalker
Twitter: @carolannwalker

Education

THE WHARTON SCHOOL of the UNIVERSITY OF PENNSYLVANIA,
Philadelphia, PA
Ph.D. in Finance, 5/2015

UNIVERSITY OF WISCONSIN, Milwaukee, WI
M.S. in Business Administration ("Executive Curriculum"), 5/2002

INDIANA UNIVERSITY, Bloomington, IN
B.S. in Business Administration, Emphasis in Finance, 5/2000

Affiliations
• Association for Investment Management and Research (AIMR),
  Member, 2002 to Present
• Association for Corporate Financial Planning (ACFP), Senior Member,
  2004 to Present

Portfolio of Financial Plans Available on Request

FIGURE 9-13. Advanced Résumé (Combining Functional and Chronological
Elements) (*continued*)

If you have performed volunteer work during such a period, list that
experience. Volunteer work often results in the same experience as does
full-time, paid work, a fact that your résumé should reflect, as in the
following example:

▶ **School Association Coordinator, 2014–2016** Managed special
   activities of the high school Parent-Teacher Association. Planned
   and coordinated meetings, scheduled events, and supervised fund-
   drive operations. Raised $70,000 toward refurbishing the school
   auditorium.

Organizing Your Résumé (Sections)

The following résumé sections and section headings are typical and, depending on the subject matter, may use alternative terminology as shown in the following list. The sections you choose to include in your résumé and the order in which you list them should depend on your experience, your goals, the employer's needs, and any standard practices in your profession.

- Heading (name and contact information)
- Job Objective vs. Headline
- Qualifications Summary (Professional Profile, Key Attributes)
- Education (Academic Background, Certifications)
- Employment Experience (Career History, Career Chronology)
- Related Knowledge, Skills, and Abilities (Professional Affiliations, Volunteer Work, Networking Assets)
- Honors and Activities (Awards, Recognition, Notable Contributions, Volunteer Work, Publications, or Affiliations)
- References and Portfolios

There really is no right or wrong way to organize your résumé, and any number of organizational patterns can be effective. For example, whether you place "education" before "employment experience" depends on the job you are seeking. Organize your information in the sequence that emphasizes the credentials that will strengthen your résumé the most. A recent graduate without much work experience should list education first. A candidate with many years of job experience, including jobs directly related to the target position, may decide to list employment experience first. When you list information in the education and employment sections, use a reverse chronological sequence: List the most recent employer or credential first, the next most recent experience second, and so on.

Heading.   At the top of your résumé, include your name, the best phone number where you can be reached, professional e-mail (Tab 2) address, and links to social-media sites where you have a professional presence. Make sure that your name stands out on the page. If you are in transition, list the city, state, and ZIP codes of your residences along with relevant telephone numbers and e-mail addresses underneath your name (see Figure 9–8). You can omit your street address for privacy reasons.

Job Objective vs. Headline.   Your résumé needs a clear career focus. Hiring managers spend mere seconds for the initial résumé review, so your career goal should be immediately evident. Job objectives and résumé headlines (or *taglines*) both introduce the material and help the reader quickly understand your goal. An objective is a narrative statement about the type of job that interests you, and it can include your career level and credentials. A headline is similar to a newspaper headline and is meant to quickly grab the employer's attention. A headline contains a brief description of your job target and one or two of your strongest qualifications. A headline can provide visual impact, especially if it appears as a banner near the top of your résumé (see Figure 9–10). The following examples illustrate the difference between objectives and headlines.

SAMPLE OBJECTIVE STATEMENTS

▶ A computer-science position aimed at solving online security vulnerabilities.

▶ A position involving meeting the concerns of women, such as family planning, career counseling, or crisis management.

▶ A programming internship requiring software-development and debugging skills.

SAMPLE JOB TITLE AND HEADLINE COMBINATIONS

▶ FINANCIAL SERVICES / BANKING PROFESSIONAL
"Ensuring the Financial Success of Customers, Clients, and Communities"

▶ MECHANICAL ENGINEER
"Developing Innovative, Efficient, Environmentally Friendly Energy Solutions"

▶ FIREFIGHTER / EMT
"Prevention, Mitigation, Response" or "Protecting Life, Property, and the Environment"

▶ **PROFESSIONALISM NOTE** If you include an objective on your résumé, avoid using clichés, such as "seeking a challenging opportunity with potential for advancement" and other overused statements. ▶

Qualifications Summary. Include a brief summary of your qualifications to persuade hiring managers to select you for an interview. Sometimes called a *professional profile, summary statement,* or *career summary,* a qualifications summary can include skills, expertise, experience, or personal qualities that make you especially well suited to the position. You may give this section a unique heading or simply use a job title, as shown in Figures 9–12 and 9–13.

Education. List the school(s) you have attended, the degree(s) you received and the dates you received them, your major field(s) of study, and any academic honors you have earned. Most career-development professionals recommend that you should include your grade point average (GPA) only if it is 3.0 or higher. Omit your GPA if you earned your degree long ago and are focusing on experience rather than education. List individual courses if they are unusually impressive, if they provide the opportunity to include keywords, if they are relevant to your career goals, or if your résumé is otherwise sparse (see Figure 9–10). Consider including any special skills developed or projects completed in your course work. Mention high school only if you do not possess higher education or if you want to call attention to special high school achievements, awards, projects, programs, internships, or study abroad.

Employment Experience.   Organize your employment experience in reverse chronological order, starting with your most recent job and working backward under a single heading. You can also organize your experience functionally by clustering similar types of jobs into several sections with specific section headings, such as "Management," "Leadership," "Administration," or "Logistics."

Depending on the situation, one type of arrangement might be more persuasive than the other. For example, if you are applying for an accounting job but have no employment experience in accounting, simply list past and present jobs in reverse chronological order (most recent to least recent). If you are applying for a supervisory position and have had three supervisory jobs in addition to two nonsupervisory positions, you could create a section heading called "Supervisory Experience" and list the three supervisory jobs, followed by another section labeled "General Experience" to include the nonsupervisory jobs.

In general, consider the following guidelines when working on the "Experience" section of your résumé:

- Include jobs or internships when they relate directly to the position you are seeking. Including such experiences can make a résumé more persuasive if they have helped you develop relevant skills.
- Include extracurricular experiences, such as taking on a leadership position in a college organization or directing a community-service project, if they demonstrate the skills valued by a potential employer.
- List military service as a job, even though the occupational specialties may not be directly applicable to the positions for which you are applying. Give the dates served, the duty specialty, and the rank at discharge. Discuss military duties if they relate to the job you are seeking, and translate military terminology to be easily understood by hiring managers.
- For each job or experience, list both the job title and the employer name. Throughout each section, consistently begin with either the

job or the company name, depending on which will likely be more impressive to potential employers.

- Under each job or experience, provide a concise description of your accomplishments. By listing your accomplishments and quantifying them with numbers, percentages, or monetary value, you will let the employer know what separates you from the competition. That said, do not omit job duties entirely from your résumé; employers still want to see the scope of what you were responsible for. A good strategy for effectively organizing both duties and responsibilities is to create a brief paragraph outlining your responsibilities, followed by a bulleted list of your strongest accomplishments in the position.

- Focus as much as possible on your achievements in your work history. ("Increased employee retention rate by 16 percent by developing a training program.") Employers will picture themselves as benefiting from the same types of accomplishments.

- Use action verbs ("managed," "supervised," "developed," "achieved," and "analyzed"). Be consistent when using past or present tense. Even though the résumé is about you, do not use "I" (for example, instead of "I was promoted to Section Leader," use "Promoted to Section Leader").

Related Knowledge, Skills, and Abilities.   Employers are interested in hiring applicants with a variety of skills or the ability to learn new ones quickly. Depending on the position, you might list items such as fluency in foreign languages, writing and editing abilities, specialized technical knowledge, or computer skills (including knowledge of specific languages, software, and hardware).

Honors and Activities.   List any honors and unique activities near the end of your résumé, unless they are exceptionally notable or would be more persuasive for a particular objective. Include items such as student or community activities, professional or club memberships, awards received, and published works. Do not duplicate information given in other categories, and include only information that supports your employment objective. Use a heading for this section that fits its contents, such as "Activities," "Honors," "Professional Affiliations," "Memberships," and "Publications."

References and Portfolios.   Avoid specifying on your résumé that references are available unless that is standard practice in your profession or your résumé is sparse. Employers assume that a well-prepared job seeker will provide a list of professional references. Create a separate list of references in the same format design and layout as your résumé, and be ready to provide this page to prospective employers during the interview. Always seek permission from anyone you list as a reference and notify each person in advance when you provide the information to a prospective employer.

A portfolio is a collection of samples in a binder or on a Web site of your most impressive work and accomplishments. The portfolio can include successful documents you have produced, letters of praise from employers, copies of awards and certificates, and samples of your work. If you have developed a portfolio, you can include the phrase "Portfolio available on request" in your résumé. If portfolios are standard in your profession, you might even include a small section that outlines the contents of your portfolio.

▌ PROFESSIONALISM NOTE Avoid listing your desired salary on the résumé. On the one hand, you may price yourself out of a job you want if the salary you list is higher than a potential employer is willing to pay. On the other hand, if you list a low salary, you may not get the best possible offer. ▌

Digital Formats and Media

Once you have developed a strong résumé, consider adapting it for multiple media and digital formats.

E-mail–Attached Résumés.   An employer may request that you submit a résumé attached to an e-mail. If a file-format preference is not specified, send the résumé in Adobe PDF or MS Word format. Then attach the file and treat the e-mail-message body as your cover letter.

Applicant Tracking System Résumés.   When you submit your résumé via e-mail or to an employer's Web site, it may be added to an electronic applicant tracking system (ATS). These systems parse, store, manage, and rank résumés based on criteria specified by the hiring manager. Although these systems vary, some guidelines are universal:

• Avoid fancy graphics and icons because they will not be readable.
• Choose common titles for headers, such as "Professional Experience" and "Education."
• Incorporate keywords that are relevant to your career field in descriptions, but avoid a separate "Keyword" section that wastes valuable space.
• Use a consistent format in the placement of employer names and job titles.

In general, when developing your résumé for an ATS, try thinking like a computer and focus on logic and consistency.

Plain-Text Résumés. Some employers request ASCII or plain-text résumés via e-mail or their Web site, enabling the file to be easily added to résumé databases. ASCII résumés allow employers to read the file no matter what type of software they are using. You can copy and paste a plain-text résumé directly into the body of an e-mail message. To create an ASCII résumé, look for an option to "Save as" Plain Text in your word-processing program. After you save as a text file with a .txt extension, re-open the file in a text editor (such as Notepad for PCs or TextWrangler for Macs) and clean up the file as needed. For more, visit *resumepower.com/ascii-resumes.html.*

Scannable Résumés. A scannable-résumé format is a paper document that you mail to the employer. After it is received, the document will be scanned into an automated program and then downloaded into the company's searchable database. For such résumés, avoid decorative fonts, underlining, shading, letters that touch each other, or other features that will not scan easily. Before sending, scan the résumé yourself to make sure that it is legible.

Web-Posted Résumés. You can use a personal Web site to post your résumé and display other items that portray your value as a candidate, such as awards and samples of your work. You can list a link to your Web site in your candidate documents and correspondence with prospective employers. For such Web sites, keep the following in mind:

- Follow the general advice for writing for the Web (Tab 2), and view your résumé and materials on several browsers.
- Consider building a multipage site for displaying a work portfolio, publications, reference letters, and other related materials.
- Provide just below your name a series of internal page links to such important categories as "experience" and "education."
- Do not include your phone number or home address on the Web site—include an e-mail "contact link" that prospective employers and recruiters can use to reach you.
- Do not advertise that you are actively seeking a job if you are currently employed; if your employer learns about your search, your job could be in jeopardy.
- Post copies of your résumé in various file formats so that employers can select the best format for their needs.

If you do not have your own Web site, you can upload your files to an online cloud storage service, such as Dropbox (*www.dropbox.com*), and send employers the link to your folder.

▶ PROFESSIONALISM NOTE When applying for a position within the U.S. government, America's largest employer, make sure your résumé's content and style are suitable for a federal application. Protocol for your federal résumé varies depending on the specific agency you are targeting, but your résumé must address how your qualifications match the requirements outlined in the vacancy announcement. Kathyrn Troutman provides excellent resources for preparing federal résumés (visit *www.resume-place.com/services/federal-resume-writing*). See also job search. ▶

10

Style and Clarity

Preview

The entries in this section are intended to help you develop a style that is clear and effective — and that follows the conventions of standard English. For a number of related entries, see Tab 1, "The Writing Process"; Tab 11, "Grammar"; and the Appendix, "Usage."

Some entries in this section — <u>awkwardness</u>, <u>coherence</u>, <u>parallel structure</u>, and <u>sentence variety</u> — will help you construct clear sentences and paragraphs. Other entries discuss such word-choice issues as <u>abstract / concrete words</u>, <u>idioms</u>, and <u>jargon</u>. Finally, this section covers the important subjects of <u>biased language</u>, <u>business writing style</u>, and the <u>"you" viewpoint</u>.

10

Style and Clarity

abstract / concrete words

Abstract words refer to general ideas, qualities, conditions, acts, or relationships — intangible things that cannot be detected by the five senses (sight, hearing, touch, taste, and smell), such as *learning, leadership*, and *technology*. *Concrete words* identify things that can be perceived by the five senses, such as *diploma, manager*, and *keyboard*.

Abstract words must often be further defined or described.

> The marketing team needs freedom.
> *to develop its own customer database*

Abstract words are best used with concrete words to help make intangible concepts specific and vivid.

> Public *transportation* [abstract] in Chicago includes *buses* [concrete] and *commuter trains* [concrete].

See also context and word choice.

10

Style and Clarity

affectation

Affectation is the use of language that is more formal, technical, or showy than necessary to communicate information to the reader. Affectation is a widespread writing problem in the workplace because many people feel that affectation lends a degree of authority to their writing. In fact, affectation can alienate customers, clients, and colleagues because it forces readers to work harder to understand the writer's meaning.

Affected writing typically contains inappropriate abstract, highly technical, or foreign words and is often liberally sprinkled with trendy buzzwords.

❖ ETHICS NOTE Jargon and euphemisms can become affectation, especially if their purpose is to hide relevant facts or give a false impression of competence. See ethics in writing (Tab 1). ❖

Writers easily slip into affectation through the use of long variants — words created by adding prefixes and suffixes to simpler words (*orientate* for *orient; utilization* for *use*). Unnecessarily formal words (such as *penultimate* for *next to last*), created words using *ese* (such as *managementese*), and outdated words (such as *aforesaid*) can produce affectation. Elegant variation — attempting to avoid repeating a word within a paragraph by substituting a pretentious synonym — is also a form of affectation. Either repeat the term or use a pronoun.

▶ The use of digital modules in our assembly process has increased
production. ~~Modular digitization has also~~ cut costs.

and

Another type of affectation is gobbledygook, which is wordy, round-about writing with many legal- and technical-sounding terms (such as *wherein* and *morphing*). See also clichés, conciseness, nominalizations, and word choice.

10 | awkwardness

Any writing that strikes readers as awkward—that is, as forced or unnatural—impedes their understanding. The following checklist and the entries indicated will help you smooth out most awkward passages.

Writer's Checklist: Eliminating Awkwardness

- ☑ Strive for clarity and **coherence** during **revision** (Tab 1).
- ☑ Check for **organization** (Tab 1) to ensure your writing develops logically.
- ☑ Keep **sentence construction** (Tab 11) as direct and simple as possible.
- ☑ Use **subordination** appropriately and avoid needless **repetition**.
- ☑ Correct any **logic errors** within your sentences.
- ☑ Revise for **conciseness** and avoid **expletives** where possible.
- ☑ Use the active **voice** (Tab 11) unless you have a justifiable reason to use the passive voice.
- ☑ Eliminate jammed or misplaced **modifiers** (Tab 11) and, for particularly awkward constructions, apply the tactics in **garbled sentences**.

biased language

Biased language refers to words and expressions that offend because they make inappropriate assumptions or reinforce stereotypes about gender, ethnicity, physical or mental disability, age, or sexual orientation. Even if used unintentionally, biased language can damage your credibility.

Style and Clarity

▶ PROFESSIONALISM NOTE The easiest way to avoid bias is simply not to mention differences among people unless the differences are relevant to the discussion. Keep current with accepted usage and, if you are unsure of the appropriateness of an expression or the tone of a passage, have several colleagues review the material and give you their assessments. ▶

Sexist Language

Sexist language is the arbitrary stereotyping of men and women. Avoid sexism in your writing with nonsexist occupational descriptions, parallel terms, and pronoun references.

INSTEAD OF	CONSIDER
chairman, chairwoman	chair, chairperson
foreman	supervisor, manager
man-hours	staff hours, worker hours
policeman, policewoman	police officer
salesman, saleswoman	salesperson, sales associate

Use parallel terms to describe men and women.

INSTEAD OF	USE
ladies and men	ladies and gentlemen; women and men
man and wife	husband and wife
Ms. Jones and	Ms. Jones and Mr. Weiss;
Bernard Weiss	Mary Jones and Bernard Weiss

One common way of handling <u>pronoun references</u> (Tab 11) that could apply equally to a man or a woman is the use of the expression *his or her*. To avoid this awkward usage, try rewriting the sentence in the plural.

> *All employees*   *their*   *reports*
> ▶ ~~Every employee~~ should submit ~~his or her~~ expense ~~report~~ by
>
> Monday.

Another solution is to omit pronouns completely if they are not essential to the meaning of the sentence.

>   *an*
> ▶ Every employee should submit ~~his or her~~ expense report by
>
> Monday.

Other Types of Biased Language

Identifying people by racial, ethnic, or religious categories is simply not relevant in most workplace writing. Telling readers that an accountant is Native American or an attorney is Jewish almost never conveys useful information.

Also consider how you refer to people with disabilities. If you refer to "a disabled employee," you imply that the part (*disabled*) is as significant as the whole (*employee*). Use "an employee with a disability" instead. Similarly, the preferred usage is "a person who uses a wheelchair" rather than "a wheelchair-bound person," an expression that inappropriately equates the wheelchair with the person. Likewise, references to a person's age can be inappropriate, as in expressions like "middle-aged manager" or "young social-media coordinator." See also <u>ethics in writing</u> (Tab 1).

10

Style and Clarity

business writing style

Business writing has evolved from a formal and elaborate style to one that is more personal and direct. Business writing today varies from the conversational style you might use in a <u>text message</u> (Tab 2) to the formal, legalistic style found in contracts. In most e-mails, letters, and memos, a style between those two extremes generally is appropriate. (See <u>correspondence</u>, Tab 3.) Writing that is too formal can alienate your <u>audience</u> (Tab 1). But an inappropriate attempt to be casual and informal may strike readers as insincere and unprofessional, especially to clients or those you do not know well.

▶ ~~Hey~~ Jane*,* *Dear*

> *Your proposal arrived today, and it looks good.*
> ~~Just got your proposal. It's awesome!~~

The use of personal <u>pronouns</u> (Tab 11) is important in letters and e-mails. In fact, one way you can make your business writing natural and persuasive is to use the <u>"you" viewpoint</u>, which often (but not always) uses the pronoun *you* to place the readers' interest foremost.

❖ ETHICS NOTE Be careful when you use the pronoun *we* in writing to clients and others outside your organization because you are committing your organization to what you have written. In general, when a statement is your opinion, use *I*; when it is company policy, use *we*. Do not refer to yourself in the third person by using *one* or *the writer*. It is perfectly natural and appropriate to refer to yourself as *I* and to the reader as *you*. In a report, however, you may be writing to more than one reader and may not necessarily want to refer to collective readers as *you*. See also <u>ethics in writing</u> (Tab 1), <u>persuasion</u> (Tab 1), and <u>point of view</u> (Tab 1). ❖

The best writers strive to write in a style that is so clear that their message cannot be misunderstood. In fact, you cannot be persuasive without being clear. One way to achieve clarity, especially during revision (Tab 1), is to eliminate overuse of the passive voice (Tab 11), which plagues most poor business writing. Although the passive voice is sometimes necessary, often it not only makes your writing dull but also makes it ambiguous, indirect, or overly impersonal.

You can also achieve clarity with conciseness. Proceed cautiously here, however, because business writing should not be an endless series of short, choppy sentences that are blunt or deliver too little information to be helpful to the reader. (See also sentence variety and telegraphic style.) Appropriate and effective word choice is also essential to clarity. Finally, the careful use of punctuation can promote clarity, as discussed in Tab 12, "Punctuation and Mechanics." See also "Five Steps to Successful Writing" (page xxvii).

buzzwords

Buzzwords are popular words or phrases that, because of an intense period of overuse, tend to lose their freshness and preciseness. They often become popular through their associations with technology, popular culture, or even sports. See also jargon and word choice.

▶ win/win, F2F meeting, 24/7, touch base, take-away [as a noun], same page, action items, face time, impact [as a verb]

Obviously, the words in this list are appropriate when used in the right context (Tab 1).

▶ We must establish an *interface* between our system and the satellite hardware. [*Interface* is appropriately used as a noun.]

When writers needlessly shift from the normal function of a word, however, they often create a buzzword that is imprecise.

       cooperate
▶ We must ~~interface~~ with the Human Resources Department.
      ^

[*Interface* is inappropriately used as a verb; *cooperate* is more precise.]

We include such words in our vocabulary because they *seem* to give force and vitality to our language. Actually, buzzwords often sound like an affectation in business writing.

10

Style and Clarity

clichés

Clichés are expressions that have been used for so long that they are no longer fresh but come to mind easily because they are so familiar. Clichés are often wordy as well as vague and can be confusing, especially to speakers of <u>English as a second language</u> (Tab 11). A better, more direct word or phrase is given for each of the following clichés.

INSTEAD OF	USE
all over the map	scattered; unfocused
the game plan	strategy; schedule
last but not least	last; finally

Some writers use clichés in a misguided attempt to appear casual or spontaneous, just as other writers try to impress readers with <u>buzzwords</u>. Although clichés may come to mind easily while you are writing a draft, eliminate them during revision. See also <u>affectation</u>, <u>conciseness</u>, and <u>international correspondence</u> (Tab 3).

10

Style and Clarity

coherence

Writing is coherent when the relationships among ideas are clear to readers. The major components of coherent writing are a logical sequence of related ideas and clear transitions between those ideas. See also <u>organization</u> (Tab 1).

Presenting ideas in a logical sequence is the most important requirement in achieving coherence. The key to achieving a logical sequence is a good outline. (See <u>outlining</u>, Tab 1.) An outline forces you to establish a beginning, a middle, and an end. That structure contributes greatly to coherence by enabling you to experiment with sequences and lay out the most direct route to your <u>purpose</u> (Tab 1) without digressing.

Thoughtful <u>transition</u> is also essential; without it, your writing cannot achieve the smooth flow from sentence to sentence and paragraph to paragraph that results in coherence.

During <u>revision</u> (Tab 1), check your draft carefully for coherence. If possible, have someone else review your draft for how well it expresses the relationships between ideas. See also <u>unity</u>.

compound words

A compound word is made from two or more words that function as a single concept. A compound may be hyphenated, written as one word, or written as separate words.

▶ high-energy, nevertheless, post office, low-level, underestimate, blood pressure

If you are not certain whether a compound word should use a <u>hyphen</u> (Tab 12), check a dictionary.

Be careful to distinguish between compound words (*greenhouse*) and words that simply appear together but do not constitute compound words (*green house*). For plurals of compound words, generally add *s* to the last letter (*bookcases* and *Web sites*). However, when the first word of the compound is more important to its meaning than the last, the first word takes the *s* (*editors in chief*). Possessives are formed by adding *'s* to the end of the compound word (the *editor in chief's* desk, the *pipeline's* diameter, the *post office's* hours). See also <u>possessive case</u> (Tab 11).

10

Style and Clarity

conciseness

Concise writing is free of unnecessary words, phrases, clauses, and sentences without sacrificing clarity or appropriate detail. Conciseness, however, is not a synonym for brevity; a long report may be concise, while its <u>abstract</u> (Tab 6) may be brief and concise. Conciseness is always desirable, but brevity may or may not be desirable in a given passage, depending on the writer's purpose. (See also <u>text messaging</u>, Tab 2.) Although concise sentences are not guaranteed to be effective, wordy sentences always sacrifice some of their readability and <u>coherence</u>.

Causes of Wordiness

<u>Modifiers</u> (Tab 11) that repeat an idea implicit or present in the word being modified contribute to wordiness by being redundant.

▶ *basic* essentials   *completely* finished
  final outcome   *present* status

Coordinated synonyms that merely repeat each other contribute to wordiness.

▶ *each and every*   *basic and fundamental*
  finally and for good   *first and foremost*

Excess qualification also contributes to wordiness.

▶ *perfectly* clear   *completely* accurate

Expletives, relative pronouns, and relative adjectives, although they have legitimate purposes, often result in wordiness.

WORDY	*There are* [expletive] many Web designers *who* [relative pronoun] are planning to attend the conference, at *which* [relative adjective] time we should meet.
CONCISE	Because many Web designers plan to attend the conference, we should meet then.

Circumlocution (a long, indirect way of expressing things) is a leading cause of wordiness.

WORDY	The payment to which a subcontractor is entitled should be made promptly so that in the event of a subsequent contractual dispute we, as general contractors, may not be held in default of our contract by virtue of nonpayment.
CONCISE	Pay subcontractors promptly. Then, if a contractual dispute occurs, we cannot be held in default of our contract because of nonpayment.

Balance is important. When conciseness is overdone, writing can become choppy and ambiguous. (See also **telegraphic style**.) Too much conciseness can produce a style that is not only too brief but also too blunt, especially in **correspondence** (Tab 3).

Writer's Checklist: Achieving Conciseness

Wordiness is understandable when you are **writing a draft** (Tab 1), but it should not survive **revision** (Tab 1).

☑ Use **subordination** to achieve conciseness.

> *five-page*
> ▶ The financial report was carefully documented, and it covered five
>
> pages.

☑ Avoid **affectation** by using simple words and phrases.

WORDY	It is the policy of the company to provide Internet access to enable employees to conduct the online communication necessary to discharge their responsibilities; such should not be utilized for personal communications or nonbusiness activities.
CONCISE	Employee Internet access should be used only for appropriate company business.

Writer's Checklist: Achieving Conciseness (continued)

☑ Eliminate redundancy.

WORDY   Post-installation testing, which is offered to all our customers at no further cost to them whatsoever, is available with each Line Scan System One purchased from this company.

CONCISE   Free post-installation testing is offered with each Line Scan System One.

☑ Change the passive <u>voice</u> (Tab 11) to the active voice and the indicative <u>mood</u> (Tab 11) to the imperative mood whenever possible.

WORDY   Bar codes normally are used when an order is intended to be displayed on a monitor, and inventory numbers normally are used when an order is to be placed with the manufacturer.

CONCISE   Use bar codes to display the order on a monitor, and use inventory numbers to place the order with the manufacturer.

☑ Eliminate or replace wordy introductory phrases or pretentious words and phrases (*in the case of, it may be said that, it appears that, needless to say*).

REPLACE	WITH
in order to, with a view to	to
due to the fact that, for the reason that, owing to the fact that, the reason for	because
by means of, by using, in connection with, through the use of	by, with
at this time, at this point in time, at present, at the present	now, currently

☑ Do not overuse <u>intensifiers</u>, such as *very, more, most, best, quite, great, really,* and *especially*. Instead, provide specific and useful details.

☑ Use the "search and replace" command to locate and revise wordy expressions, including *to be* and unnecessary helping <u>verbs</u> (Tab 11) such as *will*.

connotation / denotation

The *denotations* of a word are its literal meanings, as defined in a dictionary. The *connotations* of a word are its meanings and associations beyond its literal definitions. For example, the denotations of *Hollywood* are "a district of Los Angeles" and "the U.S. movie industry as a whole"; its connotations for many are "glamour, opulence, and superficiality."

10

Style and Clarity

Often words have particular connotations for <u>audiences</u> (Tab 1) within professional groups and organizations. Choose words with both the most accurate denotations and the most appropriate connotations for the <u>context</u> (Tab 1). See also <u>defining terms</u> (Tab 1) and <u>word choice</u>.

emphasis

Emphasis in writing means highlighting the facts and ideas you consider important and subordinating those of secondary importance. You can achieve emphasis through one or more of the following techniques: position, climactic order, sentence length, sentence type, active <u>voice</u> (Tab 11), <u>repetition</u>, <u>intensifiers</u>, direct statements, long <u>dashes</u> (Tab 12), and typographical devices.

Achieving Emphasis

Position. Place the idea in a conspicuous position. The first and last words of a sentence, paragraph, or document stand out in readers' minds.

▶ Moon craters are important to understanding the earth's history because they reflect geological history.

The term *moon craters* is emphasized because it appears at the beginning of the sentence, and *geological history* is emphasized because it appears at the end of the sentence. See also <u>subordination</u>.

Climactic Order. List the ideas or facts within a sentence in sequence from least to most important, as in the following example. See also <u>lists</u> (Tab 7).

▶ Discontinuation of the HGX212 line of circuit boards would cause some technicians to be relocated to other cities, some to be reclassified to a lower grade, and some to lose their jobs.

Sentence Length. Vary sentence length strategically. A short sentence that follows a long sentence or a series of long sentences stands out in the reader's mind, as in the short sentence ("We must cut costs") that ends the following paragraph. See also <u>sentence construction</u> (Tab 11).

▶ We have already reviewed the problem the accounting department has experienced during the past year. We could continue to examine the causes of our problems and point an accusing finger at all the culprits beyond our control, but in the end it all leads to one simple conclusion. We must cut costs.

Sentence Type.   Vary sentences by the strategic use of a compound sentence, a complex sentence, or a simple sentence. See <u>sentence variety</u>.

▶ The report submitted by the committee was carefully illustrated, and it covered five pages of single-spaced copy.
[This compound sentence carries no special emphasis; it contains two coordinate independent clauses.]

▶ The committee's report, which was carefully illustrated, covered five pages of single-spaced copy.
[This complex sentence emphasizes the size of the report.]

▶ The carefully illustrated report submitted by the committee covered five pages of single-spaced copy.
[This simple sentence emphasizes that the report was carefully illustrated.]

Active Voice.   Use the active voice to emphasize the performer of an action: Make the performer the subject of the verb.

▶ Our department designed the new system.
[This sentence emphasizes *our department*, which is the performer and the subject of the verb, *designed*.]

Repetition.   Repeat key terms, as in the use of the word *remains* and the phrase *come and go* in the following sentence.

▶ Similarly, atoms *come and go* in a molecule, but the molecule *remains*; molecules *come and go* in a cell, but the cell *remains*; cells *come and go* in a body, but the body *remains*; persons *come and go* in an organization, but the organization *remains*.

—Kenneth Boulding, *Beyond Economics*

Intensifiers.   Although you can use intensifiers (*most, much, very*) for emphasis, this technique is so easily abused that it should be used with caution.

▶ The final proposal is *much* more persuasive than the first one.
[The intensifier *much* emphasizes the contrast.]

Direct Statements.   Use direct statements, such as "most important," "foremost," or someone's name in a direct address.

▶ Most important, keep in mind that everything you do affects the company's bottom line.

▶ John, I believe we should rethink our plans.

10

Style and Clarity

Long Dashes.   Use a dash to call attention to a particular word or statement.

▶ The job will be done — after we are under contract.

Typographical Devices.   Use *italics*, **bold type**, underlining, color, and CAPITAL LETTERS — but use them sparingly because overuse can create visual clutter and cause readers to ignore truly important information. See also capitalization (Tab 12), italics (Tab 12), and layout and design (Tab 7).

euphemisms

A euphemism is an inoffensive substitute for a word or phrase that could be distasteful, offensive, or too blunt: *passed away* for *died*; *previously owned* or *preowned* for *used*; *lay off* or *downsize* for *fire* or *terminate* employees. Used judiciously, euphemisms can help you avoid embarrassing or offending someone.

❖ ETHICS NOTE Euphemisms can also hide the facts of a situation (*incident* or *event* for *accident*) or be a form of affectation if used carelessly. Avoid them especially in international correspondence (Tab 3) and other forms of global communication (Tab 1) where their meanings could be not only confusing but also misleading. See also ethics in writing (Tab 1). ❖

expletives

An expletive is a word that fills the position of another word, phrase, or clause. *It* and *there* are common expletives.

▶ *It* is certain that he will be promoted.

In the example, the expletive *it* occupies the position of subject in place of the real subject, *that he will be promoted.* Expletives are sometimes necessary to avoid awkwardness, but they are commonly overused, and most sentences can be better stated without them.

  Many   *were*
▶ ~~There were many~~ files lost when we converted to the new server.
   ^   ^

In addition to its grammatical use, the word *expletive* means a profane exclamation or oath.

figures of speech

A figure of speech is an imaginative expression that often compares two things that are basically not alike but have at least one thing in common. For example, if a device is cone-shaped and has an opening at the narrow end, you might say that it looks like a volcano.

Figures of speech can clarify the unfamiliar by relating a new concept to one with which readers are familiar. In that respect, they help establish understanding between the specialist and the nonspecialist. (See also <u>audience</u>, Tab 1.) Figures of speech can help translate the abstract into the concrete; in the process of doing so, they can also make writing more colorful and graphic. (See also <u>abstract / concrete words</u>.) A figure of speech must make sense, however, to achieve the desired effect.

ILLOGICAL   Without the fuel of tax incentives, our economic engine would operate less efficiently. [An engine would not operate at all without fuel.]

Figures of speech also must be consistent to be effective.

▶ We must get our sales program *back on course*, and we are counting on you to *steer the effort.* ~~carry the ball.~~
                          ^

A figure of speech should not overshadow the point the writer is trying to make. In addition, it is better to use no figure of speech at all than to use a trite one. A surprise that comes "like a bolt out of the blue" seems stale and not much of a surprise. See also <u>clichés</u> and <u>idioms</u>.

garbled sentences

A garbled sentence is one that is so tangled with structural and grammatical problems that it cannot be repaired. Garbled sentences often result from an attempt to squeeze too many ideas into one sentence.

▶ My job objectives are accomplished by my having a diversified background which enables me to operate effectively and efficiently, consisting of a degree in computer science, along with twelve years of experience, including three years in Staff Engineering-Packaging, sets a foundation for a strong background in areas of analyzing problems and assessing economical and reasonable solutions.

10

Style and Clarity

Do not try to patch such a sentence; rather, analyze the ideas it contains, list them in a logical sequence, and then construct one or more entirely new sentences. An analysis of the preceding example yields the following five ideas:

- My job requires that I analyze problems to find economical and workable solutions.
- My diversified background helps me accomplish my job.
- I have a computer-science degree.
- I have twelve years of job experience.
- Three of these years have been in Staff Engineering-Packaging.

Using those five ideas—together with parallel structure, sentence variety, subordination, and transition—the writer might have described the job as follows:

▶ My job requires that I analyze problems to find economical and workable solutions. Both my education and my experience help me achieve this goal. Specifically, I have a computer-science degree and twelve years of job experience, three of which have been in the Staff Engineering-Packaging Department.

See also awkwardness, mixed constructions (Tab 11), and sentence construction (Tab 11).

idioms

An idiom is a group of words that has a special meaning apart from its literal meaning. Someone "*runs* for political office" in the United States, for example, while a candidate "*stands* for office" in the United Kingdom. Because such expressions are specific to a culture, nonnative speakers must memorize them.

Idioms are often constructed with prepositions that follow adjectives (*similar to*), nouns (*need for*), and verbs (*approve of*). Some idioms can change meaning slightly with the preposition used, as in *agree to* ("consent") and *agree with* ("in accord"). The following are typical idioms that give nonnative speakers trouble.

call off [cancel]	hand in [submit]
call on [visit a client]	hand out [distribute]
drop in on [visit unexpectedly]	look up [research a subject]
find out [discover information]	run into [meet by chance]
get through with [finish]	run out of [deplete supply]
give up [quit]	watch out for [be careful]

Idioms often provide helpful shortcuts. In fact, they can make writing more natural and lively. Avoid them, however, if your writing is to be translated into another language or read in other English-speaking countries. Because no language system can fully explain such usages, a reader must check dictionaries or usage guides to interpret the meaning of idioms. See also <u>English as a second language (ESL)</u> (Tab 11), <u>global communication</u> (Tab 1), and <u>international correspondence</u> (Tab 3).

intensifiers

Intensifiers are <u>adverbs</u> (Tab 11) that emphasize degree, such as *very, quite, rather, such,* and *too.* (See also <u>emphasis</u>.) Although intensifiers serve a legitimate and necessary function, unnecessary intensifiers can weaken your writing. Eliminate those that do not make an obvious contribution or replace them with specific details.

▶ The team learned the ~~very~~ good news that it had been awarded
   $10,000
   a ~~rather substantial monetary~~ prize for its design.
   ^

Some words (such as *perfect, impossible,* and *final*) do not logically permit intensification because, by definition, they do not allow degrees of comparison. Although usage often ignores that logical restriction, avoid such comparisons in business writing. See also <u>adjectives</u> (Tab 11); <u>adverbs</u> (Tab 11); <u>conciseness</u>; and the Appendix, "Usage."

jargon

Jargon is a specialized slang that is unique to an occupational or a professional group. For example, human resource personnel use the term *headhunters* to describe specialists who recruit professional and executive personnel. Jargon is at first understood only by insiders; over time, it may become known more widely and become a <u>buzzword</u>. If all your readers are members of a particular occupational group, jargon may provide an efficient means of communicating. However, if you have any doubt that your entire <u>audience</u> (Tab 1) is part of such a group, avoid using jargon. See also <u>affectation</u>.

logic errors

Logic is the study of the principles of reasoning. In most writing, especially in writing intended to persuade an audience, logic is essential to demonstrating that your conclusions are valid. This entry describes typical errors in logic that can undermine the point you are trying to communicate and your credibility. See also <u>persuasion</u> (Tab 1).

❖ ETHICS NOTE Many logic errors occur unintentionally. However, when they are used intentionally to mislead readers, that practice is unethical. See also <u>ethics in writing</u> (Tab 1). ❖

Lack of Reason

When a statement is contrary to the reader's common sense, that statement is not reasonable. If, for example, you stated, "New York City is a small town," your reader would immediately question your statement. However, if you stated, "Although New York City's population is over eight million, it is composed of neighborhoods that function as small towns," your reader could probably accept the statement as reasonable.

Sweeping Generalizations

Sweeping generalizations are statements that are too broad or all-inclusive to be supportable. They are general statements that disregard exceptions: a flat statement such as "Management is never concerned about employees" ignores evidence that many managers are in fact concerned for their employees. Using such generalizations weakens your credibility.

Non Sequiturs

A non sequitur is a statement that does not logically follow a previous statement.

▶ I cleared off my desk, and the report is due today.

The missing link in these statements is that the writer cleared his or her desk to make space for materials to help finish the report that is due today. Avoid non sequiturs by making sure you explicitly state the logical connections of ideas and facts in your writing.

False Cause

A false cause (also called *post hoc, ergo propter hoc*) refers to the logical fallacy that because one event followed another event, the first somehow caused the second.

▶ I didn't bring my umbrella today. No wonder it is now raining.

▶ Because we now have our board meetings at the Education Center, our management turnover rate has declined.

10

Style and Clarity

Such errors in reasoning can happen when the writer hastily concludes that two events are related without examining whether a causal connection between them, in fact, exists.

Biased or Suppressed Evidence

A conclusion reached as a result of biased or suppressed evidence—self-serving data, questionable sources, purposely omitted or incomplete facts—is both illogical and unethical. Suppose you are preparing a report on the acceptance of a new policy among employees. If you distribute questionnaires only to those who think the policy is effective, the resulting evidence will be biased. Intentionally ignoring relevant data that might not support your position not only produces inaccurate results but also is unethical.

Fact Versus Opinion

Distinguish between fact and opinion. Facts include verifiable data or statements, whereas opinions are personal conclusions that may or may not be based on facts. For example, it is verifiable that distilled water boils at 100°C; that it tastes better or worse than tap water is an opinion. Distinguish the facts from your opinions in your writing so that your readers can draw their own conclusions.

Loaded Arguments

When you include an opinion in a statement and then reach conclusions that are based on that statement, you are loading the argument. Consider the following opening for a memo:

▶ I have several suggestions to improve the poorly written policy manual. First, we should change . . .

Unless everyone agrees that the manual is poorly written, readers may reject a writer's entire message because they disagree with this loaded premise. Conclusions reached with such loaded statements are weak and can produce negative reactions in readers who detect the loading.

nominalizations

A nominalization is a noun form of a verb that is often combined with vague and general (or "weak") verbs like *make, do, give, perform,* and *provide.* Avoid nominalizations when you can use specific verbs that communicate the same idea more directly and concisely.

        evaluate
▶ The staff should ~~perform an evaluation of~~ the new software.

If you use nominalizations solely to make your writing sound more formal, the result will be <u>affectation</u>. See also <u>business writing style</u>, <u>conciseness</u>, <u>plain language</u>, and <u>voice</u> (Tab 11).

parallel structure

Parallel structure requires that sentence elements that are alike in function be alike in grammatical form as well. This structure achieves an economy of words, clarifies meaning, expresses the equality of the ideas, and achieves <u>emphasis</u>. Parallel structure assists readers because it allows them to anticipate the meaning of a sentence element on the basis of its construction.

Parallel structure can be achieved with words, phrases, or clauses.

▶ If you want to benefit from the jobs training program, you must be *punctual, courteous,* and *conscientious.* [parallel words]

▶ If you want to benefit from the jobs training program, you must recognize the importance *of punctuality, of courtesy,* and *of conscientiousness.* [parallel phrases]

▶ If you want to benefit from the jobs training program, *you must arrive punctually, you must behave courteously,* and *you must respond conscientiously.* [parallel clauses]

Correlative conjunctions (*either . . . or, neither . . . nor, not only . . . but also*) should always join elements that use parallel structure. Both parts of the pairs should be followed immediately by the same grammatical form: two similar words, two similar phrases, or two similar clauses.

▶ Viruses carry either *DNA* or *RNA,* never both. [parallel words]

▶ Clearly, neither *serological tests* nor *virus isolation studies* alone would have been adequate. [parallel phrases]

▶ Either *we must increase our production efficiency* or *we must decrease our production goals.* [parallel clauses]

To make a parallel construction clear and effective, it is often best to repeat an article, a pronoun, a helping verb, a preposition, a subordinating conjunction, or the mark of an infinitive (*to*).

▶ The association has *a* mission statement and *a* code of ethics. [article]

▶ The software is popular *because* it is compatible across platforms and *because* it is easily customized. [subordinating conjunction]

Parallel structure is especially important in creating <u>lists</u> (Tab 7), outlines, <u>tables of contents</u> (Tab 6), and <u>headings</u> (Tab 7) because it lets

10

Style and Clarity

readers know the relative value of each item in a table of contents and each heading in the body of a document. See also <u>outlining</u> (Tab 1).

Faulty Parallelism

Faulty parallelism results when joined elements are intended to serve equal grammatical functions but do not have equal grammatical form.

Faulty parallelism sometimes occurs because a writer tries to compare items that are not comparable.

> **NOT PARALLEL** The company offers special college training to help hourly employees move into professional careers like engineering management, software development, service technicians, and sales trainees. [Notice faulty comparison of occupations—*engineering management* and *software development*—to people—*service technicians and sales trainees.*]

To avoid faulty parallelism, make certain that each element in a series is similar in form and structure to all others in the same series.

> **PARALLEL** The company offers special college training to help hourly employees move into professional careers like *engineering management, software development, technical services,* and *sales.*

plain language

Plain language is writing that is logically organized and understandable on the first reading. Such writing avoids unnecessary <u>jargon</u>, <u>affectation</u>, and technical terminology. Even with the best of intentions, however, you cannot always avoid using specialized terms and concepts. Accordingly, assess your <u>audience</u> (Tab 1) carefully to ensure that your language connects with their level of knowledge. Replace jargon and complex legal wording with familiar words or terms when possible.

> **COMPLEX** The systems integration specialist must be able to visually perceive the entire directional response module.
>
> **PLAIN LANGUAGE** The operator must be able to see the entire control panel.

If you are a health-care provider, for example, use the appropriate plain-language equivalent for medical terminology with patients in conversations and written guidelines: *bleeding* instead of *hemorrhaging*; *heart attack* instead of *myocardial infarction*; *cast* instead of *splint*;

stitches instead of *sutures*. If a plain-language alternative does not exist, define or explain a technical term on its first use and use visuals where necessary.

Writer's Checklist: Using Plain Language

☑ Identify your average reader's level of technical knowledge.

☑ Avoid unnecessary jargon and legal language.

☑ Avoid confusing terms and constructions.

- Define necessary **abbreviations** (Tab 12) and acronyms.
- Use the same words consistently for the same things.
- Do not give an obscure meaning to a word.

☑ Use the active **voice** (Tab 11) for directness and for identifying the doer of an action.

☑ Use the second **person** (Tab 11) (*you / yours*) or imperative **mood** (Tab 11) to write directly to the reader.

☑ Write coherent sentences.

- Aim for one message in each sentence.
- Break up complex information into smaller, easier-to-understand units.
- Use **positive writing** and the present **tense** (Tab 11) as much as possible.

☑ Select word placement carefully.

- Keep subjects and **objects** (Tab 11) close to their **verbs** (Tab 11).
- Put *only*, *always*, and other conditional words next to the words they modify.

Plain-language principles are especially useful when writing **international correspondence** (Tab 3). For format and visual elements that promote clarity, see **layout and design** (Tab 7) and **lists** (Tab 7). See also **English as a second language** (Tab 11). For information on plain-language laws and practices, see *www.plainlanguage.gov/site/about.cfm* and *www.plainlanguagenetwork.org.*

positive writing

Presenting positive information as though it were negative is confusing to readers.

NEGATIVE   If the error does *not* involve data transmission, the backup function will *not* be used.

In this sentence, the reader must reverse two negatives to understand the exception that is being stated. The following sentence presents the exception in a positive and straightforward manner.

POSITIVE   The backup function is used only when the error involves data transmission.

❖ ETHICS NOTE Negative facts or conclusions, however, should be stated negatively; stating a negative fact or conclusion positively is deceptive because it can mislead the reader.

DECEPTIVE   In the first quarter of this year, employee exposure to airborne lead averaged within 10 percent of acceptable state health standards.

ACCURATE   In the first quarter of this year, employee exposure to airborne lead averaged 10 percent below acceptable state health standards.

See also ethics in writing (Tab 1). ❖

Even if what you are saying is negative, do not state it more negatively than necessary.

NEGATIVE   We are withholding your shipment because we have not received your payment.

POSITIVE   We will forward your shipment as soon as we receive your payment.

See also correspondence (Tab 3), plain language, and "you" viewpoint.

repetition

The deliberate use of repetition to build a sustained effect or to emphasize a feeling or an idea can be a powerful device. See also emphasis.

▶ Similarly, atoms *come and go* in a molecule, but the molecule *remains*; molecules *come and go* in a cell, but the cell *remains*; cells *come and go* in a body, but the body *remains*; persons *come and go* in an organization, but the organization *remains*.

—Kenneth Boulding, *Beyond Economics*

Repetition of keywords from a previous sentence or paragraph can also be used effectively to achieve transition.

▶ For many years, *oil* has been a major industrial energy source. However, *oil* supplies are limited, and other sources of energy must be developed.

Be consistent in the word or phrase you use to refer to something. In business writing, it is generally better to repeat a word or use a clear pronoun reference (so readers know that you mean the same thing) than to use synonyms to avoid repetition. See also <u>affectation</u>.

SYNONYMS	Several recent *analyses* support our conclusion. These *studies* cast doubt on the feasibility of long-range forecasting. The *reports*, however, are strictly theoretical.
CONSISTENT TERMS	Several recent *studies* support our conclusion. These *studies* cast doubt on the feasibility of long-range forecasting. *They* are, however, strictly theoretical.

Purposeless repetition, however, makes a sentence awkward and hides its key ideas. See also <u>conciseness</u>.

▶ She said that the customer ~~said that he~~ was canceling the order.

---

sentence variety

Sentences can vary in length, structure, and complexity. As you revise, vary your sentences so that they do not become tiresomely alike. See also <u>sentence construction</u> (Tab 11).

Sentence Length

A series of sentences of the same length is monotonous, so varying sentence length makes writing less tedious to the reader. For example, avoid stringing together a number of short independent clauses. Either connect them with subordinating connectives, thereby making some dependent clauses, or make some clauses into separate sentences.

STRING	The river is 63 miles long, and it averages 50 yards in width, and its depth averages 8 feet.
IMPROVED	The river, which is 63 miles long and averages 50 yards in width, has an average depth of 8 feet.
IMPROVED	The river is 63 miles long. It averages 50 yards in width and 8 feet in depth.

You can often effectively combine short sentences by converting verbs into adjectives.

failed
▶ The digital shift indicator ~~failed. It~~ was pulled from the market.

Although too many short sentences make your writing sound choppy and immature, a short sentence can be effective following a long one.

► During the past two decades, many changes have occurred in American life—the extent, durability, and significance of which no one has yet measured. *No one can.*

In general, short sentences are good for emphatic, memorable statements. Long sentences are good for detailed explanations and support. Nothing is inherently wrong with a long sentence, or even with a complicated one, as long as its meaning is clear and direct. Sentence length becomes an element of style when varied for emphasis or contrast; a conspicuously short or long sentence can be used to good effect.

Word Order

When a series of sentences all begin in exactly the same way (usually with an article and a noun), the result is likely to be monotonous. You can make your sentences more interesting by occasionally starting with a modifying word, phrase, or clause.

► *To salvage the project*, she presented alternatives when existing policies failed to produce results. [modifying phrase]

However, overuse of this technique can itself be monotonous, so use it in moderation.

Inverted word order can be an effective way to achieve variety, but be careful not to create an awkward construction.

AWKWARD	So good sales have never been.
EFFECTIVE	Never have sales been so good.

For variety, you can alter normal sentence order by inserting a phrase or clause.

► Titanium fills the gap, *both in weight and in strength*, between aluminum and steel.

The technique of inserting a phrase or clause is good for achieving emphasis, providing detail, breaking monotony, and regulating pace.

Loose and Periodic Sentences

A loose sentence makes its major point at the beginning and then adds subordinate phrases and clauses that develop or modify the point. A loose sentence could end at one or more points before it actually ends, as the periods in brackets illustrate in the following example:

► It went up[.], a great ball of fire about a mile in diameter[.], an elemental force freed from its bonds[.] after being chained for billions of years.

A periodic sentence delays its main idea until the end by presenting modifiers or subordinate ideas first, thus holding the readers' interest until the end.

▶ During the past century, the attitude of Americans toward technology underwent a profound change.

Experiment with shifts from loose sentences to periodic sentences in your own writing, especially during <u>revision</u> (Tab 1). Avoid the monotony of a long series of loose sentences, particularly a series containing coordinate clauses joined by <u>conjunctions</u> (Tab 11). Using <u>subordination</u> not only provides emphasis but also makes your sentences more interesting.

10

Style and Clarity

subordination

Subordination is the use of sentence structure to show the appropriate relationship between ideas of unequal importance.

▶ Envirex Systems now employs 500 people. It was founded just three years ago. [The two ideas are equally important.]

▶ Envirex Systems, *which now employs 500 people*, was founded just three years ago. [The number of employees is subordinated; the founding date is emphasized.]

▶ Envirex Systems, *which was founded just three years ago*, now employs 500 people. [The founding date is subordinated; the number of employees is emphasized.]

Subordination allows you to emphasize your main idea by putting less-important ideas in subordinate <u>clauses</u> (Tab 11) or <u>phrases</u> (Tab 11).

DEPENDENT CLAUSE	The regional manager's report, *which covered five pages*, was carefully illustrated.
PHRASE	The regional manager's report, *covering five pages*, was carefully illustrated.
SINGLE MODIFIER	The regional manager's *five-page* report was carefully illustrated.

Subordinating conjunctions (*because, if, while, when, although*) achieve subordination effectively.

▶ An increase in local sales is unlikely *because* the local population has declined.

You may use a coordinating conjunction (*and, but, for, nor, or, so, yet*) to concede that an opposite or balancing fact is true; however, a subordinating conjunction can often make the point more smoothly.

▶ *Although* their bank has a lower interest rate on loans, ours provides a wider range of essential services.

The relationship between a conditional statement and a statement of consequences is clearer if the condition is expressed as a subordinate clause.

▶ *Because* the bill was incorrect, the customer was angry.

Relative pronouns (*who, whom, which, that*) can be used effectively in subordinate clauses. See <u>pronouns</u> (Tab 11).

▶ OnlinePro, *which* protects computers from malicious programs, makes your system "invisible" to hackers.

Avoid subordinate constructions that overlap and depend on the preceding construction. Overlapping can make the relationship between a relative pronoun and its antecedent less clear.

OVERLAPPING	Shock, *which* often accompanies severe injuries and infections, is a failure of the circulation, *which* is marked by a fall in blood pressure *that* initially affects the skin (*which* explains pallor) and later the vital organs such as the kidneys and brain.
CLEAR	Shock often accompanies severe injuries and infections. Marked by a fall in blood pressure, it is a failure of the circulation, initially to the skin (thus producing pallor) and later to the vital organs like the kidneys and the brain.

Effective subordination can be used to achieve <u>conciseness</u>, <u>emphasis</u>, and <u>sentence variety</u>.

telegraphic style

Telegraphic style condenses writing by omitting articles, pronouns, conjunctions, and <u>transitions</u>. Although <u>conciseness</u> is important, especially in instructions, writers sometimes try to achieve conciseness by omitting necessary words and thus producing misunderstandings. Compare the following two passages and notice how much easier the revised version reads (the added words are italicized).

| TELEGRAPHIC | Per 5/21 e-mail, 12 instruction booklets/question-naires enclosed. Report can be complete when above materials received. July filling quickly, so let's set date. Pls advise. |
| CLEAR | *As promised in my May 21* e-mail, enclosed *are* 12 *copies of the* instruction booklet *and the* questionnaire. *We* can complete *the* report when *we* receive *the questionnaires. Our* July *calendar is* filling quickly, so *please call me to* set *a meeting* date *as soon as possible.* |

Telegraphic style can also produce ambiguity, as the following example demonstrates.

AMBIGUOUS	The director wants report written by New York office. [Does the director want a report that the New York office *wrote in the past,* or does the director want the New York office *to write a report in the future*?]
CLEAR	The director wants the report *that was* written by the New York office.
CLEAR	The director wants the report *to be* written by the New York office.

▶ PROFESSIONALISM NOTE Although you may save yourself work by writing telegraphically, you may produce serious misunderstandings and your readers will have to work that much harder to decipher your meaning. Professional courtesy requires that you help your <u>reader</u> (Tab 1). Even in <u>text messaging</u> (Tab 2), you need to make sure your reader will understand your message. ▶

tone

Tone is the attitude a writer expresses toward the subject and his or her readers. In workplace writing, tone may range widely—depending on the purpose, situation, context, audience, and even the medium of a communication. For example, in an e-mail message to be read only by an associate who is also a friend, your tone might be casual.

▶ Your proposal to Smith and Kline is awesome. We'll just need to hammer out the schedule. If we get the contract, I owe you lunch!

In a message to your manager or superior, however, your tone might be more formal and respectful.

▶ Your proposal to Smith and Kline is excellent. I have marked a couple of places where I'm concerned that we are committing ourselves to a schedule that we might not be able to keep. If I can help further, please let me know.

In a message that serves as a report to numerous readers, the tone would be professional, without the more-personal style that you would use with an individual reader.

▶ The Smith and Kline proposal appears complete and thorough, based on our department's evaluation. Several small revisions, however, would ensure that the company is not committing itself to an unrealistic schedule. These revisions are marked on the copy of the report attached to this message.

The word choice, the introduction, and even the title contribute to the overall tone of your document. For instance, a title such as "Ecological Consequences of Diminishing Water Resources in California" clearly sets a different tone from "What Happens When We've Drained California Dry?" The first title would be appropriate for a report; the second title would be more appropriate for a popular blog or article. See also blogs and forums (Tab 2), business writing style, correspondence (Tab 3), and titles (Tab 4).

10

Style and Clarity

transition

Transition is the means of achieving a smooth flow of ideas from sentence to sentence, paragraph to paragraph, and subject to subject. Transition is a two-way indicator of what has been said and what will be said; it provides readers with guideposts for linking ideas and clarifying the relationship between them.

Transition can be obvious.

▶ *Having considered* the benefits of a new facility, *we move next* to the question of adequate staffing.

Transition can be subtle.

▶ *Even if* this facility can be built at a reasonable cost, there *still remains* the issue of adequate staffing.

Either way, you now have your readers' attention fastened on the subject of adequate staffing, which is exactly what you set out to do.

Methods of Transition

Transition can be achieved in many ways: (1) using transitional words and phrases, (2) repeating keywords or key ideas, (3) using pronouns (Tab 11) with clear antecedents, (4) using enumeration (1, 2, 3, or first, second, third), (5) summarizing a previous paragraph, (6) asking a question, and (7) using a brief transitional paragraph.

Certain words and phrases are inherently transitional. Consider the following terms and their functions:

FUNCTION	TERMS
Result	*therefore, as a result, consequently, thus, hence*
Example	*for example, for instance, specifically, as an illustration*
Comparison	*similarly, likewise, in comparison*
Contrast	*but, yet, still, however, nevertheless, on the other hand*
Addition	*moreover, furthermore, also, too, besides, in addition*
Time	*now, later, meanwhile, since then, after that, before that time*
Sequence	*first, second, third, initially, then, next, finally*

Within a paragraph, such transitional expressions clarify and smooth the movement from idea to idea. Conversely, the lack of transitional devices can make for disjointed reading. See also <u>telegraphic style</u>.

Transition Between Sentences

You can achieve effective transition between sentences by repeating key-words or key ideas from preceding sentences and by using pronouns that refer to antecedents in previous sentences. Consider the following short paragraph, which uses both of those means.

▶ Representative of many American university towns is Middletown. *This midwestern town*, formerly *a sleepy farming community*, is today the home of a large and vibrant *academic community*. Attracting students from all over the Midwest, *this university town* has grown very rapidly in the last ten years.

Enumeration is another device for achieving transition.

▶ The recommendation rests on *two conditions*. *First*, the department staff must be expanded to handle the increased workload. *Second*, sufficient time must be provided for training the new staff.

Transition Between Paragraphs

The means discussed so far for achieving transition between sentences can also be effective for achieving transition between paragraphs. For paragraphs, however, longer transitional elements are often required. One technique is to use an opening sentence that summarizes the preceding paragraph and then moves on to a new paragraph.

> One property of material considered for manufacturing processes is hardness. Hardness is the internal resistance of the material to the forcing apart or closing together of its molecules. Another property is ductility, the characteristic of material that permits it to be drawn into a wire. Material also may possess malleability, the property that makes it capable of being rolled or hammered into thin sheets of various shapes. Purchasing managers must consider these properties before selecting manufacturing materials for use in production.
>
> *The requirements of hardness, ductility, and malleability* account for the high cost of such materials. . . .

Another technique is to ask a question at the end of one paragraph and answer it at the beginning of the next.

> New technology has often been feared because it has at times displaced some jobs. However, it invariably created many more jobs than it eliminated. Almost always, the jobs eliminated by technological advances have been unskilled jobs, and workers who have been displaced have been forced to increase their skills, which resulted in better and higher-paying jobs for them. *In view of this history, should we now uncritically embrace new technology?*
>
> Certainly technology has given us unparalleled access to information and created many new roles for employees. . . .

A purely transitional paragraph may be inserted to aid readability.

> The problem of poor management was a key factor that caused the weak performance of the company.
>
> *Two other setbacks to the company's fortunes also marked the company's decline: the loss of many skilled workers through the early retirement program and the intensification of the rate of employee turnover.*
>
> The early retirement program resulted in engineering staff . . .

If you provide logical <u>organization</u> (Tab 1) and have prepared an outline, your transitional needs will easily be satisfied and your writing will have <u>unity</u> and <u>coherence</u>. During revision, look for places where transition is missing and add it. Look for places where it is weak and strengthen it.

10

Style and Clarity

unity

Unity is singleness of <u>purpose</u> (Tab 1) and focus; a unified <u>paragraph</u> (Tab 1) or document has a central idea and does not digress into unrelated topics.

The logical sequence provided through <u>outlining</u> (Tab 1) is essential to achieving unity. An outline enables you to lay out the most direct route from introduction to conclusion, and it enables you to build each paragraph around a topic sentence that expresses a single idea. Effective <u>transition</u> helps build unity as well as <u>coherence</u>, because transitional terms clarify the relationship of each part to what precedes it.

vague words

10

Style and Clarity

A vague word is one that is imprecise in the context in which it is used. Some words are vague because they encompass such a broad range of meanings that there is no focus for their definition. Words such as *real, nice, important, good, bad, contact, thing,* and *fine* are often called "omnibus words" because they can have so many meanings and interpretations. In speech, our vocal inflections help make the meanings of such words clear. Because you cannot rely on vocal inflections when you are writing, avoid using vague words. Be concrete and specific. See also <u>abstract / concrete words</u> and <u>word choice</u>.

VAGUE	It was a *good* meeting. [Why was it good?]
SPECIFIC	The meeting resolved three questions: pay scales, fringe benefits, and workloads.

word choice

Mark Twain once said, "The difference between the almost right word and the right word is . . . the difference between the lightning-bug and the lightning." The most important goal in choosing the right word in business writing is the preciseness implied by Twain's comment. Vague words and abstract words defeat preciseness because they do not convey the writer's meaning directly and clearly.

VAGUE	It was a *productive* meeting.
PRECISE	The meeting resulted in the approval of the health-care benefits package.

In the first sentence, *productive* sounds specific but conveys little information; the revised sentence says specifically what made the meeting "productive." Although abstract words may at times be appropriate to your topic, using them unnecessarily will make your writing difficult to understand. See also <u>abstract / concrete words</u>.

Being aware of the connotations and denotations of words will help you anticipate the reactions of your <u>audience</u> (Tab 1) to the words you choose. Understanding antonyms (*fresh / stale*) and synonyms (*notorious / infamous*) will increase your ability to choose the proper word. For help with some common usage decisions, see the Appendix, "Usage." See also <u>connotation / denotation</u>.

Although many entries throughout this book will help you improve your word choices and avoid impreciseness, the following entries should be particularly helpful:

<u>affectation</u> 303	<u>euphemisms</u> 314
<u>biased language</u> 304	<u>idioms</u> 316
<u>buzzwords</u> 307	<u>jargon</u> 317
clichés 308	<u>logic errors</u> 317
<u>conciseness</u> 309	<u>vague words</u> 332

A key to choosing the correct and precise word is to keep current in your reading and to be aware of new words in your profession and in the language. In your quest for the right word, use a reputable and current dictionary. See also <u>English as a second language (ESL)</u> (Tab 11) and <u>plain language</u>.

10

Style and Clarity

"you" viewpoint

The "you" viewpoint places the reader's interest and perspective foremost. It is based on the principle that most readers are naturally more concerned about their own needs than they are about those of a writer or a writer's organization. See <u>audience</u> (Tab 1).

The "you" viewpoint often, but not always, means using the words *you* and *your* rather than *we, our, I,* and *mine.* Consider the following sentence that focuses on the needs of the writer and organization (*we*) rather than on those of the reader. (See also <u>refusals</u>, Tab 3.)

▶ *We must receive* your signed approval before *we can process* your payment.

Even though the sentence uses *your* twice, the words in italics suggest that the <u>point of view</u> (Tab 1) centers on the writer's need to receive the signed approval in order to process the payment. Consider the following revision, written with the "you" viewpoint.

▶ *So you can receive* your payment promptly, please send your signed approval.

Because the benefit to the reader is stressed, the writer is more likely to motivate the reader to act. See also <u>persuasion</u> (Tab 1).

In some instances, as suggested earlier, you may need to avoid using the pronouns *you* and *your* to achieve a positive <u>tone</u> and maintain goodwill. Notice how the first of the following examples (with *your*) seems to accuse the reader. But the second (without *your*) uses <u>positive writing</u> to emphasize a goal that reader and writer share—meeting a client's needs.

ACCUSATORY   *Your* budget makes no allowance for setup costs.

POSITIVE   The budget should include an allowance for setup costs to meet all the concerns of our client.

As this example illustrates, the "you" viewpoint means more than using the pronouns *you* and *your* or adopting a particular writing style. By genuinely considering the readers' interests as you write, you can achieve your <u>purpose</u> (Tab 1) not only in <u>correspondence</u> (Tab 3) but also in <u>proposals</u> (Tab 4), many <u>reports</u> (Tab 4), and <u>presentations</u> (Tab 8).

Grammar

Preview

Grammar is the systematic description of the way words work together to form a coherent language. *Parts of speech* is a term used to describe the class of words to which a particular word belongs, according to its function in a sentence. For example, <u>nouns</u> and <u>pronouns</u> name things, <u>verbs</u> express action, <u>adjectives</u> and <u>adverbs</u> describe and modify, and <u>conjunctions</u> and <u>prepositions</u> join elements of sentences. The entries in this section are intended to help you understand grammar and parts of speech so that you can diagnose and correct problems that may occur in your writing.

However, to be an effective writer, you also need to know the conventions of usage that help writers select the appropriate word or expression, as well as the principles of effective business writing style. Therefore, you may wish to consult Tab 10, "Style and Clarity"; Tab 12, "Punctuation and Mechanics"; and the Appendix, "Usage."

adjectives

An adjective is any word that modifies a **noun** or **pronoun**. *Descriptive adjectives* identify a quality of a noun or pronoun. *Limiting adjectives* impose boundaries on the noun or pronoun.

► *hot* surface [descriptive]

► *three* phone lines [limiting]

Limiting Adjectives

Limiting adjectives include the following categories:

* Articles (*a, an, the*)
* Demonstrative adjectives (*this, that, these, those*)
* Possessive adjectives (*my, your, his, her, its, our, their*)
* Numeral adjectives (*two, first*)
* Indefinite adjectives (*all, none, some, any*)

Articles.   Articles (*a, an, the*) are traditionally classified as adjectives because they modify nouns by either limiting them or making them more specific. See also **articles** and **English as a second language (ESL)**.

Demonstrative Adjectives.   A demonstrative adjective points to the thing it modifies, specifying the object's position in space or time. *This* and *these* specify a closer position; *that* and *those* specify a more remote position.

► *This* version is more current than *that* version produced last month.

► *These* sales figures are more recent than *those* reported last week.

Demonstrative adjectives often cause problems when they modify the nouns *kind, type,* and *sort.* Demonstrative adjectives used with those nouns should agree with them in number.

   this kind, *these* kinds; *that* type, *those* types

Confusion often develops when the preposition *of* is added (*this kind of, these kinds of*) and the object of the preposition does not conform in number to the demonstrative adjective and its noun. See also **agreement** and **prepositions**.

► *This kind of* human resources ~~policies are~~ standard.
   policy is

► *These kinds of* human resources ~~policy is~~ standard.
   policies are

11

Grammar

Avoid using demonstrative adjectives like *kind*, *type*, and *sort* that can easily lead to vagueness. Instead, be more specific.

Possessive Adjectives.   Because possessive adjectives (*my*, *your*, *his*, *her*, *its*, *our*, *their*) directly modify nouns, they function as adjectives, even though they are pronoun forms (*my* idea, *her* plans, *their* projects).

Numeral Adjectives.   Numeral adjectives identify quantity, degree, or place in a sequence. They always modify count nouns. Numeral adjectives are divided into two subclasses: cardinal and ordinal. A *cardinal adjective* expresses an exact quantity (*one* pencil, *two* computers); an *ordinal adjective* expresses degree or sequence (*first* quarter, *second* edition).

In most writing, an ordinal adjective should be spelled out if it is a single word (*tenth*) and written in figures if it is more than one word (*312th*). Ordinal numbers can also function as adverbs. ("John arrived *first*.") See also <u>numbers</u> (Tab 12).

Indefinite Adjectives.   Indefinite adjectives do not designate anything specific about the nouns they modify (*some* monitors, *all* designers). The articles *a* and *an* are included among the indefinite adjectives (*a* chair, *an* application).

Comparison of Adjectives

Most adjectives in the positive form show the comparative form with the suffix *-er* for two items and the superlative form with the suffix *-est* for three or more items.

▶ The first report is *long*. [positive form]

▶ The second report is *longer*. [comparative form]

▶ The third report is *longest*. [superlative form]

Many two-syllable adjectives and most three-syllable adjectives are preceded by the word *more* or *most* to form the comparative or the superlative.

▶ The new media center is *more* impressive than the old one. It is the *most* impressive in the county.

A few adjectives have irregular forms of comparison (*much*, *more*, *most*; *little*, *less*, *least*).

Some adjectives (*round*, *unique*, *exact*, *accurate*), often called *absolute words*, are not logically subject to comparison.

Placement of Adjectives

When limiting and descriptive adjectives appear together, the limiting adjectives precede the descriptive adjectives, with the articles usually in the first position.

▶ *The ten yellow* taxis were sold at auction.
[article (*The*), limiting adjective (*ten*), descriptive adjective (*yellow*)]

Within a sentence, adjectives may appear before the nouns they modify (the attributive position) or after the nouns they modify (the predicative position).

▶ *The small* jobs are given priority. [attributive position]

▶ The exposure is *brief*. [predicative position]

Use of Adjectives

Nouns often function as adjectives to clarify the meaning of other nouns.

▶ The *accident* report prompted a *product* redesign.

When adjectives modifying the same noun can be reversed and still make sense or when they can be separated by *and* or *or*, they should be separated by commas.

▶ The company seeks *bright, energetic, creative* managers.

Notice that there is no comma after *creative*. Never use a comma between a final adjective and the noun it modifies. When an adjective modifies a phrase, no comma is required.

▶ We need an *updated Web-page design*.
[*Updated* modifies the phrase *Web-page design*.]

Writers sometimes string together a series of nouns used as adjectives to form a unit modifier, thereby creating stacked (jammed) <u>modifiers</u>, which can confuse readers. See also <u>word choice</u> (Tab 10).

11

Grammar

ESL TIP for Using Adjectives

Do not add *-s* or *-es* to an adjective to make it plural.

▶ the *long* trip

▶ the *long* trips

(*continued*)

> **ESL TIP** for Using Adjectives (*continued*)
>
> Capitalize adjectives of origin (city, state, nation, continent).
>
> ▶ the *Venetian* canals
>
> ▶ the *Texas* longhorn steer
>
> ▶ the *French* government
>
> ▶ the *African* continent
>
> In English, verbs of feeling (for example, *bore, interest, surprise*) have two adjectival forms: the present participle (*-ing*) and the past participle (*-ed*). Use the present participle to describe what causes the feeling. Use the past participle to describe the person who experiences the feeling.
>
> ▶ We heard the *surprising* election results.
> [The *election results* cause the feeling.]
>
> ▶ Only the losing candidate was *surprised* by the election results.
> [The *candidate* experienced the feeling of surprise.]
>
> Adjectives follow nouns in English in only two cases: when the adjective functions as a subjective complement ("That project is not *finished*") and when an adjective phrase or clause modifies the noun ("The project that *was suspended temporarily*"). In all other cases, adjectives are placed before the noun.
>
> When a sentence has multiple adjectives, it is often difficult to know the right order. The guidelines illustrated in the following example would apply in most circumstances, but there are exceptions. (Normally do not use a phrase with so many stacked <u>modifiers</u>.) See also <u>articles</u>.
>
> ▶ The six extra-large rectangular brown cardboard take-out containers
>
>

adverbs

An adverb modifies the action or condition expressed by a <u>verb</u>.

▶ The wrecking ball hit the side of the building *hard*.
[The adverb tells *how* the wrecking ball hit the building.]

An adverb also can modify an <u>adjective</u>, another adverb, or a <u>clause</u>.

▶ The brochure design used *remarkably* bright colors.
[*Remarkably* modifies the adjective *bright*.]

▶ The redesigned brake pad lasted *much* longer than the previous one.
[*Much* modifies the adverb *longer*.]

▶ *Surprisingly*, the engine failed.
[*Surprisingly* modifies the clause *the engine failed*.]

Use adverbs sparingly in business writing. Because they are often subjective (hot/cold, hard/soft, long/short), consider providing specifics that define them or provide context. How hot? (Give the temperature.) How fast? (State the speed or rate.) How short or long? (State the length.) How expensive or efficient? (Compare relative costs or provide data on time savings.)

Types of Adverbs

A simple adverb can answer one of the following questions:

Where? (adverb of place)
• Move the display *forward* slightly.

When? or *How often?* (adverb of time)
• Replace the thermostat *immediately*.
• I worked overtime *twice* this week.

How? (adverb of manner)
• Add the solvent *cautiously*.

How much? (adverb of degree)
• The *nearly* completed report was sent to the director.

An interrogative adverb can ask a question (*Where? When? Why? How?*):

▶ *How* many hours did you work last week?

▶ *Why* was the hard drive reformatted?

A conjunctive adverb can modify the clause that it introduces as well as join two independent clauses with a <u>semicolon</u> (Tab 12). The most common conjunctive adverbs are *however, nevertheless, moreover, therefore, further, then, consequently, besides, accordingly, also,* and *thus*.

▶ I rarely work on weekends; *however*, this weekend will be an exception.

In this example, note that a semicolon precedes and a comma follows *however*. The conjunctive adverb (*however*) introduces the independent

11

Grammar

clause (*this weekend will be an exception*) and indicates its relationship to the preceding independent clause (*I rarely work on weekends*). See also transition (Tab 10).

Comparison of Adverbs

Most one-syllable adverbs show comparison with the suffixes *-er* and *-est*.

▶ This motor runs *fast*. [positive form]

▶ This motor runs *faster* than the old one. [comparative form]

▶ This motor runs the *fastest* of the three tested. [superlative form]

Most adverbs with two or more syllables end in *-ly*, and most adverbs ending in *-ly* are compared by inserting the comparative *more* or *less* or the superlative *most* or *least* in front of them.

▶ The patient recovered *more quickly* than the staff expected.

▶ *Most surprisingly*, the engine failed during the final test phase.

A few irregular adverbs require a change in form to indicate comparison (*well, better, best; badly, worse, worst; far, farther, farthest*).

▶ The training program functions *well*.

▶ Our training program functions *better* than most others in the industry.

▶ Many consider our training program the *best* in the industry.

Placement of Adverbs

An adverb usually should be placed in front of the verb it modifies.

▶ The pilot *methodically* performed the preflight check.

An adverb may, however, follow the verb (or the verb and its object) that it modifies.

▶ The system failed *unexpectedly*.

▶ They replaced the hard drive *quickly*.

An adverb may be placed between a helping verb and a main verb.

▶ In this temperature range, the pressure will *quickly* drop.

Adverbs such as *only, nearly, almost, just*, and *hardly* should be placed immediately before the words they limit. See also modifiers.

agreement

Grammatical agreement is the correspondence in form between different elements of a sentence to indicate number, <u>person</u>, gender, and case. A subject and its <u>verb</u> must agree in number.

▶ The *design is* acceptable.
[The singular subject, *design*, requires the singular verb, *is*.]

▶ The new *products are* going into production soon.
[The plural subject, *products*, requires the plural verb, *are*.]

A subject and its verb must agree in person.

▶ *I am* the designer.
[The first-person singular subject, *I*, requires the first-person singular verb, *am*.]

▶ *They are* the designers.
[The third-person plural subject, *they*, requires the third-person plural verb, *are*.]

A <u>pronoun</u> and its antecedent must agree in person, number, gender, and case.

▶ The *employees* report that *they* are more efficient in the new facility.
[The third-person plural subject, *employees*, requires the third-person plural pronoun, *they*.]

▶ *Kaye McGuire* will meet with the staff on Friday, when *she* will assign duties.
[The third-person singular subject, *Kaye McGuire*, requires *she*, the third-person feminine pronoun, in the subjective case.]

See also <u>sentence construction</u>.

11

Grammar

appositives

An appositive is a <u>noun</u> or noun <u>phrase</u> that follows and amplifies another noun or noun phrase. It has the same grammatical function as the noun it complements.

▶ George Thomas, *the noted economist*, summarized the president's speech in a confidential memo.

▶ The noted economist *George Thomas* summarized the president's speech in a confidential memo.

For detailed information on the use of commas with appositives, see restrictive and nonrestrictive elements.

If you are in doubt about the case of an appositive, check it by substituting the appositive for the noun it modifies. See also pronouns.

▶ My boss gave the two of us, Jim and ~~I~~ *me*, the day off.

[You would not say, "My boss gave *I* the day off."]

articles

Articles (*a, an, the*) function as adjectives because they modify the items they designate by either limiting them or making them more specific. Articles may be indefinite or definite.

The indefinite articles, *a* and *an*, denote an unspecified item.

▶ *A* package was delivered yesterday. [*not* a specific package]

The choice between *a* and *an* depends on the sound rather than on the letter following the article. Use *a* before words or abbreviations beginning with a consonant sound, including *y* or *w* (*a* person, *a* historic event, *a* year's salary, *a* one-page report, *a* DNR order).

The definite article, *the*, denotes a particular item.

▶ *The* package was delivered yesterday. [*one* specific package]

Do not omit all articles from your writing in an attempt to be concise. Including articles costs nothing; eliminating them makes reading more difficult. (See also telegraphic style, Tab 10.) However, do not overdo it. An article can be superfluous.

▶ I'll meet you in *a* half *an* hour.
[Choose one article and eliminate the other.]

Do not capitalize articles in titles except when they are the first word ("*The Economist* reviewed *Winning the Talent Wars*").

ESL TIP for Using Articles

Whether to use a definite or an indefinite article is determined by what you can safely assume about your audience's knowledge. In each of these sentences, you can safely assume that the reader can clearly identify the noun. Therefore, use a definite article.

▶ *The* sun rises in the east.
  [The Earth has only one *sun*.]

▶ Did you know that yesterday was *the* coldest day of the year so far?
  [The modified noun refers to *yesterday*.]

▶ *The* man who left his briefcase in the conference room was in a hurry.
  [The relative phrase *who left his briefcase in the conference room* restricts and, therefore, identifies the meaning of *man*.]

In the following sentence, however, you cannot assume that the reader can clearly identify the noun.

▶ *A* package is on the way.
  [It is impossible to identify specifically what package is meant.]

A more important question for some nonnative speakers of English is when *not* to use articles. These generalizations will help. Do not use articles with the following:

> Singular proper nouns
> ▶ Utah, Main Street, Harvard University, Mount Hood
> Plural nonspecific count nouns (when making generalizations)
> ▶ Helicopters are the new choice of transportation for the rich and famous.
> Singular mass nouns
> ▶ She loves coffee.
> Plural count nouns used as complements
> ▶ Those women are physicians.

See also English as a second language (ESL).

11

Grammar

---

clauses

A clause is a group of words that contains a subject and a predicate and that functions as a sentence or as part of a sentence. (See sentence construction.) Every subject-predicate word group in a sentence is a clause, and every sentence must contain at least one independent clause; otherwise, it is a <u>sentence fragment</u>.

   A clause that could stand alone as a simple sentence is an *independent clause*. ("*The scaffolding fell* when the rope broke.") A clause that could not stand alone if the rest of the sentence were deleted is a *dependent* (or *subordinate*) *clause*. ("I was at the St. Louis branch *when the decision was made*.")

   Dependent (or subordinate) clauses are useful in making the relationship between thoughts clearer and more succinct than if the ideas were presented in a series of simple sentences or compound sentences.

FRAGMENTED	The recycling facility is located between Millville and Darrtown. Both villages use it. [The two thoughts are of approximately equal importance.]
SUBORDINATED	The recycling facility, *which is located between Millville and Darrtown*, is used by both villages. [One thought is subordinated to the other.]

Subordinate clauses are especially effective for expressing thoughts that describe or explain another statement. Too much <u>subordination</u> (Tab 10), however, can be confusing and foster wordiness. See also <u>conciseness</u> (Tab 10).

11

Grammar

▶ He selected instructors whose classes ~~had a slant that was~~ specifi-
   ^{were}

cally designed for ~~students who intended to go into accounting.~~
   ^{accounting students.}

A clause can be connected with the rest of its sentence by a coordinating <u>conjunction</u>, a subordinating conjunction, a relative <u>pronoun</u>, or a conjunctive <u>adverb</u>.

▶ It was 500 miles to the facility, *so* we made arrangements to fly. [coordinating conjunction]

▶ Drivers will need to be alert *because* snow may cause hazardous conditions near the entrance to the warehouse. [subordinating conjunction]

▶ Robert M. Fano was the scientist *who* developed the earliest multiple-access computer system at MIT. [relative pronoun]

▶ We arrived in the evening; *nevertheless*, we began the tour of the facility. [conjunctive adverb]

complements

A complement is a word, <u>phrase</u>, or <u>clause</u> used in the predicate of a sentence to complete the meaning of the sentence.

- ▶ Pilots fly *airplanes*. [word]

- ▶ To invest is *to risk losses*. [phrase]

- ▶ John knew *that he would be late*. [clause]

Four types of complements are generally recognized: direct <u>object</u>, indirect object, objective complement, and subjective complement. See also <u>sentence construction</u>.

A *direct object* is a <u>noun</u> or noun equivalent that receives the action of a transitive <u>verb</u>; it answers the question *What?* or *Whom?* after the verb.

- ▶ I designed *a Web site*. [noun phrase]

- ▶ I like *to work*. [verbal]

- ▶ I like *it*. [pronoun]

- ▶ I like *what I saw*. [noun clause]

An *indirect object* is a noun or noun equivalent that occurs with a direct object after certain kinds of transitive verbs such as *give, wish, cause,* and *tell*. It answers the question *To whom or what?* or *For whom or what?*

- ▶ We should buy the *office* a *scanner*.
  [*Scanner* is the direct object, and *office* is the indirect object.]

An *objective complement* completes the meaning of a sentence by revealing something about the object of its transitive verb. An objective complement may be either a noun or an <u>adjective</u>.

- ▶ They call him *a genius*. [noun phrase]

- ▶ We painted the building *white*. [adjective]

A *subjective complement*, which follows a linking verb rather than a transitive verb, describes the subject. A subjective complement may be either a noun or an adjective.

- ▶ His sister is *a consultant*. [noun phrase follows linking verb *is*]

- ▶ His brother is *ill*. [adjective follows linking verb *is*]

11

Grammar

conjunctions

A conjunction connects words, <u>phrases</u>, or <u>clauses</u> and can also indicate the relationship between the elements it connects.

A *coordinating conjunction* joins two sentence elements that have identical functions. The coordinating conjunctions are *and, but, or, for, nor, yet,* and *so.*

- ▶ Nature *and* technology affect petroleum prices. [joins two <u>nouns</u>]

- ▶ To hear *and* to listen are two different things. [joins two phrases]

- ▶ I would like to include the survey, *but* that would make the report too long. [joins two clauses]

Coordinating conjunctions in the titles of books, articles, plays, and movies should not be capitalized unless they are the first or last word in the title.

- ▶ Our library contains *Consulting and Financial Independence* as well as *So You Want to Be a Consultant?*

Occasionally, a conjunction may begin a sentence; in fact, conjunctions can be strong transitional words and at times can provide <u>emphasis</u> (Tab 10). See also <u>transition</u> (Tab 10).

- ▶ I realize that the project is more difficult than expected and that you have encountered staffing problems. *But* we must meet our deadline.

Correlative conjunctions are used in pairs. The correlative conjunctions are *either . . . or, neither . . . nor, not only . . . but also, both . . . and,* and *whether . . . or.*

- ▶ The auditor will arrive on *either* Wednesday *or* Thursday.

A *subordinating conjunction* connects sentence elements of different relative importance, normally independent and dependent clauses. Frequently used subordinating conjunctions are *so, although, after, because, if, where, than, since, as, unless, before, that, though,* and *when.*

- ▶ I left the office *after* I had finished the report.

A *conjunctive adverb* functions as a conjunction because it joins two independent clauses. The most common conjunctive <u>adverbs</u> are *however, moreover, therefore, further, then, consequently, besides, accordingly, also,* and *thus.*

- ▶ The engine performed well in the laboratory; *however,* it failed under road conditions.

dangling modifiers

Phrases that do not clearly and logically refer to the correct <u>noun</u> or <u>pronoun</u> are called *dangling modifiers*. Dangling modifiers usually appear at the beginning of a sentence as an introductory <u>phrase</u>.

DANGLING	*While eating lunch*, the computer malfunctioned. [*Who* was eating lunch?]
CORRECT	While *I* was eating lunch, the computer malfunctioned.

Dangling modifiers can appear at the end of the sentence as well.

DANGLING	The program gains efficiency *by eliminating the superfluous coding*. [*Who* eliminates the superfluous coding?]
CORRECT	The program gains efficiency *when you* eliminate the superfluous coding.

To correct a dangling modifier, add the appropriate subject to either the dangling modifier or the main <u>clause</u>.

DANGLING	After finishing the research, the proposal was easy to write. [The appropriate subject is *I*, but it is not stated in either the dangling phrase or the main clause.]
CORRECT	After *I* finished the research, the proposal was easy to write. [The pronoun *I* is now the subject of an introductory clause.]
CORRECT	After finishing the research, *I* found the proposal easy to write. [The pronoun *I* is now the subject of the main clause.]

For a discussion of misplaced modifiers, see <u>modifiers</u>.

11

Grammar

English as a second language (ESL)

Learning to write well in a second language takes a great deal of effort and practice. The most effective way to improve your command of written English is to read widely beyond the reports and professional articles your job requires, such as magazines, newspapers, articles, novels, biographies, and any other writing that interests you. In addition, listen carefully to native speakers on television, on radio, on podcasts, and in person. Do not hesitate to consult a native speaker of English, especially for important writing tasks, such as <u>e-mails</u> (Tab 2), <u>memos</u> (Tab 3), and <u>reports</u> (Tab 4). Focus on those particular areas of English that give you trouble. This entry covers several areas often confusing to nonnative speakers and writers of English. See also <u>global communication</u> (Tab 1).

Count and Mass Nouns

Count nouns refer to things that can be counted (*tables, pencils, projects, employees*). *Mass nouns* (also called *noncount nouns*) identify things that cannot be counted (*electricity, air, loyalty, information*). This distinction can be confusing with words like *electricity* and *water*. Although we can count kilowatt-hours of electricity and bottles of water, counting becomes inappropriate when we use the words *electricity* and *water* in a general sense, as in "*Water* is an essential resource." Following is a list of typical mass <u>nouns</u>.

advice	education	money	technology
biology	equipment	news	transportation
business	furniture	oil	waste
clothing	health	precision	weather
coffee	honesty	research	work

The distinction between something that can and something that cannot be counted determines the form of the noun to use (singular or plural), the kind of <u>article</u> that precedes it (*a, an, the*, or no article), and the kind of limiting <u>adjective</u> it requires (such as *fewer* or *less* and *much* or *many*). (See also <u>fewer / less</u> in the Appendix, "Usage.") Notice that count and mass nouns are always common nouns; they are not proper nouns (such as the names of people).

Articles and Modifiers

Every singular count noun must be preceded by an article (*a, an, the*), a demonstrative adjective (*this, that, these, those*), a possessive adjective (*my, your, her, his, its, their*), or some expression of quantity (such as *one, two, several, many, a few, a lot of, some, none*). The article, adjective, or expression of quantity appears either directly in front of the noun or in front of the whole noun phrase.

▶ Beth read *a* report last week. [article]

▶ *Those* reports Beth read were long. [demonstrative adjective]

▶ *Their* report was long. [possessive adjective]

▶ *Some* reports Beth read were long. [indefinite adjective]

The articles *a* and *an* are used with count nouns that refer to one item of the whole class of like items.

▶ Matthew has *a* pen.
[Matthew could have any pen.]

The article *the* is used with nouns that refer to a specific item that both the reader and the writer can identify.

▶ Matthew has *the* pen.
[Matthew has a specific pen that is known to both the reader and the writer.]

When making generalizations with count nouns, writers can either use *a* or *an* with a singular count noun or use no article with a plural count noun. Consider the following generalization using an article.

▶ *An* egg is a good source of protein. [any egg, all eggs, eggs in general]

However, the following generalization uses a plural count noun with no article.

▶ *Eggs* are good sources of protein. [any egg, all eggs, eggs in general]

When you are making a generalization with a mass noun, do not use an article in front of the mass noun.

▶ *Sugar* is bad for your teeth.

Gerunds and Infinitives

Nonnative writers of English are often puzzled about whether to use a gerund or an infinitive as a direct object of a <u>verb</u> because no structural rule exists for distinguishing which form to use. Any specific verb may take an infinitive as its object, others may take a gerund, and yet others take either an infinitive or a gerund. At times, even the base form of the verb is used.

▶ He enjoys *working*. [gerund as a complement]

▶ She promised *to fulfill* her part of the contract. [infinitive as a complement]

▶ The president had the manager *assign* her staff to another project. [basic verb form as a complement]

To make such distinctions accurately, rely on what you hear native speakers use or what you read. You might also consult a reference book for ESL students.

11

Grammar

Adjective Clauses

Because of the variety of ways adjective clauses are constructed in different languages, they can be particularly troublesome. The following guidelines will help you form adjective clauses correctly.

Place an adjective clause directly after the noun it modifies.

▶ The tall woman *who is standing across the room* is a vice president of the company ~~who is standing across the room.~~

The adjective clause *who is standing across the room* modifies *woman*, not *company*, and thus comes directly after *woman*.

Avoid using a relative pronoun with another pronoun in an adjective clause.

▶ The man who ~~he~~ sits at that desk is my boss.

Present-Perfect Verb Tense

In general, use the present-perfect <u>tense</u> to refer to events completed in the past that have some implication for the present.

PRESENT PERFECT   She *has performed* the experiment three times. [She might perform it again.]

When a specific time is mentioned, however, use the simple past.

SIMPLE PAST   I *wrote* the letter yesterday morning. [The action, *wrote*, does not affect the present.]

Use the present perfect with a *since* or *for* phrase to describe actions that began in the past and continue in the present.

▶ This company *has been* in business *for* 14 years.

▶ This company *has been* in business *since* 2003.

Present-Progressive Verb Tense

The present-progressive tense is especially difficult for those whose native language does not use this tense. The present-progressive tense is used to describe some action or condition that is ongoing (or in progress) in the present and may continue into the future.

PRESENT PROGRESSIVE   I *am searching* for an error in the spreadsheet. [The search is occurring now and may continue.]

In contrast, the simple present tense more often relates to routine actions.

SIMPLE PRESENT   I *search* for errors in my spreadsheets.
[I regularly search for errors, but I am not necessarily searching now.]

See *ESL Tip for Using the Progressive Form* on page 379.

ESL Entries

Most entries in Tabs 10 through 12 and the Appendix may interest writers of English as a second language; however, the entries listed in the Contents by Topic under ESL Tips address issues that often cause problems.

mixed constructions

A mixed construction is a sentence in which the elements do not sensibly fit together. The problem may be a grammar error, a logic error (Tab 10), or both.

► Because the copier wouldn't start̕ ~~explains why~~ we called a

technician.

The original sentence mixes a subordinate clause (*Because the copier wouldn't start*) with a verb (*explains*) that attempts to incorrectly use the subordinate clause as its subject. The revision correctly uses the pronoun *we* as the subject of the main clause. See also sentence construction.

modifiers

Modifiers are words, phrases, or clauses that expand, limit, or make otherwise more specific the meaning of other elements in a sentence. Although we can create sentences without modifiers, we often need the detail and clarification they provide.

WITHOUT MODIFIERS   Production decreased.
WITH MODIFIERS   *Glucose* production decreased *rapidly*.

Most modifiers function as adjectives or adverbs. Adjectives describe qualities or impose boundaries on the words they modify.

► *noisy* machinery, *ten* files, *this* printer, *a* workstation

11

Grammar

An adverb modifies an adjective, another adverb, a <u>verb</u>, or an entire clause.

▶ Under test conditions, the brake pad showed *much* less wear than it did under actual conditions.
   [The adverb *much* modifies the adjective *less*.]

▶ The redesigned brake pad lasted *much* longer.
   [The adverb *much* modifies another adverb, *longer*.]

▶ The wrecking ball hit the wall of the building *hard*.
   [The adverb *hard* modifies the verb *hit*.]

▶ *Surprisingly*, the motor failed even after all the durability and performance tests it had passed.
   [The adverb *surprisingly* modifies an entire clause.]

Adverbs are <u>intensifiers</u> (Tab 10) when they increase the impact of adjectives (*very* fine, *too* high) or adverbs (*very* slowly, *rather* quickly). Be cautious using intensifiers; their overuse can lead to vagueness and a resulting lack of precision.

Stacked (Jammed) Modifiers

Stacked (or *jammed*) modifiers are strings of modifiers preceding <u>nouns</u> that make writing unclear or difficult to read.

▶ Your *staffing-level authorization reassessment* plan should result in a major improvement.

The noun *plan* is preceded by three long modifiers, a string that forces the reader to slow down to interpret its meaning. Stacked modifiers often result from the overuse of <u>buzzwords</u> (Tab 10) or <u>jargon</u> (Tab 10). See how breaking up the stacked modifiers makes the example easier to read.

▶ Your plan for reassessing the staffing-level authorizations should result in a major improvement.

Misplaced Modifiers

A modifier is misplaced when it modifies the wrong word or phrase. A misplaced modifier can cause ambiguity.

▶ We *almost* lost all of the files.
   [The files were *almost* lost but were not.]

▶ We lost *almost* all of the files.
   [Most of the files were in fact lost.]

Note the two meanings possible when the phrase is shifted in the following sentences:

▶ The equipment *without the accessories* sold the best.
[Different types of equipment were available, some with and some without accessories.]

▶ The equipment sold the best *without the accessories.*
[One type of equipment was available, and the accessories were optional.]

To avoid ambiguity, place clauses as close as possible to the words they modify.

REMOTE   We sent the brochure to several local firms *that had four-color art.*

CLOSE   We sent the brochure *that had four-color art* to several local firms.

Squinting Modifiers

A squinting modifier is one that can be interpreted as modifying either of two sentence elements simultaneously, thereby confusing readers about which is intended.

▶ We agreed *on the next day* to make the adjustments.
[Did they agree *to make the adjustments* on the next day? Or *on the next day*, did they agree to make the adjustments?]

A squinting modifier can sometimes be corrected simply by changing its position, but often it is better to rewrite the sentence.

▶ We agreed that *on the next day* we would make the adjustments.
[The adjustments were to be made *on the next day*.]

▶ *On the next day*, we agreed that we would make the adjustments.
[The agreement was made *on the next day*.]

See also <u>dangling modifiers</u>.

11

Grammar

mood

The grammatical term *mood* refers to the <u>verb</u> functions that indicate whether the verb is intended to make a statement, ask a question, give a command, or express a hypothetical possibility.

The *indicative mood* states a fact, gives an opinion, or asks a question.

▶ The setting *is* correct.
▶ *Is* the setting correct?

The *imperative mood* expresses a command, suggestion, request, or plea. In the imperative mood, the implied subject *you* is not expressed. ("*Install* the system today.")

The *subjunctive mood* expresses something that is contrary to fact or that is conditional, hypothetical, or purely imaginative; it can also express a wish, a doubt, or a possibility. In the subjunctive mood, *were* is used instead of *was* in clauses that speculate about the present or future, and the base form (*be*) is used following certain verbs, such as *propose*, *request*, or *insist*. See also progressive <u>tense</u>.

▶ If we *were* to close the sale today, we would meet our monthly goal.

▶ The senior partner insisted that she [I, you, we, they] *be* the project leader.

The most common use of the subjunctive mood is to express clearly that the writer considers a condition to be contrary to fact. If the condition is not considered to be contrary to fact, use the indicative mood.

SUBJUNCTIVE   If I *were* president of the firm, I would change several hiring policies.

INDICATIVE   Although I *am* president of the firm, I don't control every aspect of its policies.

(ESL) TIP for Determining Mood

In written and especially in spoken English, the tendency increasingly is to use the indicative mood where the subjunctive traditionally has been used. Note the differences between traditional and contemporary usage in the following examples.

TRADITIONAL (FORMAL) USE OF THE SUBJUNCTIVE MOOD

▶ I wish he *were* here now.

▶ If I *were* going to the conference, I would travel with him.

▶ I requested that she *arrive* on time.

CONTEMPORARY (INFORMAL) USE OF THE INDICATIVE MOOD

▶ I wish he *was* here now.

▶ If I *was* going to the conference, I would travel with him.

▶ I requested that she *arrives* on time.

In professional writing, it is better to use the more traditional expressions.

11

Grammar

nouns

A noun names a person, a place, a thing, a concept, an action, or a quality.

Types of Nouns

The two basic types of nouns are proper nouns and common nouns. *Proper nouns*, which are capitalized, name specific people, places, and things (*H. G. Wells*, *Boston*, *United Nations*, *Nobel Prize*). See also <u>capitalization</u> (Tab 12).

Common nouns, which are not capitalized unless they begin sentences or appear in titles, name general classes or categories of persons, places, things, concepts, actions, and qualities (*writer*, *city*, *organization*, *award*). Common nouns include concrete nouns, abstract nouns, collective nouns, count nouns, and mass nouns.

Concrete nouns are common nouns used to identify those things that can be discerned by the five senses (*paper*, *keyboard*, *glue*, *nail*, *grease*).

Abstract nouns are common nouns that name ideas, qualities, or concepts that cannot be discerned by the five senses (*loyalty*, *pride*, *valor*, *peace*, *devotion*).

Collective nouns are common nouns that indicate a group or collection. They are plural in meaning but singular in form (*audience*, *jury*, *brigade*, *staff*, *committee*). (See the subsection Collective Nouns on page 358 for advice on using singular or plural forms with collective nouns.)

Count nouns are concrete nouns that identify things that can be separated into countable units (*desks*, *envelopes*, *printers*, *pencils*, *books*).

Mass nouns are concrete nouns that identify things that cannot be separated into countable units (*water*, *air*, *electricity*, *oil*, *cement*). See also <u>English as a second language (ESL)</u>.

Noun Functions

Nouns function as subjects of <u>verbs</u>, direct and indirect objects of verbs and <u>prepositions</u>, subjective and objective <u>complements</u>, or <u>appositives</u>.

▶ The *metal* failed during the test.
[subject]

▶ The bricklayer cemented the *blocks* efficiently.
[direct object of a verb]

▶ The state presented our *department* a safety award.
[indirect object]

▶ The event occurred within the *year*.
[object of a preposition]

11

Grammar

▶ A dynamo is a *generator*.
[subjective complement]

▶ The regional manager was appointed *chairperson*.
[objective complement]

▶ Philip Garcia, the *treasurer*, gave his report last.
[appositive]

Words normally used as nouns can also be used as <u>adjectives</u> and <u>adverbs</u>.

▶ It is *company* policy.
[adjective]

▶ He went *home*.
[adverb]

Collective Nouns

When a collective noun refers to a group as a whole, it takes a singular verb and pronoun.

▶ The staff *was* divided on the issue and could not reach *its* decision until May 15.

When a collective noun refers to individuals within a group, it takes a plural verb and pronoun.

▶ The staff *have returned* to *their* offices after the conference.

A better way to emphasize the individuals on the staff would be to use the phrase *the staff members*.

▶ The staff members *have returned* to *their* offices after the conference.

Treat organization names and titles as singular.

▶ LRM Associates *has* grown 30 percent in the last three years; *it* will move to a new facility in January.

Plural Nouns

Most nouns form the plural by adding -*s* (*desk/desks*, *pen/pens*). Nouns ending in *ch*, *s*, *sh*, *x*, and *z* form the plural by adding -*es*.

▶ search/searches, glass/glasses, wish/wishes, six/sixes, buzz/buzzes

Nouns that end in a consonant plus *y* form the plural by changing the *y* to *ies* (*delivery/deliveries*). Some nouns ending in *o* add -*es* to form the plural, but others add only -*s* (*tomato/tomatoes*, *dynamo/dynamos*). Some nouns ending in *f* or *fe* add -*s* to form the plural; others change the *f* or *fe* to *ves*.

▶ cliff/cliffs, cafe/cafes, hoof/hooves, knife/knives

Some nouns require an internal change to form the plural.

▶ woman/women, man/men, mouse/mice, goose/geese

Some nouns do not change in the plural form.

▶ many *fish*, several *deer*, fifty *sheep*

Some nouns remain in the plural form whether singular or plural.

▶ headquarters, means, series, crossroads

Hyphenated and open compound nouns form the plural in the main word.

▶ sons-in-law, high schools, editors in chief

Compound nouns written as one word add *-s* to the end (two *table-spoonfuls*).

If you are unsure of the proper usage, check a dictionary. See <u>possessive case</u> for a discussion of how nouns form possessives.

objects

Objects are <u>nouns</u> or noun equivalents: <u>pronouns</u>, verbals, and noun <u>phrases</u> or <u>clauses</u>. The three kinds of objects are direct objects, indirect objects, and objects of <u>prepositions</u>. See also <u>complements</u>.

A *direct object* answers the question *what?* or *whom?* about a <u>verb</u> and its <u>subject</u>.

▶ We sent a *full report*.
  [We sent *what?*]

▶ Michelle e-mailed the *client*.
  [Michelle e-mailed *whom?*]

An *indirect object* is a noun or noun equivalent that occurs with a direct object after certain kinds of transitive verbs, such as *give, wish, cause,* and *tell*. The indirect object answers the question *to whom or what?* or *for whom or what?* The indirect object always precedes the direct object.

▶ We sent the *general manager* a full report.
  [*Report* is the direct object; the indirect object, *general manager*, answers the question, "We sent a full report *to whom?*"]

The *object of a preposition* is a noun or pronoun that is introduced by a preposition, forming a prepositional phrase.

▶ At the *meeting*, the district managers approved the contract.
  [*Meeting* is the object, and *at the meeting* is the prepositional phrase.]

11

Grammar

person

Person refers to the form of a personal <u>pronoun</u> that indicates whether the pronoun represents the speaker, the person spoken to, or the person or thing spoken about. A pronoun representing the speaker is in the *first* person. ("*I* could not find the answer in the manual.") A pronoun that represents the person or people spoken to is in the *second* person. ("*You* will be a good manager.") A pronoun that represents the person or people spoken about is in the *third* person. ("*They* received the news quietly.") The following list shows first-, second-, and third-person pronouns.

PERSON	SINGULAR	PLURAL
First	I, me, my, mine	we, us, our, ours
Second	you, your, yours	you, your, yours
Third	he, him, his, she, her, hers, it, its	they, them, their, theirs

phrases

A phrase is a meaningful group of words that does not make a complete statement because it lacks both a subject and a predicate, as <u>clauses</u> do. Phrases, which are based on <u>nouns</u>, nonfinite <u>verb</u> forms, or verb combinations, provide context within a clause or sentence in which they appear. See also <u>sentence construction</u>.

▶ She reassured her staff *by her calm confidence.* [phrase]

A phrase may function as an <u>adjective</u>, an <u>adverb</u>, a noun, or a verb.

▶ The subjects *on the agenda* were all discussed. [adjective]

▶ We discussed the project *with great enthusiasm.* [adverb]

▶ *Working hard* is her way of life. [noun]

▶ The human resources director *should have been notified.* [verb]

Even though phrases function as adjectives, adverbs, nouns, or verbs, they are normally named for the kind of word around which they are constructed — <u>preposition</u>, participle, infinitive, gerund, verb, or noun. A phrase that begins with a preposition is a *prepositional phrase*, a phrase that begins with a participle is a *participial phrase*, and so on. For typical verb phrases and prepositional phrases that can cause difficulty for speakers of <u>English as a second language (ESL)</u>, see <u>idioms</u> (Tab 10).

possessive case

A **noun** or **pronoun** is in the possessive case when it represents a person, place, or thing that *possesses* something. Possession is generally expressed with an **apostrophe** (Tab 12) and an *s* ("the *report's* title"), with a prepositional **phrase** using *of* ("the title *of the report*"), or with the possessive form of a pronoun ("*our* report").

Practices vary for some possessive forms, but the following guidelines are widely used. Above all, be consistent.

Singular Nouns

Most singular nouns show the possessive case with *'s*.

▶ the *hospital's* medical staff   the *witness's* testimony
   an *employee's* paycheck   the *bus's* schedule

When pronunciation with *'s* is difficult or when a multisyllable noun ends in a *z* sound, you may use only an apostrophe.

▶ *New Orleans'* convention hotels

Plural Nouns

Plural nouns that end in *-s* or *-es* show the possessive case with only an apostrophe.

▶ the *managers'* reports   the *companies'* joint project
   the *employees'* paychecks   the *witnesses'* testimony

Plural nouns that do not end in *-s* show the possessive with *'s*.

▶ *children's* clothing, *women's* resources, *men's* room

Apostrophes are not always used in official names ("*Consumers* Union") or for words that may appear to be possessive nouns but function as **adjectives** ("a *computer peripherals* supplier").

Compound Nouns

Compound words form the possessive with *'s* following the final letter.

▶ the *attorney general's* decision, the *editor-in-chief's* desk, the *pipeline's* diameter

Plurals of some compound expressions are often best expressed with a prepositional phrase ("presentations *of the editors in chief*").

Coordinate Nouns

Coordinate nouns show joint possession with *'s* following the last noun.

▶ *Fischer and Goulet's* partnership was the foundation of their business.

Coordinate nouns show individual possession with *'s* following each noun.

▶ The difference between *Barker's* and *Washburne's* test results was not statistically significant.

Possessive Pronouns

Pronouns that show possession (*its, whose, his, her, our, your, my, their*) do not require apostrophes. ("Even good systems have *their* flaws.") Only the possessive form of a pronoun should be used with a gerund (a noun formed from an *-ing* <u>verb</u>).

▶ The safety officer insisted on *our* wearing protective clothing. [*Wearing* is the gerund.]

Possessive pronouns are also used to replace nouns. ("The responsibility was *theirs*.") See also <u>its / it's</u> in the Appendix, "Usage."

Indefinite Pronouns

Some indefinite pronouns (*all, any, each, few, most, none, some*) form the possessive case with the <u>preposition</u> *of*.

▶ We tested both covers and found flaws on the surface *of each*.

Other indefinite pronouns (*everyone, someone, anyone, no one*), however, use *'s*.

▶ *Everyone's* contribution is welcome.

11

Grammar

prepositions

A preposition is a word that links a <u>noun</u> or <u>pronoun</u> to another sentence element by expressing such relationships as direction (*to, into, across, toward*), location (*at, in, on, under, over, beside, among, by, between, through*), time (*before, after, during, until, since*), or position (*for, against, with*). Together, the preposition, its object (the noun or pronoun), and the object's <u>modifiers</u> form a prepositional <u>phrase</u> that acts as a modifier.

▶ Answer help-line questions *in a courteous manner*. [The prepositional phrase *in a courteous manner* modifies the <u>verb</u> *answer*.]

The object of a preposition (the word or phrase following the preposition) is always in the objective case. When the object is a compound, both nouns and pronouns should be in the objective case. For example, the phrase "between you and *me*" is frequently and incorrectly written as "between you and *I*." *Me* is the objective form of the pronoun, and *I* is the subjective form.

Many words that function as prepositions also function as <u>adverbs</u>. If the word takes an object and functions as a connective, it is a preposition; if it has no object and functions as a modifier, it is an adverb.

PREPOSITIONS	The thermostat is *behind* the column *in* the conference room.
ADVERBS	The customer lagged *behind*; then he came *in* and sat down.

Certain verbs, adverbs, and adjectives are normally used with certain prepositions (interested *in*, aware *of*, equated *with*, adhere *to*, capable *of*, object *to*, infer *from*). See also <u>idioms</u> (Tab 10).

Prepositions at the End of a Sentence

A preposition at the end of a sentence can be an indication that the sentence is awkwardly constructed.

> *She was at the*
> ▶ ~~The~~ branch office ~~is where she was at.~~

However, if a preposition falls naturally at the end of a sentence, leave it there. ("I don't remember which file name I saved it *under*.")

Prepositions in Titles

Capitalize prepositions in <u>titles</u> (Tab 4) when they are the first or last words, or when they contain five or more letters (unless you are following a style that recommends otherwise). See also <u>capitalization</u> (Tab 12).

> ▶ The newspaper column "*In* My Opinion" included a review of the article "New Concerns *About* Distance Education." [*In* and *About* are prepositions.]

Preposition Errors

Do not use redundant prepositions, such as "off *of*," "in back *of*," "inside *of*," and "at *about*."

EXACT	The client will arrive at ~~about~~ four o'clock.
APPROXIMATE	The client will arrive ~~at~~ about four o'clock.

Avoid unnecessarily adding the preposition *up* to verbs.

▶ Call ~~up and~~ ^{to} see if he is in his office.

Do not omit necessary prepositions.

▶ He was oblivious ^{to} and not distracted by the view from his office window.

See also <u>conciseness</u> (Tab 10) and <u>English as a second language (ESL)</u>.

---

pronoun reference

A <u>pronoun</u> should refer clearly to a specific antecedent. Avoid vague and uncertain references.

▶ We got the account as a result of our proposal. *, which was a big one,* ~~It was a big one.~~

For <u>coherence</u> (Tab 10), place pronouns as close as possible to their antecedents—distance increases the likelihood of ambiguity.

▶ The office building next to City Hall *, praised for its architectural design, is* ~~is praised for its architectural design.~~

A general (or broad) reference or one that has no real antecedent is a problem that often occurs when the word *this* is used by itself.

▶ He deals with human relations problems in his work. This *experience* helps him in his personal life.

Another common problem is a hidden reference, which has only an implied antecedent.

▶ A high-lipid, low-carbohydrate diet is "ketogenic" because it favors ~~their~~ *the* formation *of ketone bodies*.

Do not repeat an antecedent in parentheses following the pronoun. If you feel you must identify the pronoun's antecedent in that way, rewrite the sentence.

AWKWARD	The senior partner first met Bob Evans when he (Evans) was a trainee.
IMPROVED	Bob Evans was a trainee when the senior partner first met him.
IMPROVED	When the senior partner first met him, Bob Evans was a trainee.

For advice on avoiding pronoun-reference problems with gender, see <u>biased language</u> (Tab 10).

pronouns

A pronoun is a word that is used as a substitute for a <u>noun</u> (the noun for which a pronoun substitutes is called the *antecedent*). Using pronouns in place of nouns relieves the monotony of repeating the same noun over and over. See also <u>pronoun reference</u>.

Personal pronouns refer to the person or people speaking (*I, me, my, mine; we, us, our, ours*); the person or people spoken to (*you, your, yours*); or the person, people, or thing(s) spoken of (*he, him, his; she, her, hers; it, its; they, them, their, theirs*). See also <u>person</u> and <u>point of view</u> (Tab 1).

▶ If *their* figures are correct, *ours* must be in error.

Demonstrative pronouns (*this, these, that, those*) indicate or point out the thing being referred to.

This is my desk. *These* are my coworkers. *That* will be a difficult job. *Those* are incorrect figures.

Relative pronouns (*who, whom, which, that*) perform a dual function: (1) They take the place of nouns, and (2) they connect and establish the relationship between a dependent <u>clause</u> and its main clause.

▶ The department manager decided *who* would be hired.

Interrogative pronouns (*who, whom, what, which*) are used to ask questions.

▶ *What* is the trouble?

Indefinite pronouns specify a class or group of persons or things rather than a particular person or thing (*all, another, any, anyone, anything, both, each, either, everybody, few, many, most, much, neither, nobody, none, several, some, such*).

▶ Not *everyone* liked the new procedures; *some* even refused to follow them.

11

Grammar

A *reflexive pronoun*, which always ends with the suffix *-self* or *-selves*, indicates that the subject of the sentence acts upon itself. See also <u>sentence construction</u>.

▶ The electrician accidentally shocked *herself*.

The reflexive pronouns are *myself, yourself, himself, herself, itself, oneself, ourselves, yourselves,* and *themselves*. *Myself* is not a substitute for *I* or *me* as a personal pronoun.

▶ Victor and ~~myself~~ completed the report on time.

▶ The assignment was given to Ingrid and ~~myself~~.

Intensive pronouns are identical in form to the reflexive pronouns, but they perform a different function: Intensive pronouns emphasize their antecedents.

▶ I *myself* asked the same question.

Reciprocal pronouns (*one another, each other*) indicate the relationship of one item to another. *Each other* is commonly used when referring to two persons or things and *one another* when referring to more than two.

▶ Lashell and Kara work well with *each other*.

▶ The crew members work well with *one another*.

Case

Pronouns have forms to show the subjective, objective, and possessive cases.

SINGULAR	SUBJECTIVE	OBJECTIVE	POSSESSIVE
First person	I	me	my, mine
Second person	you	you	your, yours
Third person	he, she, it	him, her, it	his, her, hers, its

PLURAL	SUBJECTIVE	OBJECTIVE	POSSESSIVE
First person	we	us	our, ours
Second person	you	you	your, yours
Third person	they	them	their, theirs

> **ESL** TIP for Using Possessive Pronouns
>
> In many languages, possessive pronouns agree in number and gender with the nouns they modify. In English, however, possessive pronouns agree in number and gender with their antecedents (nouns or noun forms). Check your writing carefully for agreement between a possessive pronoun and the word, phrase, or clause to which it refers.
>
> ▶ The *woman* brought *her* brother a cup of coffee. [*her* (pronoun) refers to *woman* (antecedent/noun)]
>
> ▶ *Robert* sent *his* mother flowers on Mother's Day. [*his* (pronoun) refers to *Robert* (antecedent/noun)]
>
> ▶ *The FedEx truck* made *its* final delivery. [*its* (pronoun) refers to *the FedEx truck* (antecedent/noun phrase)]
>
> ▶ *The three judges* made *their* decision. [*their* (pronoun) refers to *the three judges* (antecedent/noun phrase)]

A pronoun that functions as the subject of a clause or sentence is in the subjective case (*I, we, he, she, it, you, they, who*). The subjective case is also used when the pronoun follows a linking <u>verb</u>.

▶ *She* is my boss.

▶ My boss is *she*.

A pronoun that functions as the object of a verb or <u>preposition</u> is in the objective case (*me, us, him, her, it, you, them, whom*).

▶ Ms. Davis hired Tom and *me*. [object of verb]

▶ Between *you* and *me*, she's wrong. [object of preposition]

A pronoun that expresses ownership is in the <u>possessive case</u> (*my, mine, our, ours, his, her, hers, its, your, yours, their, theirs, whose*).

▶ He took *his* notes with him on the business trip.

▶ We took *our* notes with us on the business trip.

A pronoun <u>appositive</u> takes the case of its antecedent.

▶ Two systems analysts, Joe and *I*, were selected to represent the company. [*Joe and I* is in apposition to the subject, *two systems analysts*, and must therefore be in the subjective case.]

▶ The manager selected two representatives—Joe and *me*. [*Joe and me* is in apposition to *two representatives*, which is the object of the verb, *selected*, and therefore must be in the objective case.]

If you have difficulty determining the case of a compound pronoun, try using the pronoun singly.

▶ In his letter, Eldon mentioned *him* and *me*.
In his letter, Eldon mentioned *him*.
In his letter, Eldon mentioned *me*.

▶ *They* and *we* must discuss the terms of the merger.
They must discuss the terms of the merger.
We must discuss the terms of the merger.

When a pronoun modifies a noun, try it without the noun to determine its case.

▶ [*We / Us*] pilots fly our own planes.
We fly our own planes.
[You would not write, "*Us* fly our own planes."]

▶ He addressed his remarks directly to [*we / us*] technicians.
He addressed his remarks directly to *us*.
[You would not write, "He addressed his remarks directly to *we*."]

Gender

A pronoun must agree in gender with its antecedent. A problem sometimes occurs because the masculine pronoun has traditionally been used to refer to both sexes. To avoid the sexual bias implied in such usage, use *he or she* or the plural form of the pronoun, *they*.

▶ ~~Each~~ may stay or go as ~~he chooses.~~
   All   *they choose.*

As in this example, when the singular pronoun (*he*) changes to the plural (*they*), the singular indefinite pronoun (*each*) must also change to its plural form (*all*). See also <u>biased language</u> (Tab 10).

Number

Number is a frequent problem with only a few indefinite pronouns (*each, either, neither*, and those ending with *-body* or *-one*, such as *anybody, anyone, everybody, everyone, nobody, no one, somebody, someone*) that are normally singular and so require singular verbs and are referred to by singular pronouns.

▶ As *each member arrives* for the meeting, please hand *him or her* a copy of the confidential report. *Everyone* must return the copy before *he or she* leaves. *Everybody* on the committee *understands* that *neither* of our major competitors *is* aware of the new process we have developed.

Person

Third-person personal pronouns usually have antecedents.

▶ Gina presented the report to the members of the board of directors. *She* [Gina] first summarized *it* [the report] for *them* [the directors] and then asked for questions.

First- and second-person personal pronouns do not normally require antecedents.

▶ *I* like my job.

▶ *You* were on vacation at the time.

▶ *We* all worked hard on the project.

restrictive and nonrestrictive elements

Modifying phrases and clauses may be either restrictive or nonrestrictive. A *nonrestrictive phrase or clause* provides additional information about what it modifies, but it does not restrict the meaning of what it modifies. A nonrestrictive phrase or clause can be removed without changing the essential meaning of the sentence. It is a parenthetical element that is set off by commas (Tab 12) to show its loose relationship with the rest of the sentence.

NONRESTRICTIVE   The annual report, *which was distributed yesterday,* shows that sales increased 20 percent last year.

A *restrictive phrase or clause* limits, or restricts, the meaning of what it modifies. If it were removed, the essential meaning of the sentence would change. Because a restrictive phrase or clause is essential to the meaning of the sentence, it is never set off by commas.

RESTRICTIVE   All employees *wishing to donate blood* may take Thursday afternoon off.

Writers need to distinguish between nonrestrictive and restrictive elements. The same sentence can take on two entirely different meanings, depending on whether a modifying element is set off by commas (because it is nonrestrictive) or is not (because it is restrictive). A slip by the writer can not only mislead readers but also embarrass the writer.

11

Grammar

MISLEADING   He gave a poor performance evaluation to the staff members who protested to the Human Resources Department.
[This suggests that he gave the poor evaluation because the staff members had protested.]

ACCURATE   He gave a poor performance evaluation to the staff members, who protested to the Human Resources Department.
[This suggests that the staff members protested because of the poor evaluation.]

Use *which* to introduce nonrestrictive clauses and *that* to introduce restrictive clauses.

NONRESTRICTIVE   After John left the restaurant, *which* is one of the finest in New York, he came directly to my office.

RESTRICTIVE   Companies *that* diversify usually succeed.

sentence construction

A sentence is the most fundamental and versatile tool available to writers. Sentences generally flow from a subject to a <u>verb</u> to any <u>objects</u>, <u>complements</u>, or <u>modifiers</u>, but they can be ordered in a variety of ways to achieve emphasis. When shifting word order for emphasis, however, be aware that word order can make a great difference in the meaning of a sentence.

▶ He was *only* the accountant. [suggests importance]

▶ He was the *only* accountant. [defines the number]

The most basic components of sentences are subjects and predicates.

Subjects

The *subject* of a sentence is a <u>noun</u> or <u>pronoun</u> (and its modifiers) about which the predicate of the sentence makes a statement. Although a subject may appear anywhere in a sentence, it most often appears at the beginning. ("*To increase sales* is our goal.") Grammatically, a subject must agree with its verb in number.

▶ *These departments have* much in common.

▶ *This department has* several functions.

11 Grammar

The subject is the actor in sentences using the active <u>voice</u>.

▶ *The webmaster reported* an increase in site visits for May.

A *compound subject* has two or more substantives (nouns or noun equivalents) as the subject of one verb.

▶ *The president* and *the treasurer* agreed to begin the audit.

ESL **TIP** for Understanding the Subject of a Sentence

In English, every sentence, except commands, must have an explicit subject.

         He established
▶ *Paul* worked fast. ~~Established~~ the parameters for the project.
              ^

In commands, the subject *you* is understood and is used only for emphasis.

▶ (*You*) Meet me at the airport at 6:30 tomorrow morning.

▶ (*You*) Do your homework, young man. [parent to child]

If you move the subject from its normal position (subject-verb-object), English often requires you to replace the subject with an expletive (*there, it*). In this construction, the verb agrees with the subject that follows it.

▶ *There are* two files on the desk.
   [The subject is *files*.]

▶ *It is* presumptuous for me to speak for Jim.
   [The subject is *to speak for Jim*.]

Time, distance, weather, temperature, and environmental expressions use *it* as their subject.

▶ *It* is ten o'clock.

▶ *It* is ten miles down the road.

▶ *It* seldom snows in Florida.

▶ *It* is very hot in Jorge's office.

11

Grammar

Predicates

The *predicate* is the part of a sentence that makes an assertion about the subject and completes the thought of the sentence.

▶ Bill *has piloted the corporate jet.*

The *simple predicate* is the verb and any helping verbs (*has piloted*). The *complete predicate* is the verb and any modifiers, objects, or complements (*has piloted the corporate jet*). A *compound predicate* consists of two or more verbs with the same subject.

► The company *tried* but *did not succeed* in that field.

Such constructions help achieve <u>conciseness</u> (Tab 10) in writing. A *predicate nominative* is a noun construction that follows a linking verb and renames the subject.

► She is *my attorney.* [noun]

► His excuse was *that he had been sick.* [noun clause]

Sentence Types

Sentences may be classified according to *structure* (simple, compound, complex, compound-complex); *intention* (declarative, interrogative, imperative, exclamatory); and *stylistic use* (loose, periodic, minor).

Structure.   A *simple sentence* consists of one independent clause. At its most basic, a simple sentence contains only a subject and a predicate.

► Profits [subject] rose [predicate].

A *compound sentence* consists of two or more independent clauses connected by a comma and a coordinating <u>conjunction</u>, by a <u>semicolon</u> (Tab 12), or by a semicolon and a conjunctive <u>adverb</u>.

► Drilling is the only way to collect samples of the layers of sediment below the ocean floor, *but* it is not the only way to gather information about these strata. [comma and coordinating conjunction]

► The chemical composition of seawater bears little resemblance to that of river water; the various elements are present in entirely different proportions. [semicolon]

► It was 500 miles to the site; *therefore*, we made arrangements to fly. [semicolon and conjunctive adverb]

A *complex sentence* contains one independent clause and at least one dependent clause that expresses a subordinate idea.

► The generator will shut off automatically [independent clause] if the temperature rises above a specified point [dependent clause].

A *compound-complex sentence* consists of two or more independent clauses plus at least one dependent clause.

> ▶ Productivity is central to controlling inflation [independent clause]; when productivity rises [dependent clause], employers can raise wages without raising prices [independent clause].

Intention. A *declarative sentence* conveys information or makes a factual statement. ("The motor powers the conveyor belt.") An *interrogative sentence* asks a direct question. ("Does the conveyor belt run constantly?") An *imperative sentence* issues a command. ("Restart in SAFE mode.") An *exclamatory sentence* is an emphatic expression of feeling, fact, or opinion. It is a declarative sentence that is stated with great feeling. ("The files were deleted!")

Stylistic Use. A *loose sentence* makes its major point at the beginning and then adds subordinate phrases and clauses that develop or modify that major point. A loose sentence could end at one or more points before it actually does end, as the periods in brackets illustrate in the following sentence:

> ▶ It went up[.], a great ball of fire about a mile in diameter[.], an elemental force freed from its bonds[.] after being chained for billions of years.

A *periodic sentence* delays its main ideas until the end by presenting subordinate ideas or modifiers first.

> ▶ During the past century, the attitude of the American citizen toward automation underwent a profound change.

A *minor sentence* is an incomplete sentence that makes sense in its context because the missing element is clearly implied by the preceding sentence.

> ▶ In view of these facts, is the service contract really useful? *Or economical?*

Constructing Effective Sentences

The subject-verb-object pattern is effective because it is most familiar to readers. In "The company increased profits," we know the subject (*company*) and the object (*profits*) by their positions relative to the verb (*increased*).

An *inverted sentence* places the elements in unexpected order, thus emphasizing the point by attracting the readers' attention.

11

Grammar

▶ A better job I never had. [direct object-subject-verb]

▶ More optimistic I have never been. [subjective complement-subject-linking verb]

▶ A poor image we presented. [direct object-subject-verb]

Use uncomplicated sentences to state complex ideas. If readers have to cope with a complicated sentence in addition to a complex idea, they are likely to become confused. Just as simpler sentences make complex ideas more digestible, a complex sentence construction makes a series of simple ideas more smooth and less choppy.

Avoid loading sentences with a number of thoughts carelessly tacked together. Such sentences are monotonous and hard to read because all the ideas seem to be of equal importance. Rather, distinguish the relative importance of sentence elements with <u>subordination</u> (Tab 10). See also <u>garbled sentences</u> (Tab 10).

LOADED   We started the program three years ago, only three members were on the staff, and each member was responsible for a separate state, but it was not an efficient operation.

IMPROVED   When we started the program three years ago, only three members were on the staff, each responsible for a separate state; however, that arrangement was not efficient.

Express coordinate or equivalent ideas in similar form. The structure of the sentence helps readers grasp the similarity of its components, as illustrated in <u>parallel structure</u> (Tab 10).

ESL TIP for Understanding the Requirements of a Sentence

- A sentence must start with a capital letter.
- A sentence must end with a period, a question mark, or an exclamation mark.
- A sentence must have a subject.
- A sentence must have a verb.
- A sentence must conform to subject-verb-object word order (or inverted word order for questions or emphasis).
- A sentence must express an idea that can stand on its own (called the main, or independent, clause).

sentence faults

A number of problems can create sentence faults, including faulty sub-ordination (Tab 10), clauses with no subjects, rambling sentences, omitted verbs, and illogical assertions.

Faulty subordination occurs when a grammatically subordinate element contains the main idea of the sentence or when a subordinate element is so long or detailed that it obscures the main idea. Both of the following sentences are logical, depending on what the writer intends as the main idea and as the subordinate element.

▶ Although the new filing system saves money, many of the staff are unhappy with it.
[If the main point is that *many of the staff are unhappy*, this sentence is correct.]

▶ The new filing system saves money, although many of the staff are unhappy with it.
[If the main point is that *the new filing system saves money*, this sentence is correct.]

In the following example, the subordinate element overwhelms the main point.

FAULTY   Because the noise level in the assembly area on a typical shift is as loud as a smoke detector's alarm ten feet away, employees often develop hearing problems.

IMPROVED   Employees in the assembly area often develop hearing problems because the noise level on a typical shift is as loud as a smoke detector's alarm ten feet away.

Missing subjects occur when writers inappropriately assume a subject that they do not state in the clause. See also sentence fragments.

INCOMPLETE   Your application program can request to end the session after the next command.
[Your application program can request *who* or *what* to end the session?]

COMPLETE   Your application program can request *the host program* to end the session after the next command.

Rambling sentences contain more information than the reader can comfortably absorb. The obvious remedy for a rambling sentence is to divide it into two or more sentences. When you do that, put the main message of the rambling sentence into the first of the revised sentences.

11

Grammar

| RAMBLING | The payment to which a subcontractor is entitled should be made promptly in order that in the event of a subsequent contractual dispute we, as general contractors, may not be held in default of our contract by virtue of nonpayment. |
| DIRECT | Pay subcontractors promptly. Then if a contractual dispute occurs, we cannot be held in default of our contract because of nonpayment. |

Missing verbs produce some sentence faults.

▶ I never have *written* and probably never will write the annual report.

Faulty logic results when a predicate makes an illogical assertion about its subject. "Mr. Wilson's *job* is a sales representative" is not logical, but "*Mr. Wilson* is a sales representative" is logical. "Jim's *height* is six feet tall" is not logical, but "*Jim* is six feet tall" is logical. See also <u>logic errors</u> (Tab 10).

sentence fragments

A sentence fragment is an incomplete grammatical unit that is punctuated as a sentence.

| FRAGMENT | And quit his job. |
| SENTENCE | He quit his job. |

A sentence fragment lacks either a subject or a <u>verb</u> or is a subordinate <u>clause</u> or <u>phrase</u>. Sentence fragments are often introduced by relative <u>pronouns</u> (*who, whom, which, that*) or subordinating <u>conjunctions</u> (such as *although, because, if, when,* and *while*).

▶ The new manager instituted several new procedures*, although* <del>Although</del> she didn't clear them with Human Resources.

A sentence must contain a finite verb; verbals (nonfinite) do not function as verbs. The following sentence fragments use verbals (*providing, to work*) that cannot function as finite verbs.

FRAGMENT	*Providing* all employees with disability insurance.
SENTENCE	The company *provides* all employees with disability insurance.
FRAGMENT	*To work* a 40-hour week.
SENTENCE	Most of our employees *must work* a 40-hour week.

Explanatory phrases beginning with *such as, for example,* and similar terms often lead writers to create sentence fragments.

▶ The staff wants additional benefits. ~~For example,~~ the use of company cars.

, such as

A hopelessly snarled fragment simply must be rewritten. To rewrite such a fragment, pull the main points out of the fragment, list them in the proper sequence, and then rewrite the sentence, as illustrated in <u>garbled sentences</u> (Tab 10). See also <u>sentence construction</u> and <u>sentence faults</u>.

tense

Tense is the grammatical term for <u>verb</u> forms that indicate time distinctions. The six tenses in English are past, past perfect, present, present perfect, future, and future perfect. Each tense also has a corresponding progressive form.

TENSE	BASIC FORM	PROGRESSIVE FORM
Past	I began	I was beginning
Past perfect	I had begun	I had been beginning
Present	I begin	I am beginning
Present perfect	I have begun	I have been beginning
Future	I will begin	I will be beginning
Future perfect	I will have begun	I will have been beginning

Perfect tenses allow you to express a prior action or condition that continues in a present, past, or future time.

PRESENT PERFECT	I *have begun* to write the annual report and will continue for the rest of the month.
PAST PERFECT	I *had begun* to read the manual when the fire alarm sounded.
FUTURE PERFECT	I *will have begun* this project by the time funds are allocated.

Progressive tenses allow you to describe some ongoing action or condition in the present, past, or future.

PRESENT PROGRESSIVE	I *am beginning* to be concerned that we will not meet the deadline.
PAST PROGRESSIVE	I *was beginning* to think we would not finish by the deadline.
FUTURE PROGRESSIVE	I *will be requesting* a leave of absence when this project is finished.

11

Grammar

Past Tense

The simple past tense indicates that an action took place in its entirety in the past. The past tense is usually formed by adding -*d* or -*ed* to the root form of the verb. ("We *closed* the office early yesterday.")

Past-Perfect Tense

The past-perfect tense (also called *pluperfect*) indicates that one past event preceded another. It is formed by combining the helping verb *had* with the past-participle form of the main verb. ("He *had finished* by the time I arrived.")

Present Tense

The simple present tense represents action occurring in the present, without any indication of time duration. ("I *ride* the train to work.")

A general truth is always expressed in the present tense. ("Time *heals* all wounds.") The present tense can be used to present actions or conditions that have no time restrictions. ("Water *boils* at 212 degrees Fahrenheit.") Similarly, the present tense can be used to indicate habitual action. ("I *pass* the coffee shop every day.") The present tense is also used for the "historical present," as in newspaper headlines ("Dow Jones *Reaches* a High for the Year") or as in references to an author's opinion or a work's contents—even though it was written in the past and the author is no longer living. ("Orwell argues for plain language in his 1946 essay.")

Present-Perfect Tense

The present-perfect tense describes something from the recent past that has a bearing on the present—a period of time before the present but after the simple past. The present-perfect tense is formed by combining a form of the helping verb *have* with the past-participle form of the main verb. ("We *have finished* the draft and can now revise it.")

Future Tense

The simple future tense indicates a time that will occur after the present. It uses the helping verb *will* (or *shall*) plus the main verb. ("I *will finish* the job tomorrow.") Do not use the future tense needlessly; doing so merely adds complexity.

▶ This system ~~will be~~ explained on page 3.
  is

▶ When you press this button, the feeder ~~will move~~ the paper into position.
  moves

Future-Perfect Tense

The future-perfect tense indicates action that will have been completed at the time of or before another future action. It combines *will have* and the past participle of the main verb. ("She *will have driven* 1,400 miles by the time she returns.")

Shift in Tense

Be consistent in your use of tense. The only legitimate shift in tense records a real change in time. Illogical shifts in tense will only confuse your readers.

▶ Before he toured the facility, the manager ~~meets~~ *met* with the staff.

ESL TIP for Using the Progressive Form

The progressive form of the verb is composed of two features: a form of the helping verb *be* and the *-ing* form of the base verb.

PRESENT PROGRESSIVE	I *am updating* the Web site.
PAST PROGRESSIVE	I *was updating* the Web site last week.
FUTURE PROGRESSIVE	I *will be updating* the Web site regularly.

The present progressive is used in three ways:

1. To refer to an action that is in progress at the moment of speaking or writing:

   ▶ The technician *is repairing* the copier.

2. To highlight that a state or an action is not permanent:

   ▶ The office temp *is helping* us for a few weeks.

3. To express future plans:

   ▶ The summer intern *is leaving* to return to school this Friday.

The past progressive is used to refer to a continuing action or condition in the past, usually with specified limits.

   ▶ I *was failing* calculus until I got a tutor.

The future progressive is used to refer to a continuous action or condition in the future.

   ▶ We *will be monitoring* his condition all night.

Verbs that express mental activity (*believe, know, see,* and so on) are generally not used in the progressive.

   ▶ I ~~am believing~~ *believe* the defendant's testimony.

11

Grammar

verbs

A verb is a word or group of words that describes an action ("The copier *jammed* at the beginning of the job"), states how something or someone is affected by an action ("He *was disappointed* that the proposal was rejected"), or affirms a state of existence ("She *is* a district manager now").

Types of Verbs

Verbs are either transitive or intransitive. A *transitive verb* requires a direct <u>object</u> to complete its meaning.

▶ They *laid* the foundation on October 24.
[*Foundation* is the direct object of the transitive verb *laid*.]

▶ Rosalie Anderson *wrote* the treasurer a memo.
[*Memo* is the direct object of the transitive verb *wrote*.]

An *intransitive verb* does not require an object to complete its meaning. It makes a full assertion about the subject without assistance (although it may have <u>modifiers</u>).

▶ The engine *ran*.

▶ The engine *ran* smoothly and quietly.

A *linking verb* is an intransitive verb that links a <u>complement</u> to the subject.

▶ The carpet *is* stained.
[*Is* is a linking verb; *stained* is a subjective complement.]

Some intransitive verbs, such as *be, become, seem,* and *appear,* are almost always linking verbs. A number of others, such as *look, sound, taste, smell,* and *feel,* can function as either linking verbs or simple intransitive or transitive verbs. If you are unsure about whether one of those verbs is a linking verb, try substituting *seem;* if the sentence still makes sense, the verb is probably a linking verb.

▶ Their antennae *feel* delicate.
[*Seem* can be substituted for *feel*—thus *feel* is a linking verb.]

▶ Their antennae *feel* delicately for their prey.
[*Seem* cannot be substituted for *feel*; in this case, *feel* is a simple intransitive verb.]

Forms of Verbs

Verbs are described as being either finite or nonfinite.

Finite Verbs.   A finite verb is the main verb of a <u>clause</u> or sentence. It makes an assertion about its subject and often serves as the only verb in its clause or sentence. ("The telephone *rang*, and the receptionist *answered* it.") See also <u>sentence construction</u>.

A helping verb (sometimes called an *auxiliary verb*) is used in a verb <u>phrase</u> to help indicate <u>mood</u>, <u>tense</u>, and <u>voice</u>. ("The phone *had* rung.") Phrases that function as helping verbs are often made up of combinations with the sign of the infinitive, *to* (for example, *am going to, is about to, has to,* and *ought to*). The helping verb always precedes the main verb, although other words may intervene. ("Machines *will* never completely *replace* people.")

Nonfinite Verbs. Nonfinite verbs are verbals—verb forms that function as <u>nouns</u>, <u>adjectives</u>, or <u>adverbs</u>.

A *gerund* is a noun that is derived from the *-ing* form of a verb. ("*Seeing* is *believing*.") An *infinitive*, which uses the root form of a verb (usually preceded by *to*), can function as a noun, an adverb, or an adjective.

▶ He hates *to complain*. [noun, direct object of *hates*]

▶ The valve closes *to stop* the flow. [adverb, modifies *closes*]

▶ This is the proposal *to consider*. [adjective, modifies *proposal*]

A *participle* is a verb form that can function as an adjective.

▶ The *rejected* proposal may be resubmitted when the concerns are addressed.
[*Rejected* is a verb form that is used as an adjective modifying *proposal*.]

Properties of Verbs

Verbs must (1) agree in <u>person</u> with personal pronouns functioning as subjects, (2) agree in tense and number with their subjects, and (3) be in the appropriate voice.

ESL TIP for Avoiding Shifts in Voice, Mood, or Tense

To achieve clarity in your writing, maintain consistency and avoid abrupt changes in voice, mood, or tense. Pay special attention when you edit your writing to check for the following types of shifts.

VOICE

▶ The captain permits his crew to go ashore, but ~~they are not~~ *he does not permit*
~~permitted~~ *them* to go downtown.

[The entire sentence is now in the active voice.]

(continued)

ESL **TIP** for Avoiding Shifts in Voice, Mood, or Tense (*continued*)

MOOD

▶ Reboot your computer,/ and ~~you should~~ empty the cache.
[The entire sentence is now in the imperative mood.]

TENSE

                           fell

▶ I was working quickly, and suddenly a box ~~falls~~ off the conveyor

  broke

belt and ~~breaks~~ my foot.

[The entire sentence is now in the past tense.]

Person is the term for the form of a personal pronoun that indicates whether the pronoun refers to the speaker, the person spoken to, or the person (or thing) spoken about. Verbs change their forms to agree in person with their subjects.

▶ I *see* [first person] a yellow tint, but she *sees* [third person] a yellow-green hue.

Tense refers to verb forms that indicate time distinctions. The six tenses are past, past perfect, present, present perfect, future, and future perfect.

Number refers to the two forms of a verb that indicate whether the subject of a verb is singular ("The copier *was* repaired") or plural ("The copiers *were* repaired").

Most verbs show the singular of the present tense by adding -*s* or -*es* (he *stands*, she *works*, it *goes*), and they show the plural without -*s* or -*es* (they *stand*, we *work*, they *go*). The verb *to be*, however, normally changes form to indicate the singular ("I *am* ready") or plural ("We *are* ready").

Voice refers to the two forms of a verb that indicate whether the subject of the verb acts or receives the action. The verb is in the *active voice* if the subject of the verb acts ("The bacteria *grow*"); the verb is in the *passive voice* if it receives the action ("The bacteria *are grown* in a petri dish").

voice

In grammar, *voice* indicates the relation of the subject to the action of the <u>verb</u>. When the verb is in the *active voice*, the subject acts; when it is in the *passive voice*, the subject is acted upon.

ACTIVE   David Cohen *wrote* the newsletter article.
            [The subject, *David Cohen*, performs the action; the
            verb, *wrote*, describes the action.]

PASSIVE   The newsletter article *was written* by David Cohen.
            [The subject, *the newsletter article*, is acted upon; the
            verb, *was written*, describes the action.]

The two sentences say the same thing, but each has a different emphasis: the first emphasizes the writer (*David Cohen*); the second emphasizes what was written (*the newsletter article*). In business writing, it is often important to emphasize who or what performs an action. Further, the passive-voice version is indirect because the performer of the action generally follows the verb instead of preceding it. Because the active voice is more direct, more concise, and easier for readers to understand, use the active voice unless the passive voice is more appropriate, as described on pages 384–85. Whether you use the active voice or the passive voice, be careful not to shift voices in a sentence.

▶ David Cohen corrected the error as soon as ~~it was identified by~~
                         identified it
   the editor.
              ^

Using the Active Voice

Improving Clarity.   The active voice improves clarity and avoids confusion, especially in instructions and policies and procedures.

PASSIVE   Sections B and C *should be checked* for errors.
            [Are they already checked?]

ACTIVE   *Check* sections B and C for errors.
            [The performer of the action, *you*, is understood:
            (You) *Check* the sections.]

Active voice can also help avoid <u>dangling modifiers</u>.

PASSIVE   Hurrying to complete the work, the cables *were
            connected* improperly.
            [*Who* was hurrying? The implication is the cables were
            hurrying!]

ACTIVE   Hurrying to complete the work, the technician
            connected the cables improperly.
            [Here, *hurrying to complete the work* properly modifies
            the performer of the action: *the technician*.]

11

Grammar

Highlighting Subjects. One difficulty with passive sentences is that they can bury the performer of the action within <u>expletives</u> (Tab 10) and prepositional <u>phrases</u>.

PASSIVE It *was reported by* the testing staff that the new model is defective.

ACTIVE The testing staff *reported* that the new model is defective.

Sometimes writers using the passive voice fail to name the performer—information that might be missed.

PASSIVE The error *was reported* yesterday.

ACTIVE The attending physician *reported* the error yesterday.

Achieving Conciseness. The active voice helps achieve <u>conciseness</u> (Tab 10) because it eliminates the need for an additional helping verb as well as an extra <u>preposition</u> to identify the performer of the action.

PASSIVE Arbitrary changes in policy *are resented by* employees.

ACTIVE Employees *resent* arbitrary changes in policy.

The active-voice version takes one verb (*resent*); the passive-voice version takes two verbs (*are resented*) and an extra preposition (*by*).

11

Grammar

Using the Passive Voice

The passive voice is sometimes effective or even necessary. Indeed, for reasons of tact and diplomacy, you might need to use the passive voice to avoid an implied accusation.

ACTIVE Your staff *did not meet* the sales quota last month.

PASSIVE The sales quota *was not met* last month.

❖ ETHICS NOTE Be careful not to use the passive voice to evade responsibility or to obscure an issue or information that readers should know, as in the following examples.

► Several mistakes *were made.*
[*Who* made the mistakes?]

► It *has been decided.*
[*Who* has decided?]

See also <u>ethics in writing</u> (Tab 1). ❖

When the performer of the action is either unknown or unimportant, of course, use the passive voice. ("The copper mine *was discovered* in 1929.") When the performer of the action is less important than the receiver of that action, the passive voice is sometimes more appropriate. ("Ann Bryant *was presented* with a Sales Award by the president.") Even in such cases, another verb may enable you to use the active voice. ("Ann Bryant *received* a Sales Award from the president.")

When you are explaining an operation in which the reader is not actively involved or when you are explaining a process or a procedure, the passive voice may be more appropriate. In the following example, anyone — it really does not matter who — could be the performer of the action.

▶ Area strip mining *is used* in regions of flat to gently rolling terrain, like that found in the Midwest. Depending on applicable reclamation laws, the topsoil *may be removed* from the area *to be mined*, *stored*, and later *reapplied* as surface material during reclamation of the mined land. After the removal of the topsoil, a trench *is cut* through the overburden to expose the upper surface of the coal to be mined. The overburden from the first cut *is placed* on the unmined land adjacent to the cut. After the first cut *has been completed*, the coal *is removed*.

Do not, however, simply assume that any such explanation should be in the passive voice; in fact, as in the following example, the active voice is often more effective.

▶ In the operation of an internal combustion engine, an explosion in the combustion chamber *forces* the pistons down in the cylinders. The movement of the pistons in the cylinders *turns* the crankshaft.

Ask yourself, "Would it be of any advantage to the reader to know the performer of the action?" If the answer is yes, use the active voice, as in the previous example.

11

Grammar

ESL TIP for Choosing Voice

Different languages place different values on active-voice and passive-voice constructions. In some languages, the passive is used frequently; in others, hardly at all. As a nonnative speaker of English, you may have a tendency to follow the pattern of your native language. As this entry describes, even though business writing may sometimes require the passive voice, active verbs are highly valued in English.

12

Punctuation and Mechanics

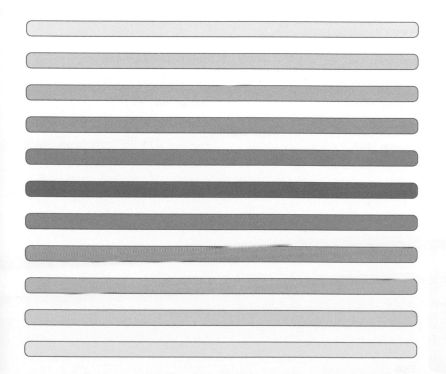

Preview

Understanding punctuation and mechanics enables you as a writer to communicate clearly and precisely. Punctuation is a system of symbols that helps readers understand the structural relationships within a sentence. The use of punctuation is determined by grammatical convention and a writer's intention.

Marks of punctuation may link, separate, enclose, indicate omissions, terminate, and classify. This section provides detailed information on each of 14 marks of punctuation. This section also includes entries on such conventions of writing as when to capitalize letters, whether to write a number as a word or figure, the format for writing dates, and how and when to use acronyms.

12

Punctuation
and Mechanics

abbreviations

Abbreviations are shortened versions of words or combinations of the first letters of words (*Corp.* / Corp*oration*, *URL* / u*niform* r*esource* l*ocator*). If used appropriately, abbreviations can be convenient for both the reader and the writer. Like symbols, they can be important space savers in business writing.

Abbreviations that are formed by combining the initial letter of each word in a multiword term are called *initialisms.* Initialisms are pronounced as separate letters (*SEC* / *Securities and Exchange Commission*). Abbreviations that combine the first letter or letters of several words — and can be pronounced — are called *acronyms* (*PIN* / p*ersonal* i*dentification* *number, LAN* / l*ocal* a*rea* n*etwork*).

Using Abbreviations

The most important consideration in the use of abbreviations is whether they will be understood by your <u>audience</u> (Tab 1). The same abbreviation, for example, can have two different meanings (NEA stands for both National Education Association and the National Endowment for the Arts). Like <u>jargon</u> (Tab 10), shortened forms are easily understood within a group of specialists; outside the group, however, shortened forms might be incomprehensible. In fact, abbreviations can be easily overused, either as an <u>affectation</u> (Tab 10) or in a misguided attempt to make writing concise, even with <u>instant messaging</u> (Tab 10) where abbreviations are often appropriate. Remember that <u>memos</u> (Tab 3), <u>e-mail</u> (Tab 2), or <u>reports</u> (Tab 4) addressed to specific people may be read by others, so consider those secondary audiences as well. A good rule to follow: "When in doubt, spell it out."

12

**Punctuation
and Mechanics**

Writer's Checklist: Using Abbreviations

☑ Except for commonly used abbreviations (*U.S.*, *a.m.*), spell out a term to be abbreviated the first time it is used, followed by the abbreviation in parentheses. Thereafter, the abbreviation may be used alone.

☑ In long documents, repeat the full term in parentheses after the abbreviation at regular intervals to remind readers of the abbreviation's meaning, as in "Submit the CAR (Capital Appropriations Request) by October 15." For digital texts, consider linking abbreviations to a glossary or providing the definition in a pop-up that appears when the cursor hovers over an abbreviation.

☑ Do not add an additional period at the end of a sentence that ends with an abbreviation. ("The official name of the company is DataBase, Inc.")

☑ For abbreviations specific to your profession or discipline, use a style guide recommended by your professional organization or company.

☑ Write acronyms in capital letters without periods. The only exceptions are acronyms that have become accepted as common nouns, which are written in lowercase letters, such as *scuba* (*s*elf-*c*ontained *u*nderwater *b*reathing *a*pparatus).

☑ Generally, use periods for lowercase initialisms (*a.k.a.*, *p.m.*) but not for uppercase ones (*GDP*, *IRA*). Exceptions include geographic names (*U.S.*, *U.K.*, *E.U.*) and the traditional expression of academic degrees (*B.A.*, *M.S.E.E.*, *Ph.D.*).

☑ Form the plural of an acronym or initialism by adding a lowercase *s*. Do not use an **apostrophe** (*CARs*, *DVDs*).

☑ Do not follow an abbreviation with a word that repeats the final term in the abbreviation (*ATM location* not *ATM machine location*).

☑ Avoid creating your own abbreviations; they will confuse readers.

Forming Abbreviations

Names of Organizations.   A company may include in its name a term such as *Brothers, Incorporated, Corporation, Company,* or *Limited Liability Company.* If the term is abbreviated in the official company name that appears on letterhead stationery or on its Web site, use the abbreviated form: *Bros., Inc., Corp., Co.,* or *LLC.* If the term is not abbreviated in the official name, spell it out in writing, except with addresses, footnotes, bibliographies, and lists where abbreviations may be used. Likewise, use an ampersand (&) only if it appears in the official company name. For names of divisions within organizations, terms such as *Department* and *Division* should be abbreviated only when space is limited (*Dept.* and *Div.*).

Measurements. Except for abbreviations that may be confused with words (*in.* for *inch* and *gal.* for *gallon*), abbreviations of measurement do not require periods (*yd* for *yard* and *qt* for *quart*). Abbreviations of units of measure are identical in the singular and plural: *1 cm* and *15 cm* (not *15 cms*). Some abbreviations can be used in combination with other symbols (*°F* for *degrees Fahrenheit* and *ft²* for *square feet*).

For a listing of abbreviations for the basic units used in the International System of Units (SI), see *http://physics.nist.gov/cuu/Units /units.html*. For additional definitions and background, search the National Institute of Standards and Technology Web site at *www.nist .gov* and generally online for *units of information*. For information on abbreviating dates and time, see numbers.

Personal Names and Titles. Personal names generally should not be abbreviated: *Thomas* (not *Thos.*) and *William* (not *Wm.*). An academic, civil, religious, or military title should be spelled out and in lowercase when it does not precede a name. ("The *captain* checked the orders.") When they precede names, some titles are customarily abbreviated (*Dr. Smith*, *Mr. Mills*, *Ms. Katz*). See also Ms. / Miss / Mrs. in the Appendix: Usage (page 425).

An abbreviation of a title may follow the name; however, be certain that it does not duplicate a title before the name (*Angeline Martinez, Ph.D.* or *Dr. Angeline Martinez*). When addressing correspondence (Tab 3) and including names in other documents, you normally should spell out titles (*The Honorable Mary J. Holt*; *Professor Charles Matlin*). Traditionally, periods are used with academic degrees, although some style guides suggest omitting these (*M.A. / MA, M.B.A. / MBA, Ph.D. / PhD*).

Common Scholarly Abbreviations and Terms. The following is a partial list of abbreviations commonly used in reference books and for documenting sources in research papers and reports. Other than in such documents, generally avoid such abbreviations.

anon.	anonymous
bibliog.	bibliography, bibliographer, bibliographic
ca., c.	*circa*, "about" (used with approximate dates: *ca. 1756*)
cf.	*confer*, "compare"
chap.	chapter
diss.	dissertation
ed., eds.	edited by, editor(s), edition(s)

e.g.	*exempli gratia*, "for example"
esp.	especially
et al.	*et alii*, "and others"
etc.	*et cetera*, "and so forth"
f., ff.	and the following page(s) or line(s)
GPO	Government Printing Office, Washington, D.C.
i.e.	*id est*, "that is"
MS, MSS	manuscript, manuscripts
n., nn.	note, notes (used immediately after page number: *56n.*, *56n.3*, *56nn.3–5*)
N.B., n.b.	*nota bene*, "take notice, mark well"
n.d.	no date (of publication)
n.p.	no place (of publication); no publisher; no page
p., pp.	page, pages
proc.	proceedings
pub.	published by, publisher, publication
rev.	revised by, revised, revision; review, reviewed by (Spell out "review" where "rev." might be ambiguous.)
rpt.	reprinted by, reprint
sec., secs.	section, sections
sic	so, thus; inserted in brackets ([*sic*]) after a misspelled or misused word in quotations
supp., suppl.	supplement
trans.	translated by, translator, translation
UP	University Press (used in MLA style, as in *Oxford UP*)
viz.	*videlicet*, "namely"
vol., vols.	volume, volumes
vs., v.	*versus*, "against" (*v.* preferred in titles of legal cases)

Postal Abbreviations.   Official state and place-name abbreviations used by the United States Postal Service are listed at *www.usps.com*.

apostrophes

12

An apostrophe (') is used to show possession or to indicate the omission of letters. Sometimes it is also used to avoid confusion with certain plurals of words, letters, and abbreviations.

Showing Possession

An apostrophe is used with an *s* to form the possessive case of some nouns (the *report's* title). For further advice on using apostrophes to show possession, see possessive case (Tab 11).

Indicating Omission

An apostrophe is used to mark the omission of letters or <u>numbers</u> in a <u>contraction</u> or a date (*can't*, *I'm*, *I'll*; the class of *'15*).

Forming Plurals

An apostrophe can be used in forming the plurals of letters, words, or lowercase abbreviations if confusion might result from using *s* alone and thus forming a word.

▶ The search program does not find *a*'s and *i*'s.

▶ Do not replace all *of which*'s in the document.

▶ *I*'s need to be distinguished from the number 1.

▶ The prescription included several *bid*'s [*bid* is an abbreviation used for "twice-daily medications."].

In general, however, add only *-s* in roman (or regular) type when referring to words as words or capital letters. See also <u>italics</u>.

▶ Five *and*s appear in the first sentence.

▶ The applicants received *A*s and *B*s in their courses.

Do not use an apostrophe for plurals of abbreviations with all capital letters (*PDFs*) or a final capital letter (*ten PhDs*) or for plurals of numbers (*7s*, *the late 1990s*).

brackets

The primary use of brackets ([ ]) is to enclose a word or words inserted by the writer or editor into a quotation.

▶ The text stated, "Web sites can be categorized as either static [nonchanging] or interactive [responding to user activity]."

Brackets are used to set off a parenthetical item within parentheses.

▶ We must credit Emanuel Foose (and his brother Emilio [1912–1982]) for founding the institute.

Brackets are also used to insert the Latin word *sic*, indicating that a writer has quoted material exactly as it appears in the original, even though it contains a misspelled or wrongly used word. See also <u>abbreviations</u> and <u>quotations</u> (Tab 5).

▶ The contract states, "Tinted windows will be installed to protect against son [*sic*] damage."

capitalization

The use of capital, or uppercase, letters is determined by custom. Capital letters are used to call attention to certain words, such as proper nouns and the first word of a sentence. Use capital letters carefully because they can affect a word's meaning (march / March, china / China) and because a spell checker would fail to identify such an error.

Proper Nouns

Capitalize proper nouns that name specific persons, places, or things (Pat Wilde, Peru, Business Writing 205, Microsoft). When in doubt, consult a general or subject-area dictionary.

Common Nouns

Common nouns name general classes or categories of people, places, things, concepts, or qualities rather than specific ones and are not capitalized (person, country, business writing class, company).

First Words

The first letter of the first word in a sentence is always capitalized. ("Of the plans submitted, ours is best.") The first word after a <u>colon</u> is capitalized when the colon introduces two or more sentences (independent clauses) or if the colon precedes a statement requiring special emphasis.

▶ The meeting will address only one issue: What is the firm's role in environmental protection?

If a subordinate element follows the colon or if the thought is closely related, use a lowercase letter following the colon.

▶ We kept working for one reason: the approaching deadline.

The first word of a complete sentence in <u>quotation marks</u> is capitalized.

▶ Peter Drucker said, "The most important thing in communication is to hear what isn't being said."

The first word in the salutation (Dear Mr. Smith:) and in the complimentary close (Sincerely yours,) are capitalized, as are the names of the recipients. See also <u>letters</u> (Tab 3).

Specific Groups

Capitalize the names of ethnic groups, religions, and nationalities (Native American, Christianity, Mongolian). Do not capitalize the names of social and economic groups (middle class, unemployed).

Specific Places

Capitalize the names of all political divisions (Ward Six, Chicago, Cook County, Illinois) and geographic divisions (Europe, Asia, North America, the Middle East). Do not capitalize geographic features unless they are part of a proper name.

▶ The *mountains* in some areas, such as the *Great Smoky Mountains*, make cell phone reception difficult.

The words *north*, *south*, *east*, and *west* are capitalized when they refer to sections of the country. They are not capitalized when they refer to directions.

▶ I may relocate further *west*, but my family will remain in the *South*.

Specific Institutions, Events, and Concepts

Capitalize the names of institutions, organizations, and associations (U.S. Department of Health and Human Services). An organization usually capitalizes the names of its internal divisions and departments (Aeronautics Division, Human Resources Department). Types of organizations are not capitalized unless they are part of an official name (a business communication association; Association for Business Communication). Capitalize historical events (the Great Depression of the 1930s). Capitalize words that designate holidays, specific periods of time, months, or days of the week (Labor Day, the Renaissance, January, Monday). Do not capitalize seasons of the year (spring, summer, autumn, winter) unless they are used in a title (Winter Semester Schedule).

Titles of Works

Capitalize the initial letters of the first, last, and major words in the title of a book, an article, a play, or a film. Do not capitalize <u>articles</u> (Tab 11), coordinating <u>conjunctions</u> (Tab 11), or <u>prepositions</u> (Tab 11) unless they begin or end the title (*The Lives of a Cell*). Capitalize prepositions within titles when they contain five or more letters (*Between, Within, Until, After*), unless you are following a style that recommends otherwise. The same rules apply to the subject lines of e-mails or memos.

Professional and Personal Titles

Titles preceding proper names are capitalized (Ms. Berger, Senator King). Appositives following proper names normally are not capitalized (Angus King, *senator* from Maine). However, the word *president* is often capitalized when it refers to the chief executive of a national government. See <u>appositives</u> (Tab 11).

Job titles used with personal names are capitalized (H. S. Kim, *Division Manager*). Job titles used without personal names are not capitalized. (The *division manager* will meet us tomorrow.) Use capital letters to designate family relationships only when they occur before a name (my uncle, Uncle Fred).

Abbreviations and Letters

Capitalize <u>abbreviations</u> if the words they stand for would be capitalized, such as MBA (Master of Business Administration). Capitalize letters that serve as names or indicate shapes (vitamin B, T-square, U-turn, I-beam).

Miscellaneous Capitalizations

The first word of a complete sentence enclosed in <u>dashes</u>, <u>brackets</u>, or <u>parentheses</u> is not capitalized when it appears as part of another sentence.

► We must improve our safety record this year (accidents last year were up 10 percent).

Certain units, such as parts and chapters of books and rooms in buildings, when specifically identified by number, are capitalized (Chapter 5, Ch. 5; Room 72, Rm. 72). Minor divisions within such units are not capitalized unless they begin a sentence (page 11, verse 14, seat 12).

colons

The colon (:) is a mark of introduction that alerts readers to the close connection between the preceding statement and what follows.

Colons in Sentences

A colon links independent clauses to words, phrases, clauses, or lists that identify, rename, explain, emphasize, amplify, or illustrate the sentence that precedes the colon.

► Two topics will be discussed: *the new accounting system and the new bookkeeping procedures.* [phrases that identify]

► Only one thing will satisfy Mr. Sturgess: *our finished report.* [appositive (renaming) phrase for emphasis]

▶ Any organization is confronted with two separate, though related, information problems: *It must maintain an effective internal communication system and an effective external communication system.* [clause to amplify and explain]

▶ Heart patients should make key lifestyle changes: *stop smoking, exercise regularly, eat a low-fat diet, and reduce stress.* [list to identify and illustrate]

Colons with Salutations, Titles, Citations, and Numbers

A colon follows the salutation in formal <u>correspondence</u> (Tab 3), even when the salutation refers to a person by first name.

▶ Dear Professor Jeffers: *or* Dear Mary:

Colons separate titles from subtitles and separate references to sections of works in citations. See also <u>documenting sources</u> (Tab 5).

▶ "'We Regret to Inform You': Toward a New Theory of Negative Messages"

▶ *International Journal of Business Communication* 51:279–303 [volume 51, pages 279–303]

Colons separate numbers in time references and indicate numerical ratios.

▶ 9:30 a.m. [9 hours and 30 minutes]

▶ The cement is mixed with water and sand at a ratio of 5:3:1. [The colon is read as the word *to.*]

Punctuation and Capitalization with Colons

A colon always goes outside <u>quotation marks</u>.

▶ This was the real meaning of the manager's "suggestion": Cooperation within our department must improve.

As this example shows, the first word after a colon may be capitalized if the statement following the colon is a complete sentence and functions as a formal statement or question. If the element following the colon is subordinate, however, use a lowercase letter to begin that element. See also <u>capitalization</u>.

▶ We have only one way to stay within our present budget: to reduce expenditures for research and development.

Unnecessary Colons

Do not place a colon between a <u>verb</u> (Tab 11) and its objects.

▶ Three fluids that clean pipettes are⁄ water, alcohol, and acetone.

12

Likewise, do not use a colon between a <u>preposition</u> (Tab 11) and its object.

► I may be transferred to: Tucson, Boston, or Miami.

Do not insert a colon after *including,* *such as,* or *for example* to introduce a simple list.

► Do not use the office Internet access for personal activities such as: social networking, online shopping, downloading music, and accessing personal e-mail.

One common exception is made when a verb or preposition is followed by a stacked <u>list</u> (Tab 7); however, it may be possible to introduce the list with a complete sentence instead.

The following corporations
► ~~Corporations that~~ manufacture computer systems : ~~include:~~

Apple	Acer	Gateway
HP	Philips	Samsung

comma splice

A comma splice is a grammatical error in which two independent <u>clauses</u> (Tab 11) are joined by only a <u>comma</u>.

INCORRECT   It was 500 miles to the facility, we arranged to fly.

A comma splice can be corrected in several ways.

1. Substitute a <u>semicolon,</u> a semicolon and a conjunctive <u>adverb</u> (Tab 11) followed by a comma, or a comma and a coordinating <u>conjunction</u> (Tab 11).
   • It was 500 miles to the facility; we arranged to fly. [semicolon]
   • It was 500 miles to the facility; *therefore,* we arranged to fly. [conjunctive adverb]
   • It was 500 miles to the facility, *so* we arranged to fly. [coordinating conjunction]
2. Create two sentences.
   • It was 500 miles to the facility. *We* arranged to fly.
3. Subordinate one clause to the other. (See <u>subordination,</u> Tab 10.)
   • *Because it was 500 miles to the facility,* we arranged to fly.

See also <u>sentence construction</u> (Tab 11) and <u>sentence faults</u> (Tab 11).

12

Punctuation
and Mechanics

commas

DIRECTORY

Like all punctuation, the comma (,) helps readers understand the writer's meaning and prevents ambiguity. Notice how the comma helps make the meaning clear in the second example.

AMBIGUOUS	To be successful managers with MBAs must continue their education.
CLEAR	To be successful, managers with MBAs must continue their education. [The comma makes clear where the main part of the sentence begins.]

Do not follow the old myth that you should insert a comma wherever you would pause if you were speaking. Although you would pause wherever you encounter a comma, you should not insert a comma wherever you might pause. Effective use of commas depends on an understanding of <u>sentence construction</u> (Tab 11).

Linking Independent Clauses

Use a comma before a coordinating conjunction (*and*, *but*, *or*, *nor*, and sometimes *so*, *yet*, and *for*) that links independent <u>clauses</u> (Tab 11).

▶ The new microwave disinfection system was delivered, *but* the installation will require an additional week.

However, if two independent clauses are short and closely related—and there is no danger of confusing the reader—the comma may be omitted. Both of the following examples are correct.

▶ The cable snapped and the power failed.

▶ The cable snapped, and the power failed.

12

Punctuation
and Mechanics

Enclosing Elements

Commas are used to enclose nonessential information in nonrestrictive clauses, phrases, and parenthetical elements. See also restrictive and nonrestrictive elements (Tab 11).

▶ Our new factory, *which began operations last month,* should add 25 percent to total output. [nonrestrictive clause]

▶ The accountant, *working quickly and efficiently,* finished early. [nonrestrictive phrase]

▶ We can, *of course,* expect their lawyer to call us. [parenthetical element]

Yes and *no* are set off by commas.

▶ *Yes,* I think we can finish by the deadline.

A direct address should be enclosed in commas.

▶ You will note, *Jeff,* that the budget figure matches our estimate.

An appositive phrase (which re-identifies another expression in the sentence) is enclosed in commas.

▶ Our company, *NT Insurance Group,* won several awards last year.

Interrupting parenthetical and transitional words or phrases are usually set off with commas. See also transition (Tab 10).

▶ The report, *therefore,* needs to be revised.

Commas are omitted when the word or phrase does not interrupt the continuity of thought.

▶ I *therefore* recommend that we begin construction.

For other means of punctuating parenthetical elements, see dashes and parentheses.

Introducing Elements

Clauses and Phrases.   Generally, place a comma after an introductory clause or phrase, especially if it is long, to identify where the introductory element ends and the main part of the sentence begins.

▶ *Because we have not yet reached our hiring goals for the Sales Division,* we recommend the development of an aggressive recruiting program.

A long modifying phrase that precedes the main clause should always be followed by a comma.

▶ *During the first series of field-performance tests at our Colorado proving ground,* the new engine failed to meet our expectations.

When an introductory phrase is short and closely related to the main clause, the comma may be omitted.

▶ *In two seconds* a 5°C temperature rise occurs in the test tube.

A comma should always follow an absolute phrase, which modifies the whole sentence.

▶ *The presentation completed,* we returned to our offices.

Words and Quotations. Certain types of introductory words are followed by a comma. One example is a transitional word or phrase (*however, in addition*) that connects the preceding clause or sentence with the thought that follows.

▶ *Furthermore,* we should include college job fairs in our recruiting plans, provided our budget is approved.

▶ *For example,* this change will make us more competitive in the global marketplace.

When an <u>adverb</u> (Tab 11) closely modifies the <u>verb</u> (Tab 11) or the entire sentence, it should not be followed by a comma.

▶ *Perhaps* we can still solve the turnover problem. *Certainly* we should try.
[*Perhaps* and *certainly* closely modify each statement.]

A proper noun used in an introductory direct address is followed by a comma, as is an interjection (such as *oh, well, why, indeed, yes,* and *no*).

▶ *Nancy,* enclosed is the article you asked me to review. [direct address]

▶ *Indeed,* I will ensure that your request is forwarded. [interjection]

Use a comma to separate a direct quotation from its introduction.

▶ Morton and Lucia White *said,* "People live in cities but dream of the countryside."

Do not use a comma when giving an indirect quotation.

▶ Morton and Lucia White *said that* people dream of the countryside, even though they live in cities.

Separating Items in a Series

Although the comma before the last item in a series is sometimes omitted, it is generally clearer to include it.

▶ Random House, Bantam, Doubleday, and Dell were once separate publishing companies. [Without the final comma, "Doubleday and Dell" might refer to one company or two.]

Phrases and clauses in coordinate series are also punctuated with commas.

▶ Plants absorb noxious gases, act as receptors of dirt particles, and cleanse the air of other impurities.

When phrases or clauses in a series contain commas, use <u>semicolons</u> rather than commas to separate the items.

▶ Among those present were John Howard, President of the Howard Paper Company; Thomas Martin, CEO of AIR Recycling, Inc.; and Larry Stanley, President of Northland Papers.

When <u>adjectives</u> (Tab 11) modifying the same noun can be reversed and make sense, or when they can be separated by *and* or *or*, they should be separated by commas.

▶ The aircraft featured a *modern, sleek, swept-wing* design.

When an adjective modifies a phrase, no comma is required.

▶ She was investigating the *damaged inventory-control system*. [The adjective *damaged* modifies the phrase *inventory-control system*.]

Never separate a final adjective from its noun.

▶ He is a conscientious, honest, reliable/ worker.

Clarifying and Contrasting

Use a comma to separate two contrasting thoughts or ideas.

▶ The project was finished on time, but not within the budget.

Use a comma after an independent clause that is only loosely related to the dependent clause that follows it or that could be misread without the comma.

▶ I should be able to finish the plan by July, even though I lost time because of illness.

Showing Omissions

A comma sometimes replaces a verb in certain elliptical constructions.

▶ Some were punctual; *others, late.*
[The comma replaces *were*.]

It is better, however, to avoid such constructions in business writing.

Using with Numbers and Names

Commas are conventionally used to separate distinct items. Use commas between the elements of an address written on the same line (but not between the state and the ZIP code).

▶ Kristen James, 4119 Mill Road, Dayton, Ohio 45401

A full date that is written in month-day-year format uses a comma preceding and following the year.

▶ November 30, 2025, is the payoff date.

Do not use commas for dates in the day-month-year format, which is used in many parts of the world and by the U.S. military. See also inter-national correspondence (Tab 3).

▶ Note that 30 November 2025 is the payoff date.

Do not use commas when showing only the month and year or month and day in a date.

▶ The target date of May 2017 is optimistic, so I would like to meet on March 4 to discuss our options.

Use commas to separate the elements of Arabic numbers.

▶ 1,528,200 feet

Be aware that in many countries the comma is a decimal marker, with periods or spaces used for large numbers (1.528.200 meters or 1 528 200 meters).

A comma may be substituted for the colon in the salutation of a personal letter or e-mail. Do not, however, use a comma in the salutation of a formal business letter or e-mail, even if you use the person's first name.

▶ Dear Marie, [personal letter or e-mail]

▶ Dear Marie: [business letter or e-mail]

Use commas to separate the elements of geographic names.

▶ Toronto, Ontario, Canada

Use a comma to separate names that are reversed (*Smith, Alvin*) and commas with professional <u>abbreviations</u>.

▶ Jim Rogers Jr., M.D., chaired the conference.
  [*Jr.* or *Sr.* does not require a comma.]

Using with Other Punctuation

Conjunctive adverbs (*however, nevertheless, consequently, for example, on the other hand*) that join independent clauses are preceded by a <u>semicolon</u> and followed by a comma. Such adverbs function both as <u>modifiers</u> (Tab 11) and as connectives.

▶ The idea is good; *however,* our budget is not sufficient.

As shown earlier in this entry, use semicolons rather than commas to separate items in a series when the items themselves contain commas.

When a comma should follow a phrase or clause that ends with words in parentheses, the comma always appears outside the closing parenthesis.

▶ Although we left late (at 7:30 p.m.), we arrived in time for the keynote address.

Commas always go inside <u>quotation marks</u>.

▶ The status display indicates "*ready,*" but the unit requires an additional warm-up period.

Except with abbreviations, a comma should not be used with a <u>dash</u>, an <u>exclamation mark</u>, a <u>period</u>, or a <u>question mark</u>.

▶ "Have you finished the project?/" she asked.

Avoiding Unnecessary Commas

A number of common writing errors involve placing commas where they do not belong. As stated earlier, such errors often occur because writers assume that a pause in a sentence should be indicated by a comma.

Do not place a comma between a subject and verb or between a verb and its <u>object</u> (Tab 11).

▶ The location of our booth at this year's conference/ made attracting visitors difficult.

▶ She has often said/ that one company's failure is another's opportunity.

Do not use a comma between the elements of a compound subject or compound predicate consisting of only two elements.

▶ The director of the design department / and the supervisor of the quality-control section were opposed to the new schedules.

▶ The design director listed five major objections / and asked that the new schedule be reconsidered.

Do not include a comma after a coordinating conjunction such as *and* or *but*.

▶ The chairperson formally adjourned the meeting, but / the members of the committee continued to argue.

Do not place a comma before the first item or after the last item of a series.

▶ The products we discounted include / desks, chairs, and tables.

▶ It was a fast, simple, inexpensive / process.

Do not use a comma to separate a prepositional phrase from the rest of the sentence unnecessarily.

▶ We discussed the final report / on the new project.

contractions

A contraction is a shortened spelling of a word or phrase with an **apostrophe** substituting for the missing letter or letters (*cannot / can't, have not / haven't, will not / won't, it is / it's*). Contractions are often used in speech and informal writing; they are generally not appropriate in reports, proposals, and formal correspondence. See also **business writing style** (Tab 10).

dashes

The dash (—) can perform all the punctuation duties of linking, separating, and enclosing. The dash, sometimes indicated by two consecutive **hyphens**, can also indicate the omission of letters. ("Mr. A— admitted his error.")

Use the dash cautiously to indicate more emphasis, informality, or abruptness than the other punctuation marks would show. A dash can emphasize a sharp turn in thought.

▶ The project will end May 13—unless we receive additional funding.

A dash can indicate an emphatic pause.

▶ The project will begin—after we are under contract.

Sometimes, to emphasize contrast, a dash is used with *but*.

▶ We completed the survey quickly—*but* the results were not accurate.

A dash can be used before a final summarizing statement or before repetition that has the effect of an afterthought.

▶ It was hot near the heat-treating ovens—steaming hot.

Such a statement may also complete the meaning of the clause preceding the dash.

▶ We try to write as we speak—or so we believe.

Dashes set off parenthetical elements more sharply and emphatically than <u>commas</u>. Unlike dashes, <u>parentheses</u> tend to deemphasize what they enclose. Compare the following sentences:

▶ Only one person—the president—can authorize such activity.

▶ Only one person, the president, can authorize such activity.

▶ Only one person (the president) can authorize such activity.

Dashes can be used to set off parenthetical elements that contain commas.

▶ Three of the applicants—John Evans, Rosalita Fontiana, and Kyong-Shik Choi—seem well qualified for the job.

The first word after a dash is capitalized only if it is a proper <u>noun</u> (Tab 11).

dates

12

In the United States, full dates are generally written in the month-day-year format, with a comma preceding and following the year.

▶ November 30, 2025, is the payoff date.

Do not use <u>commas</u> in the day-month-year format, which is used in many parts of the world and by the U.S. military.

▶ Note that 30 November 2025 is the payoff date.

No commas are used when showing only the month-year or month-day in a date.

▶ The target date of May 2020 is optimistic, so I would like to meet on March 4 to discuss our options.

When writing days of the month without the year, use the cardinal number ("March 4") rather than the ordinal number ("March 4th"). Of course, in speech or <u>presentations</u> (Tab 8), use the ordinal number ("March fourth").

Avoid the strictly numerical form for dates (11/6/17) because the date is not always immediately clear, especially in <u>international corre-spondence</u> (Tab 3). In many countries, 11/6/17 means June 11, 2017, rather than November 6, 2017. Writing out the name of the month makes the entire date immediately clear to all readers.

Centuries often cause confusion with <u>numbers</u> because their spelled-out forms, which are not capitalized, do not correspond to their numeral designations. The twentieth century, for example, is the 1900s: 1900–1999.

When the century is written as a noun, do not use a <u>hyphen</u>.

▶ During the twentieth century, technology transformed business practices.

When the centuries are written as adjectives, however, use hyphens.

▶ Twenty-first-century technology relies on dependable power sources.

ellipses

An ellipsis is the omission of words from quoted material; it is indi-cated by three spaced <u>periods</u> called *ellipsis points* (. . .). When you use ellipsis points, omit original punctuation marks, unless they are neces-sary for clarity or the omitted material comes at the end of a quoted sentence.

ORIGINAL TEXT	"Promotional material sometimes carries a fee, particularly in high-volume distribution to schools, although prices for these publications are much lower than the development costs when all factors are considered."
WITH OMISSION AND ELLIPSIS POINTS	"Promotional material sometimes carries a fee . . . although prices for these publications are much lower than the development costs. . . ."

Notice in the preceding example that the final period is retained and what remains of the quotation is grammatically complete. When the omitted part of the quotation is preceded by a period, retain the period and add the three ellipsis points after it, as in the following example.

ORIGINAL TEXT	"Of the 172 major ethics cases reported, 57 percent were found to involve unsubstantiated concerns. Misinformation was the cause of unfounded concerns of misconduct in 72 cases. Forty-four cases, or 26 percent of the total cases reported, involved incidents partly substantiated by ethics officers as serious misconduct."
WITH OMISSION AND ELLIPSIS POINTS	"Of the 172 major ethics cases reported, 57 percent were found to involve unsubstantiated concerns. . . . Forty-four cases, or 26 percent of the total cases reported, involved incidents partly substantiated by ethics officers as serious misconduct."

Do not use ellipsis points when the beginning of a quoted sentence is omitted. Notice in the following example that the comma is dropped to prevent a grammatical error. See also <u>quotations</u> (Tab 5).

▶ The ethics report states that "26 percent of the total cases reported involved incidents partly substantiated by ethics officers as serious misconduct."

exclamation marks

The exclamation mark (!) indicates strong feeling, urgency, elation, or surprise ("Hurry!" "Great!" "Wow!"). However, it cannot make an argument more convincing, lend force to a weak statement, or call attention to an intended irony.

An exclamation mark can be used after a whole sentence or an element of a sentence.

▶ This meeting—please note it well!—concerns our budget deficit.

When used with <u>quotation marks</u>, the exclamation mark goes outside, unless what is quoted is an exclamation.

▶ The paramedic shouted, "Don't touch the victim!" The bystander then, according to a witness, "jumped like a kangaroo"!

In instructions, the exclamation mark is often used in cautions and warnings ("Danger!" "Stop!") or enclosed within a triangle ⚠. See also <u>emphasis</u> (Tab 10).

hyphens

The hyphen (-) is used primarily for linking and separating words and parts of words. The hyphen often improves clarity (as in *re-sign* and *resign*). The hyphen is sometimes confused with the <u>dash</u> (—), which has many other functions.

Hyphens with Compound Words

Some compound words are formed with hyphens (*able-bodied, over-the-counter*). Hyphens are also used with multiword <u>numbers</u> *twenty-one* through *ninety-nine* and fractions when they are written out (*three-quarters*). Most current dictionaries indicate whether compound words are hyphenated, written as one word, or written as separate words.

Hyphens with Modifiers

Two- and three-word <u>modifiers</u> (Tab 11) that express a single thought are hyphenated when they precede a <u>noun</u> (Tab 11).

▶ It was a *well-written* report.

However, a modifying phrase is not hyphenated when it follows the noun it modifies.

▶ The report was *well written.*

If each of the words can modify the noun without the aid of the other modifying word or words, do not use a hyphen (a *new laser* printer). If the first word is an <u>adverb</u> (Tab 11) ending in *-ly*, do not use a hyphen (a *privately held* company). A hyphen is always used as part of a letter or number modifier (*A-frame house, 22-inch screen*).

In a series of unit modifiers that all have the same term following the hyphen, the term following the hyphen need not be repeated throughout the series; for greater smoothness and brevity, use the term only at the end of the series.

▶ The third-, fourth-, and fifth-floor laboratories were inspected.

Hyphens with Prefixes and Suffixes

A hyphen is used with a prefix when the root word is a proper noun (*pre-Columbian, anti-American, post-Newtonian*). A hyphen may be used when the prefix ends and the root word begins with the same vowel (*re-enter, anti-inflammatory*). A hyphen is used when *ex-* means "former" (*ex-president, ex-spouse*) and may be used to emphasize a prefix. ("He is *anti-change.*") The suffix *-elect* is hyphenated (*president-elect*).

12

Punctuation
and Mechanics

Hyphens and Clarity

The presence or absence of a hyphen can alter the meaning of a sentence.

AMBIGUOUS   We need a biological waste management system.

That sentence could mean one of two things: (1) We need a system to manage "biological waste," or (2) We need a "biological" system to manage waste.

CLEAR   We need a *biological-waste* management system. [1]

CLEAR   We need a biological *waste-management* system. [2]

To avoid confusion, some words and modifiers should always be hyphenated. *Re-cover* does not mean the same thing as *recover*, for example; the same is true of *un-ionized* and *unionized*.

Other Uses of the Hyphen

Hyphens are used between letters showing how a word is spelled.

▶ In his e-mail, he misspelled *believed* as b-e-l-e-i-v-e-d.

A hyphen can stand for *to* or *through* between letters and numbers (*pages 44-46, the Detroit-Toledo Expressway, A-L and M-Z*).

Hyphens are commonly used in telephone numbers (*800-555-1212*), Web addresses (*computer-parts.com*), file names (*report-15.doc*), and similar number / symbol combinations. See also <u>dates</u>.

Hyphens are also used to divide words at the end of a line, especially for full-justified margins within small columns. The following are standard guidelines for using hyphens to divide words at the end of lines.

- Do not divide one-syllable words.
- Divide words at syllable breaks, which you can determine with a dictionary.
- Do not divide a word if only one letter would remain at the end of a line or if fewer than three letters would start a new line.
- Do not divide a word at the end of a page; carry the word over to the next page.
- If a word already has a hyphen in its spelling, divide the word at the existing hyphen.
- Do not use a hyphen to break a URL or an e-mail address at the end of a line. See also <u>documenting sources</u> (Tab 5).

italics

Italics is a style of type used to denote emphasis (Tab 10) and to distinguish book titles, foreign expressions, and certain other elements. Italic type is often signaled by underlining in material submitted for typesetting or where italic font is not available. You may need to italicize words that require special emphasis in a sentence. ("Contrary to projections, sales have *not* improved.") Do not overuse italics for emphasis, however. ("*This* will hurt *you* more than *me*.")

Foreign Words and Phrases

Foreign words and phrases are italicized: *bonjour*, *guten tag*, the sign said "*Se habla español*." Foreign words that have been fully assimilated into English need not be italicized: cliché, etiquette, vis-à-vis, de facto, résumé. When in doubt about whether to italicize a word, consult a current dictionary.

Titles

Italicize the titles of separately published documents (print or electronic), such as books, Web and blog sites, periodicals, newspapers, pamphlets, brochures, and legal cases.

▶ *Turning Workplace Conflicts into Collaboration* [book] was reviewed in the *New York Times* [newspaper].

▶ *CNN Money* [Web site] reports that "written communication skills remain a top priority for U.S. businesses."

Abbreviations of such titles are italicized if their spelled-out forms would be italicized.

▶ The *NYT* is one of the nation's oldest newspapers.

Italicize the titles of CDs, DVDs, movies, plays, long poems, paintings, sculptures, and long musical works.

DVD-ROM	*Computer Security Tutorial*
PLAY	Arthur Miller's *Death of a Salesman*
LONG POEM	T. S. Eliot's *The Waste Land*
MUSICAL WORK	Gershwin's *Porgy and Bess*

Use quotation marks for parts of publications, such as chapters of books and sections within larger works.

▶ *Small Business Trends* (smallbiztrends.com) [blog] posted "Microbusiness Economic Trends: Into the Future." [article]

12

Punctuation and Mechanics

Proper Names

The names of ships, trains, and aircraft (but not the companies or governments that own them) are italicized: U.S. aircraft carrier *Independence*, Amtrak's passenger train *Coast Starlight*. Craft that are known by model or serial designations are not italicized: DC-7, Boeing 747.

Words, Letters, and Figures

Words, letters, and figures discussed as such are italicized.

▶ The word *inflammable* is often misinterpreted.

▶ The *S* and *6* keys on my keyboard do not function.

Subheads

Subheads in a report are sometimes italicized.

▶ *Training Managers.* We are leading the way in developing first-line managers who not only are professionally competent but . . .

Exceptions

Some titles are not set off by italics, quotation marks, or underlining, although they are capitalized.

▶ Professional Writing [college course title], the Constitution, the Bible, Lincoln's Gettysburg Address, the Lands' End Catalog

Keep in mind your <u>context</u> (Tab 1), especially as you prepare material for screen display as in <u>writing for the Web</u> (Tab 2). See also <u>headings</u> (Tab 7) and <u>layout and design</u> (Tab 7).

numbers

12

Punctuation and Mechanics

The standards for using numbers vary; however, unless you are following an organizational or a professional style manual, observe the following guidelines.

Numerals or Words

Write numbers from zero through ten as words, and write numbers above ten as numerals.

▶ I rehearsed my presentation *three* times.

▶ The association added *152* new members.

Spell out numbers that begin a sentence, however, even if they would otherwise be written as numerals.

▶ *One hundred and fifty-two* new members joined the association.

If spelling out such a number seems awkward, rewrite the sentence so that the number does not appear at the beginning ("We added *152* new members").
Spell out approximate and round numbers.

▶ We've had *more than a thousand* requests this month.

In most writing, spell out small ordinal numbers, which express degree or sequence (*first*, *second*; but *27th*, *42nd*), when they are single words (*our nineteenth year*), or when they modify a century (*the twenty-first century*). However, avoid ordinal numbers in <u>dates</u> (use *March 30* or *30 March*, not *March 30th*).

Plurals

Indicate the plural of numerals by adding -*s* (*7s*, *the late 1990s*). Form the plural of a written number (like any noun) by adding -*s* or -*es* or by dropping the *y* and adding -*ies* (*elevens*, *sixes*, *twenties*). See also <u>apostrophes</u>.

Measurements

Express units of measurement as numerals (*3 miles*, *45 cubic feet*, *9 meters*). When numbers run together in the same phrase, write one as a numeral and the other as a word.

▶ The order was for ~~12 6-foot tables.~~
  _{12 six-foot tables.}

Generally give percentages as numerals and write out the word *percent*. ("Approximately *85 percent* of the land has been sold.") However, in a table, use a numeral followed by the percent symbol (*85%*).

Fractions

Express fractions as numerals when they are written with whole numbers (*27½ inches*, *4¼ miles*). Spell out fractions when they are expressed without a whole number (*one-fourth, seven-eighths*). Always write decimal numbers as numerals (*5.21 meters*).

Money

In general, use numerals to express exact or approximate amounts of money.

▶ We need to charge *$28.95* per unit.

▶ The new system costs *$60,000.*

Use words to express indefinite amounts of money.

▶ The printing system may cost *several thousand dollars.*

Use numerals and words for rounded amounts of money over one million dollars.

▶ The contract is worth *$6.8 million.*

Use numerals for more-complex or exact amounts.

▶ The corporation paid *$2,452,500* in taxes last year.

For amounts under a dollar, ordinarily use numerals and the word *cents* ("The pens cost *75 cents* each"), unless other numerals that require dollar signs appear in the same sentence.

▶ The business-card holders cost *$10.49* each, the pens cost *$.75* each, and the pencil-cup holders cost *$6.49* each.

Time

Divide hours and minutes with <u>colons</u> when *a.m.* or *p.m.* follows (*7:30 a.m., 11:30 p.m.*). Do not use colons with the 24-hour system (*0730, 2330*). Spelled-out time is not followed by *a.m.* or *p.m.* (*seven o'clock in the evening*).

Dates

In the United States, dates are usually written in a month-day-year sequence (*August 11, 2017*). Never use the strictly numerical form for dates (*8/11/17*) because the date is not immediately clear, especially in <u>international correspondence</u> (Tab 3).

Addresses

Spell out numbered streets from one through ten unless space is at a premium (*East Tenth Street*). Write building numbers as numerals. The only exception is the building number *one* (*One East Monument Street*). Write highway numbers as numerals (*U.S. 40, Ohio 271, I-94*).

Documents

Page numbers are written as numerals in manuscripts (*page 37*). Chapter and volume numbers may appear as numerals or words (*Chapter 2* or *Chapter Two, Volume 1* or *Volume One*), but be consistent. Express figure and table numbers as numerals (*Figure 4, Table 3*).

Do not follow a word representing a number with a numeral in parentheses that represents the same number. Doing so is redundant.

▶ Send five ~~(5)~~ copies of the report.

ESL TIP for Punctuating Numbers

Some rules for punctuating numbers in English are summarized as follows:

Use a comma to separate numbers with four or more digits into groups of three, starting from the right (*$5,289,112,001 in worldwide sales*).

Do not use a comma in years, house numbers, ZIP codes, and page numbers.

▶ June *2017*

▶ *92401* East Alameda Drive

▶ The ZIP code is *91601-1243*.

▶ Page *1204*

Use a period to represent the decimal point (*4.2 percent, $3,742,097.43*). See also global communication (Tab 1) and global graphics (Tab 7).

---

parentheses

Parentheses are used to enclose explanatory or digressive words, phrases, or sentences. Material in parentheses often clarifies or defines the preceding text without altering its meaning.

▶ She severely bruised her tibia (or shinbone) in the accident.

Parenthetical information may not be essential to a sentence (in fact, parentheses deemphasize the enclosed material), but it may be helpful to some readers.

12

Punctuation
and Mechanics

Parenthetical material does not affect the punctuation of a sentence, and any punctuation (such as a <u>comma</u> or <u>period</u>) should appear following the closing parenthesis.

▶ She could not fully extend her knee because of a torn meniscus (or cartilage), and she suffered pain from a severely bruised tibia (or shinbone).

When a complete sentence within parentheses stands independently, the ending punctuation is placed inside the final parenthesis.

▶ The project director listed the problems her staff faced. (This was the third time she had complained to the board.)

For some constructions, however, you should consider using <u>subordination</u> (Tab 10) rather than parentheses.

▶ The early tests showed little damage ⟨, which pleased the attending physician,⟩ ~~(the attending physician was pleased),~~ but later scans revealed abdominal trauma.

Parentheses also are used to enclose numerals or letters that indicate sequence.

▶ The following sections deal with (1) preparation, (2) research, (3) organization, (4) writing, and (5) revision.

Do not follow spelled-out <u>numbers</u> with numerals in parentheses representing the same numbers.

▶ Send five ~~(5)~~ copies of the report.

Use <u>brackets</u> to set off a parenthetical item that is already within parentheses.

▶ We should be sure to give Emanuel Foose (and his brother Emilio [1912–1982]) credit for his part in founding the institute.

See also <u>documenting sources</u> (Tab 5) and <u>quotations</u> (Tab 5).

---

12 | periods

A period usually indicates the end of a declarative or an imperative sentence. Periods also indicate omissions when used as <u>ellipses</u> and link when used as leaders, as in rows of periods in <u>tables of contents</u> (Tab 6). Periods are also used to end questions that are actually polite requests, or instructions to which an affirmative response is assumed. ("Will you call me as soon as he arrives.") See also <u>sentence construction</u> (Tab 11).

Periods in Quotations

Use a <u>comma</u>, not a period, after a declarative sentence that is quoted in the context of another sentence.

► "There is every chance of success," she stated.

A period is placed inside <u>quotation marks</u>. See also <u>quotations</u> (Tab 5).

► He stated clearly, "My vote is yes."

Periods with Parentheses

Place a period outside the final parenthesis when a parenthetical element ends a sentence.

► The institute was founded by Harry Denman (1902–1972).

Place a period inside the final parenthesis when a complete sentence stands independently within <u>parentheses</u>.

► The project director listed the problems her staff faced. (This was the third time she had complained to the board.)

Other Uses of Periods

Use periods following the numerals in a numbered <u>list</u> (Tab 7) and following complete sentences in a list.

► 1. Enter your name and PIN.
  2. Enter your address with ZIP code.
  3. Enter your preferred phone number.

Use periods after initials in names (*Wilma T. Grant, J. P. Morgan*). Use periods as decimal points with <u>numbers</u> (*27.3 degrees Celsius, $540.26, 6.9 percent*). Use periods to indicate certain <u>abbreviations</u> (*Ms., Dr., Inc.*). When a sentence ends with an abbreviation that ends with a period, do not add another period. ("Please meet me at 3:30 p.m.")

Period Faults

When a period is inserted prematurely, the result is a <u>sentence fragment</u> (Tab 11).

| FRAGMENT | After a long day at the office during which we finished the quarterly report. We left hurriedly for home. |
| SENTENCE | After a long day at the office, during which we finished the quarterly report, we left hurriedly for home. |

When two independent clauses are joined without any punctuation, the result is a *fused*, or *run-on*, *sentence*. Adding a period between the clauses is one way to correct a run-on sentence.

RUN-ON   Bill was late for ten days in a row Ms. Sturgess had to dismiss him.

CORRECT Bill was late for ten days in a row. Ms. Sturgess had to dismiss him.

Other options are to add a comma and a coordinating conjunction (*and, but, for, or, nor, so, yet*) between the clauses, to add a <u>semicolon</u>, or to add a semicolon with a conjunctive <u>adverb</u> (Tab 11), such as *therefore* or *however*.

question marks

The question mark (?) most often ends a sentence that is a direct question or request.

▶ Did you finish the tax report? [direct question]

▶ Will you e-mail me if your shipment does not arrive by June 10? [request]

Use a question mark to end a statement that has an interrogative meaning— a statement that is declarative in form but asks a question.

▶ The tax report is finished? [question in declarative form]

Question marks may follow a series of separate items within an interrogative sentence.

▶ Do you remember the date of the contract? Its terms? Whether you signed it?

Use a question mark to end an interrogative clause within a declarative sentence.

▶ It was not until July (or was it August?) that we submitted the report.

Retain the question mark in a title that is being cited, even though the sentence in which it appears has not ended.

▶ *Can Investments Be Protected?* is the title of her book.

Never use a question mark to end a sentence that is an indirect question.

▶ He asked me if I finished the tax report.

When a question is a polite request or an instruction to which an affirmative response is assumed, a question mark is not necessary.

▶ Will you call me as soon as he arrives. [polite request]

When used with quotations (Tab 5), the placement of the question mark is important. When the writer is asking a question, the question mark belongs outside the quotation marks.

▶ Did she actually say, "I don't think the project should continue"*?*

If the quotation itself is a question, the question mark goes inside the quotation marks.

▶ She asked, "Do we have enough funding*?*"

If both cases apply—the writer is asking a question and the quotation itself is a question—use a single question mark inside the quotation marks.

▶ Did she ask, "Do we have enough funding*?*"

quotation marks

Quotation marks (" ") are used to enclose a direct quotation of spoken or written words. Quotation marks have other special uses, but they should not be used for emphasis (Tab 10).

Direct Quotations

Enclose in quotation marks anything that is quoted word for word (a direct quotation) from speech or written material.

▶ The contract was explicit: "Monthly deliverables for the duration of this contract are due by close of business the last workday of each month."

Do not enclose indirect quotations—usually introduced by the word *that*—in quotation marks. Indirect quotations are paraphrases of a writer's or speaker's words or ideas. See also paraphrasing (Tab 5).

▶ She said that she wanted the progress report by three o'clock.

❖ ETHICS NOTE When you use quotation marks to indicate that you are quoting word for word, do not make any changes or omissions inside the quoted material unless you clearly indicate what you have done. For further information on incorporating quoted material and inserting comments, see plagiarism (Tab 5) and quotations (Tab 5). ❖

12

Punctuation
and Mechanics

Use single quotation marks (' ') to enclose a quotation that appears within a quotation.

▶ John said, "Jane told me that she was going to 'stay with the project if it takes all year.' "

Words and Phrases

Use quotation marks to set off special words or terms only when such terms are used in context for a unique or special purpose (that is, in the sense of the term *so-called*).

▶ A remarkable chain of events caused the sinking of the "unsinkable" *Titanic* on its maiden voyage.

Slang, colloquial expressions, and attempts at humor, although infrequent in workplace writing, should seldom be set off by quotation marks.

▶ Our first six months amounted to a "shakedown cruise." [*shakedown cruise.* written as correction above "shakedown cruise."]

Titles of Works

Use quotation marks to enclose titles of reports, short stories, articles, essays, single episodes of radio and television programs, and short musical works (including songs). However, do not use quotation marks for titles of books and periodicals, which should appear in underlined.

▶ "Effects of Government Regulations on Motorcycle Safety" [report] cited "No-Fault Insurance and Motorcycles" [article] published in *American Motorcyclist* [periodical].

Use quotation marks for parts of publications, such as chapters of books and sections within larger works.

▶ "Microbusiness Economic Trends: Into the Future" [article] appeared in *Small Business Trends* (smallbiztrends.com) [blog].

Some titles are not set off by quotation marks, italics, or underlining, although they are capitalized.

▶ Professional Writing [college course title], the Constitution, the Bible, Lincoln's Gettysburg Address, the Lands' End Catalog

Punctuation

Commas and periods always go inside closing quotation marks.

▶ "Reading *Computer World* gives me the insider's view," he says, adding, "It's like a conversation with the top experts."

<u>Semicolons</u> and <u>colons</u> always go outside closing quotation marks.

▶ He said, "I will pay the full amount"; this statement surprised us.

All other punctuation follows the logic of the context: If the punctuation is part of the material quoted, it goes inside the quotation marks; if the punctuation is not part of the material quoted, it goes outside the quotation marks.

semicolons

The semicolon (;) links independent <u>clauses</u> (Tab 11) or other sentence elements of equal weight and grammatical rank when they are not joined by a <u>comma</u> and a <u>conjunction</u> (Tab 11). The semicolon indicates a greater pause between clauses than does a comma but not as great a pause as a <u>period</u>.

Independent clauses joined by a semicolon should balance or contrast with each other, and the relationship between the two statements should be so clear that further explanation is not necessary.

▶ The new Web site was a success; every division reported increased online sales.

Do not use a semicolon between a dependent clause and its main clause.

▶ No one applied for the position; even though it was heavily advertised.

With Strong Connectives

In complicated sentences, a semicolon may be used before transitional words or phrases (*that is, for example, namely*) that introduce examples or provide further explanation. See also <u>transition</u> (Tab 10).

▶ The press understands Commissioner Curran's position on the issue; *that is*, local funds should not be used for the highway project.

A semicolon should also be used before conjunctive adverbs (*therefore, moreover, consequently, furthermore, indeed, in fact, however*) that connect independent clauses.

▶ The test results are not complete; *therefore*, I cannot make a recommendation.
[The semicolon in the example shows that *therefore* belongs to the second clause.]

For Clarity in Long Sentences

Use a semicolon between two independent clauses connected by a coordinating conjunction (*and, but, for, or, nor, so, yet*) if the clauses are long and contain other punctuation.

▶ In most cases, these individuals are executives, bankers, or lawyers; *but* they do not, as the press seems to believe, simply push the button of their economic power to affect local politics.

A semicolon may also be used if any items in a series contain commas.

▶ Among those present were John Howard, President of the Omega Paper Company; Carol Delgado, President of Environex Corporation; and Larry Stanley, President of Stanley Papers.

Use <u>parentheses</u> or <u>dashes</u>, not semicolons, to enclose a parenthetical element that contains commas.

▶ All affected job classifications (receptionist, secretary, transcriptionist, and clerk) will be upgraded this month.

Use a <u>colon</u>, not a semicolon, as a mark of anticipation or enumeration.

▶ Three decontamination methods are under consideration; a zeolite-resin system, an evaporation system, and a filtration system.

The semicolon always appears outside closing <u>quotation marks</u>.

▶ The attorney said, "You must be accurate"; her client replied, "I will."

slashes

The slash (/) — also called *slant line, diagonal, virgule, bar,* and *solidus* — both separates and shows omission. The slash can indicate alternatives or combinations.

▶ Our telephone numbers are (800) 549-2278/2235.

▶ Repair the on/off switch on the meter.

The slash often indicates omitted words and letters.

▶ miles/hour (miles per hour); w/o (without)

In fractions and mathematical expressions, the slash separates the numerator from the denominator (3/4 for three-fourths; x/y for x over y).

Although the slash is used informally with <u>dates</u> (*5/9/17*), avoid this form in business writing, especially in <u>international correspondence</u> (Tab 3).

The forward slash often separates items in URL (uniform resource locator) addresses for sites on the Internet (***macmillanlearning.com /bwc8e***). The backward slash is used to separate parts of file names (*c:\myfiles\reports\annual17.doc*).

spelling

Because spelling errors in your documents can confuse readers and damage your credibility, careful <u>proofreading</u> (Tab 1) is essential. The use of a spell checker is crucial; however, it will not catch all mistakes, especially those in personal and company names. It cannot detect a spelling error if the error results in a valid word; for example, if you mean *coarse* but inadvertently type *course*, the spell checker will not detect the error. If you are unsure about the spelling of a word, do not rely on guesswork or a spell checker—consult a dictionary.

Appendix: Usage

Preview

Usage describes the choices we make among the various words and constructions available in our language. The line between standard and nonstandard English, or between formal and informal English, is determined by these choices. Your choices in any writing situation should be guided by appropriateness: Is the word or expression appropriate to your audience and subject? When it is, you are practicing good usage. A good dictionary is also an invaluable aid in helping you select the right word. (See Tab 10, "Style and Clarity.")

a lot   *A lot* is often incorrectly written as one word (*alot*). The phrase *a lot* is informal and often too vague for business writing. Use *many* or *numerous* for estimates or give a specific number or amount.

152

▶ We received ~~a lot of~~ e-mails supporting the new policy.

above   Avoid using *above* to refer to a preceding passage or visual because its reference is often vague and often an <u>affectation</u> (Tab 10). The same is true of *aforesaid* and *aforementioned*. To refer to something previously mentioned, repeat the noun or pronoun, or construct your paragraph so that your reference is obvious.

your travel voucher

▶ Please complete and submit ~~the above~~ by March 1.

accept / except   *Accept* is a verb meaning "consent to," "agree to take," or "admit willingly." ("I *accept* the responsibility.") *Except* is normally used as a preposition meaning "other than" or "excluding." ("We agreed on everything *except* the schedule.")

affect / effect   *Affect* is a verb that means "influence." ("The decision could *affect* the company's stock value.") *Effect* can function as a noun that means "result" ("The decision had a positive *effect*") or as a verb that means "bring about" or "cause." However, avoid *effect* as a verb when you can replace it with a less-formal word, such as *make* or *produce*.

make

▶ The new manager will ~~effect~~ several changes to improve morale.

also   *Also* is an adverb that means "additionally." ("Two 5,000-gallon tanks are on-site, and several 2,500-gallon tanks are *also* available.") *Also* should not be used as a connective in the sense of "and."

and

▶ He brought the reports, the memos, ~~also~~ the director's

recommendations.

Avoid opening sentences with *also*. It is a weak transitional word that suggests an afterthought rather than planned writing.

In addition,

▶ ~~Also~~ he prepared a cost-benefit analysis to support his proposal.

He also

▶ ~~Also, he~~ prepared a cost-benefit analysis to support his proposal.

amount / number   *Amount* is used with things that are thought of in bulk and that cannot be counted (mass nouns), as in "the *amount* of electricity." *Number* is used with things that can be counted as individual items (count nouns), as in "the *number* of employees."

and/or   *And/or* means that either both circumstances are possible or only one of two circumstances is possible. This term is awkward and confusing because it makes the reader stop to puzzle over your distinction.

AWKWARD   Use A *and/or* B.
IMPROVED   Use A or B or both.

as / because / since   *As, because*, and *since* are commonly used to mean "because." To express cause, *because* is the strongest and most specific connective in unequivocally stating a causal relationship. ("*Because* she did not have an MBA, she was not offered the job.")

    Since is a weak substitute for *because* as a connective to express cause. However, *since* is an appropriate connective when the emphasis is on circumstance, condition, or time rather than on cause and effect. ("*Since* it went public, the company has earned a profit every year.")

    As is the least definite connective to indicate cause; its use for that purpose is best avoided.

as such   The phrase *as such* is seldom useful and should be omitted.

▶ Patients, ~~as such,~~ should be partners in their treatment decisions.

as well as   Do not use *as well as* with *both*. The two expressions have similar meanings; use one or the other and adjust the verb as needed.

              and   *are*
▶ Both General Motors ~~as well as~~ Ford ~~is~~ marketing hybrid vehicles.

▶ ~~Both~~ General Motors as well as Ford is marketing hybrid vehicles.

average / median / mean   The *average* (or arithmetic *mean*) is determined by adding two or more quantities and dividing the sum by the number of items totaled. For example, if one report is 10 pages, another is 30 pages, and a third is 20 pages, their *average* length is 20 pages. It is incorrect to say that "each report averages 20 pages" because each report is a specific length.

   The three reports average
▶ ~~Each report averages~~ 20 pages.

The *median* is the middle number in a sequence of numbers. For example, the *median* of the series 1, 3, 4, 7, 8 is 4.

bad / badly   *Bad* is the adjective form that follows such linking verbs as *feel* and *look*. ("We don't want to look *bad* at the meeting.") *Badly* is an adverb. ("The shipment was *badly* damaged.") To say "I feel *badly*" would mean, literally, that your sense of touch is impaired.

between / among   *Between* is normally used to relate two items or persons. ("Preferred stock offers a middle ground *between* bonds and common stock.") *Among* is used to relate more than two. ("The subcontracting was distributed *among* three firms.")

bi- / semi-   When used with periods of time, *bi-* means "two" or "every two," as in *published biweekly*, meaning "once in two weeks." *Semi-* means "half of" or "occurring twice within a period of time," as in *published semimonthly*, meaning "twice a month." Because these prefixes often cause confusion, substitute expressions like *every two months* or *twice a month* where possible. Normally, *bi-* and *semi-* are joined with the following element without a space or hyphen.

can / may   In writing, *can* refers to capability. ("I *can* have the project finished today.") *May* refers to possibility ("I *may* be in Boston on Monday.") or permission ("*May* I leave early?").

criteria / criterion   *Criterion* is a singular noun meaning "an established standard for judging or testing." *Criteria* and *criterions* are both acceptable plural forms of *criterion*, but *criteria* is generally preferred.

data   In formal and scholarly writing, *data* is generally used as a plural, with *datum* as the singular form. In much informal writing, however, *data* is considered a collective singular noun. Base your usage on whether your readers should consider the data as a single collection or as a group of individual facts. Whichever you use, be sure that your pronouns and verbs agree in number with the selected usage.

different from / different than   In formal writing, the preposition *from* is used with *different*. ("The product I received is *different from* the one I ordered.") *Different than* is used when it is followed by a clause. ("The actual cost was *different than* we estimated in our proposal.")

each   When *each* is used as a subject, it takes a singular verb or pronoun. ("*Each* of the reports *is* to be submitted ten weeks after *it* is assigned.") When *each* refers to a plural subject, it takes a plural verb or pronoun. ("The reports *each have* company logos on *their* title pages.")

e.g. / i.e. The abbreviation *e.g.* stands for the Latin *exempli gratia*, meaning "for example"; *i.e.* stands for the Latin *id est*, meaning "that is." Because the English expressions (*for example* and *that is*) are clear to all readers, avoid the Latin *e.g.* and *i.e.* abbreviations except to save space in notes and visuals. If you must use *i.e.* or *e.g.*, do not italicize either and punctuate them as follows. If *i.e.* or *e.g.* connects two independent clauses, a semicolon should precede the abbreviation and a comma should follow it.

▶ The conference drew international participants; e.g., speakers included Germans, Italians, Japanese, Chinese, and Americans.

If *i.e.* or *e.g.* connects a noun and an appositive, a comma should precede it and follow it.

▶ The conference included speakers from five countries, i.e., Germany, Italy, Japan, China, and the United States.

etc. *Etc.* is an abbreviation for the Latin *et cetera*, meaning "and others" or "and so on." Therefore, do not use the redundant phrase *and etc.* Likewise, do not use *etc.* at the end of a series introduced by the phrases *such as* and *for example* — those phrases already indicate unnamed items of the same category. Use *etc.* with a logical progression (1, 2, 3, etc.) and when at least two items are named. Do not italicize *etc.*

▶ The sorting machine processes coins (~~for example~~ pennies, nickels, ~~and~~ etc.) and then packages them for redistribution.

Otherwise, avoid *etc.* because the reader may not be able to infer what other items a list might include.

VAGUE	He will bring notepads, paper clips, etc., to the trade show.
CLEAR	He will bring notepads, paper clips, and other office supplies to the trade show.

explicit / implicit An *explicit* statement is one expressed directly, with precision and clarity.

▶ He gave us *explicit* directions to the Wausau facility.

An *implicit* meaning is one that is not directly expressed.

▶ Although the CEO did not mention the lawsuit directly, the company's commitment to ethical practices was *implicit* in her speech.

fact Expressions containing the word *fact* ("due to the *fact* that," "except for the *fact* that," "as a matter of *fact*," or "because of the *fact* that") are often wordy substitutes for more accurate terms.

> *Because*
> ▶ ~~Due to the fact that~~ the sales force has a high turnover rate, sales
>   ^
> have declined.

Do not use the word *fact* to refer to matters of judgment or opinion.

> *In my opinion,*
> ▶ ~~It is a fact that~~ sales are poor in the Midwest because of insuffi-
>   ^
> cient market research.

The word *fact* is, of course, valid when facts are what is meant.

> ▶ Our study uncovered numerous *facts* to support your conclusion.

few / a few   In certain contexts, *few* carries more negative overtones than does the phrase *a few*.

NEGATIVE	The report offers *few* helpful ideas.
POSITIVE	The report offers *a few* helpful ideas.

fewer / less   *Fewer* refers to items that can be counted (count nouns). ("*Fewer* employees retired than we expected.") *Less* refers to mass quantities or amounts (mass nouns). ("We had much *less* rain this year than forecasts predicted.")

first / firstly   *First* and *firstly* are both adverbs. Avoid *firstly* in favor of *first*, which sounds less stiff than *firstly*. The same is true of other ordinal numbers, such as *second, third*, and so on.

former / latter   *Former* and *latter* should be used to refer to only two items in a sentence or paragraph.

> ▶ The president and his aide emerged from the conference, the *former* looking nervous and the *latter* looking glum.

Because these terms make the reader look to previous material to identify the reference, they complicate reading and are best avoided.

good / well   *Good* is an adjective and *well* is an adverb.

ADJECTIVE	Janet presented a *good* plan.
ADVERB	She presented the plan *well*.

Well also can be used as an adjective to describe health (a *well* child, *wellness* programs).

he / she   The use of either *he* or *she* to refer to both sexes excludes half of the population. To avoid this problem, you could use the phrases *he or she* and *his or her*. ("Whoever is appointed will find *his or her* task difficult.") However, *he or she* and *his or her* are clumsy when used repeatedly, as are *he/she* and similar constructions. One solution is to reword the sentence to use a plural pronoun; if you do, change the nouns or other pronouns to match the plural form.

>   *Administrators*   *their jobs*   *they understand*
> ▶ ~~The administrator~~ cannot do ~~his or her job~~ until ~~he or she under-~~
>
> ~~stands~~ the organization's culture.

In other cases, you may be able to avoid using a pronoun altogether.

>   *an*
> ▶ Everyone must submit ~~his or her~~ expense report by Monday.

Of course, a pronoun cannot always be omitted without changing the meaning of a sentence.

Another solution is to omit troublesome pronouns by using the imperative mood.

>   *Submit all*   *s*
> ▶ ~~Everyone must submit his or her~~ expense report by Monday.

imply / infer   If you *imply* something, you hint at or suggest it. ("Her e-mail *implied* that the project would be delayed.") If you *infer* something, you reach a conclusion based on evidence or interpretation. ("The manager *inferred* from the e-mail that the project would be delayed.")

in / into   *In* means "inside of"; *into* implies movement from the outside to the inside. ("We were *in* a meeting when the intern brought copies of the contract *into* the conference room.")

its / it's   *Its* is a possessive pronoun and does not use an apostrophe. *It's* is a contraction of *it is.*

> ▶ *It's* important that the sales department meet *its* quota.

kind of / sort of   The phrases *kind of* and *sort of* should be used only to refer to a class or type of things. ("We require a special *kind of* training to ensure employee safety.") Do not use *kind of* or *sort of* to mean "rather," "somewhat," or "somehow."

lay / lie   *Lay* is a transitive verb—a verb that requires a direct object to complete its meaning—that means "place" or "put."

▶ We will *lay* the foundation one section at a time.

The past-tense form of *lay* is *laid.*

▶ We *laid* the first section of the foundation last month.

The perfect-tense form of *lay* is also *laid.*

▶ Since June, we *have laid* all but two sections of the foundation.

Lay is frequently confused with *lie*, which is an intransitive verb—a verb that does not require an object to complete its meaning—that means "recline" or "remain."

▶ A person in shock should *lie* down with legs slightly elevated.

The past-tense form of *lie* is *lay* (not *lied*). This form causes the confusion between *lie* and *lay.*

▶ The injured employee *lay* still for approximately five minutes.

The perfect-tense form of *lie* is *lain.*

▶ The injured employee *had lain* still for five minutes before the EMTs arrived.

like / as   To avoid confusion between *like* and *as*, remember that *like* is a preposition and *as* (or *as if*) is a conjunction. Use *like* with a noun or pronoun that is not followed by a verb.

▶ The new supervisor behaves *like* a novice.

Use *as* before clauses, which contain verbs.

▶ He responded *as* we hoped he would.

▶ The presentation seemed *as if* it would never end.

Like and *as* are used in comparisons: *Like* is used in constructions that omit the verb, and *as* is used when the verb is retained.

▶ He adapted to the new system *like* a duck to water.

▶ He adapted to the new system *as* a duck adapts to water.

media / medium   *Media* is the plural of *medium* and should always be used with a plural verb.

▶ Many communication *media are* available today.

▶ The Internet *is* a multifaceted *medium.*

Ms. / Miss / Mrs.   *Ms.* is used in business and public life to address or refer to a woman. Some women may indicate a preference for *Ms.*, *Miss,* or *Mrs.,* which you should honor. If a woman has an academic or a professional title, use the appropriate form of address (*Doctor, Professor, Captain*) instead of *Ms., Miss,* or *Mrs.*

nature   *Nature,* when used to mean "kind" or "sort," is vague. Avoid this usage in your writing. Say exactly what you mean.

> ► The ~~nature of~~ the contract caused the problem.
>   *exclusionary clause in*

on / onto / upon   *On* is normally used as a preposition meaning "attached to" or "located at." ("Install the shelf *on* the north wall.") *On* also stresses a position of rest. ("The victim lay *on* the stretcher.") *Onto* implies movement to a position on or movement up and on. ("The commuters surged *onto* the platform.") *Upon* emphasizes movement or a condition. ("The report is due *upon* completion of the project.")

only   The word *only* should be placed immediately before the word or phrase it modifies.

> ► We ~~only~~ lack financial backing.
>   *only*

Be careful with the placement of *only* because it can change the meaning of a sentence.

> ► *Only* he said that he was tired. [He alone said that he was tired.]

> ► He *only* said that he was tired. [He actually was not tired, although he said he was.]

> ► He said *only* that he was tired. [He said nothing except that he was tired.]

> ► He said that he was *only* tired. [He said that he was nothing except tired.]

per   When *per* is used to mean "for each," "by means of," "through," or "on account of," it is appropriate (*per* gallon, *per* capita, *per* diem). When used to mean "according to" (*per* your request, *per* your order), the expression is jargon and should be avoided.

> ► As ~~per our discussion~~, I will send revised instructions.
>   *we discussed*

percent / percentage *Percent* is normally used instead of the symbol % ("only 15 *percent*"), except in tables, where space is at a premium. *Percentage,* which is never used with numbers, indicates a general size ("only a small *percentage*").

persons / people The word *persons* is used to refer to a specific category or number of people, often in legal or official contexts. ("Admittance is limited to *persons* age 18 and over.") In all other contexts, use *people.* ("We need more qualified *people* to fill the vacant positions.")

really *Really* is an adverb meaning "actually" or "in fact." Although both *really* and *actually* are often used as intensifiers for emphasis or sarcasm in speech, avoid such use in formal and professional writing.

▶ Did he ~~really~~ finish the report on time?

▶ I ~~really~~ support the conclusions in your report.

reason is [because] Replace the redundant phrase *the reason is because* with *the reason is that* or simply *because.*

regardless Always use *regardless* instead of the nonstandard *irregardless,* which expresses a double negative. The prefix *ir-* renders the base word negative, but *regardless*—meaning "unmindful"—is already negative.

that / which / who The word *that* is often overused and can foster wordiness.

> When   I think
▶ ~~I think that when~~ this project is finished, ~~that~~ you should publish

the results.

However, include *that* in a sentence if it avoids ambiguity or improves the pace.

>   that
▶ Some designers fail to appreciate the workers who operate equip-

ment constitute an important safety system.

Use *which,* not *that,* with nonrestrictive clauses (clauses that do not change the meaning of the basic sentence).

NONRESTRICTIVE	After John left the law firm, *which* is the largest in the region, he started a private practice.
RESTRICTIVE	Companies *that* diversify usually succeed.

That and *which* should refer to animals and things; *who* should refer to people.

▶ Dr. Cynthia Winter, *who* recently joined the clinic, treated a dog *that* was severely burned.

there / their / they're   *There* is an expletive (a word that fills the position of another word, phrase, or clause) or an adverb.

EXPLETIVE	*There* were more than 1,500 people at the conference.
ADVERB	More than 1,500 people were *there*.

Their is the possessive case form of *they*. ("Managers check *their* e-mail regularly.") *They're* is a contraction of *they are*. ("Clients tell us *they're* pleased with our services.")

to / too / two   *To, too,* and *two* are frequently confused because they sound alike. *To* is used as a preposition or to mark an infinitive.

▶ Send the report *to* the district manager. [preposition]

▶ I do not wish *to* attend. [mark of the infinitive]

Too is an adverb meaning "excessively" or "also."

▶ The price was *too* high. [excessively]

▶ I, *too*, thought it was high. [also]

Two is a number (*two* buildings, *two* concepts).

utilize   Do not use *utilize* as a long variant of *use,* which is the general word for "employ for some purpose." *Use* will almost always be clearer and less pretentious.

via   *Via* is Latin for "by way of." The term should be used only in routing instructions.

▶ The package was shipped *via* FedEx.

as a result of
▶ Her project was funded ~~via~~ the recent legislation.

when / where / that　*When and if* (or *if and when*) is a colloquial expression that should not be used in writing.

▶ When ~~and if~~ funding is approved, you will get the position.

　　　　If
▶ ~~When and if~~ funding is approved, you will get the position.
　　^

In phrases using the *where . . . at* construction, *at* is unnecessary and should be omitted.

▶ Where is his office ~~at~~?

Do not substitute *where* for *that* to anticipate an idea or a fact to follow.

　　　　　　　　　　　　　　that
▶ I read in the newsletter ~~where~~ sales increased last quarter.
　　　　　　　　　　　　　^

whether　*Whether* communicates the notion of a choice. The use of *whether or not* to indicate a choice between alternatives is redundant.

▶ The client asked whether ~~or not~~ the proposal was finished.

The phrase *as to whether* is clumsy and redundant. Either use *whether* alone or omit it altogether.

　We have decided to　　　　　　　　　　　　　*contract.*
▶ ~~As to whether we will~~ commit to a long-term ~~contract, we have~~
　^　　　　　　　　　　　　　　　　　　　　　^

~~decided to do so.~~

while　*While,* meaning "during an interval of time," is sometimes substituted for connectives like *and, but, although,* and *whereas.* Used as a connective in that way, *while* often causes ambiguity.

　　　　　　　　　　　　and
▶ Ian Evans is media director, ~~while~~ Joan Thomas is a vice president
　　　　　　　　　　　　　　^

for research.

Do not use *while* to mean *although* or *whereas.*

　Although
▶ ~~While~~ Ryan Sims is retired, he serves as our financial consultant.
　^

Restrict *while* to its meaning of "during the time that."

▶ I'll have to catch up on my reading *while* I am on vacation.

who / whom *Who* is a subjective-case pronoun, and *whom* is the objective-case form of *who*. When in doubt about which form to use, substitute a personal pronoun to see which one fits. If *he, she,* or *they* fits, use *who.*

▶ *Who* is the training coordinator? [You would say, "*She* is the training coordinator."]

If *him, her,* or *them* fits, use *whom.*

▶ It depends on *whom?* [You would say, "It depends on *them.*"]

who's / whose / of which *Who's* is the contraction of *who is.* ("*Who's* scheduled today?") *Whose* is the possessive case of *who.* ("Consider *whose* budget should be cut.")

Normally, *whose* is used with persons, and *of which* is used with inanimate objects.

▶ The employee *whose* car had been towed away was angry.

▶ The report recommended over 100 changes, more than half *of which* the client approved.

If *of which* causes a sentence to sound awkward, *whose* may be used with inanimate objects. (Compare "The business the profits *of which* steadily declined . . ." versus "The business *whose* profits steadily declined . . .".)

your / you're *Your* is a possessive pronoun ("*your* wallet"); *you're* is the contraction of *you are* ("*You're* late for the meeting"). If you tend to confuse *your* with *you're,* use the "find" function to review for both terms during <u>proofreading</u> (Tab 1).

Acknowledgments (*continued from page iv*)

Figure 7–1: Ken Cook/DeSantis Collection
Figure 7–2: FEMA
Figure 7–4: Portland Real Estate Blog
Figure 7–5: American National Standards Inst.
Figure 7–6: Department of Health and Human Services; Unknown
Figure 7–7: International Organization for Standardization (ISO) Symbols
Figure 7–13: USDA
Figure 9–9: Kim Isaacs, Advanced Career Systems
Figure 9–13 (a–b): Kim Isaacs, Advanced Career Systems

Index

Words and phrases in **bold type** indicate main entries. Usage terms appear in *italic type*.

internships, 279
interrogative adverbs, 341
interrogative pronouns, 365
interrogative sentences, 372, 418
interrupting elements, commas with, 400
interruptive person, 245
interviewing for a job, 266–72
  behavior and responses during, 267–68
  behavioral interviews, 267
  ethics note on, 268–69
  follow-up procedures, 271
  preparing for, 266–68
  professionalism and, 268–69
  requesting an interview, 261, 266
  résumés and, 283
interviewing for information, 159–61
  choosing interviewees, 159
  conducting interview, 160
  for job searches, 275–76
  note-taking and, 160
  preparing for, 159
  professionalism and, 159
  Writer's Checklist for, 161
interviews, documenting, 155, 156
in-text citations. *See* citations, in-text
intranet, 47, 60
intransitive verbs, 380, 434
introductions, xxxiii, 17–21
  context in, 10
  for correspondence, 77–78
  for formal proposals, 122
  for formal reports, 183, 191–93
  full-scale, 21
  for grant proposals, 129
  for presentations, 249–50
  for process explanations, 33
  for reports, 111, 117, 134
  revising, 39
  setting tone with, 329
  strategies for, 18–21
  See also openings
introductory elements
  commas with, 400–1
  dangling modifiers as, 349
  wordiness and, 311
  See also sentence openings
inverted sentences, 325, 373
investigative reports, 115–16
invitation for bids (IFB), 125
irregardless, 436
"is when" / "is where" definitions, 11
ISO symbols. *See* International
    Organization for Standardization
    symbols

it
  as expletive, 314, 371
  and *its,* 365
  as subject, 371
IT (information technology) specialists,
    45
italics, 411–12
  for emphasis, 223, 314, 411
  for foreign words, 411
  for headings and subheadings, 224,
    412
  for proper names, 412
  for titles, 135–36, 411, 412
  for words, letters, and numbers, 412
items in a series. *See* series of items
its / it's, 433

jammed modifiers. *See* stacked modifiers
jargon, 317
  affectation and, 303
  ethics in writing and, 13
  in global communication, 94
  plain language *vs.*, 321
  revising for, 39
  stacked modifiers as, 354
job advertisements
  cover letter to, 263
  partial, 261
job alerts, 277
job applications, 267, 280–82
  ethics note on, 281, 282
  Writer's Checklist for, 281–82
job interviews. *See* interviewing for a job
job objective
  in résumés, 293–94, 297
  sexist language and, 305
  See also names and titles
job search, 272–82
  acceptance / refusal letters, 259–60, 271
  advertisements, 277
  application cover letters, 260–65
  campus career services, 276
  career goals and, 273, 283
  direct inquiries, 280
  employment agencies, 278
  follow-up correspondence, 265, 271
  internships, 279
  interviewing, 266–72, 274
  job applications, 280–82
  networking, 275–76
  online resources for, 276, 278, 280
  organizing, 274
  personal branding for, 274, 275
  professionalism and, 274, 277

COMPLETE LIST OF MODEL DOCUMENTS

The Business Writer's Companion offers abundant examples of successful business writing and visuals of effective design. All of these elements are listed here for easy access.

4. BUSINESS WRITING DOCUMENTS AND ELEMENTS

5. RESEARCH AND DOCUMENTATION

6. FORMAL REPORTS

7. DESIGN AND VISUALS

8. PRESENTATIONS AND MEETINGS

9. JOB SEARCH AND APPLICATION